'No one who has read Julia Lovell's marvelous book on the Great Wall of China will be surprised that she has written such a great history of the Opium War. This defining passage in China's history – the beginning of a grisly century and a half of exploitation and misery – provides a rich seam of material which Julia Lovell draws on with huge narrative skill. Not the least of her attributes is her ability to show how these events have resonated down the years. A real cracker of a book.'

CHRIS PATTEN,
former Governor and Commander in Chief of Hong Kong

'A welcome piece of myth-busting . . . This book serves a crucial purpose in reminding Britain of a shameful episode in its past that still shapes relations with China today. But official China could also learn from it that reconciliation with the past comes by understanding its complexities, rather than turning it into a simple morality tale.'

RANA MITTER,
author of *Forgotten Ally: China's World War II, 1937-1945*

'Making the most of her considerable gifts as a story teller and deep familiarity with the contrasting ways that the tale of the Opium War has been told inside and outside of China, Julia Lovell offers us a fresh perspective on a pivotal episode in nineteenth-century history. The result is a compulsively readable and consistently thought-provoking work. It is filled with both lively accounts of things that happened long ago and insightful comments on the powerful shadows that these old events continue to cast in our still-young century.'

JEFFREY WASSERSTROM,
author of *China in the 21st Century: What Everyone Needs to Know*

'You cannot understand China today without understanding the huge impact the Opium Wars have had on restructuring Chinese national pride. This is the first western book I have read that does justice to that complicated story.'

XINRAN, author of *The Good Women of China*
and *Message From an Unknown Chinese Mother*

'In this riveting book, Julia Lovell explores the myths surrounding opium trading and the titanic clash between Britain and China, which shaped China's perception of its place in the world for more than a century. This book is at its heart a powerful plea for deeper mutual sympathy between the West and China; with Western economies under stres de imbalances, the parallel between the 1830s a e would be wise to heed the ancient warning t n history are doomed to repeat it.' *a*

THE OPIUM WAR

JULIA LOVELL teaches modern Chinese history at Birkbeck College, University of London. She is the author of *The Great Wall: China Against the World* and *The Politics of Cultural Capital: China's Quest for a Nobel Prize in Literature* and writes on China for the *Guardian*, the *Independent* and the *Times Literary Supplement*. Her many translations of modern Chinese fiction include, most recently, Lu Xun's *The Real Story of Ah-Q, and Other Tales of China*.

Also by Julia Lovell

THE POLITICS OF CULTURAL CAPITAL
China's Quest for a Nobel Prize in Literature

THE GREAT WALL
China Against the World, 1000 BC – AD 2000

JULIA LOVELL

THE OPIUM WAR

Drugs, Dreams and the Making of China

The Overlook Press
New York, NY

This edition first published in paperback in the United States in 2015 by
The Overlook Press, Peter Mayer Publishers, Inc.

141 Wooster Street
New York, NY 10012
www.overlookpress.com
For bulk and special sales, please contact sales@overlookny.com,
or write us at the above address

Maps drawn by Martin Lubikowski, ML Design, assisted by originals in Peter Ward Fay,
The Opium War, 1840–42 (Chapel Hill: University of North Carolina Press, 1975);
Peter Perdue, *China Marches West: The Qing Conquest of Central Eurasia*
(Cambridge, Mass.: Harvard University Press, 2005); Jonathan Spence,
The Search for Modern China (New York: Norton, 1999).

Cataloging-in-Publication Data is available from the Library of Congress.
Printed in the United States of America

ISBN 978-1-4683-1173-0
3 5 7 9 8 6 4

To Rob

Preface

On 8 November 2010, the British prime minister, David Cameron, led a substantial embassy to China. He was accompanied by four of his most senior ministers, and fifty or so high-ranking executives, all hoping to sign millions of pounds' worth of business deals with China (for products ranging from whisky to jets, from pigs to sewage-stabilization services). To anyone familiar with the history of Sino-British relations, the enterprise would have brought back some unhappy memories. Britain's first two trade-hungry missions to China (in 1793 and 1816) ended in conflict and frustration when their ambassadors – proud Britons, both – declined to prostrate themselves before the Qing emperor. These failures led indirectly to decades of intermittent wars between the two countries, as Britain abandoned negotiation and resorted instead to gunboat diplomacy to open Chinese markets to its goods – chief among which was opium.

Despite happy snaps of David Cameron smiling and walking along the Great Wall in the company of schoolchildren, the 2010 visit was not without its difficulties. On 9 November, as Cameron and company arrived to attend their official welcoming ceremony at the Great Hall of the People at Tiananmen Square, a Chinese official allegedly asked them to remove their Remembrance Day poppies, on the grounds that the flowers evoked painful memories of the Opium War fought between Britain and China from 1839 to 1842.

Someone in China's official welcoming party had, it seemed, put considerable effort into feeling offended on behalf of his or her 1.3 billion countrymen (for one thing, Remembrance Day poppies are clearly

modelled on field, not opium, poppies). Parts of the Chinese Internet
– which, since it came into existence some fifteen years ago, has been
home to an oversensitive nationalism – responded angrily. 'As rulers
of the greatest empire in human history,' remembered one netizen,
'the British were involved in, or set off, a great many immoral wars,
such as the Opium Wars that we Chinese are so familiar with.'
'Whose face is the English prime minister slapping, when he insists
so loftily on wearing his poppy?' asked one blogger. 'How did the
English invade China? With opium. How did the English become
rich and strong? Through opium.'

In Britain, meanwhile, the incident was quickly spun to the credit
of the country's leadership: our steadfast ministers, it was reported,
had refused to bow to the Chinese request. 'We informed them the
poppies meant a great deal to us,' said a member of the Prime
Minister's party, 'and we would be wearing them all the same.' (In
recent years, Remembrance Day activities have become infected by
political humbug, as right-wing rags lambast public figures caught
without poppies in their lapels. In November 2009, the then-
opposition leader, David Cameron, and the Prime Minister, Gordon
Brown, used the commemoration to engage in PR brinkmanship,
both vying to be photographed laying wreaths for the war dead.) In
certain quarters of the British press, the incident was read as an echo
of the 1793 and 1816 stand-offs, with plucky little Britain again
refusing to kowtow to the imperious demands of the Chinese giant.

Behind all this, however, reactions to the incident were more
nuanced. For one thing, beneath the stirring British headlines of
'David Cameron rejects Chinese call to remove "offensive" poppies', it
proved hard to substantiate who, exactly, in the Chinese government
had objected. Beyond the occasional expression of outrage, as in the
examples above, the Chinese cyber-sphere and press did not actually
seem particularly bothered, with netizens and journalists calmly
discussing the symbolic significance of British poppy-wearing, and
even bemoaning the fact that China lacked similar commemorations
of her war dead. The wider public response in Britain also appeared
restrained. Reader comments on coverage of the incident in Britain's
normally jingoistic *Daily Mail* were capable of empathy and even
touches of guilt. 'Just because [poppy-wearing] is important in Britain
doesn't mean it means the same the world over. I'm sure some of us

in Britain are highly ignorant of the importance of Chinese history in China – especially . . . the Opium War . . . no wonder they are a bit sensitive about it'.

David Cameron's poppy controversy was only the most recent example of the antagonisms, misunderstandings and distortions that the Opium War has generated over the past hundred and seventy years. Since it was fought, politicians, soldiers, missionaries, writers and drug smugglers inside and outside China have been retelling and reinterpreting the conflict to serve their own purposes. In China, it has been publicly demonized as the first emblematic act of Western aggression: as the beginning of a national struggle against a foreign conspiracy to humiliate the country with drugs and violence. In nations like Britain, meanwhile, the waging of the war transformed prevailing perceptions of the Middle Kingdom: China became, in Western eyes, an arrogant, fossilized empire cast beneficially into the modern world by gunboat diplomacy. The reality of the conflict – a tangle of overworked emperors, mendacious generals and pragmatic collaborators – was far more chaotically interesting. This book is the story of the extraordinary war that has been haunting Sino-Western relations for almost two centuries.

Contents

Maps

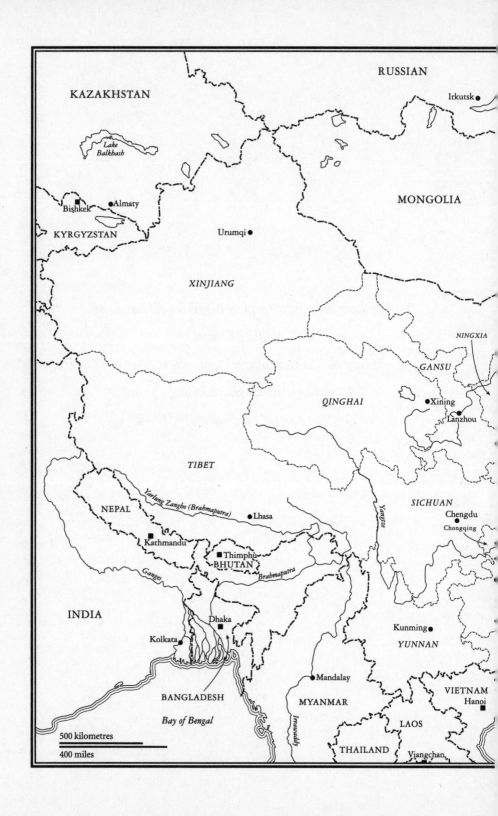

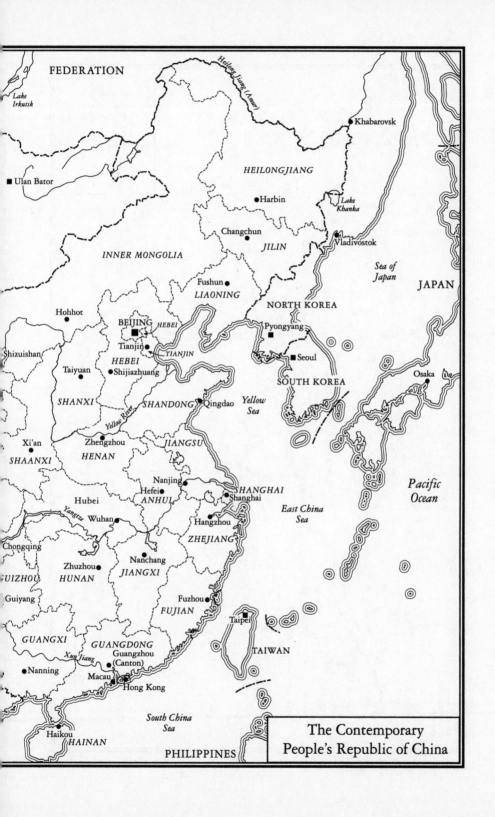

FEDERATION

*Lake
Irkutsk*

■ Ulan Bator

Heilong Jiang (Amur)

● Khabarovsk

HEILONGJIANG

● Harbin

*Lake
Khanka*

Changchun ●

JILIN

● Vladivostok

*Sea of
Japan*

JAPAN

INNER MONGOLIA

Fushun ●
LIAONING

NORTH KOREA

Pyongyang ■

Hohhot
●

BEIJING *HEBEI*
■

Tianjin ●
TIANJIN

■ Seoul

Shizuishan

HEBEI
Shijiazhuang
●

SOUTH KOREA

Osaka
●

Taiyuan ●

SHANXI

SHANDONG ● Qingdao

*Yellow
Sea*

Yellow River

Xi'an ●

Zhengzhou ●

JIANGSU

*Pacific
Ocean*

SHAANXI

HENAN

Nanjing ●
Hefei ●
ANHUI

SHANGHAI
● Shanghai

*East China
Sea*

Hubei

Yangtze
Wuhan ●

Hangzhou ●

Chongqing ●

ZHEJIANG

Nanchang ●

Zhuzhou ●
GUIZHOU   HUNAN

JIANGXI

Guiyang ●

Fuzhou ●

FUJIAN

Taipei ■

GUANGXI   GUANGDONG

Xun Jiang
● Nanning

Guangzhou
(Canton) ●
Macau ●
● Hong Kong

TAIWAN

*South China
Sea*

Haikou ●
HAINAN

PHILIPPINES

The Contemporary
People's Republic of China

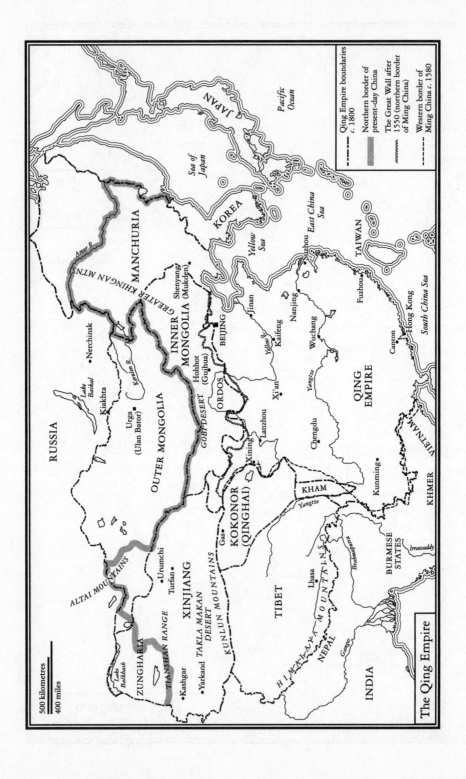

The Qing Empire

500 kilometres
400 miles

RUSSIA

Lake Baikal
Kiakhta
Nerchinsk
Amur R.

Urga (Ulan Bator)
Kerulen R.

OUTER MONGOLIA

GOBI DESERT

MANCHURIA
GREATER KHINGAN MTNS

Shenyang (Mukden)

INNER MONGOLIA

Hohhot (Guihua)
ORDOS

BEIJING

Yellow R.
Jinan
Kaifeng
Nanjing
Wuchang
Xi'an

Yangtze

KOREA

JAPAN

Sea of Japan

Pacific Ocean

Yellow Sea

East China Sea

Suzhou
Fuzhou
TAIWAN

South China Sea

Hong Kong

Canton

QING EMPIRE

Chengdu

Kunming

Lanzhou
Xining

KOKONOR (QINGHAI)

KHAM

Yangtze

VIETNAM

KHMER

ALTAI MOUNTAINS

Urumchi
Turfan

XINJIANG

TAKLA MAKAN DESERT

TIANSHAN RANGE

Lake Balkhash

ZUNGHARIA

Kashgar
Yarkand

KUNLUN MOUNTAINS

Gas

TIBET

Lhasa

Brahmaputra

HIMALAYA MOUNTAINS

NEPAL

Ganges

INDIA

BURMESE STATES

Irrawaddy

Qing Empire boundaries c. 1800

Northern border of present-day China

The Great Wall after 1550 (northern border of Ming China)

Western border of Ming China c. 1580

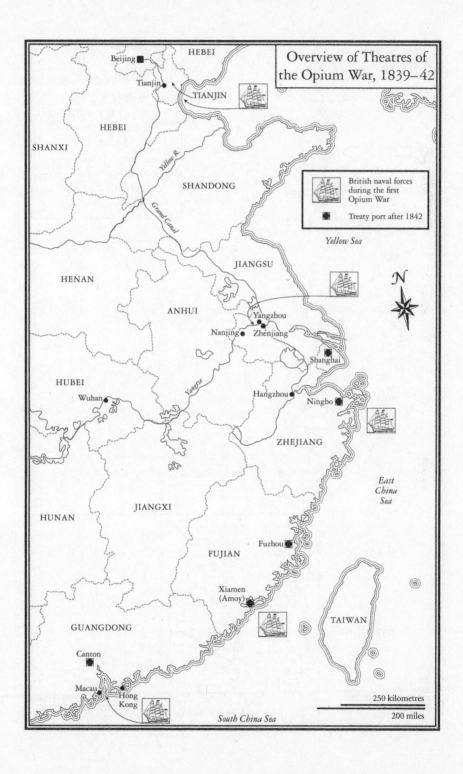

Overview of Theatres of
the Opium War, 1839–42

British naval forces
during the first
Opium War

Treaty port after 1842

HEBEI
Beijing
Tianjin
TIANJIN

HEBEI

SHANXI

SHANDONG

Yellow R.

Grand Canal

Yellow Sea

HENAN

JIANGSU

ANHUI

Yangzhou
Nanjing   Zhenjiang
Shanghai

N

HUBEI

Wuhan

Yangtze

Hangzhou
Ningbo

ZHEJIANG

East
China
Sea

HUNAN

JIANGXI

Fuzhou

FUJIAN

Xiamen
(Amoy)

TAIWAN

GUANGDONG

Canton

Macau
Hong
Kong

South China Sea

250 kilometres

200 miles

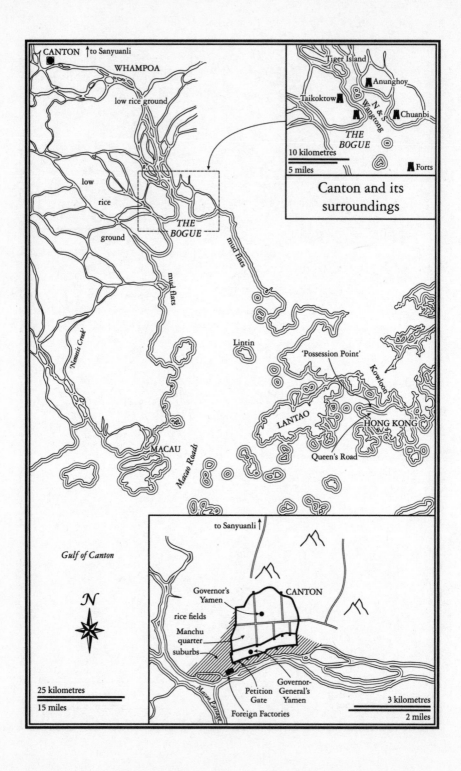

CANTON ↑to Sanyuanli

WHAMPOA

low rice ground

low

rice

ground

THE BOGUE

mud flats

mud flats

'Nemesis Creek'

Lintin

'Possession Point'

Kowloon

LANTAO

HONG KONG

Queen's Road

MACAU

Macao Roads

Gulf of Canton

N

Tiger Island

Taikoktow

Anunghoy

N & S Wangtong

Chuanbi

THE BOGUE

10 kilometres

5 miles

Forts

Canton and its surroundings

25 kilometres

15 miles

to Sanyuanli ↑

Governor's Yamen

rice fields

Manchu quarter

suburbs

Petition Gate

Foreign Factories

CANTON

Governor-General's Yamen

Macao Passage

3 kilometres

2 miles

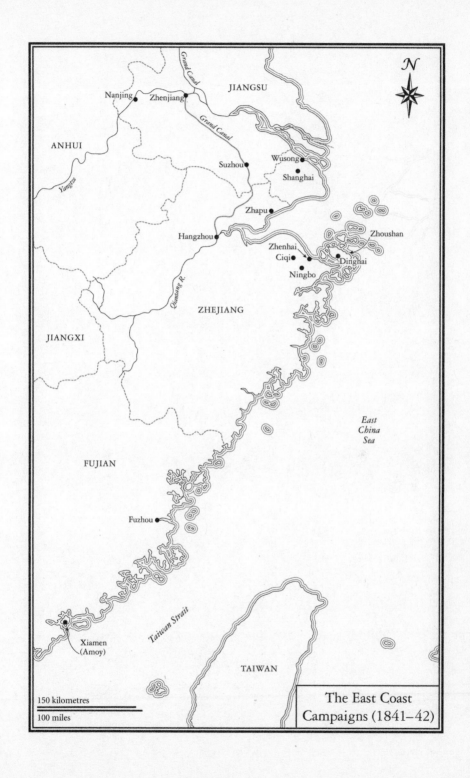

The East Coast
Campaigns (1841–42)

A Note About Chinese Names and Romanization

In Chinese names, the surname is given first, followed by the given name. Therefore, in the case of Liang Qichao, Liang is the surname and Qichao the given name.

I have used the pinyin system of romanization throughout, except for a few spellings best known outside China in another form, such as Chiang Kai-shek (Jiang Jieshi in pinyin). In addition, I have occasionally used the old, nineteenth-century anglophone spellings of some Chinese place names (for example Canton, for the city known in Mandarin Chinese as Guangzhou) to reduce confusion resulting from more than one name being cited in the main text and in quotations from primary sources, and also because anglophone historians still call the pre-1839 rules governing European trade with China 'the Canton system'.

In pinyin, transliterated Chinese is pronounced as in English, apart from the following sounds:

VOWELS

a (when the only letter following a consonant): *a* as in ah
ai: *eye*
ao: *ow* as in how
e: *uh*
ei: *ay* as in say
en: *en* as in happen
eng: *ung* as in sung

i (as the only letter following most consonants): *e* as in me
i (when following c, ch, s, sh, z, zh): *er* as in driver
ia: *yah*
ian: *yen*
ie: *yeah*
iu: *yo* as in yo-yo
o: *o* as in stork
ong: *oong*
ou: *o* as in so
u (when following most consonants): *oo* as in loot
u (when following j, q, x, y): *ü* as the German ü
ua: *wah*
uai: *why*
uan: *wu-an*
uang: *wu-ang*
ui: *way*
uo: *u-woah*
yan: *yen*
yi: *ee* as in feed

CONSONANTS

c: *ts* as in bits
g: *g* as in good
q: *ch* as in choose
x: a slightly more sibilant version of *sh* as in sheep
z: *ds* as in woods
zh: *j* as in job

Introduction

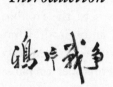

In 1832, a lord of the King's bedchamber by the name of William Napier lost his seat as a Scottish peer and started looking for gainful employment. Within a year, something had come up: Superintendent of British trade in China – a new government position (at an attractive, ambassadorial-level £6,000 per annum) to replace the old Select Committee of the East India Company, whose monopoly over the China trade had just been abolished. Though Napier immediately made a play for the post, the Prime Minister, Lord Grey, stalled him on the grounds that he needed Cabinet approval. For on paper, Napier was not the strongest of applicants. He was a man of many talents: navigation; sheep-farming (on which subject he was a published authority); bagpipe-mending; playing the flute. Unpicking delicate diplomatic wrangles with one of the largest and most intricately cultured empires in the world was not, however, part of his skill-set.

Yet Grey was not overwhelmed by more suitable candidates. The post had already been turned down by a colonial stalwart and future Governor of India, Lord Auckland, who had named Canton – the southern city in Guandong province to which European traders had been restricted since 1760 – 'perhaps the least pleasant residence for a European on the face of the earth'.[1] Britain's relationship with China's current overlords, the Manchu Qing dynasty, should have been straightforward. Britain wanted tea, and other desirables such as silk and porcelain; the Qing were happy to sell. The trade was thoroughly regulated. The dynasty's fourth emperor, Qianlong, had in 1760 limited foreign commerce to a monopolistic Canton guild of merchants known to Europeans as the 'Hong' (Cantonese for company): purchases and sales, transit taxes, complaints, customs tariffs – everything was to go first through the Hong, who might pass outstanding queries on to the local official in charge of trade. He might, in turn, forward matters on to the provincial governor; and from there, eventually, they might move on to the emperor in Beijing. Rather than put themselves to the trouble of finding lodgings and warehouses in the city of Canton itself, China's government ruled that European traders were to make themselves at home through the trading season (roughly September to January) in a row of 'factories' leased to them by the Hong. Situated deliberately outside Canton's thirty-foot-high city walls, the factories offered merchants around fifteen acres of living and warehouse space, overlooking the Pearl River that led up to the city from the sea. Outside these months, the foreigners were to withdraw to the Portuguese-leased enclave of Macao, about seventy miles away, or return home. The Europeans, in sum, were at all times to be kept at a careful, bureaucratic distance from the authorities and populace.

But if relations between the Chinese government and foreign merchants were wary, the true source of bad feeling was not bureaucracy – it was economics. By the 1780s, Britain was running up a serious trade deficit: while China's government was quite happy to service the growing British tea addiction, it seemed to want little except silver in return. As East India Company profits failed to offset the costs of rule in India, British tea-drinkers pushed Asia trade figures further into the red. From 1780 to 1790, the combined returns of the India and China trades failed to make even a £2 million dent in the £28 million debt left over from the conquest of India.[2]

By the 1820s, the British thought they had found a perfect solution to their difficulty: Indian opium, for which Chinese consumers had increasingly developed a taste over the preceding couple of decades. Between 1752 and 1800, a net 105 million silver dollars (approximately £26.25 million) flowed into China; between 1808 and 1856, 384 million travelled in the opposite direction, the balance apparently tipped by booming opium imports. From 1800 to 1818, the average annual traffic held steady at around 4,000 chests (each chest containing around 140 pounds of opium); by 1831, it was nearing 20,000. After 1833, when the Free Trade lobby terminated the East India Company's monopoly on the tea trade, the market was flooded by private merchants hungry for tea and profits. Opium – in ever greater quantities – was the barter. By the close of the decade, sales had more than doubled again.[3]

The greater part of the profits fell into the pockets of the British government, whose agents in Asia controlled opium production in Bengal. The East India Company did not publicly dirty its hands by bringing the drug to China. It commissioned and managed plantations of opium poppies across hundreds of thousands of Indian acres. It took care of the processing (the painstaking lancing of individual poppy seed pods for raw opium gum, setting and drying the gum in trays, pressing it into cakes, and coating these in crushed, dried poppy stems and leaves). Finally, it oversaw the packing of the drug into mango-wood chests, its shipping to Calcutta, and auctioning off. At that moment, the Company washed its hands of it, letting private merchants sail for the Chinese coast, where they anchored off the island of Lintin, at the mouth of the Pearl River. Eager Chinese wholesalers would then use silver to buy certificates from private trading offices in Canton and exchange them for opium; this silver would in turn secure tea for the English market. And before the tea disappeared into British cups, the government would exact its import duties. Through the nineteenth century, these duties would be put to careful use: they covered a substantial part of the costs of the Royal Navy which, naturally, kept the British empire afloat.

On the face of it, the arrangement was as tidy as the earlier silver–tea trade: one side having something to sell, the other having something it wanted in exchange. But anxious members of the Qing government were no happier to lose silver than their British counterparts had been a few decades earlier, and were fretting about the corrupting effects of a booming drug culture. After a handful of attempted crackdowns in the eighteenth century, the Qing state's war on opium began in earnest in the 1830s, and would continue – intermittently, inconsistently – over the next hundred years. Britain's private opium-sellers were also dissatisfied. For India could provide as much opium as China would take and they resented the fact that the Qing's trade controls had pushed them into the black economy. They craved a more respectable image, to establish commerce on a footing 'equally advantageous and honourable', and wanted a lawful way in

to the China market, either through the legalization of opium, or
through the opening of ports to other British goods – and preferably
both, to which end they began, through the 1830s, impudently
edging the trade further north up the coast.[4]

These merchants were for the most part a crew of buccaneering
money-makers, full of mockery for the empire outside whose walls
they were held (or at any rate for the unrepresentative southern
fragment that they glimpsed at Canton). They objected to what they
saw as its pompous, often venal bureaucracy; its determination to
keep them and their trade at a prudent remove; its antiquity, its
smells, its absence of Christianity and decent water-closets; the
offensive Chinese habit of staring at foreigners; the arrogant Chinese
failure to stare at foreigners; and so on. The Chinese, as summarized
by James Matheson, a Scottish pillar of the smuggling community
and co-founder with William Jardine of the great opium house
Jardine–Mathesons, were 'a people characterized by a marvellous
degree of imbecility, avarice, conceit and obstinacy . . . It has been
the policy of this extraordinary people to shroud themselves and all
belonging to them in mystery impenetrable . . . [to] exhibit a spirit
of exclusiveness on a grand scale.'[5]

Matheson and his colleagues were joined in their impatience by
the Protestant missionary community. The London Missionary Society
had sent out their first man to south China, Robert Morrison, in
1807. Not long after his arrival, he had been asked whether he hoped
to have any spiritual impact on the country: 'No,' he responded, 'but
I expect God will'.[6] Thirty years later, he and his colleagues found
themselves unable either to name or enumerate more than a handful
of converts. Ill, depressed, stalled on the edge of the mainland,
frustrated missionary observers of the 1830s spoke a pure dialect of
imperialist paternalism: 'China still proclaims her proud and unap-
proachable supremacy and disdainfully rejects all pretensions in any
other nation to be considered as her equal. This feeling of contemptible vanity Christianity alone will effectually destroy. Where other
means have failed, the gospel will triumph; this will fraternize the
Chinese with the rest of mankind . . . [linking] them in sympathy
with other portions of their species, and thus add to the triumphs
it has achieved.'[7] The missionaries became natural allies of the smugglers: when they first arrived on the coast of China, they docked

among opium traders on the island of Lintin; they interpreted for them in exchange for passages up the coast, distributing tracts while the drug was taken onshore; and in the *Chinese Repository*, Canton's leading English-language publication, they shared a forum for spreading their views on the urgent need to open China, by whatever means necessary. By the 1830s, merchants and missionaries alike favoured violence. '[W]hen an opponent supports his argument with physical force, [the Chinese] can be crouching, gentle, and even kind', observed Karl Gützlaff, a stout Pomeranian missionary who would, during the Opium War, lead the British military occupation of parts of eastern China, running armies of Chinese spies and collaborators.[8] The slightest provocation would do. In 1831, traders had written to the government in India, demanding a fleet of warships to avenge the Chinese authorities' partial demolition of a front garden that the British had illegally requisitioned.[9]

The appointment Napier sought was to oversee this untidy, though broadly profitable modus vivendi. His brief was to maintain a legal tea trade financed by illegal drug imports. Eventually, after asking the king to intervene on his behalf, Napier won Britain's first official resident posting to China. The new superintendent had a simple solution to the difficulties before him: blast the country into submission. 'The Empire of China is my own', he confided excitedly to his diary. 'What a glorious thing it wd be to have a blockading squadron on the Coast of the Celestial Empire . . . how easily a gun brig wd raise a revolution and cause them to open their ports to the trading world. I should like to be the medium of such a change.'[10]

Grey took care to put him right in a private letter of instructions: 'Nothing must be done to shock [Chinese] prejudices & excite their fears . . . Persuasion & Con-ciliation should be the means employed, rather than anything approaching to the tone of hostile & menacing language'.[11] The warning fell on deaf ears. In the course of his six-month sea voyage to China, Napier drew the following conclusions: first, that the key to British interest in China was tea, and second, that 'every act of violence on our part has been productive of instant redress and other beneficial results'.[12] The British 'must *use* force, not menace it', he reminded himself, somewhere past Madeira.[13] There will come a time, Napier resolved as his ship crossed the tropic seas, when their folly will 'bring down upon them the chastisement of

Great Britain, when every point may be gained with the greatest ease, and secured for all time to come'.[14]

Burnt raw by the south China sun, Napier sailed into Canton at 2 a.m. on 25 July 1834; by daybreak, the Union flag was flying high over the old East India Company factory. Within two days he had succeeded in breaking six long-established rules of Anglo-Chinese trade. Chief among these offences were that he had sailed into Canton without a passport, and without a permit to take up residence there, and that he tried to communicate in writing directly with officials – thereby asserting his diplomatic equality – rather than through the merchants imperially appointed to deal with foreigners.

Napier's disregard for the rules did not endear him to the governor-general responsible for Canton, Lu Kun, who began trying to edge him back into line, instructing him to retreat to Macao and not return without a permit. Irritated by all this diplomatic fuss (Napier's determination to hand a letter of self-introduction directly to the governor-general had embroiled English and Chinese underlings in a three-hour stand-off at the city gate under the midday sun), the Chinese administration allowed itself a little linguistic mischief. In public edicts, Napier's name appeared in characters that, the British translator awkwardly explained, seemed to mean 'laboriously vile'. In return, Napier named the governor-general 'a presumptuous savage', mutinously distributed Chinese-language broadsheets enumerating the local government's sins, and swore to punish the insult to the British crown: 'Three or four frigates and brigs,' he quickly wrote to his foreign secretary, Lord Palmerston, 'with a few steady British troops . . . would settle the thing in a space of time inconceivably short. Such an undertaking would be worthy the greatness and the power of England . . . the exploit is to be performed with a facility unknown even in the capture of a paltry West India Island'.[15]

Given his irascibility towards the Chinese authorities, Napier developed a surprising tenderness for the Chinese people themselves. 'I never met with more civility,' he remarked some three weeks into his stay, 'or so little of a disposition to act with insult or rudeness than I constantly see among these hardworking and industrious people.'[16] He became convinced that they looked to him for liberation from China's oppressive authorities. '[S]ay to the Emperor – adopt this or abide the consequences – and it is done . . . I anticipate not the loss of a single soul, and we have justice on our side ... The Chinese are most anxious to trade with us.' Provided it was kept sufficiently informed of the British grievance, he reasoned, the populace 'might look to the arrival of such a force as the happy means of their emancipation from a most arbitrary system of oppression ... surely it would be an act of Charity to take them into one's hands altogether, and no difficult job.'[17]

By 2 September 1834, Napier's defiance had driven Lu Kun to stop trade and blockade the British factory. Within another week, it had provoked armed conflict. After dispatching a request to Lord Grey for a British force from India, Napier called the two frigates under his command (stationed along the coast) up river towards Canton, expecting to frighten his adversary into submission. The Chinese were not so easily intimidated, however. The forts at the mouth of the river exchanged fire with the frigates, killing at least two British sailors and injuring others. Lu Kun had, moreover, ordered a series of boats to be sunk behind the frigates, which then (too big to advance further, their way back blocked) found themselves stranded. Now sickening badly from malaria, Napier was forced to abandon the British factory and Canton. On his way back down to the coast, Napier was left floating for a week in the Pearl River by vengeful Cantonese bureaucrats, until the frigates were confirmed as having returned to the ocean. Weakened by the delay on board, after another two weeks he died of fever in Macao.

Never mind that plenty of British onlookers thought Napier foolishly violent and precipitate, that trade should be won by peace and not war. (The British were, the sinophone MP for Hampshire George Staunton argued, 'in a national point of view, totally and entirely in the wrong'.[18]) Never mind, either, that Napier had broken rule upon rule, and ignored the greater part of his official instructions. Or, again, that until Lu Kun threatened to behead him for spreading seditious notices about the Qing government, the Cantonese authorities had resisted him peaceably enough. ('Suppose a Chinaman', Napier himself wrote to Palmerston concerning his lack-of-passport controversy, 'were to land under similar circumstances at Whitehall, your Lordship would not allow him to "loiter" as they have permitted me.'[19]) Britain had now been offered its first decent pretext for open conflict with China, should it be of a mind to make use of it: the emperor's man in Canton had menaced the life of the king's man in Canton; British life, liberty and property had been insulted and lost – insults that British hawks now insisted could only be avenged by an armed response.

Despite his many diplomatic failures (and death), then, Napier succeeded superbly in two respects: first, in moving Anglo-Chinese relations closer towards the possibility of armed conflict, as relatively peaceful pragmatism was ousted by economic self-interest and pompous national principle; and second, in recasting the British impulse towards war as a moral obligation, an 'act of Charity' towards the Chinese that would sow only friendship for British gunboats. Although the advocates of war would not win over Britain's decision-makers until 1839, their denunciations of insufferable Chinese arrogance were busily working on British public opinion in the interim. Constructed around the time of the Opium War to justify violence against China (the hostile Chinese, the argument went, have *forced* us to defend ourselves), this stereotype of the obtusely anti-foreign Chinese would haunt Western attitudes to the empire through the nineteenth and twentieth centuries.[20] China, declared the *Chinese Repository* in the last days of 1836, was 'a nation nursing itself in solitary, sulky grandeur, and treating as inferior all other nations, most far superior in civilization, resources, courage, arts and arms . . . It seems indeed strange that the whole fabric of the Chinese Empire does not fall asunder of itself'. One 'vigorous and well directed blow from a foreign power', and 'it will totter to its base'.[21]

In 1839, the British government resolved to administer that blow, after the Qing government refused British smugglers food, water and trade until they promised to stop hauling their shipfuls of opium into China, and Canton's merchant lobby bore down on Foreign Secretary Palmerston to intervene. On 18 October, Palmerston informed his man in China, Captain Charles Elliot, that a fleet would reach China the following year to fight the Qing. 'All the world must rejoice that such a force is here', crowed the *Chinese Repository* from south China, watching the expedition's ships sail off in late June 1840 into their first war with China.[22]

*

In China today, the Opium War is the traumatic inauguration of the country's modern history. History books, television documentaries and museums chorus a received wisdom about the conflict, which goes something like this. In the early nineteenth century, unscrupulous British traders began forcing enormous quantities of Indian opium on Chinese consumers. When the Chinese government declared war on opium, in order to avert the moral, physical and financial disaster threatened by the empire's growing drug habit, British warships bullied China out of tens of millions of dollars, and its economic and political independence. Gunboat diplomacy, opium and the first 'Unequal Treaty' of 1842 (followed by a second in 1860, concluding the 'second Opium War' begun in 1856) brought China – until the end of the eighteenth century, probably the richest and most powerful civilization in the world – to its knees, leaving its people slavish addicts, incapable of resisting subsequent waves of European, American and Japanese colonizers.[23] This account of the Opium War is now one of the founding episodes of Chinese nationalism: the first great call to arms against a bullying West; but also the start of China's 'century of humiliation' (a useful pedagogical shorthand for everything that happened in China between 1842 and 1949) at the hands of imperialism.[24] It marks the beginning of China's struggle to free itself from 'semi-colonial semi-feudalism' (Mao's own summary of the century of Chinese experience after 1842), and to 'stand up' (Mao again) as a strong modern nation – a battle that ends, naturally, with Communist triumph in 1949. 'The story of China's modern history [from the Opium War to the present day]', summarizes a 2007 history textbook in use in one of China's elite institutions of higher education, Beijing University,

> is the history of the courageous struggle by the good-hearted masses for national survival and to accomplish the great revival of the Chinese race. It is the history of every nationality in the country, under the leadership of the Chinese Communist Party, undertaking a great and painful struggle to win national independence and liberation through the 1949 Revolution; it is the history of an extremely weak, impoverished and old China gradually growing, thanks to the socialist revolution . . . into a prosperous, flourishing and vital new socialist China . . . What are the aims of studying our modern history? . . . To gain deep

insight into how History and the People came to choose Marxism, came to choose the Chinese Communist Party and came to choose socialism.[25]

As the rulers of the contemporary People's Republic swing between self-confidence about its miracle rise and suspicion of a West supposedly determined to contain it, the Opium War is kept at the front of national memory. Particularly since the 1990s, when the Communist Party began rallying anti-foreign nationalism to shore up its own legitimacy after the Tiananmen crackdown, the Opium War has been called into service in successive 'patriotic education' campaigns waged on monuments and in textbooks, newspapers and films.[26] With the turmoil of the Tiananmen uprising of 1989 blamed on 'Western bourgeois liberalization', the hundred and fiftieth anniversary of the first Opium War in 1990 offered a public relations gift to the government, the opportunity to splash stirring editorials across the media about this 'national tragedy' inflicted by the gunboats of the West.[27] 'In order to protect its evil opium trade,' the *People's Daily* (the Communist Party's official news organ) reminded its readers,

> the British government poisoned the Chinese people, stole huge quantities of silver, and openly engaged upon imperialist aggression – as a result of which the Chinese fell into an abyss of suffering. This, as Comrade Mao Zedong pointed out, began the Chinese people's resistance against imperialism and its running dogs. The Opium War and the acts of aggression that followed it awoke in the Chinese people a desire for development and survival, initiating their struggles for independence and liberation . . . The facts undeniably tell us that the Chinese people have only managed to stand up thanks to the leadership of the Chinese Communist Party . . . only socialism can save and develop China . . . Raise ever higher the glorious banner of patriotism, commemorate the 150th anniversary of the Opium War.[28]

Unorthodox reappraisals of the Opium Wars can jangle high-level political nerves. In 2006, the government closed down China's leading liberal weekly, *Freezing Point* (*Bingdian*), because it ran an article by a philosophy professor called Yuan Weishi challenging textbook doctrine on (amongst other things) the second Opium War, which 'viciously attacked the socialist system [and] attempted to vindicate criminal acts by the imperialist powers in invading China. It seriously distorted historical facts; it seriously contradicted news propaganda discipline; it seriously damaged the national feelings of the Chinese people ... and created bad social influence.'[29] (To offer a roughly equivalent anglophone analogue: imagine *Prospect* being shut down for running a revisionist article on the Scottish Clearances or the Irish Famine.) Around this same moment, the government decided to replace the soporific lectures in Marxism-Leninism compulsory across undergraduate courses with classes in modern Chinese history – beginning, of course, with the Opium War – ensuring that China's brightest and best emerged from their university careers with a correct understanding of the past, and its relationship to the present.

At the time that it was fought, by contrast, most of the Chinese empire – including a number of those who were supposed to be directing proceedings – had some difficulty acknowledging an Opium War with the English was happening at all. The emperor had practically no idea he was supposed to be at war until the end of July 1840, almost a year after the British judged that armed hostilities had commenced. He had little clue as to why English guns were pummelling his empire's east coast until the second week of August that year, when the fleet sailed in to Tianjin, the nearest port to Beijing, to deliver a letter from the British foreign secretary to 'the Minister of the Emperor'. After the conflict's existence was at last officially acknowledged, the emperor and his men still had trouble dignifying it with the term 'war', preferring to name it a 'border provocation' or 'quarrel' (*bianxin*), atomized into a series of local clashes along China's maritime perimeter. Even while they were routing, with the newest military technology of the day, badly trained and directed Chinese armies, the British were identified in court documents of the time as 'clowns', 'bandits', 'pirates', 'robbers', 'rebels' (occasionally, the 'outrageous rebels')[30] – temporary insurgents against a world order still firmly centred in the Qing state.[31] This, in the eyes of China's rulers, was just another aggravation no more worrying than the other domestic and frontier revolts the government was struggling to suppress around the same time.

Yet somehow, in the century and a half since it was fought, the

Opium War has been transformed from a mere 'border provocation' into the tragic beginning of China's modern history, and a key prop for Communist One-Party rule. This contemporary recasting of the conflict conveniently reminds the Chinese people of their country's victimization by the West, and of everything that was wrong about the 'old society' before the Communist Party came along to make things right again. When the West tries to criticize China, most often for its human-rights record, or for its lack of an independent judiciary and press, Chinese voices – both inside and outside the government – can fight back with the Opium War. A 2004 reader's comment article for the *China Daily* (the government's English-language newspaper) denounced the whole business as 'treachery by the West on a scale never before experienced . . . the use of the drug opium set the standard of the mistakes of the west for the next 150 years . . . The Western bigots and zealots, however, have never ceased to have designs on China and on China's wealth and prosperity, even today . . . If the West and their running dogs of war now expect mercy from China for all these past invasions and thefts, they are seriously mistaken.'[32]

Look beyond current Chinese historical orthodoxy, however, and a very different picture of China, and of its first declared clash with a Western power, begins to emerge. Nineteenth-century China was not a country instinctively set against all things foreign, but rather a splintered society capable (like most societies) of a broad range of reactions – uncertainty, suspicion, condescension, curiosity – to the outside world. The mere fact that twentieth-century China came to attach so much importance to the Opium War is testament to the country's openness, rather than hostility, to the West. As it was fought, the war struck Western observers as epochal, but appeared to many of its Chinese observers subsidiary to grander narratives of local disorder and trouble on the empire's other frontiers. Yet by rechristening, since the 1920s, the Opium War as the start of modern Chinese history, China's establishment has subscribed to a thoroughly Western-centric view of the country's past that views antebellum China as a 'nation in a profound sleep', waiting to be woken by the West. Read many mid-nineteenth-century anglophone accounts of China and the war, and you might reasonably suppose that China did not possess any history before its encounter with British gunboats. Glance across a moderately detailed chronology of modern China, and it becomes very obvious that internal causes of violence far out-number external: the rural rebellions of the nineteenth century that left millions dead or displaced; the civil wars of the twentieth century, both before and after 1949. Yet while contemporary China's media and publishing industries loudly commemorate the British expedition of 1839–42, the self-inflicted disasters of the Communist period – the man-made famine of the early 1960s, the political persecutions that culminated in the extraordinary violence of the Cultural Revolu-tion, the bloodletting of 1989 – go largely ignored.

The PRC's state media work hard to convince readers and viewers that modern China is the story of the Chinese people's heroic struggles against 'imperialism and its running dogs'. (In reality, the story of modern China could probably be told just as convincingly as a history of collusion with 'imperialism and its running dogs'; China has about as rich a tradition of collaboration with foreigners as any country that has suffered regular invasion and occupation.) But self-loathing and introspection, rather than the quest for foreign scapegoats, have dominated China's efforts to modernize. Eyewitness Chinese accounts of the first Opium War blamed the empire's defeat not on external aggression but on the disorganization and cowardice of its own offi-cials and armies.

The complicated history of Chinese reactions to the Opium War, and to imperialism in general, does not remotely lessen the racist stridency of many nineteenth- and twentieth-century Western atti-tudes to China, as expressed in the writings and actions of politicians, soldiers and popular commentators. Even as he argued, in *Discovering History in China*, that historians had simplified the impact of imperi-alism on China, Paul Cohen wrote: 'Let there be no question about it. Everyone – or, at any rate, almost everyone – today regards im-perialism as bad.'[33] As many have demonstrated, China's encounter with Western imperialism was often deforming and dehumanizing.[34] Neither does this history mitigate in any way the essential, shame-inducing facts of the conflict: that the British government fought a war to protect a profitable illegal trade in narcotics. But the Opium War and its aftermath do expose how fragmented this place we call

China is: how even a seemingly straightforward act of external aggression can generate a variety of responses (indignation, admiration, self-loathing) and loyalties.

And today, many Chinese people waste little time fuming over British gunboat diplomacy when left in peace by the state's patriotic education campaign. Ask Beijing taxi-drivers (an overworked, underpaid labour-force more than entitled to a generalized sense of grievance against the world) what they think of Britain, and you are more likely to get a sigh of admiration (about how modern and developed Britain is, relative to China) than vitriol. Ask them about the Opium War, and they'll often tell you what's past is past; they're too busy thinking about managing in the present (or they don't listen to anything the government says). Even as secondary-school history textbooks and examinations still strive to indoctrinate young minds with the 'China as Victim' account of modern history, always starting with the Opium War, classroom discussions of the Opium War easily lapse out of anger towards the West, and into disgust at nineteenth-century China's corruption and military weakness. Start a conversation about the Opium War and someone, sooner or later, is bound to come out with the catchphrase *luohou jiu yao aida* – a social Darwinist sentiment that translates as 'if you're backward, you'll take a beating'; China, they mean to imply, had it coming. Beneath the angry, hate-filled narrative of the Opium War and its aftermath told by Chinese nationalism, then, lies a more intriguing story: that of a painfully self-critical and uncertain, but open-minded quest to make sense of the country's crisis-ridden last two centuries.

This book will begin with the dramas of the war itself – Qing China's expansive interactions with the world beyond its borders; the miscalculations of the court's anti-opium lobby; the mutual incomprehension that pushed both sides towards war; the opportunistic hypocrisy of the British; the terrible bloodshed resulting from Britain's overwhelming superiority and China's dearth of military realism. It will then range across the subsequent hundred and seventy years, plotting out the construction of the Opium War myth in both China and the West, via China's intensifying sense of *guochi* (national humiliation) at the hands of imperialism – the second Opium War of 1856–60, the Sino-Japanese War of 1894–95, the Boxer Uprising and subsequent Allied expedition against China of 1900, the Japanese invasion of the 1930s – and ending in the Communist Party's self-interested efforts to harness historical memory.[35] Through this larger narrative will be woven the strange, contradictory stories of opium's attackers: the prohibitionist hysteria of Western missionaries; the doctors who tried to detox smokers with arsenic, heroin and cocaine; the narcotic puritanism of twentieth-century China's two great dictators, Chiang Kai-shek and Mao Zedong – both sworn public enemies of opium, both bankrolled by drug-trade profits.

I will close in a journey around contemporary China's opinion-makers (politicians, journalists, schoolteachers, bloggers) and sites of public history (exhibitions, museums, memorials), to reflect on the paradoxes of Chinese nationalism today. Why, when China is more open to (and dependent on) global forces than at any other time in its history, has the government chosen to mobilize a nationalism fuelled by resentment of the West's historical crimes against China? Why, at a time when China is supposed to be on the edge of superpower status, are its people so regularly reminded of an abject history of 'humiliation'? To what extent is the Communist Party in control of the anti-foreign nationalism in which it has schooled its people? Behind the screens of nationalist and imperialist legend, the Opium War and its afterlives expose the struggles and dilemmas that have beset the search for modern China: how Western misperceptions and misdeeds have fuelled China's national myths; and how these myths have rebounded to mould China's interactions with the West.

Before I go on, I would like to add a brief note about the coverage of the book. Chinese histories tend to merge the first Opium War into the second, seeing them as part of a single continuum of Western aggression. The second Opium War is, without doubt, as interesting a conflict as the first: for its political symbolism, its historical ironies and its confusion of domestic and international violence. But for two reasons, this book concentrates more on the historical detail of the first Opium War. One is intellectual. Given its importance in Chinese historiography – as the beginning of the 'Century of Humiliation' – I particularly wanted to explore its realities and the way in which distorted understandings of the war have shaped the last century and a half of the Chinese past. My treatment of the second Opium War here becomes part of the first war's afterlife, showing how the delusions about China sown by the earlier conflict generate further spirals of violence, prejudice and guilt. The second reason is practical. At the time of writing, there was (to my knowledge) no book-length account of the first Opium War in English that made use of both anglophone accounts and the large collections of Chinese sources compiled and published in the 1990s. As I began to write, I realized that the richness of this material and of the historical questions that it suggested (concerning Sino-Western relations, Chinese–Manchu tensions, the functioning and malfunctioning of the Qing empire) was a good deal more than enough for one book. Although historians such as John Wong and James Hevia have produced brilliant accounts of key aspects of the second Opium War (its legality, its symbolism, its economic and political context), anglophone readers still lack a conventional narrative history of this later conflict that thoroughly combines and compares Western and Chinese sources. Regrettably, for reasons of space, I could not incorporate such a study into the present book. I hope very much, however, that the events of 1856–60 will in time receive the definitive, multilateral treatment that they deserve.

Chapter One

OPIUM AND CHINA

Consider a late-imperial photograph of Chinese opium-smokers. In one typical shot, two men recline on a couch, enveloped in long, padded jacquard silk gowns. One has an arm draped around a young woman, who is also reclining back on top of him (and looking a touch discomforted – perhaps by the smoker's attentions, perhaps by the camera). Necks propped up against the headboard, both men stare down the couch at the camera: eyes half-closed, mouths expressionless. (One of the smokers happens inexplicably to be clutching a model dog.) Even today, when synthetic opiates make opium look tame, and decades after Brassaï photographed the Parisian avant-garde rebranding the drug as bohemian chic, the image is somehow troubling; more so than a comparable shot of, for instance, a couple of Caucasian drinkers, even though the pair of smokers here are clearly well-to-do, and appear not to be indulging to great extremes. Perhaps to modern eyes there is something particularly decadent about lying down to take your narcotic of choice, something abject about the supine state. As the smokers gaze levelly back at us, through (we imagine) dope-clouded eyes, they seem to be defying us: 'We are deliberately, happily smoking ourselves into oblivion. What are you going to do about it?'

However liberal our politics, we are likely to have absorbed a mix of moral and scientific prejudice against opium that began accumulating in the West (and China) just over a hundred years ago: that reinvented it as a sinister vice enjoyed by social degenerates or masters of villainy. Beyond the opprobrium, though, that is now attached to

A late-nineteenth-century photograph of Chinese opium smokers.

opium-smoking lies a more complex social phenomenon: one that was widely debated through the nineteenth century, before Western missionary and medical opinion, and then the Chinese state, decided to condemn China's opium habit as sick and deviant – a national disease of the will that lay at the base of all the country's problems.

Opium has been an extraordinary shape-shifter in both the countries that would fight a war in its name in the early 1840s. In Britain and China, it began as a foreign drug (Turkish and Indian, respectively) that was first naturalized during the nineteenth century, then – at the end of that same century – sternly repatriated as an alien poison. For most of the century, neither popular nor expert medical opinion could agree on anything concerning opium, beyond the fact that it relieved pain. Was it more or less harmful than alcohol? Did it bestialize its users? Did it make your lungs go black and crawl with opium-addicted maggots? No one could say for sure. 'The disaster spread everywhere as the poison flowed into the hinterlands ... Those fallen into this obsession will ever utterly waste themselves', mourned one late-Qing smoker, Zhang Changjia, before observing a few pages on, 'Truly, opium is something that the world cannot do without.'[1] The clichéd image of opium-smoking is of prostration and narcolepsy; to many (including Thomas de Quincey, who walked the London streets by night sustained by laudanum), it was a stimulant. China's coolie masses would refresh their capacity for backbreaking labour with midday opium breaks. One reverend in the late-nineteenth century observed that such groups 'literally live on the opium; it is their meat and drink'.[2] Things were little different in the Victorian Fens: 'A man who is setting about a hard job takes his [opium] pill as a preliminary,' wrote one mid-century observer, 'and many never take their beer without dropping a piece of opium into it'.[3] To add to the confusion about opium's effects, British commanders in China between 1840 and 1842 noticed that Qing soldiers often prepared themselves for battle by stoking themselves up on the drug: some it calmed; others it excited for the fight ahead; others again, it sent to sleep.

Even now, after far more than a century of modern medicine, much remains unknown about opium's influence on the human constitution. Whether eaten, drunk or smoked, the drug's basic effects are the same: its magic ingredient is morphine, a lipid-soluble alkaloid that is absorbed into the bloodstream and (within seconds or minutes, depending on the strength of the preparation, the route of administration and the individual's susceptibility) presses buttons – the opioid receptors – in our cells. Once triggered, one of these buttons – the μ receptor – reduces the release of chemical transmitters from the nerve endings involved in the sensation of pain. The analgesia produced by morphine and its many analogues, such as diamorphine (heroin), can seem almost miraculous, relieving agony in minutes. And opium is good for far more than analgesia. As it enters the blood, it travels to the intestines to slow the movement of the gut, giving pause to diarrhoea and dysentery. It soothes coughs, by suppressing the brain centres that control the coughing impulse. Most famously, perhaps, it encourages the release of dopamine, the hormone that governs the brain's pleasure principle. Put more simply, opium makes us euphoric.

Like all drugs, opium has its unwanted downsides. One disadvantage is its talent for generating nausea (a response elicited in 40 per cent of patients to whom morphine is administered).[4] If taken for pain relief rather than diarrhoea, it can cause troublesome constipation.

Its greatest immediate drawback is its habit of slowing, or even putting to sleep, the centres in the brain that control breathing. In excess, opium will kill you by fatally depressing respiration. Because of the quietness with which opium overdosers generally meet their ends, opium has of old been the friend of faint-hearted suicides and the ally of assassins. While dopamine intensifies feelings of contentment, moreover, it can also heighten other, less enjoyable sensations. Encouraging and enlarging perceptions of fear and menace, it is an agent of paranoia, suspicion and schizophrenia – hence De Quincey's visions.

Opium's final flaw is that (like many dopamine-generated responses, governed as they are by the sense of pleasurable reward generated), it induces a craving for the whole thing to begin again. Without external stimulation from substances such as opium, the opioid and dopamine receptors exist quietly within us in unnoticed equilibrium. Once a receptor is triggered, however, it can become desensitized and unbalanced, demanding a regular, and perhaps increasing supply of the original stimulant. If the neural and chemical balance in the body has come to rely on external medication, a sudden withdrawal of the supply will bring unpleasant (and indeed dangerous) symptoms in response – trembling, exhaustion, fever, goosepimples (the origin of the phrase 'cold turkey'), nausea, diarrhoea and insomnia – relieved only by hair of the dog.

Opium's historical guises through the past century and a half of Chinese history have been almost as diverse as its chemical effects. For Europeans (who began trading it early in the seventeenth century), it offered first a way into Chinese markets ('transactions seemed to partake of the nature of the drug', reminisced one smuggler from retirement, 'they imparted a soothing frame of mind with three percent commission on sales, one percent on returns, and no bad debts!'), and then ethical justification for saving China from its bad, addictive tendencies ('the Chinese are all of them more or less morally weak,' explained one post-1842 British missionary, 'as you would expect to find in any heathen nation; but with the opium smoker it is worse').[5] After around 1870, Western disapproval of China's opium habit joined with other, older prejudices to create the Yellow Peril. The non-Christian Chinese love of opium, the logic went, destroyed any possibility of normal human response in them: it

was 'a form of mania', a 'potent necromancer' that left them all the
more inscrutably amoral, a mindlessly drugged army of xenophobes
plotting revenge on the West.[6] To many Chinese, opium brought
benefits (as well as the perils of addiction): profit, relief from minor
or chronic ailments, and narcotic, even aesthetic pleasure. And even
after it metamorphosed, at the close of the century, into a foreign
poison foisted upon China by scheming imperialists, it did not stay
that way for long. Indignation at the West easily subsided into self-
disgust: the British might have brought us the opium, went the
subtext of nationalist moral panic, but *we* allowed ourselves to become
addicted. In 1839, on the eve of the crackdown that would trigger a
war with Britain, Chinese anti-opium campaigners – including the
uncompromising Lin Zexu – confidently condemned it as a plague
'worse than floods and wild beasts'; as a 'life-destroying drug threatening to degrade the entire Chinese people to a level with reptiles,
dogs and swine'.[7] If only it had been that simple.

Opium began life in the Chinese empire as an import from the
vaguely identified 'Western regions' (ancient Greece and Rome,
Turkey, Syria, Iraq, Persia and Afghanistan); the earliest Chinese
reference (in a medical manual) occurs in the first half of the eighth
century. Eaten or drunk, prepared in many different ways (ground,
boiled, honeyed, infused, mixed with ginger, ginseng, liquorice,
vinegar, black plums, ground rice, caterpillar fungus), it served for all
kinds of ailments (diarrhoea and dysentery, arthritis, diabetes, malaria,
chronic coughs, a weak constitution). By the eleventh century, it was
recognized for its recreational, as well as curative uses. 'It does good
to the mouth and to the throat', observed one satisfied user. 'I have
but to drink a cup of poppy-seed decoction, and I laugh, I am
happy.'[8] 'It looks like myrrha', elaborated a court chronicle some four
hundred years later. 'It is dark yellow, soft and sticky like ox glue. It
tastes bitter, produces excessive heat and is poisonous . . . It enhances
the art of alchemists, sex and court ladies . . . Its price equals that
of gold.'[9] Opium was supposed to help control ejaculation which,
as sexological theory told it, enabled the sperm to retreat to feed the
male brain. Opium-enriched aphrodisiacs became a boom industry in

Ming China (1368–1644) – possibly contributing to the high death-rate of the dynasty's emperors (eleven out of a total of sixteen Ming rulers failed to get past their fortieth birthday). In 1958, as part of a final push to root out the narcotic in China, the new Communist government excavated the tomb of Wanli, the hypochondriac (though long-lived) emperor of the late Ming, and found his bones saturated with morphine. Enterprising Ming cooks even tried to stir-fry it, fashioning poppy seeds into curd as a substitute for tofu. Opium was one of the chief ingredients of a Ming-dynasty cure-all, the 'big golden panacea' (for use against toothache, athlete's foot and too much sex), in which the drug was combined with (amongst other things) bezoar, pearl, borneol, musk, rhinoceros horn, antelope horn, catechu, cinnabar, amber, eaglewood, aucklandia root, white sandalwood; all of which had first to be gold-plated, then pulverized, turned into pellets with breast-milk, and finally swallowed with pear juice. (Take one at a time, the pharmacological manuals recommended.[10])

It was yet another import – in the shape of tobacco from the New World – that led to the smoking of opium. Introduced to China at some point between 1573 and 1627 (around the same time as the peanut, the sweet potato and maize), by the middle of the seventeenth century tobacco-smoking had become an empire-wide habit. As the Qing established itself in China after 1644, the dynasty made nervous attempts to ban it as 'a crime more heinous even than that of neglecting archery': smokers and sellers could be fined, whipped and even decapitated.[11] But by around 1726, the regime had given up the empire's tobacco addiction as a bad job, with great fields of the stuff swaying just beyond the capital's walls. And somewhere in the early eighteenth century, a new, wonderful discovery had reached China from Java, carried on Chinese ships between the two places: that tobacco was *even better* if you soaked it first in opium syrup (carried mainly in Portuguese cargoes). First stop for this discovery was the Qing's new conquest, Taiwan; from there it passed to the mainland's maritime rim, and then the interior.

It was smoking that made Chinese consumers take properly to opium. Smoking was sociable, skilled and steeped in connoisseurship (with its carved, bejewelled pipes of jade, ivory and tortoiseshell, its silver lamps for heating and tempering the drug, its beautiful red sandalwood couches on which consumers reclined). It was also less likely to kill the consumer than the eaten or drunk version of the drug: around 80–90 per cent of the morphia may have been lost in fumes from the pipe or exhaled. Through the late eighteenth and early nineteenth centuries, China made opium-smoking its own: a chic post-prandial; an essential lubricant of the sing-song (prostitution) trade; a must-have hospitality item for all self-respecting hosts; a favourite distraction from the pressures of court life for the emperor and his household.[12] Opium houses could be salubrious, even luxurious institutions, far from the Dickensian den-of-vice stereotype (like an 'intimate beer-house', a surprised Somerset Maugham pronounced in 1922 – a mature stage in China's drug plague), in which companionable groups of friends might enjoy a civilized pipe or two over tea and dim-sum.[13]

Somewhere near the start of the nineteenth century, smokers began to dispense with the diluting presence of tobacco – perhaps because pure opium was more expensive, and therefore more status-laden. Around this time, thanks to the quality control exercised by the diligent rulers of British India (who established a monopoly over opium production in Bengal in 1793), the supply also became more reliable, no longer regularly contaminated by adulterants such as horse dung and sand. A way of burning money, smoking was the perfect act of conspicuous consumption. Every stage was enveloped in lengthy, elaborate, costly ritual: the acquisition of exquisite paraphernalia; the intricacy of learning how to cook and smoke it (softening the dark ball of opium to a dark, caramelized rubber, inserting it into the hole on the roof of the pipe bowl, then drawing slowly, steadily on the pipe to suck the gaseous morphia out); the leisurely doze that followed the narcotic hit. The best families would go one step further in flaunting their affluence, by keeping an opium chef to prepare their pipes for them. The empire's love affair with opium can be told through the beautiful objects it manufactured for consuming the drug, through the lyrics that aficionados composed to their heavy, treacly object of desire, or in bald statistics. In 1780, a British East India Company (EIC) ship could not break even on a single opium cargo shipped to Canton. By 1839, imports were topping 40,000 chests per annum.

*

One further point needs to be made about opium as it acquired its hold over eighteenth- and nineteenth-century China: it had been illegal since 1729. Somehow, over the ensuing century, it turned into a prestigious contraband bought, sold and prized by the empire's best people (as well as by some of its worst). Contemporary China's line on opium transforms it into a moral poison forced on helpless Chinese innocents by wicked aliens. The reality was more troublingly collusive.

As the British entered the trade at the end of the eighteenth century, they insisted that they were simply providing a service: satisfying, not creating demand. Those Britons involved were at pains to present it to audiences back home as quite the most honourable line of business in the East. Invest in opium, warmly suggested William Jardine to a friend in Essex, as the 'safest and most gentlemanlike speculation I am aware of'.[14] It may have seemed that way from East Anglia. It was also a hands-off and sure source of revenue for East India Company employees in India, who only had to look after the opium as far as Government House in Calcutta, letting private British and Indian, and then Chinese sellers handle the dirty business of getting it to the Chinese coast, and inland. 'From the opium trade,' summarized an 1839 text on the subject,

> the Honourable Company have derived for years an immense revenue and through them the British Government and nation have also reaped an incalculable amount of political and financial advantage. The turn of the balance of trade between Great Britain and China in favour of the former has ... contributed directly to support the vast fabric of British dominion in the East ... and benefit[ed] the nation to an extent of £6 million yearly without impoverishing India.[15]

From closer quarters, though, the opium trade looked a good deal more raffish than its leading British supporters liked to argue. Jardine and Matheson, the two doyens of the Canton opium trade (and leading sinophobe warmongers of the 1830s), were hardly gentlemen by background, however diligently they worked to convert hard cash into respectability. Born on a Scottish farm in 1784, Jardine lost his father at the age of nine; as a teenager, he scraped through Edinburgh's medical school only thanks to his older brother's support. He learnt the East Indies trade among the bilge and gore of ship's doctoring: the pay was not terrific (£10 a month), but a perk of the job was the opportunity to develop commercial sidelines – officers were allowed two tons of their own goods to buy or sell. Jardine soon learnt to make the most of it. On his second voyage, he forfeited his £40-wages because the ship and its official freight were lost through damage incurred in a Canton typhoon, and assault by a French warship, after which he ended up a prisoner of war. Nevertheless, he still made around £175 from selling on his own tonnage, which he had been wise enough to send home by a separate ship from Bombay. By 1818, he had made the leap to management, winning a nomination as agent to a private trading house in India; within another year, he had migrated to the Canton opium business.[16]

Matheson's progress to private trader was smoother: family business influence secured him merchants' indentures from the EIC aged nine-teen, when he was fresh out of Edinburgh University. Once he had arrived in Asia, the decision to trade in opium does not seem to have required conscious thought, opium imports to China having doubled between 1800 and 1820. Although by no means a blemish-free ethical choice, the move into opium by British traders was not, as claimed by contemporary historians in the People's Republic, a deliberate con-spiracy to make narcotic slaves of the Chinese empire; it was a greedy, pragmatic response to a decline in sales of other British imports (clocks, watches, furs). 'Opium is like gold', wrote James Matheson's first partner, Robert Taylor, in 1818. 'I can sell it any time.'[17] Even that was untrue: the Qing state's erratic, ongoing campaign against the drug through the early decades of the nineteenth century, together with opportunistic over-production in India, made profit margins wildly variable. Before Matheson joined more successfully with Jardine in 1825, he twice faced ruin in Canton, from over-extension in opium. Only another unpredictable about-turn in price and an audacious push to trade along the east coast saved him.

Management faced physical risks, too: at one point, presenting a petition at the gate through which official communications could be passed from foreigners at Canton, Jardine sustained (though did not seem to notice) a severe blow to the head, thereby winning the Chinese nickname that translated as 'Iron-Headed Old Rat'. Both Jardine and Matheson were far too eager to make money to waste any time themselves on appearing like bumbling gentlemen speculators: Jardine is supposed to have kept only one chair in his office – for himself – to discourage loquacity in his visitors. But once his fortune had been made, Jardine seemed to forget all that, becoming an enthusiastic propagandist for the sedate security of the business, naming it 'by far the safest trade in China'.[18] (This in 1840, when over the past two years the Qing government had begun publicly executing native opium-smugglers in front of the foreign factories, had imprisoned the British trading community in Canton, destroyed their stock and driven them from the mainland to the edges of that barren rock, Hong Kong.)

In the end, though, opium money *did* make them gentlemen: Jardine first, returning to London in 1839, where he served as military adviser on China to Palmerston, then in 1841 took an unopposed seat in the House of Commons. (In truth, he did not succeed in quashing every sceptical view of his own past. 'Oh, a dreadful man!' Disraeli thinly fictionalized him in 1845 in *Sybil*. 'A Scotchman, richer than Croesus, one Mr Druggy, fresh from Canton, with a million in opium in each pocket, denouncing corruption and bellowing free-trade.'[19]) When Jardine died of pulmonary oedema a year after the Treaty of Nanjing that closed the Opium War, he passed both his seat and the directorship of the firm to Matheson, who then promptly retired from the trade, bought the Hebridean island of Lewis for half a million pounds and reinvented himself as a laird of good works. The inscription (composed by his wife) below a posthumous snowy-white bust of the great man looking loftily out over the Atlantic from the grounds of Lewis's Stornoway Castle tells his story truly and well:

> he was a child of God, living evidently under the influence of His Holy Spirit: 'Well done, thou good and faithful servant.' (Matthew, xxv.21) . . . [He] was long resident at Canton and Macau and was one of the founders of the eminent House of Jardine, Matheson & Co. During his and Mr. Jardine's partnership, the House acquired that high repute for honour, integrity and magnificent hospitality which gave a free passport to all using its name throughout the East.

The opium trade also struggled to glean some respectability from its association with the missionary effort, both enterprises depending on each other – the traders on the linguistic skills of the men of God, the latter on the passages up the coast that the former offered. (After 1842, of course, missionaries would take aggressive advantage of the Opium War's 'opening' of China.) There seems to have been little sense of contradiction between drugs and faith in the minds of some of the most successful of the traders: 'Employed delivering briskly', goes the diary entry for 2 December 1832 of one devout pusher, James Innes, on an audacious mission up the east coast, to Fujian. 'No time to read my bible.'[20] No single figure embodied this collaboration better than Karl Gützlaff, the Pomeranian missionary and later agent of the British occupation of China ('short, square . . . with a sinister eye', summarized his cousin-in-law), who enjoyed a career in the pay of opium interests that was both varied and remunerative (though not overly long: he died in 1851, a mere nine years after the Treaty of Nanjing, of disappointment after discovering a large-scale fraud by his converts).[21] 'Tho' it is our earnest wish', went Jardine's first petition for his services in 1832,

> that you should not in any way injure the grand object you have in view by appearing interested in what by many is considered an immoral traffic yet such a traffic is absolutely necessary to give any vessel a reasonable chance . . . the more profitable the expedition the better we shall be able to place at your disposal a sum that may hereafter be usefully employed in furthering the grand object you have in view, and for your success in which we feel deeply interested.[22]

The argument was well made, for in Gützlaff's own mind, it really was that simple – commerce (by whatever means) and Christianity went hand in hand: 'Our commercial relations', he hectored the British reading public in an influential 1832 account of China, 'are at the present moment on such a basis as to warrant a continuation of the trade along the coast. We hope that this may tend ulti- mately to the introduction of the gospel, for which many doors are opened.'[23] Fluent in both self-deception and China's south-eastern dialects (to the point that locals mistook him for a native 'son of Han'), he had more interpreting offers than he could handle: 'I would give 1,000 dollars for three days of Gützlaff', sighed Innes on his Fujian trip.[24] Gützlaff's excursions up the coast gave him an opportunity to reach potential converts, whom he lectured – as the mood took him – on their horrible gambling, idolatry, conceit, opium-smoking and so on. His Bible tracts went ashore alongside the chests of opium, finding – according to Gützlaff – many 'eager and grateful readers' (though what these precious bits of paper were really used for – patching holes in walls, perhaps, or something else altogether – we will never know).[25] He was good, moreover, for far more than interpreting and preaching: when six official boats tried to inhibit Chinese opium-dealers from approaching a Jardine–Matheson ship, 'Doctor Gützlaff, dressed in his best . . . paid them a visit . . . He demanded their instant departure and threatened them with destruction if they ever again anchored in our neighbourhood. They went away immediately saying they had anchored there in the dark by mistake, and we have seen nothing more of them.'[26]

For those at the coalface of the trade – the European captains and Chinese distributors – the business delivered a miscellany of glamour, profit and risk. By the 1820s, the maritime rigours of the drug trade had given birth to the nimble opium clipper, which outmoded the large Indiamen by its ability to beat up against the monsoon and far greater speed: 'cutting through the head sea like a knife, with . . . raking masts and sharp bows running up like the head of a grey-hound.'[27] Officers on opium ships were well paid: for shaving days off passage times, for task-mastering potentially mutinous men, for pirate-fighting. Violence was to be expected: from Qing government ships, from sea bandits, from their own crews. Local pirates (called, in Chinese, 'wasps of the ocean') were the greatest terror – from small-time fishing boats that moonlighted with a little sea robbery when the opportunity presented, to more professional, multi-vessel outfits. In 1804, Portuguese-run Macao almost fell to a seventy-strong fleet of them. Practically anything served for warfare: conventional firearms, of course, but also stink-pots (earthen pots filled with gunpowder and Chinese liquor) that they lit then tossed at merchant vessels, blinding their victims with the smoke. The desperateness of pirates' living conditions (ships swarmed with rats, which 'they encourage to breed, & eat . . . as great delicacies', recalled one prisoner) and the certainty of death if caught made them vicious to their prisoners: one captain died in 1795 having spent several days bound naked over the deck, being occasionally fed a little water and rice. This was not racially motivated violence, however: natives of the coast could be treated much worse. An officer captured from the Chinese navy had, while still alive, 'his bowels cut open and his heart taken out, which they afterwards soaked in spirits and ate'.[28]

But foreign traders of the early nineteenth century had only a partial role to play: distribution deep into the mainland was carried out by native – Chinese, Manchu, Muslim – smugglers. The clippers sailed up to Lintin, a small, nondescript island about a third of the way between Hong Kong and Canton. There, they discharged their cargo onto superannuated versions of themselves: retired hulks serving as floating depots. Long, slim Chinese smuggling boats – known in the trade as 'centipedes', 'fast crabs' or 'scrambling dragons', and rowed by twenty to seventy thoroughly armed men apiece – would then draw up, into which opium was loaded, to fulfil orders purchased at the factories in Canton. From here, the drug entered the empire's circulatory system: along the south coast's threadwork of narrow waterways, and into Canton itself – amid consignments of less contentious goods, under clothes, inside coffins. At every stage, there was employment for locals: for the brokers, couriers and 'shroffs' (who checked for counterfeit silver) on board European vessels and in European pay; for the tough Tankas who made the dragons scramble; for the smugglers who brought it ashore; for the Cantonese middle-men; for the proprietors of opium shops, restaurants, tea-houses and brothels.

And every stage in the trade required officialdom to look the other way – which for the most part they obligingly did, even as the traces of the business surrounded them. One of Matheson's Calcutta associates put it nicely, wondering sarcastically that the agency's opium clippers 'have ever been able to trade at all. A European-rigged vessel gives the alarm against herself whenever she appears, and lodges an information in the hands of every individual . . . Only think of the Chinese going to smuggle tea on the coast of England in a junk!'[29] Generally, all that was required to land opium was cash outlay and sometimes a touch of doublespeak. If an opium consignee was lucky, the responsible mandarin would simply demand a businesslike bribe per box of opium – like a species of duty, as if the cargo were nothing more controversial than cotton, or molasses. If he were less fortunate, he would suffer a lecture administered first on the evils of the opium

trade, or perhaps a personal reading of the emperor's latest edict on
the subject, *then* be allowed to hand over the bribe. But connivance
– because of the profit to be made from it – seems to have been the
basic rule: one exploratory trade mission by the EIC up the north
China coast in 1832 was greeted by disappointment all the way, as
the ship, the *Lord Amherst*, had neglected to bring opium.[30]

When – and only when – the clippers were safely unloaded and
preparing to return to India, Qing government ships would, one
sardonic observer of the mid-1830s noted, at last mount a sham
pursuit: 'twenty or thirty Chinese men-o-war junks are seen creeping
slowly . . . towards them . . . never close enough to be within reach
of a cannonball, and if, for the sake of a joke, one of the clippers
heaves to, in order to allow them to come up, they never accept the
invitation, but keep at a respectful distance . . . a proclamation is
[then] issued to the entire nation, stating that "His Celestial Majesty's
Imperial fleet, after a *desperate conflict*, has made the Fan-quis [foreign
devils] run before it, and given them such a drubbing, that they will
never dare show themselves on the coast again." '[31] Thus, summarized
an American trader of the 1830s, 'we pursued the evil tenor of our
ways with supreme indifference, took care of our business, pulled
boats, walked, dined well, and so the years rolled by as happily as
possible.'[32]

From its southern point of entry, Canton's opium made its way
to the northernmost edges of the empire: on the carrying poles of
small-time peddlers and the backs of domesticated camels; in the
caravans of Shanxi and Shaanxi merchants who shifted it into Xinjiang; in the luggage of candidates for the fiercely competitive
metropolitan civil-service examinations in Beijing. Almost everywhere
that subjects of the emperor travelled, they brought opium with
them, if they had a bit of capital to spare. In 1793, John Barrow –
comptroller on the first British embassy to China – had noted that
opium's price restricted it to use only by the 'opulent'.[33] By the
1820s, indulgence had begun to seep down the social scale: 'It started
with the rich,' one south-eastern literatus remembered of the decade,
'then the lower classes began to emulate.'[34] The size and diversity of
the opium market in nineteenth-century China showed up in the
variety of terms for the drug that existed: *yapian* (a loanword invented
at least as early as the Ming dynasty), the term in current use today,

translates literally as 'crow slices' – presumably a reference to the blackness of prepared opium. Before this rendering, though, it had already passed through *diyejia* (probably a simple transliteration from a Greek term for a treacly opiate), *yingsu* (jar millet – for the poppy's seeds' resemblance to those of millet), *mi'nang* (millet bags) and *wuxiang* (black fragrance). All through the nineteenth century, *yapian* coexisted with a host of other references: *afurong* (literally, poppy), *datu* or *xiaotu* (big mud or little mud), *yangtu* (mud from the Western seas), *yangyan* (smoke from the Western seas), *yangyao* (medicine or tonic from the Western seas). The prefix *yang*, incidentally, did not denote fear or distrust for the alien, but was part of a full-blown mania for the expensive elusiveness of things foreign: 'foreign things are the most fashionable now,' observed one mid-nineteenth-century essayist, 'foreign copper, china, paint, linen, cotton . . . the list is endless.'[35] When the Communist Party – while publicly denouncing their rivals, the Nationalists, and Western imperialists for profiting from the drug trade – secretly grew opium to make ends meet in north-west China in the early 1940s, they generated another couple of euphemisms: 'special product', and sometimes 'soap'.[36]

By the time of the Opium War, the empire was not just importing and domesticating this prized foreign drug; it was producing it, in tremendous quantities. (Nonetheless, although native opium appealed because of its cheapness, it was always a poor cousin to the foreign product, due to the greater potency of the latter.) Where it grew readily (especially in southwest China, but also along the east coast, and in Shaanxi, Gansu and Xinjiang to the north-west), it was the wonder crop: it sold well, and grew on the same land in an annual cycle alongside cotton, beans, maize and rice. Almost every part of the plant could be used: the sap, for raw opium; the leaves as a vegetable; the stem for dye; the seeds for oil. For southern peasants in the late 1830s, growing opium earned them ten times more than rice. By the time of the Opium War, the trade had spread across the entire empire: smoked (extensively) in prosperous south-eastern metropolises; trafficked; and cultivated (all along the western rim, from the mountain wildernesses of Yunnan in the south, to Xinjiang in the north).

Opium simply refused to go away: when the state moved to crack down on opium along the south and east coast by banishing smokers and smugglers to the frontier zone of Xinjiang, they merely brought their habit to the north-west. If domestic poppy-growing was cut back in south-western provinces such as Yunnan, civil servants predicted that coastal imports would increase to fill the market space made available. In 1835, officials optimistically announced that the poppy had been eradicated from Zhejiang, in east China; five years later, further investigation revealed that government representatives had lopped only the tops of the plants, carelessly leaving the roots still in the ground. That same year, thirty-four peasants fought officials sent to destroy their crops properly.[37]

Sometime in the first decade of the nineteenth century, on a crisp, bright spring day, an emperor's son sat studying his history books. Bored and tired, he asked his servant to prepare him his pipe. 'My mind suddenly becomes clear,' he exclaimed, 'my eyes and ears refreshed. People have said that wine is endowed with all the virtues, but today I call opium the satisfier. When you desire happiness, it gives you happiness.' Soon, he felt inspired to poetry: 'Watch the cloud ascend from your nose/ Inhale – exhale, the fragrance rises/ The air deepens and thickens/ As it settles, it truly seems/ That mountains and clouds emerge from a distant ocean.'[38]

In 1820, this same son, Daoguang (1782–1850), himself became the Emperor of China. In another twenty years, he would authorize a campaign against opium that would ultimately result in the disastrously counter-productive engagements of the Opium War. In the years immediately preceding the war, Daoguang – according to one rumour – even executed his own son, for his failure to give up the habit. What had happened in those four decades, to transform opium-smoking from an acceptable displacement activity for an idle emperor-in-training to a perilous scourge?

The court had, it was true, been uneasy about opium for more than a century before the crackdown of the late 1830s – ever since the first imperial prohibition in 1729, when the Yongzheng emperor (1678–1735) had noted with a shudder that 'Shameless rascals lure the sons of good families into [smoking] for their own profit . . .

youngsters become corrupted until their lives collapse, their families' livelihood vanishes, and nothing is left but trouble.'[39]

Strong words – but for sixty years, little seems to have been done. Smokers and sellers continued the habit: anyone with a head on his shoulders could argue that the opium he was consuming or selling was legally medicinal, not illegally recreational; or simply bribe the relevant parties. Between 1773 and the close of the eighteenth century, annual imports of Chinese opium more than quadrupled.[40] The ban of 1729 was reaffirmed in 1796. Again, little was apparently achieved, beyond forcing smugglers to make their deals further along the coast, rather than flagrantly at Canton. Opium was a boom industry: demand, supply and price all grew through the early nineteenth century – an open invitation to local officials to profit. 1799 saw a reaffirmation of the reaffirmation, reminding the populace that opium 'is of a violent and powerful nature, and possesses a foetid and odious flavour'.[41] 1811–13 saw the introduction of further punitive measures: a new edict, specifying one hundred blows of the heavy bamboo, a month in the cangue and – a special measure for eunuchs and retainers – slavery for life in the freezing north-east.[42] By 1839, imports would have increased tenfold from the start of the century.[43]

The Qing's difficulties in promoting a hard line on smoking were simple: no one seemed able to agree on the extent of the problem, or even whether it was a problem. Despite the rise of a vociferous anti-opium lobby at court from the 1830s onwards, there was little consensus among either Chinese or Western commentators through much of the nineteenth century concerning the effects of the drug either on the human frame, the extent of its use in China or what constituted either heavy use or an addiction. Denunciations accumulated on both sides of the trade. 'The smoke of opium is a deadly poison', ran an 1836 pamphlet published by local government in Canton; it 'never fail[s] to terminate in death', the American-run *Chinese Repository* concurred, 'if the evil habit . . . is continued . . . There is no slavery on earth, to be compared with the bondage into which opium casts its victim.'[44] Equally, both sides had apologists for the drug: 'taken as it almost invariably is, in great moderation,' one Briton observed during the Opium War, 'it is by no means noxious to the constitution, but quite the reverse, causing an exhilarating and pleasing sensation, and, in short, does [users] no more harm than a moderate quantity of wine does to us.'[45] Smoke opium on a miserable, rainy day, advised one late-eighteenth-century Chinese gentleman, and 'there is a sudden feeling of refreshment . . . Detached from all worries, you enter a world of dreams and fantasies, free as a spirit. Paradise!'[46]

Foreign observers across the rest of the nineteenth century would publicize the physical ravages of opium upon its smokers: 'inflamed eyes and haggard countenance'; skin bearing 'that peculiar glassy polish by which an opium-smoker is invariably known.'[47] 'Those who are addicted to opium', echoed one Manchu Prince of the Imperial Clan Court in 1839, 'are entranced and powerless to quit, almost as if seduced by the deadly poison, until they stand like skeletons, their bodily shape totally disfigured and no better than the crippled.'[48] But others vigorously rejected accounts of opium's universally degrading effects on the populace: William Hunter, an American trader of the 1820s and 1830s, 'rarely, if ever, saw any one physically or mentally injured by it. No evidences of a general abuse . . . were apparent . . . smoking was a habit, as the use of wine was with us, in moderation.'[49]

This vagueness was in part a symptom of the underdevelopment of a modern medical profession: opium's 'particles, by their direct and topical influence on the nerves of the lungs,' confidently speculated one British army doctor, Duncan McPherson, who saw action in China, 'guard the system against disease.'[50] But taking a hard line on opium in nineteenth-century China was primarily difficult because the drug was so ubiquitously useful: as an antispasmodic, as an analgesic, as a cough, fever and appetite suppressant. For centuries, it had been a palliative against the many commonplace complaints that afflicted the inhabitants of late-imperial China: diarrhoea, fevers, aches and pains, hunger, exhaustion. While China did not produce aspirin (which remained the case at least as late as 1934, even though it was being commercially manufactured back in the 1890s), 'opium was our medicine, it was all we had', explained one former soldier in the pay of the Nationalist government (1928–49).[51] 'There is no disease in which opium may not be employed,' reported McPherson from personal experience, 'nor do we know of any substance which can supply its place.'[52]

Neither was there agreement on the nature or extent of the empire's drug problem. Since opium was officially illegal, reliable estimates of smokers are elusive. Through the nineteenth century, guesses varied from 0.35, to 5, to 60 per cent of the population.[53] Behind these hazy statistics hide other questions: how much did all these smokers use? What constituted occasional, moderate, habitual, dangerous use? Did the addict have to steadily increase his dose? The anti-opium lobby – both Chinese and Western – portrayed the drug as inevitably enslaving its users, forcing them daily to find increasing quantities of cash to fund a destructive addiction. A highly influential set of drawings in the *Chinese Repository* from 1837 depicted the life-cycle of an opium-smoker, from over-privileged young scion to emaciated sot, his wife and child condemned to lives of pitiless toil to earn money to buy the drug he craves.[54] But there were gainsayers of such apocalyptic images, too: anecdotes that told of the entirely reliable broker who smoked opium to excess; or of the zealous reforming official, who happened also to be a confirmed opium-user and brothel-visitor. Compared with alcohol's 'evil consequences', some found the harm of opium to be 'infinitesimal'; the Chinese were 'essentially temperate'.[55] No observer could agree on what constituted a standard dose: mid-nineteenth-century estimates ran from around four grams, to twenty and beyond.[56] The subjects of the Qing empire smoked for as many reasons as Europeans consumed alcohol and tobacco: for show; for companionship; to relieve boredom and pain. Some smoked their lives and estates away; others never got past their first puff; others again limited their doses to a daily post-prandial.

The only anxiety that runs consistently through Qing attempts to do something about opium concerns the question of social control. Drugs have a universal talent for dismaying the authorities: not only do they consume otherwise usefully productive money and time but, more crucially, they loosen inner psychological constraints, and the sense of restraint that holds convention together. Disquiet about the threat to stability posed by a hedonistic opium culture lurks in every official statement on the drug in the century preceding the Opium War. The first edict of 1729 punished opium-selling by reference to 'the law on heterodox teachings that delude the masses'.[57] The menace that had been identified, therefore, was not physical, but psychological: the possibility of public disorder. 'The use of opium originally prevailed only among vagrants and disreputable persons,' lamented the imperial declaration from 1799, 'but has since extended itself among the members and descendants of respectable families [resulting] in the gratification of impure and sensual desires, whereby their respective duties and occupations are neglected.'[58]

Eleven years later, when six packages of the stuff were found on sale *in the Forbidden City*, the emperor became very angry. Opium, he fulminated, makes its smoker 'very excited, capable of doing anything he pleases', adding, almost as an afterthought, 'before long, it kills him. Opium is a poison,' he returned to his main theme, 'undermining our good customs and morality.'[59] While China's educated elites began producing reasoned medical denunciations in the second decade or so of the nineteenth century, concern for individuals' physical well-being was still prefaced by anxieties about the drug's effect on public decency. One physician began a collection of anti-opium prescriptions by condemning smoking as an 'evil pastime' favoured by 'those who violate morality and bring ruin upon their families'.[60]

The threat posed by opium to political stability was intensified by the government's financial worries. By the early decades of the nineteenth century – also years of rising opium consumption – the empire seemed to be running out of silver, crucial to the smooth running of the economy because it was the currency in which taxes and the army were paid. If silver became scarce and therefore more expensive, relative to the copper currency used for small, everyday transactions, the tax-paying populace were left squeezed and resentful. Vagrancy, strikes and riots resulted: 110 incidents of mass protest took place between 1842 and 1849, precisely because of the rising cost of silver. The government simultaneously found itself short of funds for spending on the armies and public works that would keep general discontent at bay. The result was a serious rise in social insubordination: 'Since the beginning of history,' went one official complaint of 1840, 'never has there been a people as arrogant or unwilling to obey imperial orders as that of today.'[61] Contemporary observation and circumstantial evidence blamed opium. Between 1805 and 1839, imports of opium increased considerably more than tenfold, from 3,159 to 40,200 chests per year. At the same time, China's balance of payments uncharacteristically entered the red: between 1800 and 1810, around $26 million travelled into China;

between 1828 and 1836, around $38 million travelled out.[62] Panicked observers guessed that China's wealth had been reduced by 50 per cent – the reality was probably around the 19 per cent mark. By the third and fourth decades of the nineteenth century, opium suddenly seemed to be everywhere – in north, west, south, east and central China, with Guangdong (opium's main province of origin, in the deep south) the great plughole down which the empire's silver was apparently vanishing. Opium use increased at just the right moment to be fingered as the culprit for a rich repertoire of late-Qing ills: economic stagnation, environmental exhaustion, overpopulation, decline of the army and general standards of public order.

Despite this perception, it is far from clear that opium was exclusively to blame for the silver famine. Until 1852, China never imported more than eight million pounds of opium per year. Over the next forty years, opium imports exceeded this quantity in all but four years, sometimes nearing 10.6 million. And yet, after a decline in silver revenues up to around 1855 – and a concomitant decline in the effectiveness of the Qing state – bullion supplies picked up in the second half of the century (despite increases in opium use), enabling the Qing to hold on through the massive civil crisis of the Taiping Rebellion. From 1856 to 1886, the Chinese economy was once more in credit, with some $691 million flowing back to the empire.[63] If opium truly was the villain of the piece in the first half of the century, why did the Chinese economy not go further into the red after opium imports soared after 1842? To answer this question, we have to look beyond the British–Indian–Chinese trade triangle, and at the impact of South American independence movements on global silver supply.

Curiously – for it was a dynasty preoccupied with questions of security and sovereignty – the Qing had long allowed itself to be dependent on foreign silver supplies: on imports from South America, gained through Chinese trading in the Philippines, or through exports to Europe. In the forty years up to 1829, Mexico was producing around 80 per cent of the world's silver and gold. But independence movements between the 1810s and 1820s caused an estimated 56.6 per cent decline in world silver production relative to the 1790s. Given late-imperial China's involvement in the global economy through its need for foreign silver, the sudden reduction in Latin American supplies was bound to have a noticeable effect. First of all, it diminished the amount of silver that Britain had to spend on tea and silk in China; consequently, such exports from China grew only slowly in the early decades of the nineteenth century. Secondly, British traders were obliged to reach more and more for opium, rather than for scarce bullion, to exchange for the tea and silk that they did buy. All this suggests that while opium imports certainly had an impact on China's silver reserves, the effect would not have been so crippling if the first boom-period for imports had not coincided with a serious contraction of the world silver supply. Had this not been the case, it seems possible that China could have paid for its opium habit in the time-honoured fashion: with tea and silk. In other words, it was arguably not the opium trade alone that led to the financial instability of Qing China, but also global problems in the production and distribution of silver.[64]

Rightly or wrongly, though, by the end of the 1830s, opium was starting to be identified as a scapegoat for all the empire's problems. It was the further, unfortunate collision of two elements at court – an anxious, harassed emperor, and a clique of ambitious moralizers – that led to 1839's confrontation with Britain.

Chapter Two

DAOGUANG'S DECISION

To the casual onlooker, being Emperor of China – surrounded by palaces, empresses, slaves and kowtows – might have looked exquisitely pleasurable. The reality was rather different. It was not just the workload, though that was bad enough: a Qing emperor's average day at the palace consisted of audiences and memorial-reading, followed by more audiences, then more memorial-reading, sometimes varied by having officials presented, or by assessing death penalties. Emperorship was also burdened with an oppressive sense of public obligation. During the first millennium BC (the formative centuries of Chinese statecraft) the ruling Zhou dynasty established the idea that emperors ruled by the mystical Mandate of Heaven. If a dynasty's righteousness went into steep decline, Heaven would withdraw the Mandate – publicizing its decision through cataclysms such as rebellions, civil wars and comets – and pass it to someone else.

Like most rulers of China before them, the Qing had won the country through military rather than moral supremacy. In 1644, bands of Manchu horsemen (disciplined into the Eight Banners – military units totalling between 300,000 and 500,000 men) had poured from the north-east through a pass in China's great frontier wall, defeated a vast rival army of Chinese rebels and founded the dynasty in Beijing. Within another hundred years, the three great emperors of the high Qing, Kangxi (1654–1722), Yongzheng and Qianlong (1711–1799), had forcibly doubled the dimensions of the Chinese empire inherited from their predecessors the Ming, with Manchu cavalry pushing the old frontiers back into Burma, Laos,

Vietnam, Taiwan, the Gobi desert, Outer Mongolia, into the deserts and steppes of the Jungaria and Tarim basins and Tibet. But like most rulers of China before them, the Qing conquerors quickly sought to justify their violent acquisition of the Mandate of Heaven by presenting themselves as imperial sages. Consequently, the language of Qing government dripped with paternalistic self-justification: dwelling on the emperor's 'soothing' and 'cherishing' of men from both near and far.

British traders and diplomats – reading the turgid translations of official Qing documents that their linguists assembled – jibed at the condescending tones ('our Celestial Government . . . nourishes, righteously rectifies and gloriously magnifies a vast forbearance') of imperial addresses. But this rhetoric was not just pomposity or self-love (though there was a deal of that too). Taking the moral high ground was a crucial part of the emperor's portfolio: to validate – through every public act and decision – his claims to superiority over the empire, and to the love and respect of peoples beyond. Both public and private spaces in the Forbidden City were hung with moral exhortations, in case emperors and their civil servants ever forgot their proper obligations: officials took their leave of audiences with their sovereign through the Gates of Luminous Virtue and Correct Conduct, while judicial verdicts were issued and assessed in the Halls of Diligence, Discernment, and Honesty and Open-Mindedness.

Qing emperors needed to hold their nerve beneath this heavy weight of responsibility, and the omnicompetent rulers of the seventeenth and eighteenth centuries – who oversaw such a massive expansion of China's frontiers and population – had each adapted themselves to the task in their own way. Warrior, scholar, statesman, diplomat, Kangxi multitasked his way out of self-doubt. Qianlong – the beloved philosopher-emperor of eighteenth-century Europe's chinoiserie craze – buried his anxieties (sorcery scares in the 1760s, growing fears about a decline in the martial Manchu spirit, apprehensions about British ambitions) in dazzling ritual and display. His son, Jiaqing (1760–1820), seems to have comfort-eaten his way through his reign: although one inauspicious rumour told that he had died after being struck by lightning, it was more likely a combination of obesity and heatstroke.

Daoguang, the emperor who decided to fight the Opium War with the British, was unfortunately blessed with few temperamental gifts for the job. It had all started well enough for him. As a nine-year-old, in 1791, he had won the favour of his grandfather, the great Qianlong, by dispatching his first deer with bow and arrow in front of him while out on a hunting expedition. The emperor was so delighted with his precocious grandson (who succeeded in felling his first animal at an earlier age than he himself had done) that he immediately rewarded him with a bright yellow robe and a jade-green feather. Twenty-two years later, the future ruler also pleased his father – the pleasure-loving Jiaqing – by springing to the defence of the Forbidden City against millenarian rebels who had conspired with eunuchs to storm the palace gates on a quiet lunch-hour and assassinate the emperor. While on his way to enquire after the health of one of his several stepmothers, the crown prince spotted the intruders scrambling over the wall into the Forbidden City. He immediately decided to break the rule forbidding the use of firearms within the palace precincts, sent for knife, musket and powder, and dispatched two of the rebels.

Once he took the throne in 1820, though, Daoguang's nerve seems to have deserted him. Gaze at his official portrait – arrayed in the standard-issue bulky red turban, yellow brocade gown and beaded necklace of Qing emperorship – and he looks a different creature from his predecessors: the face pinched, angular, just a touch apprehensive, compared to his father's expansive jowliness, or his grandfather's patrician gravitas. He quickly abandoned displays of machismo for the laudable, but less charismatic virtues of parsimony and diligence. He draped his apartments with exhortations to 'Be Respectful, Honest, Assiduous, Correcting of Errors'.[1] On becoming emperor, he issued a cost-cutting 'Treatise on Music, Women, Goods and Profit', began going about in patched clothes and reduced his fun-loving father's resident troupe of palace musicians and actors from some 650 to a more restrained 370-odd, while halving Jiaqing's 400-strong army of cooks. As he aged, he left instructions that – contrary to custom – he modestly wanted no panegyric tablet erected at his tomb.

Daoguang's two least successful attributes were probably indecision and a fondness for scapegoating others. A day or two after he had succeeded his father, he removed three key advisers for letting a mistake slip into his deceased father's valedictory edict; a couple of days later, he reinstated two of them.[2] He even changed his mind about a choice of final resting place. Having spent seven years building one tomb, the would-be underground palace sprang a leak; reading this as deeply inauspicious, Daoguang punished the officials responsible and abandoned the project in favour of a new site. By the time it was completed, after another four years, the 'Hall of Eminent Favour' – the only Qing imperial tomb built entirely of unpainted cedar-wood – spoke of the emperor's love of frugality. (Compare the 2.27 million taels of silver – almost 3.5 million silver dollars – and 4,590 taels of gold spent by Cixi, the last empress, on her own tomb, in which even the bricks were carved and gilded.)[3] This talent for vacillation – and for censuring and replacing any commander who did not achieve impossible victories – would serve him badly in his wars against opium and the British.

During the 1830s, there was much to occupy the mind of any emperor: a steep decline in public order, finances and – most worrying of all – in the Qing military machine, whose weaknesses were being exploited by a broad range of domestic rebels (vagrants, dispossessed ethnic minorities, secret societies).

After recovering from the horrors of the seventeenth century – its wars, plagues and crop failures – the Chinese population under the remarkable Kangxi, Yongzheng and Qianlong at least doubled between 1650 and 1800, to reach some 300 million. New World silver flowed through the empire, thanks in part to a healthy export trade, the proliferation of an empire-wide network of markets and the emancipation of previously servile labourers. But size, diversity and silver turned against the Qing at the end of its eighteenth-century heyday. At this point, the empire was approaching its limits, as demographic explosion led to fierce competition for work and resources, ecological degradation, price rises, bureaucratic chaos and corruption. Critically, things also began to go wrong in the Qing military. By the second half of the eighteenth century, the Qing's earlier capacity for dominating its borders was looking more questionable. Three invasions of Burma between 1766 and 1769 were defeated or stalemated, as Qing cavalry became bogged down along the humid south-western frontier; an occupation of Vietnam in 1788 was chased out within a month, with the loss of 4,000 troops. The root cause of decline was the same as in other spheres of government: over-extension, and failure of funds.

As the empire began to malfunction, so the population began to complain, with growing militancy. Starting in 1774, the White Lotus Rebellion – only the most sprawling and destructive of the some half-dozen major revolts of the late-Qianlong era – united north-eastern peasants, actresses, carters, monks and sellers of fish, vegetable oil and bean curd in an acute sense of grievance against the fin-de-siècle empire.[4] Thanks to the decline of Qing armies, the uprising straggled on until 1805, and was finally put down only through the government authorizing local elites to generate their own militia. After 1800, the Qing empire was for the most part far too busy maintaining its costly frontiers and interior to size up new, well-armed European antagonists along the coast. Chinese-language accounts of the Opium War reveal a divided, distrustful society, with practically every grouping in conflict with another: Han Chinese with Manchu officials; northern Chinese with southern Chinese; central southern Chinese with deep southern Chinese; provincial gentry with central government; and the increasingly desperate hoi polloi with almost every group they encountered.

But to give Daoguang his due, he dealt rather well with a variety of natural and man-made problems during the first decade of his reign: crumbling river dykes, salt-tax dysfunction and a jihad on the empire's north-western frontier, during which the entire Qing garrison at Kashgar perished ('from the vein of the earth a stream of blood boiled forth', as one contemporary account put it), and which came to an end only after seven awful years, with the jihad's leader being sliced to death in Beijing.[5] On the whole, though, the emperor's actions through the first decade of his reign were often those of a man trying to keep himself too busy to panic. He promoted, he demoted, he audited; he was a bureaucratic fidget. He obviously did not know what to do: he was facing an environmental, demo-graphic, financial and social crisis for which the Confucian or Manchu empire-management manuals had no easy answers.

The political culture of the late-imperial civil service did not help Daoguang keep a cool head. For much of imperial Chinese history, government service remained the most attractive career option for educated Chinese men (women, of course, were expressly excluded). The sanctity of emperorship – ordained, as it was, by the Mandate of Heaven – ensured that working for the imperial state would be viewed as honourable and righteous in all but the most exceptional circumstances (for example, when Heaven was in the process of handing its Mandate from an unworthy to a worthy recipient). By the Ming dynasty, the imperial government had succeeded in channelling educational aspirations almost wholly into passing the civil-service exams: the tests of Confucian orthodoxy that controlled the paths to wealth and social success.

The life cycle of an aspiring bureaucrat began in the womb, with prenatal manuals lecturing pregnant women on maintaining the posture that would best aid the development of an embryonic graduand. Around two or three years after birth, formal training began: first with hours of memorizing characters – around 2,000 by the age of eight. Next came reading and memorization of the Four Books (*The Analects, Doctrine of the Mean, Great Learning, Mencius*) and the Five Classics (*Of Poetry, Documents* and *Changes, The Record of Rites* and *The Spring and Autumn Annals*) and others – perhaps as many as 518,000 characters in total, taking a five-to-twelve-year-old boy around seven years if he was memorizing 200 characters a day.

Finally, in his teens, a youth would start to practise constructing – through more rote-study – the 'eight-legged essay': a densely allusive eight-paragraph exposition (no more than a few hundred characters long) on a laconic gobbet from one of the Classics, designed to demonstrate the candidate's mastery of the terse exchanges of Confucius and his disciples. And even after a student ventured to attempt the lowest of the three rungs of imperial examinations (theoretically possible at fifteen, though twenty-one was a more usual starting age), the odds were stacked against success. During the Qing, around two million candidates sat for the lowest, county level of examinations, an opportunity available twice every three years; only 1.5 per cent passed. No more than 5 per cent would succeed at the next, provincial stage, and less than 1.5 per cent made it past the final, metropolitan rung.[6] These ratios, if anything, probably deteriorated through the Qing dynasty, as appointment quotas failed to keep up proportionally with the eighteenth century's doubling of population.

As a result, late-imperial China was increasingly saddled with an ageing population of academic failures. In 1699, a man over a hundred was led into the examination by his great-grandson (who was trying his luck for the first time). In 1826 a hundred-and-four-year-old candidate failed the metropolitan examination yet again, but was awarded his degree out of sympathy.[7] The majority swallowed their disappointment, and set about preparing for fresh attempts. A less restrained minority collapsed, went mad, died or violently rebelled, bringing mass slaughter and destruction to great swathes of the empire. The Ming dynasty was brought down in 1644 by insurrections led by a postman who happened also to be a failed examination candidate. The most destructive popular revolt of the nineteenth century, the Taiping, was led by a provincial school-teacher who after repeatedly failing the civil-service examinations suffered a nervous breakdown in which he hallucinated that God told him he was the younger brother of Jesus Christ. When his break-away Heavenly Kingdom was finally annihilated after fourteen years in 1864, it had left tens of millions dead and almost toppled the dynasty.

Under the Qing, positive discrimination in favour of the minority of Manchu candidates made the process even more frustrating for the Han Chinese majority. In theory, Qing orthodoxy held that the Manchus formed 'one family' with the Han Chinese that they ruled. In reality, the Manchu population (outnumbered by their Han Chinese subjects three hundred and fifty to one) worked to keep a sense of their ethnic otherness alive. Emperors lectured their Bannermen on the simple, honest traditions (archery, horse-riding, proficiency in Manchu, frugality) that China's conquerors must cultivate to justify their possession of the empire. Worried about the softening influence of Chinese culture, Qianlong (who also personally kowtowed to Confucius's ancestral tablet and wrote some 40,000 classical Chinese poems) encouraged his countrymen to celebrate drunken ancestors who washed their faces in urine and used their parents' corpses to trap sables.[8] Bannermen were kept deliberately aloof from China's majority civilian populations, segregated in walled garrisons that might occupy an entire half of a city's area. Wander through the streets of Qing Beijing in the middle of the nineteenth century, and the traces of Manchu foreignness would be everywhere – not just in the thick garrison ring around the imperial city (imitating, in permanent form, the layout of tents on imperial expeditions), and in the persons of the city's some 200,000 Manchu residents. The culture of the north-east also permeated the sights, sounds and smells of civilian life: in the songs beaten out on eight-cornered drums by Manchu street entertainers; in the pastry shops selling Manchu cakes and sweets; in the shaman shacks grafted onto the capital's elegant warrens of courtyard residences. Manchu women stuck out, too, by their distinctive, sculpted hair-dos (kept rigorously in place by elephant-dung lacquer); by their flair for cart-driving; by their very presence at dinners and ceremonies – for Han Chinese women were not allowed to socialize publicly.[9]

After 1644, Manchus were privileged over Han at every point in the imperial bureaucracy. The civil-service examinations were dumbed down for Manchu candidates: if Bannermen (for whom a quota of passes was reserved) found the competitive Han curriculum too challenging, they had the option of simply translating passages from the Chinese classics (which they had memorized) into Manchu and passing an archery test. Quite simply, the maths of minority worked for the Manchus: 'The path of promotion for Manchu officials is quicker than for Han officials because they are few and posts reserved for them are many', as one nineteenth-century observer put it.[10] Han Chinese men were spending lifetimes over-educating themselves to face demoralizingly low examination pass-rates, while watching less talented foreign rivals overtake them – a sure recipe for ill-feeling.

This culture of pressure and rivalry tended to produce two, highly contrasted species of official: the creatively corrupt libertine, and the puritan. And it was the tension between the two that helped produce the Opium War, with all its unfortunate consequences.

No individual better personified the talent for venality of Qing officialdom than the Qianlong emperor's notorious Manchu favourite, Heshen, on whom the elderly ruler grew increasingly dependent – politically and personally, perhaps sexually – through the last quarter of the eighteenth century. In sole control of access to the emperor, Heshen accumulated a vast personal fortune, principally through inventive embezzlement and selling political favours. During his twenty-six years at the top of the Qing political tree after 1776, he acquired for himself appointments in four of the six key boards of central government (of Civil Office, Revenue, War and Punishments) in addition to supervising the palace examinations – all of which gave him ample scope to broaden networks of influence and obligation, filling local governments with his protégés, then extorting vast bribes to ensure future discretion. After he was impeached in 1799, an official, conservative estimate calculated his property to be double the government's annual budget, at more than ten million ounces of silver, in items that reputedly included 600 pounds of top-quality ginseng, 550 fox hides, 850 raccoon dog hides, 56,000 sheep and cattle hides of varying thicknesses, 7,000 outfits, 460 European clocks and 600 concubines, all scattered thickly over his thousands of estates and residences. At the first possible opportunity, within a month of Qianlong's death, the new emperor Jiaqing had taken the unfilial step of pronouncing a death sentence on his father's pet, and confiscating his property. 'After Heshen fell, Jiaqing ate well', went one scrap of contemporary doggerel.[11]

But long after he had obeyed the emperor's command to commit suicide amid the pleasant courtyards and lotus ponds of his palace just north of the Forbidden City, Heshen continued to leave his mark on Qing politics. After decades of scholarly grind, many graduands were anxious to make profitable use of their years in bureaucratic power. In addition to a fixed salary, an official post offered civil servants abundant opportunities for self-enrichment: in bribes and favours extracted from and granted to cronies, in access to public funds and goods, in unofficial extra charges and taxes passed on to the general populace. Reinforced by Heshen's example, patronage swiftly became a deciding principle in public life. And with profit-creaming becoming more important than imperial service, public-works budgets began to disappear. In the early nineteenth century, for example, perhaps only 10 per cent of the annual six million taels of silver earmarked for Yellow River Conservancy found their way to Yellow River Conservation, the rest washing away in official banquets and entertainments.[12] Even after Heshen's disgrace, officials were still expected to actively flaunt their wealth. When one of Daoguang's less corruptible officials retired to his native place, his family filled boats with eighty wooden crates loaded with bricks so locals would think it was gold hoarded in the course of a five-decade career.[13]

There was a counterpoise, however: such abuses could also generate

a kind of inflexible asceticism. The examination system was designed
to indoctrinate imperial China's educated elites with a humourless
service ethic, drummed into them through their decades of studying
the submissive virtues (loyalty, filiality, modesty and so on) of the
classical curriculum. Part of the great genius of the Confucian school
of political education is its talent for persuading its practitioners to
police themselves, through a reproachful emphasis on self-criticism,
as stipulated in the fourth injunction of *The Analects*: 'I examine
myself three times a day. When dealing on behalf of others, have I
been trustworthy? . . . Have I practised what I was taught?'[14] The
downside to this was a certain unyielding self-righteousness. After so
many exhausting, enervating years of training in Confucian statecraft,
it was inevitable that some civil-service literati would become fixated
on their mission to set the empire in order – a feeling sharpened by
resentment at being often excluded from the top ranks of government by a less qualified foreign minority. And by Daoguang's reign,
there was, by common acknowledgement, a good deal to set in order.
Evidence from the provinces indicated that the rot had set in deep:
that the conspiracy of self-interest and neglect encouraged by people
like Heshen was destroying the bonds of government and society.
Faced by the nineteenth century's dismaying variety of social, environmental, political and economic problems, earnest Confucian officials
began to blame the whole sorry business on a massive failure of public
standards.

After the 1810s, groups of the empire's educated Chinese elite
started to form themselves into clubs – though the overtones of the
word in English are perhaps too comfortable. At annual poetry
banquets held in Beijing, members luxuriated in a melodramatic
sense of crisis, rather than in the Chinese imperial equivalent of
cigars, fine wines and roomy leather armchairs. At one such meeting,
an associate later recorded, although no wine was served, the 'six
or seven brethren present worked themselves into a state of high
emotion': writing poetry, admiring facsimiles of fourth-century calligraphy, debating whether literary style was a true gauge of moral
character, bemoaning the general state of things and considering
radical bureaucratic solutions to the ills of the empire.[15] Tame stuff
to twenty-first-century eyes, perhaps, but in the highly regimented
world of Qing politics, to form this kind of association was a daring

step. The Manchu regime had a particular horror of private clubs like this, linking them with sedition and instability. In the years after it was founded in 1829, one of the most influential of these groups – the 'Spring Purification Circle' – searched for an opportunity to persuade the emperor that they were the men to set the empire to rights.

As China entered its troubled 1830s, then, an anxious ruler was searching for a scapegoat for the country's many troubles, while a group of ambitious literati were looking for a cause that would win imperial favour and help wrest guardianship of the empire from venal Manchu privilege. Enter opium. For China's growing habit seemed to embody all that was wrong with the place: the empty, conspicuous consumption that was sending the empire's silver up in so much smoke and causing its subjects to forget their proper social roles; and the universal disregard for state laws tolerated by slick, self-serving official corruption.

In 1832, Daoguang's fears of looming crisis converged in one defeat: thousands of Qing troops were trounced by aboriginal rebels in the subtropical hills of north-west Guangdong. An imperial commissioner sent to investigate concluded, rather lamely, that the government forces 'were not used to the mountains'. He then added, more alarmingly, that 'many of the troops from the coastal garrisons were opium smokers, and it was difficult to get any vigorous response from them'.[16] Most of the troops had been stationed along the coast before they had been dispatched into the mountains; most of them, therefore, had been busily extracting bribes from the smuggling networks, doubtless while smoking a good deal of opium themselves. By an unhappy coincidence, the empire was simultaneously struck by floods, droughts and famine. When even nature began conspiring against the Chinese empire – where political legitimacy depended so heavily on Heavenly favour – panic was likely to set in.

Daoguang was seriously shaken. On 24 July 1832, at the marble Altar of Heaven on the meridian due south of the Forbidden City – the centre of the Chinese world – and dressed in pleated yellow and embroidered purple, the emperor took the exceptional step of publicly asking the celestial powers where he had gone wrong. First, he tried propitiating them by cremating a sacrificial buffalo, offering incense, jade and silk, reciting prayers and drinking the Wine and eating the Meat of Felicity. He then spoke his mind.

> This year the drought passes all precedent . . . Mankind is bowed beneath calamity, even the beasts and insects cease to live. I, the Son of Heaven, am Lord of this World. Heaven looks to me that I preserve tranquillity. My bounded duty is to soothe the people. Yet, though I cannot sleep, nor eat with appetite; though I am grief-stricken and shake with anxiety; my grief, my fasts, my sleepless nights have but obtained a trifling shower.

Without waiting for a response, he suggested his own interpretation of events.

> The atrocity alone of my sins is the cause, too little sincerity, too little devotion . . . Have I been negligent in public business, lacking in the diligence and effort which was due? Have my rewards and punishments been equitable? . . . Have unfit persons been appointed to official posts, and petty and vexatious acts oppressed the people?

'Prostrate,' he eventually concluded, 'I implore Imperial Heaven to pardon my ignorance . . . I have made the Three Kneelings, I have made the Nine Knockings. Hasten and confer clement deliverance . . . Oh, alas, Imperial Heaven, give ear to my petition!'[17]

In the absence of a clear sign from Heaven, Daoguang decided to start by taking stern measures against opium – this dark, sticky symbol of corruption and extravagance. He sacked the official responsible for the Guangdong debacle (who had clearly been waving opium shipments up the river, after letting his soldiers take their pick of the cargoes), and ordered his successor to strike hard: to 'pull up the roots and block off the source' of the drug. 'Do not muddle along', he added, 'with your gaze wrapt only upon the immediate tasks at hand and entirely oblivious to the longer-term interests of the state!'[18]

*

Yet soon, characteristically, he wavered again. Within a few years, anti-opium ardour had been dampened by bureaucratic inertia down in Canton and by the city's chastening encounter with Lord Napier (in which two British ships had given the supposedly impregnable forts protecting Canton a very hard time). The deep maritime south could breed a more pragmatic variety of Chinese official than the dry, landlocked north: one steeped in the ambiguities (and profits) of the smuggling trade. If trade were cut off, then the silver that washed about the city would also dry up. At the time of his death, the richest of the mid-nineteenth-century Hong merchants, Howqua, was ten times wealthier than Nathan Rothschild. Something had to be done to make the emperor see reason – to persuade him that opium would in fact not prove a convenient scapegoat.

And so, in 1836, a legalization lobby spoke up. A former judicial commissioner at Canton argued that banning opium and cutting off the trade there would achieve nothing. A tough policy would spread only terror among the people: 'bandits, under the pretence of preventing the smuggling of opium by order of the government, [will] seek opportunities for plundering'. Resistance was futile: the Qing government did not possess the necessary policing muscle to engage the forces (whether native or foreign) of lawlessness along the coast. As for the physical risks of opium, he continued in Malthusian vein, 'New births are daily increasing the population of the empire . . . the smokers of opium are idle, lazy, useless vagrants – undeserving even of contempt' – let them smoke themselves to death.[19] The deal must have seemed almost done: the Governor-General of Guangdong enthusiastically endorsed the plan, and told the Hong merchants to give the opium traders the nod. The British superintendent of trade, Captain Charles Elliot, exulted at the prospect of 'very important relaxations' in the Sino-British trading relationship.[20] A happy ending was in sight.

Not long after, the anti-opium lobby found its voice – led by one Huang Jueci, a president of the Sacrificial Court and founding member of the Spring Purification Circle, who dashed off a lengthy memorial on the subject to Daoguang. After expressing unctuous regret for all the sleepless nights and disrupted mealtimes his beloved emperor was suffering, Huang's memorial nominated a single culprit for the impoverishment of the realm: opium. The opium trade, he explained, was a foreign plot that began when the red-haired Europeans 'seduced the nimble, warlike people of Java into the use of it, whereupon they were subdued, brought into subjection and their land taken possession of'.[21] 'In introducing opium into this country', echoed one of his allies, 'the English purpose has been to weaken and enfeeble the central empire. If not early aroused to a sense of our danger, we shall find ourselves, before long, on the last step toward ruin ... Of this there is clear proof in the instance of the campaign against the Yao rebels in the twelfth year of our sovereign's reign ... great numbers of the soldiers were opium smokers, so that although their numerical force was large, there was hardly any strength to be found among them.'[22]

A sharp, shocking crusade was needed, to awaken the empire from its moral daze. Huang's solution was simple: execute the consumers, and watch demand (and therefore imports) dry up. Give smokers a year to repent, he added, sweetening his advocacy with a touch of Confucian benevolence, in the course of which, he estimated, eight or nine out of ten 'will have learned to refrain ... Such are your majesty's opportunities of exhibiting abundant goodness and wide-spreading philanthropy!' And to enforce the suppression, he would make use of the punitive Legalist techniques of government invented by the ministers of one of Chinese history's most notorious tyrants, the First Emperor of China (259–210 BC): every five households would be bound together in a common bond, pledged to keep watch over the others, and denounce any infringement of the new laws; failure to report an offender would bring collective punishment down on the group. 'This', Huang concluded, 'will indeed be a fountain of happiness to the rulers and the ruled in ten thousand ages to come.' Except for those executed, of course.

Alien conspiracies, military and social decline, memories of 1832: the campaign was well judged to alarm the emperor. One other key point emerges from Huang's analysis: his ignorance of foreign traders. 'Among the red-haired race', he expounded, 'the law regarding such as daily make use of opium is to assemble all of their race as spectators while the criminal is bound to a stake, and shot from a gun into the sea ... Hence England and other nations – which imports opium into China – have only preparers, not consumers of the drug.'[23]

Huang's suggestions, moreover, seem not to have considered how the British might respond to a blow to their pocket-books.

His view was not a majority one. After receiving this fiery memorial, the emperor put the whole question out to tender, soliciting views from the empire's top officials, both civilian and military. Over the next four months, twenty-nine responses drifted back to the capital: only eight supported the death penalty for smokers; the rest wanted to concentrate suppression on opium's point of entry – Canton – and on the smugglers who brought it into the country.[24] Perhaps they objected for Confucian, humanitarian reasons; or then again, out of indolence, maybe. 'In Fujian and Guangdong', one response complained, 'seven or eight out of every ten persons smoke opium. There would have to be hundreds of thousands of executions, or even more.'[25] In addition to being grisly to implement, it would also be exhausting. If the problem of opium addiction was as severe as the prohibition party claimed, 1 per cent of the county's 400 million-plus population would theoretically face the death penalty – not to mention all those involved in the trade, a proportion estimated as being as high as 90 per cent in some parts of the country. The advantage of focusing punishment on the smugglers was that they existed beyond the pale of regular society: if you were skilful or diligent enough to catch one, you enjoyed the credit. If not, no one would find you particularly wanting. But if civilian opium smokers were the ubiquitous presence in local society that the prohibitionists reported, officials would have to work much harder to find an excuse for failing to crack down. Perhaps sensing this lack of enthusiasm, Daoguang continued to waver for months after Huang's memorial arrived. Making use of that universal bureaucratic fallback, on 23 October he put it out to another working party – this time, his grand council of advisers.

But at last, two weeks later, on 9 November 1838, he acted: summoning a Fujianese official called Lin Zexu – one of Huang Jueci's eight-strong minority of supporters – to an audience, to discuss his plans for annihilating 'the evil influence of opium . . . using strong medicine to blow up the root of the sickness.'[26] What finally swayed the indecisive Daoguang? Was it the ruthless simplicity of the scheme (particularly as he only had to authorize executions)? Or family problems, perhaps? On 25 October 1838, a report reached him that one of the princes of the blood, together with one of the 'lords of suppressing the realm', had been discovered smoking opium in one of the Forbidden City's temples. On 8 November, Daoguang received a second report, from one of his most trusted ministers, Qishan, revealing that 130,000 ounces of opium had just been seized at Tianjin – the port town a hundred miles or so south of Beijing that supplied much of the capital's needs. This was the largest single seizure of opium since 1729. Qishan added that the opium was all from Canton: bought there, transported from there, by Cantonese merchants.[27]

On the last day of 1838, the emperor decided to appoint Lin Imperial Commissioner to Canton. After a century of fits and starts, the Qing war on opium was about to begin in earnest.

Chapter Three

CANTON SPRING

Lin Zexu's background was conventional. He was born on 20 August 1785 in south-east China, into a declining landholding clan that had been slowly bankrupted by preparing their sons for the examination system. When Zexu was born, the Lin clan had not won an official posting for four costly generations. All this failure seems only to have hardened the resolve of Lin's father (who had ruined his eyesight through fruitless examination preparation) to see his own son graduate to a state job. The adult Lin – who began studying the classics at the age of three – would recall how, 'through freezing days and endless nights, in a broken-down three-roomed apartment, with the north wind howling angrily, one lamp on the wall, young and old would sit next to each other, doing our reading and our needlework . . . till the night was out.'[1]

His father's efforts paid off. Aged twelve, his son managed the lowest level of the civil-service exams, producing a solid Confucian essay on 'The Great Treasure That Is Being Benevolent to Relatives'. Aged nineteen, he passed the provincial exam; seven years later, in 1811, he advanced through the metropolitan exam on his third attempt, and finally stabilized the family finances with the iron rice-bowl of an official posting.

Once past these obstacles, Lin's career could have taken him along two different paths. The first would have been to make as much money as possible from his position, then retire on the proceeds. But his spartan upbringing pushed him in another direction. In the two and a half decades before his famous intervention in the opium question, he became renowned for his bureaucratic virtuousness: hunting down pirates, fixing dams, relieving floods, managing the salt tax. He was, in short, a tremendous administrative asset – though his work–life balance could probably have used some fine-tuning. 'He never had any hobbies', commented an early biographer. 'Although he didn't mind books, paintings and inscriptions, he never bothered much with them. Instead, he preferred to be tirelessly diligent, day and night ... When he saw the people in trouble, he felt as if his heart were on fire, his liver being stabbed.' His stint as judicial commissioner in the south-east during the 1820s won him the nick-name 'Lin Qingtian' (Lin Clear-as-the-Heavens) in recognition of his incorruptibility. Transferred subsequently to river-conservancy work, his profligate predecessors 'became terrified their misdeeds would be exposed. Lin set about washing away the filth with honesty.' Temper-amentally, he was the perfect match for the parsimonious Daoguang, from whom he received more than once the highest accolades of praise: 'I've never known such a diligent river superintendent', ran one encomium; 'you have not committed any mistakes' went a second; or a third, 'you are careful and reliable'.[2]

Lin Zexu, then, was in 1839 a man brimful of self-belief: an individual who had made his way through diligence and self-control, and who was confident that this work ethic could crack the most complex of questions. He was also a man just a touch obsessed – though not, in fact, primarily with opium, the substance that would propel his name into the history books. Back in 1833, long before he began waging war on the drug, he had actually been rather pragmatic about what to do about it, proposing that – to combat the financial damage that opium imports were inflicting – China should simply grow its own.[3] His pet ambition – on which he lavished much time and ink – was to reform the expensive system of grain transport along canals up to the capital by irrigating the dry plains that ringed Beijing. Western observers of Lin's campaign against opium reached for grand diagnoses for his actions: this was, they proclaimed, a collision of civilizations (the landlocked, anti-mercantile Qing versus the adventurous, free-trading British). The reality was more mundane, however, and con-cerned with the internal politics of the Chinese empire, as well as the activities of a gang of ill-behaved British merchants. Lin wanted to make a quick success of the Canton job, to win him governorship of the wealthy Jiangsu area, in which the capital grain-transport chain began.[4] He was no inveterately xenophobic crusader, however hard his British merchant antagonists tried to demonize him as such; he was a careful bureaucrat with a passion for freight management. Back in the nineteenth century, China – as it remains today – was a big and busy place, its priorities governed by domestic, far more than international considerations. To a degree, the Opium War – and all that it led to – was set off in a fit of bureaucratic haste.

Following his imperial summons, Lin arrived in Beijing on 26 December 1838 and, over the next month or so, enjoyed nineteen audiences with the emperor. Daoguang was showing signs of strain: 'Alas!' he wept before his official, 'how can I die and go to the shades of my imperial fathers and ancestors, until opium is removed!'[5] He lavished unusual care and attention upon Lin: on 29 December, as a very rare privilege, he authorized him to ride a horse in the Forbidden City. The next day, solicitously noting Lin's discomfort on horseback, he offered an extra concession: 'You seem unused to riding. Try a sedan chair instead.'[6]

Lin offered this overwrought emperor one precious resource: certainty. To every one of Daoguang's doubts, he had a confident answer. His first step would be to confiscate all smoking apparatus. His second step was simpler still. 'The difficulty lies not with giving opium up', Lin reasoned, 'but in changing smokers' minds.' And how was this to be done? By threats. All smokers were to be put on a year's suspended death sentence, and if they failed to reform themselves within this time, and obliged the state to execute them, they would only have themselves to blame. 'It is really no pitiable thing to inflict the death penalty on reckless souls who persist to refuse repentance and fear of the law.'[7] How were smokers to be detected? By mass public surveillance of their capacity (or lack of it) 'to subsist without smoking'. Gather all those accused of smoking in a public place, Lin advocated, search them thoroughly and lock them in a room, 'where they should be seated apart without being allowed to communicate with one another . . . from ten in the morning until after midnight.'[8] On the off-chance that fear didn't work, there was always Science. Lin boasted of knowing a failsafe prescription to treat opium addiction: 'Once you've taken it, the very smell of opium will be repellent; if you smoke it, you'll vomit . . . I've also heard there's one with white plums in . . . and that willow-peach blossom is the best of all . . . though I can't say whether that's true or not.'[9]

Like those of Huang Jueci, Lin's proposals suffer from one curious oversight: little thought was given to the effect of prohibition on foreign traders, the source of all this narcotic trouble. Even though many officials suggested that anti-opium measures be focused on Canton, the centre of legal and illegal European trade, few who supported the crackdown seem to have worried much about the reaction of the foreign community there: any opposition or procrastination would simply be 'properly dealt with'.[10] Those who raised concerns about the likely British response, by contrast, have been denounced in China for spineless treachery. On his way out from the capital on 22 December, Qishan – the man who would be vilified for negotiating an early peace with the British after the first disastrous engagements of the war – exhorted Lin 'not to set off any frontier disturbances'.[11] (The seven-year troubles just past in Xinjiang had set the imperial treasury back a dismaying ten million ounces of silver, or even more.) Two years later, as the Qing's coastal defences were falling before British bombardment, Lin would bluster that he had foreseen the entire conflict. The events of the war proved otherwise: in every engagement, the Qing were surprised by the power of the British response. It seems certain that, as Lin prepared to strike hard against opium, he had not seriously considered the possibility of war with Britain – and certainly not the kind of war that actually ensued.

On 10 March 1839, Lin was welcomed into Canton after his two-month journey from Beijing. True to his incorruptible reputation, he had travelled from the sallow plains of the north-east down to the emerald rice-fields of the south in minimalist style. His entourage he pared down to one outrider, six men-at-arms, a chief cook and two further kitchen aides, who were at all times to travel with him (to prevent them from going on ahead to squeeze local innkeepers along the route).

Once arrived, he acted quickly. His first move was to put pressure on Chinese smugglers and smokers. He organized the people of Guangdong into 'security groups' (*baojia*): units of five individuals, each responsible for guaranteeing the narcotic hygiene of the other four. He lectured the degenerates of the city ('no province has as bad a reputation for opium offences as Guangdong') that resistance was useless: 'This time we are going on until the job is finished.'[12] On his journey down to Canton, he had reviewed a few case-histories indicating the scale of the problem – that of a certain Wang Zhengao caught his eye. After being dismissed from the army for malfeasance, Wang had somehow been appointed a coastal patrol, taking bribes of forty silver dollars for every couple of hundred pounds of opium that he ignored. The hundreds of chests of opium that he *had* confiscated, he had sold on for silver, which he then pretended he had seized from smugglers. For these actions, he had been not only rewarded but also promoted.[13] Within two months of his arrival, Lin had arrested 1,600 people for opium offences, and confiscated nearly fourteen tons of opium and almost 43,000 opium pipes; within another two months, he had imprisoned five times more opium-felons than the provincial governor had in three years.[14]

Lin reserved some of his best anger for the Hong merchants, whom he summoned to an audience on 17 March at his campaign headquarters. After ordering them to kneel on the hard floor before him, he treated them to a lengthy disquisition on their perfidy. It was they – they – who were responsible for the magnitude of the opium problem, he informed them. For twenty years, they had waved up the river to trade at Canton vessels that were clearly laden with opium: 'Are you not indeed dreaming, and snoring in your dreams? . . . It is as if a man, to guard his house at night, should appoint a watchman, and that, nevertheless, his property should be bundled up and carried away, while yet the watchman should declare that there had been no thief.' Every level of the trade administration, Lin continued, was mired in smuggling (transporting, storing, buying, packaging the drug); and yet the Hong merchants did not just look in the opposite direction – they aided and abetted the foreigners. They paid them visits; they gave them secret information; they lent them sedan chairs (a criminal offence; foreigners were meant to walk). 'All now are equally involved in the stench of it, and truly I burn with shame for you.'[15] (The quotations above are taken from Lin's written edict to the merchants; the oral version was probably less circuitous in tone.) All this was perfectly true: a mere glance at the Hong merchants' accounts would have revealed how deeply entangled they were with the British, from whom they had borrowed hundreds of thousands of dollars to pay for the unpredictable extra levies that the government squeezed out of them – repayment of this money would be one of Palmerston's demands during the war to come. The richest of them all, Howqua, promptly tried to buy Lin's acquiescence. 'The Great Minister does not want your money', Lin told him. 'I want your head.'[16]

Lin next moved to put the foreigners under similar pressure. He began by drafting a lengthy letter to Queen Victoria, initially forgiving her for being ignorant of the Qing empire's recent measures against opium, then exhorting her to eliminate opium production in her dominions. 'I now give my assurance that we mean to cut off this harmful drug for ever . . . what has already been manufactured Your Majesty must immediately search out and throw to the bottom of the sea . . . Our Heavenly Court would not have won the allegiance of innumerable lands did it not wield superhuman power. Do not say you have not been warned in time.'[17] On 17 March, he told the Hong merchants to order the foreigners to submit all the opium currently in their possession at Canton and to sign a pledge not to import any more. Otherwise, both foreign traffickers and their Hong allies would be executed. 'No have see so fashion before', the alarmed Hong merchants told the foreigners as they delivered Lin's messages.[18] By 23 March, the commissioner was no longer passing his messages on in writing. Instead, he was dispatching the two richest Hong merchants in chains to repeat his demands in person.

For the time being, he felt well satisfied with the start he had made: the day after his arrival in Canton, he had crowed to the emperor that Jardine had fled for England on hearing of Lin's appointment. (The tough Scot arrived in London just in time to advise Palmerston on how to make war with China.) Lin sat back and waited for a response.

*

History has been kind to Lin Zexu. In contemporary China, he is venerated as the great pioneer of Chinese nationalism: as 'the first National Hero of our modern history . . . a true man of action of the reformist landlord class'.[19] Posterity has done less well by his chief British antagonist and later plenipotentiary to China during the Opium War, Charles Elliot. For the past century and a half, British commentators have lambasted him for being foolish and indecisive – for lacking proper imperialist firmness when it came to dealing with China. (He would be sacked halfway through the war for having persuaded Qishan to cede Hong Kong – one of the world's great natural harbours.) Chinese accounts are far less positive. In the two Mainland blockbusters about the war, *Lin Zexu* (1953) and *The Opium War* (1997), Elliot is a lecherous villain (with a particularly evil leer), machinating to enslave the Chinese people with opium. But was he as incompetent or as diabolical as his detractors have claimed, or just a harassed servant of the British state doing his best in difficult circumstances?

Historians have long struggled to make sense of how the British empire – the largest in human history – came to hold sway over a quarter of the world's land and population. Old-school answers to this question blustered about the civilizing missions of Christianity and Free Trade, or muttered something about John Seeley's theory (a brilliant appeal to the English love of amateurism) that the empire was acquired in a 'fit of absence of mind'. Twentieth-century Chinese interpretations (heavily indebted to Marx and Lenin) favoured conspiracy theories: that the empire in general, and the Opium War specifically, were a long-plotted land- and resources-grab, driven by industrial expansion and greed. More recently, in Britain, other explanations – the quest for military glory, for safe sea-routes, for new investment opportunities – have been suggested. But what big theories tend to leave out is the inevitably extemporized nature of the empire: British policy abroad was usually designed under exceptional pressure, in alien environments, by operatives without local linguistic competence and isolated (in the pre-telegraphic age) for months at a time from counsel back home.[20] Charles Elliot, architect of Britain's Opium War with China, personifies this whole confusion: of imperialist ambition and opportunism; of duty and scruple; of hypocrisy and self-deception.

Like Lin, his background was orthodox. He came of good establishment stock: grandson of an earl, son of a soldier-diplomat who had 'distinguished himself by a truly British courage' against the Turks in 1772.[21] In 1815, the fourteen-year-old Charles made a career choice popularized by national hero Nelson (who had died a decade earlier at Trafalgar): he took himself off to sea. Fourteen character-forming years' experience under naval fire – scrambling up swaying topmasts and over rolling decks, feasting on weevil-filled hard tack – would prepare him well for the perils of the China station: he steps first out onto the stage of nineteenth-century Sino-British entanglements as Master Attendant to Napier's ill-fated venture of 1834, seating himself calmly beneath an umbrella on the exposed deck of one of Lord Napier's frigates as it attempted to blast its way upriver to Canton. In 1830, he jumped ship to join the Foreign Office, serving as 'Protector of Slaves' in British Guiana, in the West Indies. Within two years, his experiences there had transformed him into a fervent abolitionist: 'What should be given to the Slaves', he wrote in 1832 to a friend, 'is such a state of Freedom as they are now fit for.'[22] (One of his uncharitable Chinese biographers nonetheless labelled him 'a long-term oppressor and enslaver of local populations in English colonies'.[23])

In 1834 he was redeployed to China, where his conscience was again tested by his official duties. For Elliot – this aristocratic abolitionist – instinctively disliked the opium trade and everything bound up with it: both its moral dubiousness and its ungentlemanly, profit-hungry merchants. His weakness was to see a little of everyone's side: he understood the economic imperative of the opium trade, even while he hated the vulgarity of its perpetrators; he understood that his duty was to protect the British flag in Canton, even while he detested what some of Britannia's children were doing in the China seas. He was a man locked into the assumptions of his time: a fervent upholder of the national dignity and dutiful servant of the British empire, bound to protect its citizens (whatever they had done) from alien attack. Above all, he believed in the liberating virtues of Free Trade: that, *in extremis*, a war to introduce these virtues was justified; and particularly if such a war would do away with Britain's unsavoury dependence on opium sales.

By 1836, Elliot had been promoted to Napier's old job: Chief

Superintendent of the China trade. Although in the two years since Napier's death the British and Chinese had avoided open warfare, the job still had its difficulties. In late 1834, Elliot – in full, decorated captain's uniform – was set upon by Qing soldiers and knocked twice over the head, as he petitioned outside the city walls for the recovery of a twelve-strong merchant crew shipwrecked up the coast and taken captive by the authorities. But Elliot's greatest problem was the lack of clarity in his official instructions. The superintendent was, his foreign secretary Lord Palmerston had ordered, 'to avoid giving offence to the Chinese authorities' while at the same time refusing to 'deal subserviently with the . . . Chinese authorities'.[24] He was to keep the peace and maintain the legal trade (to ensure the supply of tea and silk to British markets), but was given no authority over the illegal opium trade. Although Elliot personally considered the smuggling business 'a trade which every friend to humanity must deplore', he fervently hoped that the Qing court would legalize it, because it would force the Chinese to take full responsibility for its moral dubiousness and – by lowering prices of the drug – deter the British from trading in it.[25] 'It cannot be good', he reasoned in 1836, 'that the conduct of a great trade should be so dependent upon the steady continuance of a vast prohibited traffic in an article of vicious luxury, high in price, and liable to frequent and prodigious fluctuation.'[26] Elliot, it seems, barely tried to conceal from the luminaries of Canton and Macao society – Jardine, Matheson et al. – his thorough distaste for them. 'No man entertains a deeper detestation of the disgrace and sin of this forced traffic on the coast of China than the humble individual who signs this dispatch', he reminded Palmerston on the brink of the Opium War. 'I have steadily discountenanced it by all the lawful means in my power, and at the total sacrifice of my private comfort in the society in which I have lived for some years past.'[27] (Jardine and company returned the compliment in full, carping in their letters home at his 'unpopularity', 'impolicy', 'sad mismanagement', and so on.[28])

Yet without opium, Elliot knew, Britain would slide into deficit with China. 'The interruption of the opium traffic', as he put it on 2 February 1837, 'must have the effect . . . of crippling our means of purchasing in this market . . . The failure of the opium deliveries is attended with an almost entire cessation of money transactions in

Canton. And in the glutted condition of this market, your Lordship
will judge how peculiarly mischievously the present stagnation must
operate on the whole British commerce with the empire.'[29] When
faced in 1837 with the choice of joining the Qing government's
renewed campaign against smuggling (in which perpetrators faced
strangulation), or sheltering those Britons responsible, he had to side
with the latter, writing to Lord Auckland, the Governor of India,
for 'a man-of-war . . . with instructions to afford such countenance to
the general trade as may be practicable, without inconveniently committing His Majesty's Government upon any delicate question.'[30]
Deprived of clear authority, Elliot remained duty-bound to protect
the lives and property of British subjects. At the same time, though,
he asked the Foreign Office for an extension of his powers so that he
might maintain 'due order amongst the seafaring class of Her
Majesty's subjects, who visit this part of the Empire', a request that
the Admiralty refused.[31] Socially isolated by the foreign merchant
population in Macao, separated from his family (although his wife,
Clara, had sailed out to China with him, they had been forced to
leave three of their beloved children in England), politically and
linguistically challenged in Canton, and infuriated by contradictory
instructions from London, Charles Elliot in 1839 was a man under
significant strain.

He was in Macao when news of Lin's brusque new measures reached
him. On hearing about the commissioner's ultimatum, Elliot pulled
on full naval uniform and sailed straight to Canton where he docked
at the foreign factories and flew the flag (to, he reported back to
Palmerston, resounding cheers).

He found there a divided foreign community. James Matheson,
characteristically, was unfazed by Lin's demands, reporting the Hong
merchants' appearance in chains as 'the most complete exhibition
of humbug ever witnessed in China'.[32] Others lacked the British
sang-froid: Howqua, an American trader reported, was 'crushed to the
ground by his terrors . . . the Hong merchants were in instant fear of
their lives and properties'.[33] In Elliot's absence, the trading community had done its best to stall Lin, producing vague declarations

about the 'almost unanimous feeling in the community' against the opium traffic. Lin was unimpressed: 'if opium was not delivered up', the Hong merchants reported his response, 'he would be at their headquarters tomorrow at 10 o'clock, and then he would show what he would do'. The foreigners asked if Lin meant to carry out his threats of execution. 'As [His Excellency] says, so will he act', responded the Hong.[34] British traders then tried compromise: about 1,000 chests of opium would be given up. Useless, they were told; Lin wanted all the opium, and he now issued an arrest warrant for one of the leading British smugglers, Lancelot Dent. Dent refused to go and see the commissioner; Lin's deputy declared he would camp out at Dent's house until the latter came with him. Dent told him dinner and a bed would be made available.

Elliot strode fearlessly into this impasse, taking Dent under his personal protection and dashing off impassioned dispatches to Palmerston ('it was my resolution to reach those factories, or to sacrifice my life in the attempt').[35] Under pressure from Lin, Elliot seems to have undergone a curious metamorphosis. Back on 17 December 1838, he had reviled the 'deep disgrace' of the opium trade, expressing his readiness to leave British smugglers to their fate under harsh Chinese jurisdiction. Now, he solemnly vowed to resist 'aggression against foreign persons and property . . . This was my capital duty as the Queen's officer'.[36] Dent, too, had changed: no longer a diplomatic embarrassment, he became (in Elliot's words) 'one of our most respected merchants at Canton'.[37] A harassed government functionary and a fractious gaggle of foreign smugglers, in other words, were starting to reinvent themselves as a united community of persecuted innocents.

Irritated by Elliot's interference, Lin called off all trade and swore to blockade the factories until all tradable opium had been handed over. At 8 p.m. on 24 March, he ordered all Chinese servants off the premises; within half an hour, they were as 'places of the dead'.[38] (In the normal way of things, the area was internationally famed for its raucousness. Bemused Europeans wrote of the 'ten thousand different sounds coming from every quarter and with every variety of intonation', of the crowds of boats 'of all sizes, shapes and colours', of the clamour of gongs, trumpets, clarions and fire-crackers. 'The whole place teems with speculation', observed one Scottish visitor in the mid-1830s – with 'shopkeepers, barbers, quacks, thieves, rogues, vagabonds and coolies', with fruit-sellers and freak-shows, with laya-bouts catching lice from the folds of their clothing and cracking them between their teeth, with beggars and malnourished children, with foreigners shouting orders to Cantonese sailors or yelling for their servants.[39]) And there the 350-strong foreign population of Canton stayed for the next forty-seven days, the streets between the factories and the city filled with 1,000 armed police, soldiers, servants and coolies, the waterways south of the city barricaded with a triple row of junks. Even the Hong merchants were drawn into the surveillance effort, stationed in large chairs (that by night doubled as beds) just by the old East India Company building.

It was a pretty mild sort of imprisonment. Food was not a great worry: sugar, water, oil, bread and capons had been smuggled in before the blockade tightened, while a well-connected trader like William Hunter had his breakfast and dinner brought to him in boxes by one of the Hong's Chinese translators. The greatest physical risk the prisoners suffered, Jardine–Mathesons' authorized historian has concluded, was 'too much food and too little exercise'.[40] Boredom was another discomfort, alleviated by improvised entertainments: cricket, leapfrog, scrambling up the flagstaff, gossiping over beer with their guards. When these amusements grew stale, the prisoners laughed at their own domestic incompetence: at their inability to 'roast a capon, to boil an egg or potatoe'.[41]

Three days into this siege, at 11 a.m. on 27 March, Elliot did two things that Chinese historians have unanimously regarded as evidence of his scheming genius. First, he agreed to hand over to Lin 20,283 chests of British opium. Second, he promised the horrified merchant community that the Crown would take responsibility for the confiscated property. In two brisk moves, Elliot turned a private economic quarrel into a matter of state: a negotiation between the Queen of England and the Chinese emperor. When news of the blockade reached England some six months later, the British gov-ernment would find £2 million (the cost of the opium) far more persuasive as a casus belli than emotive protestations about Lin's 'insults to national dignity'. (Palmerston had barely noticed when Elliot reported in 1834 that local officials had struck him twice over the head.)

Why did Elliot act as he did?

In his despatches to Palmerston, Elliot insisted that his hand was forced by the desperateness of his situation. 'This is the first time, in our intercourse with this empire,' he wrote on 2 April, 'that its Government has taken unprovoked initiative in aggressive measures against British life, liberty and property, and against the dignity of the British Crown . . . They have deprived us of our liberty, and our lives are in their hands.'[42] Elliot's enemies, by contrast, accused him of meddling unnecessarily in the Canton stand-off between Lin and the British traders, of inflaming the situation (and provoking the blockade in the first place) by placing himself between Lin and the opium traders. British life and property, William Jardine told a House of Commons select committee in 1840, were under no threat at the time of Lin's measures.[43] Why, Elliot's detractors ask, did he oppose then abruptly capitulate to Lin's demand, and capitulate in such an extreme fashion? 'What for he pay so large?' wondered the Hong merchants at his massive pledge of opium. 'No wantee so much!'[44]

We will never know exactly what Charles Elliot meant to achieve – he left no diary or memoir for us to dissect. While noting his enemies' accusations against him (of calculation, incompetence, rashness and self-aggrandisement) we should also remember the difficulties of the situation. Lin was a different creature from his predecessors: an implacable, incorruptible anti-opium crusader. Did Elliot have any realistic alternative to involving himself in the affairs of these private traders, when Lin was issuing threats against British citizens and property? (With Lin threatening a stoppage to both smuggling and legitimate trades, his measures also had clear repercussions for Britain's supplies of tea, silk and bullion.) Although no one was starving in the factories, no one would escape either without a British climb-down of some sort. The besieged community did, moreover, fear that the phoney war might become real, under the right sort of provocation: if the armed foreign ships left at Whampoa ventured to blast through the blockade up to Canton, speculated the usually imperturbable William Hunter, 'the Chinese would probably fall upon and massacre us'.[45]

Most of all, by 1839 Elliot was an exasperated man: worn out by Palmerston's inconsistency, by his own dislike of the opium trade and by his inability to do anything to regulate it. Repeatedly, he found himself in the humiliating position of having to tell Qing officials that he had no power to expel British opium ships: 'can he yet', his Chinese interlocutors mocked him in response, 'be considered fit for the office of Superintendent?'[46] By surrendering the opium, he perhaps hoped to provoke some kind of unequivocal response from his foreign secretary. Like Napier before him, he seems genuinely to have believed in the purgative benefits (to both sides) of a short, sharp, clean war: 'I feel assured', he wrote on 11 April,

> that the single mode of saving the coasts of the empire from a shocking character of warfare, both foreign and domestic, will be the very prompt and powerful intervention of Her Majesty's government for the just vindication of all wrongs, and the effectual prevention of crime and wretchedness by permanent settlement. Comprehensively considered, this measure has become of high obligation towards the Chinese government, as well as to the public interests and character of the British nation.[47]

And that is how a publicly declared enemy of opium ended up begging his government to fight an Opium War.

Chapter Four

OPIUM AND LIME

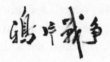

In May 1839, Humen – a small, unexceptional town on the south China coastline – bore witness to what would later become one of the most celebrated moments in nineteenth-century Chinese history: Lin Zexu's destruction of the 20,000 chests of opium surrendered by Charles Elliot. The spot is still marked, of course. The trenches from which the opium was flushed out to sea are now stagnant lotus ponds, set within a small park named after the commissioner. The local tourist board has done its best to whip up visitors' patriotic fervour. Inside the entrance stands a huge, angry, rust-red sculpture in high socialist realist mode: a montage of bare-chested, pitchfork-wielding peasant heroes, their hair and clothes rippling in the imaginary wind. 'The brave sacrifice of the people's heroes in the Opium War', reads the plaque, 'will never be forgotten!' Just behind stands a tall, dignified statue of Lin. 'The British colonialists', the inscription explains, 'used every illegal trick to smuggle in opium . . . This accursed sickness paralysed our sacred land's economy, afflicted production, and weakened the army'. It's a quiet spot these days: a pleasant refuge for China's leisured classes (the retired, the unemployed) to meditate in, or for parents to give their toddlers a run-around (the Opium War-period cannon to the left of the statue are a favourite place for a photo opportunity).

A hundred and seventy years ago, though, the place would have looked (and smelled) very different. On 11 April that year, Elliot's opium began arriving – 7,000 of the total 20,000-odd chests from the great house of Jardine–Matheson's alone. In early May, Lin began

69

destroying it, pausing only to inform the Sea Spirit apologetically that he would shortly be releasing the drug into the great ocean and that the creatures of the water should therefore be advised to vacate the area. Over the next three weeks, somewhere between six and ten million dollars' worth of opium were thrown into vast, water-filled trenches specially dug at the mouth of the Canton River, scattered with salt and lime, then washed out to sea. After 1949, the scene was immortalized at the public heart of Communist power: outlines of improbably muscular Chinese workers hurling British opium into Humen's trenches were carved onto one side of the Monument to the Heroes of the People, the grey, thirty-seven-metre-high obelisk at the centre of Tiananmen Square. Lin himself put a slightly different spin on local Chinese enthusiasm for the spectacle. 'The inhabitants of the coastal region', he wrote to Daoguang, 'are coming in throngs to witness the destruction of the opium. They are, of course, only allowed to look on from outside the fence and are not permitted access to the actual place of destruction, for fear of pilfering.'[1] Of the British merchants come to witness the work, he happily observed that 'the foreigners are trembling in awe. I should judge from their attitudes that they have the decency to feel heartily ashamed . . . probably they will not dare to repeat the same [crime].'[2] (Lin may have mistaken biliousness for bad conscience: the combination of opium, salt and lime smelled foul, he recalled.[3])

He rejoiced at his progress. 'The real sympathy and sincerity thus shown, are worthy of praise', he congratulated Charles Elliot. 'Now is the time for foreigners of all nations to repent their faults.'[4] A delighted Daoguang dispatched in late March a gift of roebuck meat – its Chinese name, *baolu*, punning with the phrase meaning 'promotion guaranteed' – to which Lin was careful to kowtow nine times. A few days after inspecting his arrangements for destroying the opium in trenches near Canton, he was in such a good mood that he composed a poem to lychees. 'Mists and rains from foreign seas darken Lintin', he recited to the (probably nonplussed) orderly who had brought him a gift of the fruit from Canton's governor-general. 'Suddenly I received a carved platterful of stars / Eighteen smiling young ladies. / Your kindness refreshes like the green of the lychees.'[5] On 22 April, the promised promotion came: Daoguang elevated him to the Governor-Generalship of Jiangnan and Jiangxi – once matters at Canton were settled. How marginal this fuss with the foreigners is, the emperor seemed to be saying; finish it up quickly and get on with the real business of the empire.

Elliot and Lin, however, were soon caught up in another sticky negotiation. Nine days after Elliot agreed to hand over the opium, Lin reminded him of his second demand: for the British to sign a bond pledging not to bring any more of the drug into the empire, on pain of death. When the Hong merchants brought him a copy of the bond to sign, Elliot responded with the Victorian equivalent of a tantrum. 'I tore it up at once [according to one account, into a thousand pieces, which he then threw into the fireplace], and desired them to tell their officers that they might take my life as soon as they saw fit, but that it was a vain thing to trouble themselves or me any further upon the subject of the bond.'[6] From this point on, his rather stiff despatches to his foreign secretary take on a more histrionic colour, telling of 'protracted outrage . . . spoliation of the very worst description . . . the most shameless violences which one nation has ever yet dared to perpetrate against another'.[7]

Elliot was against the bond for sound reasons. It meant conceding on paper the principle of extraterritoriality in China that the British had been fighting to establish for almost sixty years. (In the decades preceding the struggles of 1839, Sino-Western relations had periodically broken down during disputes over how injuries or damage caused by Western traders should be handled. The most notorious case concerned the trading vessel the *Lady Hughes*, from 1784, in which a gun salute had accidentally killed a Chinese man – open-and-shut manslaughter, by British law. The Chinese authorities stopped trade until the accidental murderer had been handed over then quietly strangled him. Among the horrified British trading community, the whole episode quickly became shorthand for the Oriental cruelty of the Qing that, under the present Canton system, they were powerless to resist.) Also, given the diligence with which the British trading community dealt in opium, agreement would have led to a bloodbath. Yet again, Elliot found himself in an impossible position: 'It is beyond dispute', he admitted to Lin at a calmer moment, 'that those who will come to Canton to trade, must act in obedience to the laws. But the new regulation regarding these bonds is incompatible with the laws of England. If . . . these bonds be absolutely required, there will remain no alternative but for the English men and vessels to depart.' Fine, responded Lin: 'After you have thus returned, you will not be allowed to come again.'[8] Elliot's difficulty was that Lin was ready to have his bluff called – he had no fear of stopping the Canton trade. For the commissioner's actions sprang from a conviction that the foreigners would die without China's tea and rhubarb (later, he conceded that only tea was truly essential to their well-being), while foreign trade was of only incidental importance to the Chinese empire. On 23 May, Elliot ordered all British ships out of Canton, and retreated to Macao to ponder his next move.

He was soon to discover the wisdom of the old Chinese proverb: when you're stuck down a well, someone is bound to throw a rock on your head.

As relations grew increasingly tense through the spring and early summer of 1839, the community of opium vessels had found a new anchorage: along the northern edge of the island of Hong Kong. They had chosen well: it was a deep natural harbour, sheltered to the west by the larger Lantao Island, and to the right by the sandy finger of Kowloon Peninsula pointing down from the mainland. Better still, the island itself was so steep and rocky – dipping in and out of granite mountains and tangled jungle – that it was practically deserted (barring a few villages of fishermen and pirates), and a safe forty-odd miles from the Bogue (the entrance to the Canton riverways). At some point in the 1830s, the opium trade had begun migrating to this new berth, anchoring at a promontory insolently renamed Possession Point. Showcasing their capacity for laissez-faire, the Qing authorities seem to have done little to interfere, beyond stationing a handful of war junks nearby to keep an eye on things. But the spot had its inconveniences, too: most notably, a shortage of fresh victuals and water, for which crews and Chinese middlemen had to go over to Kowloon. On 7 July, consequently, a group of English and American sailors had landed somewhere on the shores of the peninsula and set off through the countryside in search of refreshments. At the small village of Jianshazui, they found it: a stash of samshoo – a potent local rice liquor usually laced with arsenic. Having drunk it, they part-demolished a small temple, brawled with the villagers, one of whom (by the name of Lin Weixi) died of his injuries the next day, and returned to Hong Kong, tired but happy.

It is not recorded what Elliot said when this unwelcome news reached him. Here was yet another public-relations disaster, another source of extraterritorial conflict between the British and Chinese, another example of British disregard for law and order. Like the pragmatic diplomat that he was, however, he immediately began hushing it up, advancing (via one 'Lo San' – presumably one of many cooperative Kowloon locals) 'a sum of 1,500 dollars to the family of the deceased, a further sum of 400 dollars to protect them from the extortion of this money by the lower mandarins in the neighbourhood, and 100 dollars, to be distributed among the suffering villagers, with the hope to soothe the irritation which the late event was calculated to create.' Following all of which, he informed Palmerston, 'the relatives of the deceased have forwarded me a paper, declaring that they ascribe his death to an accident, and not wilfulness'.[9]

But the damage had been done. 'Sudden changes from fine to rain', ran Lin's diary for 12 July. 'Heard that at Kowloon Point sailors from a foreign ship beat up some Chinese peasants and killed one of them. Sent a deputy to make inquiries.' He was soon taking the matter very seriously indeed – even asking a local American doctor to translate a Swiss tract on international law, from which he learnt that 'any foreigner who commits a crime must be punished by the law of the country'. On 2 August, Lin made his position clear in notices pasted up around Macao, reporting that he knew all: 'how many sailors there were ashore – what ships they belonged to – how they possessed themselves of the club or staves with which they struck or wounded Lin Weixi, till he dropped down', as well as a number of other interesting snippets, such as the quantity and source of the hush-money. 'Produce the foreign murderer, that . . . he may forfeit the life for the life he has taken', for the 'ghost of the dead man may still be longing for revenge in the regions below . . . Is this reasonable or not?'[10]

Elliot had no intention of surrendering a Briton to Chinese adjudication. But neither could he satisfactorily resolve the case himself. Although Lin was sure that fingering the felon would be easy, Elliot would have found it tricky to work out who exactly had dealt the homicidal blow: it was a drunken group affray (involving Britons and Americans) and the man died the following day – the precise cause of death would have been almost impossible to identify. On 12–13 August, Elliot held an on-board trial of the six sailors involved, as a result of which 'five men were found guilty on an indictment of riot and assault' and given fines and prison sentences. Elliot might as well not have bothered. After the seamen were sent home, they were allowed to vanish into the civilian population – for Captain Elliot, the British judiciary deemed, possessed no such authority over British citizens. (Yet again, Elliot's attempts at legal fair play were foiled by the establishment that he served.) And the show failed to satisfy Lin Zexu, who responded that 'if Elliot genuinely maintains that, after going twice to the scene of the murder and spending day after day investigating the crime, he still does not know who committed it, then all I can say is, a wooden dummy would have done better'.[11] Lin now stepped up the pressure by forbidding local servants, compradors and shopkeepers to work for or supply in any way the English on Macao. Signs began to appear at Hong Kong springs notifying that the water had been poisoned; from one, a weighted bag was fished out, stuffed with leaves and another mysterious substance that persuaded thirsty sailors to leave well alone. Military reinforcements around Macao seemed to be thickening also: on 15 August, Lin – in the company of 2,000 troops – paid a visit to a town forty miles north of the Portuguese settlement. Fifty-seven English families – including Elliot, his wife and their two-year-old son, Frederick – now fled Macao for merchant ships floating off Hong Kong. Lin, as usual, was confident they would soon be begging for mercy: 'they have on their ship a certain stock of dried provisions', he informed the emperor as August turned to September, 'but they will very soon find themselves without the heavy, greasy meat dishes for which they have such a passion.'[12]

Driven off dry land in somewhat dubious company (a shipful of opium-smugglers and a jittery Irish painter on the run from his wife), deprived of greasy food (and, more importantly, a guaranteed supply of water), Elliot might well have concluded that the Qing empire was dedicated to making his life miserable.

In truth, the Qing authorities did not take him quite seriously enough for that. Lin would later be lionized by nationalist admirers for his wisdom in seeking out foreign intelligence to defend China against alien imperialists. Much modern Chinese ink has been spilt on analysing his zeal to understand the West: on his hiring of linguists to translate foreign books and local anglophone newspapers into Chinese, on his quizzing of foreign residents about English attitudes to opium and activities in India, and so on.[13] Yet Lin seems to have failed to apply this knowledge usefully, underestimating the nature of the British threat and dismissing them in communications to the emperor as empty 'swashbucklers'. (In any case, a question mark hangs over the competence of Lin's translators. When Lin showed a version of his letter to Queen Victoria, rendered by his chief interpreter, to a crew of shipwrecked Englishmen, one member of his audience reported that he 'could scarcely command my gravity . . . Some parts of it we could make neither head nor tail of.'[14])

On 1 May, Lin made the following report to the emperor. 'After I arrived in Canton, I investigated the feelings of the foreigners. On the outside, they seem intractable, but inside they are cowardly. If in future we fear them setting off border provocations, the ulcer of trouble they bring will grow day by day . . . They are the minority, we are the majority. Though their ships are strong and their guns quick, they can only be victorious at sea – they cannot play their tricks in port, and Guangdong is well fortified . . . Although there have been some ups-and-downs so far, the situation as a whole is under control.' On 4 June, he wrote that those who went on smuggling were courting destruction and that they could easily be destroyed by fire rafts, or by militia hired from the local fishing populations.[15] On 1 September, he informed Daoguang that, 'despite their guns, the foreign soldiers are not skilled at infantry engagements. Their legs and feet, moreover, are closely bound by their tight trousers, which makes bending and stretching inconvenient. When they reach shore, they are thus powerless, and their strength can be easily controlled.'[16] As news of the approaching British fleet reached the Chinese coast, three times Lin dismissed them as 'rumours'. When the fleet did reach Canton in the middle of June 1840, Lin insisted to the emperor that it was simply a large-scale opium-smuggling operation. By the time this assessment reached Beijing the English forces had occupied the eastern island of Zhoushan for twelve days.[17]

In September 1839, Daoguang asked Lin to verify a story that the British were buying up thousands of Chinese children. 'Abroad,' Lin replied, consulting a text at least thirty years old dictated by a sailor once employed on European ships, 'the population is very sparse, so great value is set on every human being, and as it is also well known that they prize women even more than men, it is improbable that they would kill little girls for the purposes of black magic.'[18] It has been suggested elsewhere, he further informed his sovereign, that the foreigners' opium is made by mixing poppy-juice with human flesh. 'But I have ascertained', he rationalizes, 'that it is mixed with the corpses of crows. Now it is known that foreigners expose their dead and let the crows peck away the flesh. That is why the crows shown in pictures in foreign books are of such enormous size, sometimes several feet high.'[19]

Europeans interpreted this ignorance as evidence that the Qing government felt itself far above needing to enquire seriously into the condition of these English 'barbarians'. Certainly, a note of imperial pomposity is threaded through Lin's communications with England (which, officially, the Qing regarded as one of the 'ten thousand humbly submissive countries'): 'Although it is the maxim of the Celestial Court to treat with great tenderness and mildness men from afar,' ran one typical sermon, 'yet it cannot suffer them to indulge in scornful and contemptuous trifling with us.' Lin's tone towards Elliot veers between the schoolmasterish ('Looking over the some hundred words in your address, I find but one sentence to approve of . . . How is your mind so void of clear perception?') and the Old Testament ('Repent and you will again have indulgence shown you . . . now is the time for foreigners to repent of their faults and turn themselves over to the side of virtue [in order to receive once more] the dewy influences of the favour of the Celestial Court.')[20]

But his relative blindness towards the British suggests also a basic failure of focus: neither the emperor nor his commissioner seems to have felt that Sino-British relations merited serious, long-term concentration. In early September, as the British population bobbed off Hong Kong and just before both sides began firing at each other, the emperor urged Lin once again to tidy things up quickly in Canton then hurry on east, to begin his new job. Daoguang was, like his commissioner, oblivious to the potential consequences of confrontation with the English: 'What you have done is supremely gratifying!' he noted (in the vermilion ink reserved exclusively for the emperor's annotations) on a memorial describing the confiscation of the 20,000 chests.[21] 'Terror before mercy', he would advise a few weeks later, before clarifying: 'Do not disrupt things lightly, but at the same time do not be fearful and weak'.[22] By early 1840, with the dispute no nearer resolution, he was sounding weary of the whole business, issuing Lin with a demotion following the collapse of a dam in Hubei, where Lin had previously served as governor-general.[23] By the time the British fleet arrived in the summer of that year, the emperor's attention had long drifted elsewhere.

Lin's ignorance also shows, again, how little he trusted the Cantonese locals in his struggle to bring the British to heel. Theoretically, he had to hand at least a dozen wily 'experts' who had made careers and fortunes dealing with the foreigners: the Hong merchants (not to mention the thousands of compradors, cooks, cleaners and tradesmen who made their livings servicing the needs of the foreigners). Yet Lin made it very clear that he had the greatest disgust for such individuals – one of his first acts on reaching Canton had been to lecture the Hong merchants on their collaboration with the British and threaten to behead their ringleaders. Qing China on the eve of the Opium War was a place too wrapped up in its own insecurities to put its best energies into dealing with the British.

Chapter Five

THE FIRST SHOTS

Neither the short nor the longer-term antagonisms behind the outbreak of Sino-British hostilities of 1839 were hard to discern. British merchants wanted to sell their goods (and especially contraband narcotics) legally and freely all the way along the eastern coast; the Qing imperial government wanted to confine trade to Canton and ban opium. The British wanted extraterritorial powers over their subjects; the Qing wanted to maintain judicial authority over crimes committed within their borders. In short, the British wanted everything in China to be exactly as they liked. While the Qing state, not surprisingly, disagreed.

This conflict of interest was in due course rationalized by Britain's mercantile war party into honourable justification for international armed conflict. Over the key months of 1839–40 (when the Cabinet took the decision to go to war), the unwillingness of British merchants to play by another state's rules on that state's territory (the very issue triggering the factory siege) was publicly recast as something far nobler. A well-orchestrated pamphlet and press campaign turned their cause into the modern free world's righteous resistance to an evil empire fossilized into an ancient superiority complex and determined to keep the forces of civilization and progress at bay.

Such views had long been expressed in the pages of the *Chinese Repository*. 'We,' held forth one merchant in 1834, 'with our principles of forbearance, have been fixed in a corner of China; ourselves insulted, our fellow subjects unjustly slaughtered, and insult and contumely showered upon us most unsparingly. Has not the nation been disgraced by its extreme humiliation in the face of insult of the grossest nature?'[1] After 1834, these voices took advantage of the pathos of Napier's untimely death to seek a domestic British audience for their complaints. 'This truculent, vain-glorious people', James Matheson described the Chinese in 1836, 'have been pleased to consider all other inhabitants of the earth . . . as BARBARIANS.'[2] As tensions with the Qing government intensified, so did British merchants' efforts to occupy the moral high ground in the conflict. In early 1839, the trader William Jardine had returned to London from China to lead the merchant lobby, taking with him $20,000 and some sound advice from his partner Matheson: 'You may find it expedient to secure the services of some leading newspaper to advocate the cause', and perhaps to engage 'literary men' to draw up 'the requisite memorials in the most concise and clear shape'.[3] Between 1839 and 1840, Lin's siege of the factories (throughout which Chinese merchants had made nocturnal deliveries to British smugglers of bread, capons, hams, boxed lunches and suppers) was recreated, in a series of stirring published accounts, as a second Black Hole of Calcutta in which 'a despotic and arbitrary government . . . [that] has always been unjust and oppressive in their treatment of foreigners' deprived innocent Britons 'of their liberty; debar[red] them of food or water; threaten[ed] their lives . . . Dearly will they pay for the insults and outrages offered to the British nation', wrote Hugh Hamilton Lindsay, an old East India Company hand, and another of the leaders of the merchant lobby.[4]

This animosity flowed into a broader current of anti-China feeling that in the second half of the eighteenth century had begun to compete with the more admiring views of the French and English Enlightenment. As Britain's economic dispute with China gathered pace over these years, it became intellectually fashionable to obscure the petty, pounds-shilling-and-pence nature of the quarrel (and the deep dubiousness of the opium trade) with systemic diagnoses of all that was wrong with the empire, concealing the simple fact that what Europeans really found objectionable was the Qing's desire to control trade on its own terms. Where China was a vast, conservative, static unity, European states (and especially England) were small, nimble, fast-changing. While China's slavish people had been homogenized into 'speaking one language . . . and sympathising in the same

manners', reasoned David Hume, England's 'great liberty and inde-
pendency, which every man enjoys, allows him to display the manners
peculiar to him'.[5] Herder, Hegel and others concurred, finding
China languishing in 'shameful stagnation', 'an embalmed mummy,
wrapped in silk, and painted with hieroglyphics: its internal circulation is that of a dormouse in its winter sleep'.[6] Once established in
the minds of philosophers, China's immobility became the expression
of a more fatal malaise: a refusal to improve, or to learn from other,
more civilized powers. If China carried on as it was, the assumption
went, it was doomed.

As the eighteenth century changed to the nineteenth, therefore,
China was reinvented as a rogue state: a massive, militarized, alien,
hostile nation that refused to play by the rules of the international
game so recently invented by Europe. In 1840, British merchants and
diplomats asserted that the only appropriate riposte to this impossible
country was war. 'It is earnestly expected', went a pamphlet composed
by a 'Resident in China' in 1840, 'that the wisdom of Government
will be exercised in the choice of some strong and efficient measure,
to lower the pretensions of a people so arrogant and unjust.'[7] The
quarrel with China was no longer about *Britain*'s economic greed, or
drug-smuggling: it was about *China*'s contempt for national dignity
– contempt that Britain was honour-bound to avenge through military action.

Once the decision to go to war had been made, a turning point
was reached in popular impressions of China. The story that the
impossible Chinese had driven the British to violence had to be
maintained, overriding all empirical evidence to the contrary. Passing
judgement in 1841, the sixth President of the United States, John
Quincy Adams, blamed the eruption of hostilities on 'the kowtow –
the arrogant and insupportable pretensions of China, that she will
hold commercial intercourse with the rest of mankind not upon terms
of equal reciprocity, but upon the insulting and degrading forms of
the relations between lord and vassal'.[8] The euphoria of victory
further reinforced Britain's view of its own correctness. How, if Qing
China had not taken the losing side of History, could it have been
so soundly thrashed by the forces of Progress and Free Trade?[9]

China's rulers, it should be noted, would probably not have
recognized themselves in the stereotype that Britain's war party had

devised; nor would many of those on the fringes of the empire (who had first-hand experience of the Qing's voracious interest in the world at its borders) have seen much resemblance.[10] Perhaps even British detractors would have changed their minds, if they had taken the trouble to look at a map, or study a little history. Far from a community turned in on itself, Qing China was a vast, multi-ethnic jigsaw of lands and peoples. British opinion- and policy-makers of the 1830s made the mistake of – or deliberately deceived themselves into – simplifying the territory they called China into a complacent unity: an obstinate duelling partner from whom satisfaction must be extracted. It was nothing of the sort. This was an empire that could not even agree upon a single word for itself – changing shape and name according to whichever dynastic house happened to have acquired it – until discipline-conscious nationalists took matters into their own hands at the start of the twentieth century and settled on Zhongguo (literally, the 'Middle Kingdom', an ancient term for the individual state occupying the centre of what is now China).

Before the nineteenth-century closing of the Western mind on China, a visitor touring the palaces of the Qing dynasty would have found it hard to fathom the self-identity of its ruling house. First stop might be the heartland of imperial Chinese power, the Forbidden City, its thousand-yard-long succession of audience halls and vast white-stone courtyards enclosing (within three concentric sets of walls) the Son of Heaven at the centre of his capital. Our imaginary tourist might then take the air at the emperor's summer retreat in the north-western suburbs of the city – the Yuanmingyuan (Park of Perfect Brightness). There, our traveller would encounter a conspicuously European maze, then, a little further on, a Western-gabled mansion, its interiors draped with French tapestries and glazed with the best Venetian glass. He might subsequently choose to move on to Chengde – the summer capital in the dynasty's Manchurian homeland north-east of the Great Wall, where he would find 1,300 acres of steppe hunting grounds scattered with Chinese pleasure pavilions and willow-fringed lakes. He might chance upon the Mongolian yurt in which the emperor received his Central Asian vassals; or stroll around 'Little Potala' (a red-and-white imitation of the Dalai Lama's Lhasa residence), while gazing out over the mountains of Inner Mongolia. Set next door to one another, the Qing's several palace complexes (Chinese, European, Manchurian, Mongolian, Tibetan) would have resembled a kind of eighteenth-century Las Vegas, expressing in microcosm the dynasty's robust appetite for territories, peoples, religions, ideas and objects. The story of the Qing is of a great colonial enterprise, in which a Manchurian conquest minority somehow kept in check for over two and a half centuries a great patchwork of other ethnic groups: Chinese, Mongolians, Tibetans. No mean achievement for a state whose founder, Nurhaci, had begun in the 1580s as a magpie-worshipping ginseng trader with only thirteen suits of armour to protect his followers.

Even the origins of the Manchus were untidily heterogeneous: they had started out as a blur of hunting, fishing, farming, pearl-gathering semi-Mongolicized tribes known as Jurchens, for whom Ming China had used the nervous shorthand 'wild people'.[11] The architects of the Qing conquest, Nurhaci and his extraordinarily tough son Hung Taiji, had been notably pragmatic in their hungry quest to build an empire, attracting and rewarding literate Chinese immigrants to the north-east to run the increasingly complex machinery of their rising state (formally established in 1616). The Manchu armies that conquered China to establish the Qing dynasty in 1644 were dominated by Chinese collaborators and weapons.

Although China – with its high agricultural yields, urban economies and cultivated elites – was a fine prize, it was only one of the land masses that the Qing bolted together across the seventeenth and eighteenth centuries. By 1634, Hung Taiji had secured allegiances from Inner Mongolia. Anxious that the Zunghars – a grouping of independent tribes in Outer Mongolia and eastern Turkestan (present-day Xinjiang) – might pose a threat in conjunction with Romanov Russia, the second Qing Emperor, Kangxi, turned his attention to the Zunghar leader, Galdan. Within ten years, Galdan had been isolated, betrayed and poisoned, his bones crushed and scattered through the streets of Beijing as a stern warning to other potential resisters of Qing will.[12] Scenting trouble from an alliance between the western Mongols and Tibet, Kangxi occupied and garrisoned Tibet, transforming the Panchen Lama into a Qing protégé and marking the

end of the territory's political independence – all the while bringing
to heel a Ming-loyalist regime on Taiwan. At the end of it all, Qing
emperors could realistically proclaim themselves the Lord of Lords:
the Confucian Son of Heaven, the Khan of the Mongol Khans and the
Patron-in-Chief of Tibetan Buddhism.

Expansion, then, was the keynote of Qing rule, and early Qing
emperors led by example. Kangxi delighted in the opportunity to
leave court life for the freedom of steppe campaigns. 'In two years,'
he wrote from a corpse-strewn Gobi desert, 'I made three journeys,
across deserts combed by wind and bathed with rain, eating every
other day, in the barren and uninhabited deserts . . . My life is happy,
fulfilled – I have what I wanted.'[13] Although his son and grandson –
the Yongzheng and Qianlong emperors – preferred civilian life to the
gales of the north-west, both delegated their generals to push hard on
the empire's northern and southern frontiers. In old age, Qianlong
styled himself the 'Old Man of the Ten Utter Victories', generating
some 1,500 poems and essays commemorating his wars, to be
scratched (in the several languages incorporated into the Qing conquest – Chinese, Manchu, Mongol, Arabi, Uighur) onto hundreds of
monumental war memorials littered across the empire. He revelled in
the rituals of war, presiding over the grand receptions, banquets,
elephant processions and ritual drawing and quartering of prisoners
acted out at the gate to the Forbidden City, often before international
– Dutch, Korean, Japanese – audiences.

It took, though, something more sophisticated than brute force
to keep this empire in one piece. True political omnivores, Qing
emperors took an intense interest in almost any source of cultural,
practical or religious leverage – Confucian, Buddhist or European –
over their various peoples.

Somewhere near the centre of Qing government lay a collection of
ideas about managing the world that could be termed Confucianism.
For once the population of China proper had been forcibly compelled
– on pain of death – to wear the badge of submission to their foreign
conquerors (the Manchu shaved forehead and long braided queue that
would, illogically, become the trademark of the pantomime Chinaman
in Western minds), the Qing were anxious to prove themselves faithful inheritors of ancient Chinese statecraft. Since the establishment
of the Han dynasty in 206 BC (when the Confucian Lu Jia thought

aloud to the dynasty's militantly anti-intellectual founder, 'You have vanquished the empire on horseback; but can you rule it on horseback?'), Confucianism had served as the moral glue holding together a long succession of regimes founded on violent conquest.

Confucius – who himself lived through an era of ruthless interstate conflict – preached a philosophy of harmonious submission. The Chinese world, he believed, would prosper not through violence, but through careful maintenance of hierarchy. His great, popularizing innovation was to scale his political philosophy down into the manageable analogy of family relationships: to equate the bond between father and son (or elder brother and younger brother; husband and wife) with that between ruler and subject. Good fathers and sons, his logic went, make good rulers and subjects, bringing the empire back to its rightful state of peaceful unity; perform your own social role properly, and the country will prosper. At the centre of all these relationships sat the emperor, whose mandate to rule depended on his own cultivation of the values of Confucian scripture. In 1670, therefore, the warlike Kangxi emperor had reinvented himself as a hearth-and-home Confucian, indoctrinating his millions of new subjects in the philosopher's submissive virtues of obedience, loyalty, thrift and hard work.

When it came to governing the peoples of Inner Asia, Qing rulers reinvented themselves, in turn, as the descendants of Genghis Khan, as patrons of Tibetan Lamaism, as secretive earthly mediators with the Buddhist spirit guide of the dead – all in the interests of wielding spiritual (and therefore political) power over Tibet and Mongolia. Qianlong advertised himself not only as the Confucian Son of Heaven and the Khan of Khans, but also as the messianic 'wheel-turning king' (cakravartin) of Tibetan Buddhist scripture, whose virtuous conquests were rolling the world on towards salvation.

Again in the interests of state-strengthening, the Qing borrowed happily from Europe. Taking advantage of Catholic Europe's naive eagerness to gain access to a vast new empire of conversion opportunity, Qing emperors exploited a series of talented Jesuit priests – Belgians, Germans, Italians – who rose to the many tasks set them by the imperial will: in astronomy, engineering, surveying, weaponbuilding, personal tutoring (the Kangxi emperor had a German maths and astronomy teacher); conjuring up clocks, mechanical sing-songs, harpsichord lessons, hydraulics, medicines, sextants, palaces, bluebells. European ingenuity was also put to military uses. In 1673, the Kangxi emperor threatened all Jesuits with expulsion from China unless they helped manufacture cannon to defeat a massive southern rebellion; when his Belgian director of the Imperial Bureau of Astronomy, Ferdinand Verbiest, obliged (blessing and naming after a saint each of the 500 cannon he produced), Kangxi offered him his own sable coat in gratitude. Across the next century, Jesuits served variously as cannon-makers, artillery instructors and negotiators in arms sales between the Qing and European merchants in Canton.

At the end of conquest, the Jesuits were again deployed, to draw up maps communicating the frontiers of the Qing triumph to regional competitors such as the Romanov empire. Between 1708 and 1718, the Kangxi emperor commissioned from his faithful servants a multi-lingual survey and atlas of the entire realm – from the Korean border to Tibet – that combined the latest Chinese and European cartographical techniques. The great Qianlong could barely suppress his delight at the new extent of his dominions after 1750, scrawling the gleeful 'unprecedented' over maps drawn up to mark his latest conquests.

How, then, did nineteenth-century warmongers become so ready to respond to the 'provocation' of Lin's siege of March 1839? Why, despite the obviously cosmopolitan basis of Qing power, did merchants, missionaries and policy-makers begin so confidently to denounce the empire as exclusive? What had they glimpsed or encountered that turned them against the country?

The answer, in part, lies in the ways in which the Qing sought to control its encounters with Europeans. As it looked to manage the world outside its borders, Chinese statecraft for nearly two millennia had used a form of tribute system. By this reckoning, China was a universal empire (*tianxia*, 'all under heaven'), whose authority – cohering around elaborately literate political and cultural traditions – in theory radiated indefinitely outward to civilize non-Chinese neighbours. According to Han-dynasty political geography, China was divided into five concentric zones: the inner three ruled directly by the Chinese king, while the outer two were occupied by barbarians;

all five zones owed tribute and ritual obeisance to the universally sage Chinese emperor (the 'Son of Heaven'), thereby affirming their status as vassals. Simply and economically, the tribute system transformed the Confucian principle of hierarchical submission into a universal model for foreign relations. The world, according to the sino-centric ideal at least, revolved around China.

In truth, all the way through Chinese history, the tribute system was little more than a fudge for other, more pragmatic realities. Between the Han and Qing dynasties, parts, and sometimes all of China were conquered by tribes from the northern steppe, the last of which founded the Qing in 1644. The hierarchical facade of tributary homage could serve equally as a face-saving front for trade; or as a kind of diplomatic protection racket, operating at a financial loss to the empire. The Chinese court would offer subsidies to warlike neighbours in exchange for objects of often no particular value or use and the promise not to attack Chinese territory. Imperial China's foreign policy-makers over the centuries had combined tributary etiquette with economic incentives and diplomacy, and even with the laissez-faire 'loose-rein' policy, by which distant peoples who chose to pay court to the Chinese centre would not be refused, while those who did not would be left in peace.

Nonetheless, at the start of the Ming dynasty in 1368, the sino-centric vision was at last formalized into a body of codes and rituals to which foreign visits to court were to conform. On entering the frontier, envoys would be escorted slowly to the capital, where they would be banqueted, required to kowtow to the emperor, banqueted, entertained by music, gifted, handed an edict expressing the imperial response to whatever demands they may have raised and banqueted again. With some adaptations and simplifications, the Qing dynasty inherited the principle and spirit of the Ming version, using the system to regulate relations both with its more familiar neighbours (Korea, Vietnam, Thailand) and with new visitors from Europe eager to trade for China's prized exports.

By the eighteenth century, Europeans – and Britons especially – were finding the whole farrago infuriating. As Dutch, Portuguese, sometimes Russian and (latterly) British embassies progressed sedately to the feet of the Son of Heaven, they began to mutter increasingly loudly about their frustrations at the system: at its restrictive bureau-

cratic routine; at the court's demeaning insistence on the kowtow; at
the absence of opportunity for straight-talking negotiation and for
getting what they wanted – notably free trade, consular representation
and diplomatic equality.

When the British sent their first mission in 1792–3 to establish
free trade with China, their ambassador – George, Lord Macartney –
grew openly impatient with the system's elaborate ceremonial. As
the British economy agitated over its tea-fuelled trade deficit with
China, George III dispatched his representative together with the
finest fruits of European science and culture – telescopes, clocks,
barometers, airguns, a hot-air balloon – to dazzle Qianlong into
opening free trade with Britain, by convincing him that he and his
313 million people needed Britain's technological marvels. The entire
trip took Macartney a good two years, of which several months were
spent crawling up the rivers and roads of the Chinese interior to the
emperor's summer retreat at Chengde and wrangling over issues of
diplomatic etiquette: whether or not the British gifts counted as
'tribute', or 'gifts' (from a diplomatic equal); whether Macartney
would kowtow to the emperor.

But Qianlong wanted little to do with George III's demands for
free-trading rights in China and for a permanent British embassy in
Beijing. 'We have never valued ingenious articles, nor do we have the
slightest need of your country's manufactures', Qianlong explained
in his official response to the British king – a communication that
has subsequently become shorthand for Qing China's delusions of
supremacy over the rest of the globe.[14] China, Macartney concluded,
was 'an old crazy first rate man-of-war' fated to be 'dashed to pieces
on the shore'.[15] Macartney's failure – disseminated soon after his
return in the published diary of his travels, and in the peevish travel
memoirs of his entourage – edged British public opinion on China
closer towards the shorter-tempered nineteenth-century vision of an
arrogant, ritual-obsessed empire that had to be blasted 'with a couple
of frigates' into the modern, civilized world of free trade.[16]

Again, however, the Qing world would probably not have recognized itself in Britain's caricature. Far from self-sufficient, Qing
China was fully – vulnerably – dependent on international commerce
to bring in the essentials of existence: rice, pepper, sugar, copper
and wood from south-east Asia, Taiwan, Japan and Korea; and New

World silver to pay its taxes, and therefore government and armies.[17]
Early nineteenth-century European travellers around China's fringes
reported the population's eagerness for trade and for foreign goods –
wool, opium, even Bible tracts. Neither did Chinese merchants wait
passively for useful items to come their way from abroad. Instead,
China's booming population spilled across the seas in search of business and labouring opportunities (boatbuilding, sawmilling, mining,
pawnbroking, hauling), mostly in south-east Asia, Ceylon or Africa;
a handful (of barbers, scholars, Christian converts) straggled out as far
as France, Italy, Portugal, Mexico. Only a state of emergency would
persuade the authorities to shut down maritime trade. During the war
to recover Taiwan from Ming loyalists in 1661, Kangxi shifted coastal
populations twenty miles inland, to starve out the island; the ban
was promptly rescinded in 1684, once the breakaway regime had
been ousted. A 1740 Dutch massacre in Batavia of more than 10,000
Chinese residents did not offer sufficient cause to ban trade – and
neither, for long, did the outbreak of the Opium War.

So if the British simply wanted to trade, Qianlong pointed out in
his reply to George III, they already could do so, down at Canton –
which many of them quite contentedly were doing. Reminiscing in
the 1880s, that old China hand William Hunter regretted the passing of the antebellum Canton trade – even the demolition of the old
factory buildings whose position outside the city walls was the cause
of much controversy between foreign traders and locals. 'The business
transacted within their walls was incalculable, and I think I am safe
in saying that . . . the novelty of the life, the social good feeling
and unbounded hospitality always mutually existing . . . the facility
of all dealings with the Chinese who were assigned to transact business with us, together with their proverbial honesty, combined
with a sense of perfect security to person and property.'[18] His elegy
reveals a world characterized not by mutual suspicion, bureaucratic
conceit and numbing hierarchy, but rather by trust, good will and
fine dining. He recalls jovial dinners at the houses of the imperially
appointed Hong merchants, serving up 'such delicacies as birds'-nest
soup, with plovers' eggs, and Beche-de-Mer, curiously prepared
sharks' fins and roasted snails . . . it is not true, as has been supposed,
that on these convivial occasions the guests were served with roast or
boiled "puppy" as a *bonne bouche*'.[19] Such, he claims, was the good faith

existing between Europeans and Chinese that there was no use of written receipts or promissory notes. On one occasion, a Chinese merchant – out of friendship – wrote off a foreign merchant's debt for 72,000 dollars; more often, the credit flowed in the opposite direction, with the Hong traders substantially in debt to the Europeans.

It was true, nonetheless, that the Qing state was far more devoted to regulating the European than it was the Asian junk trade. And a discontented British minority concluded from the limits imposed on them a general principle of Qing xenophobia. More careful consideration of the matter would have revealed a political design behind the entire scheme. European sailors of the two centuries before Macartney's arrival had not been on their best behaviour when approaching the Chinese coast. The Portuguese, the first Europeans to make a concerted effort to penetrate mainland China under the Ming dynasty, had barged undiplomatically up to Canton – building a fort, buying Chinese children, trading at will. The first British merchant to introduce himself memorably to the Chinese authorities was one Captain John Weddell who, in 1637, similarly forced his way up to Canton aspiring to 'do all the spoils . . . [he] could unto the Chinois.'[20] While deliberating on how to handle the Macartney embassy, the Qing court pondered accounts of the British absorption of India. 'Among the western ocean states, England ranks foremost in strength', Qianlong secretly communicated to his Grand Minister. 'It is said that the English have robbed and exploited the merchant ships of the other western ocean states so that the foreigners along the western ocean are terrified of their brutality.'[21] The British, the emperor observed, were ever-ready to take advantage of slack military discipline on the coast. The accuracy of Qianlong's assessment of British ambitions in Asia would be borne out by the events of 1839–42 and beyond.

For the Qing – as a conquering minority – uneasiness about security was a way of life, directed at every ethnic group within its sprawling frontiers, including the Han Chinese majority who helped administer the empire. 'If our government were to become weak,' the Kangxi emperor had prophesied near the end of his life,

if we were to weaken our vigilance over the Chinese in the southern provinces and over the large number of boats that leave every year for Luzon, Batavia, Japan, and other countries, or if

divisions were to erupt among us Manchus and the various
princes of my family, if our enemies the Eleuths were to succeed
in allying with the Tartars of Kokonor, as well as our Kalmuk
and Mongol tributaries, what would become of our empire?
With the Russians to the north, the Portuguese from Luzon
to the east, the Dutch to the south, [they] would be able to do
with China whatever they liked.[22]

Antagonism between Manchus and Chinese (and, for that matter,
between Chinese from different regions) would consistently undermine Qing efforts throughout the Opium War to come.

Qianlong's lofty public denial of interest in ingenious foreign
articles (belied by his French, Tibetan and Mongol residences, by his
profusion of exquisite European 'spheres, orreries, clocks and musical
automatons' that, Macartney noted, made the British gifts 'shrink
from the comparison') is perhaps best understood as part of a careful
strategy of imperialist control. The emperor was informing a potential
rival of his determination to define and monitor his empire's need for
ideas and objects.[23] His rhetoric suggests an insular overconfidence in
his empire's possessions and achievements. His contrasting actions
– his collections of exotic artefacts and religions, his expansionist
campaigns – reveal an aggressive interest in the outside world.

The Qing appetite for foreign languages, objects and ideas grew
directly out of the preoccupation with security that nineteenth-
century European accounts read as xenophobia. Emperors made excellent diplomatic use of their own cosmopolitanism: 'when the rota of
Mongols, Muslims and Tibetans come every year to the capital for
audience,' proclaimed the sexalingual Qianlong emperor, 'I use their
own languages and do not rely on an interpreter . . . to conquer them
by kindness.'[24] They used Manchu to correspond secretly with distant
officers in the field, outside Chinese lines of communication. Well
aware of the political uses of multilingualism, the Qing did its best
to prevent non-resident Europeans from acquiring Chinese and Manchu, and therefore the means to communicate independently with the
native population: in early nineteenth-century Canton, teaching a
foreigner Chinese remained a capital offence. 'The shrewd Chinaman',
William Hunter observed, 'succeeded in supplying [foreigners']
absence of the knowledge of his own language by cleverly making

himself familiar with sounds of foreign words'.[25] Most Western writers quoted pidgin – the linguistic bridge between Canton's European and Chinese merchant communities – to ridicule the Chinese into whose mouths they put it; Hunter's analysis remade it into a grand intelligence scheme.

In short, the British made an error of judgement in assessing their first, influential encounter with high Qing diplomacy in 1793, allowing the ceremonial facade of the tribute system to obscure the pragmatic reality of Qing foreign policy. According to the tributary ideal, no ruler of China ever needed to lift a finger against its neighbours as – mesmerized by the glitter of Confucian civilization – all would voluntarily prostrate themselves before the Son of Heaven. The great military enterprises of the Qing dynasty tell a different story: this was an ambitious conquest backed by all available technical or political means – Central Asian, Confucian, Tibetan, European – of securing the resulting empire. As a result, by the start of the nineteenth century, it becomes remarkably difficult to define what European observers so confidently called China. What we have instead is a cross-bred state, held together by coercive cosmopolitanism: by a sense of unbounded entitlement to rule and control, justified by the Confucian Mandate of Heaven, the Manchu Way, Tibetan spirituality and European firepower. The great Qing emperors tried to be all things to all their people: great conquerors, preaching the superiority of their ethnic heritage; learned Confucian poets, scholars, receivers of tributaries; Buddhist messiahs. While the foundation stones of the empire – the economy and the army – were prospering, success seems to have kept this multi-ethnic balancing act in place. But once these same things sank into decline at the close of the eighteenth century, the whole edifice of empire began to shake.

As European opinion on China turned through the eighteenth and nineteenth centuries, erudites from Montesquieu to J. S. Mill and beyond produced lazy general hypotheses to explain what was wrong with China (or rather, what they disliked about it): to justify why the old Qing Chinese way was doomed to be swept away by the modern European, or British, way. But these theories fell some way off the mark: economic, ecological and imperialist overextension would poise the Qing for a nineteenth-century tumble. The Chinese empire (as it remains today) is probably best seen as an impressive but improbable high-wire act, unified by ambition, bluff, pomp and pragmatism. At any one moment – as an ethnic minority cajoled, blustered and compelled into allegiance any number of territories that could just as easily have floated off into independence – there were far more logical reasons for the Qing empire to fall apart than for it to hold together. A glance across the two centuries of Qing history that preceded the outbreak of the Opium War tells us that this was a state capable of all manner of responses to Britain in spring 1839 (force, ceremonial, economic concessions or diplomatic realism). Misfortune – the distractions of protracted economic and social crisis – rather than blind conceit turned it in on itself, and pushed it towards confrontation with Palmerston's gunboats.

At 9 a.m. on 4 September 1839, Charles Elliot – in a fleet of three small ships – sailed from the northern shore of Hong Kong towards the Qing junks at Kowloon that were blocking British access to fresh food and water. Just off the mainland, he dispatched Karl Gützlaff to hand a couple of letters to the authorities, stating that if the war junks did not withdraw, violence would result. Chinese representatives declined to take them, on the grounds that they were not empowered to do so. At 2 p.m., with the Cantonese sun blazing down, Elliot communicated that if he did not get provisions in half an hour, he would fire on the Qing ships. When the deadline came and went, Elliot stuck to his word. To the British consternation, the junks did not flee, but returned the fire, and well. Nonetheless, at 4.45, as the junks drew alongside the English ships, 'we . . . gave them three such Broadsides that it made every Rope in the vessel grin again', one of Elliot's shaken clerks later wrote home. 'We loaded with Grape the fourth time, and gave them Gun for Gun. – The shrieking on board was dreadful, but it did not frighten me; this is the first day I ever shed human blood, and I hope will be the last.'[26]

But full-blown war was still not inevitable. Immediately afterwards, local traders were once more allowed to supply to the British, although at slightly higher prices than before; and the signs marked 'Poison' disappeared from watering holes. By 15 September, Lin was allowing a few of the English (including the troublesome Elliot) to drift back to Macao, and the two men succeeded in exchanging relatively peaceable communications for almost a month. Elliot offered a compromise: officials could search newly arrived ships, and cargos that contained any opium would be confiscated; he also pledged 2,000 dollars in the search for Lin Weixi's murderer. It was not exactly harmonious; but neither were the two sides firing broadsides at each other – even if Lin had amiably threatened to 'annihilate' the English on 28 September, if they continued to refuse to hand over the homicide. Trade, meantime, was thriving, because the Americans had signed their own version of a bond (which, they claimed, made no mention of a death penalty), and were shifting British goods by the boatful into Canton, then tea and silk out.

Soon, though, Elliot's luck soured again. On 14 October an old East India Company ship, the *Thomas Coutts*, approached the China coast from Singapore carrying nothing but Indian cotton, rattan and pepper, bypassed Hong Kong, and headed straight to Humen, where its captain signed Lin's bond and was waved up to Canton. Lin now abandoned the idea of compromise, and bid once more for a mass signing of the bond. How much quicker and easier, he told Elliot, the bond was than a search: sign, and the 'usual privileges would be restored'.[27] Lin, meanwhile, assembled at Chuanbi – the eastern bank of the river mouth leading up to Canton, where a mass of British merchant ships was waiting to finalize the revised bond with Lin – a fleet of war junks and fire rafts. The next day, Elliot set off from Hong Kong to mediate, in the *Volage* and the *Hyacinth*, the frigate and sloop that had arrived from India at the very end of August. When he arrived on 2 November after five anxious days beating up against adverse winds, the captain of the *Volage*, Henry Smith, planned to pass a letter to the commissioner, asking the latter to reconsider his order.

There are at least three accounts of what happened next. Elliot claimed that an infuriating diplomatic dance began: the Qing admiral, Guan Tianpei, refused to receive the letter, and yet again asked for the murderer of Lin Weixi; yet again, Elliot stated that he did not know who the murderer was. At noon, Captain Smith calculated that the risk of leaving the merchant fleet exposed over-night to possible Qing attack was too great, while retiring 'was not compatible with the honour of the flag'.[28] (Had he been dragged all the way from India, he was perhaps asking himself, merely to deliver post?) After consulting Elliot, he opened fire.

The Chinese version is rather different. According to Lin's memorial to the emperor, as the second English ship to sign the bond, the *Royal Saxon*, prepared to enter the river to approach Canton, the two English warships 'forcibly ordered [her] to return, and prevented her from entering the port'. Just when a surprised Admiral Guan was making enquiries regarding the matter, 'the Hyacinth began cannonading, and advanced her attack'.[29] The admiral now returned the fire and ordered his own fleet to advance, 'standing erect before the mast, wielding his sword and roaring "Death to deserters!" He did not flinch even when injured by a cannon ball that took the side off one of the masts'. He 'blasted the figure-head off one ship, causing many foreign sailors to fall into the sea'. ('Outstanding', noted the emperor.) As the British ships shortly tried to flee the scene, the Qing navy decided to let them limp off.[30]

Now back to Elliot. '[We] ran down the Chinese line, pouring in a destructive fire . . . the terrible effect of [which] was soon manifest. One war junk blew up at about pistol-shot distance . . . three were sunk; and several others were obviously waterlogged . . . the Admiral's conduct was worthy of his station,' Elliot conceded, 'manifesting a resolution of behaviour honourably enhanced by the hopelessness of his efforts. In less than three quarters of an hour, however, he and the remainder of his squadron were retiring in great distress to their former anchorage; and as it was not Captain Smith's disposition to protract destructive hostilities, he . . . discontinued the fire and made sail for Macao.'[31] One light injury – to a British sailor – was sustained.

Despite the difficulties (or even impossibilities) of his position, Elliot was utterly in the wrong. By 3 November, he had not only repeatedly flouted Qing law, but had also used force to prevent two British ships from complying with this same law, and authorized a clash with Chinese ships. Nevertheless, when it comes to war, the principle of natural justice sometimes needs to be sidelined by more pragmatic considerations. The engagement at Chuanbi should have confirmed to Lin that Qing ships and cannon were no match for the British and that, for the time being, open conflict was best avoided. Even if he had drawn that cautious conclusion, though, the English Cabinet would soon take the decision for war out of his hands.

Chapter Six

'AN EXPLANATORY DECLARATION'

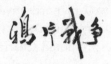

On 29 August 1839, Lord Palmerston – Free Trader, libertine, arch-villain of Chinese historiography – went to work as usual at the Foreign Office. In the 1830s, this institution was wedged into a corner of the Downing Street cul-de-sac, not far from a malfunctioning sewer. The integrity of the whole structure – a rickety amalgam of two eighteenth-century houses – was threatened by the weight of the printing apparatus up in the attic, which sent ominous cracks through the building.[1] Palmerston was so dissatisfied with the accommodation that when a fire started in one of the rooms in 1836, he reportedly could not bring himself to call for help with any great urgency. It was eventually on his recommendation that the old place was demolished in 1861, and replaced by the purpose-built classical palace that houses the FCO in Whitehall today.

That day in late summer 1839, he would have found on his desk – at which he always worked standing up, sometimes for up to seven hours at a time (his theory being that if he fell asleep at the job, he would wake up when he hit the floor)[2] – a dispatch from the Queen's man in China, Charles Elliot, with news of what was happening out there: the threats, the blockade, the extraction of the opium. Concluding his dispatch, Elliot suggested a course of action: 'It appears to me, my Lord, that the response to all these unjust violences should be made in the form of a swift and heavy blow unprefaced by one word of written communication.'[3]

According to contemporary Chinese historians, what happened next is straightforward. With his eyes on imperialist expansion,

Palmerston – in alliance with Britain's rapacious merchant lobby – grasped the pretext delivered to him by Lin's destruction of British government property and prepared for war. For Palmerston, like Elliot, is accused of many things in PRC history books. His sins go back to 1833, when he is supposed to have instigated the Napier fiasco, ordering Lord William to set off a diplomatic incident to justify a military invasion of China. (One might cautiously observe that it was not a very well-planned invasion, as he failed to tell British India to provide any ships.) In June 1836, the PRC case against him continues, he promoted Charles Elliot to the position of chief superintendent in China and abolished any junior positions, so as to give the wicked captain absolute power over China policy. (English sources give a more prosaic explanation: Palmerston wanted to reduce costs.) Palmerston, in summary, 'was the evil inciter and organiser of the Opium War . . . a total pirate'.[4] In Communist China, Palmerston's decision to send out the gunboats is read as a long-planned conspiracy, with Elliot's manoeuvring through 1839 merely providing an excuse for an inevitable war.

To which Palmerston might have ruefully responded: if only he had had time that year for such luxuries as elaborate global conspiracies. The viscount had first been appointed to the Foreign Office in 1830; in 1839, it remained an organization under severe pressure. To some, diplomacy remained a bastion of gentlemanly amateurism: 'neither more nor less than a gigantic system of outdoor relief for the aristocracy of Great Britain', went one contemptuous observation. A 'nursery' at the top of the Downing Street house was fitted out with fencing foils, boxing gloves and a piano, with which young bloods fresh out of university could entertain themselves. Palmerston's staff, both in London and abroad, certainly included its fair share of dilettanti, womanizers and gamblers, and Palmerston was periodically importuned by well-born chums, colleagues and his own prime minister for preferential placements for ill-qualified junior relatives, resulting in a number of unwise appointments. In 1851, the Consul-Generalship to the Mosquito Indians was granted to an individual, according to one account, 'as mad as Bedlam, vulgar, & mental & quarrelling with all classes & people'.[5] Palmerston's man in Belgium in the early 1830s took pride in the fact that he did not read 'the trumpery Belgian papers' or 'mix with the trumpery Belgian people ... his time was passed in a state of besotted irritation, carrying on warlike correspondence with quarrelsome English gentlemen, and amatory correspondence with accommodating French & Belgian ladies'.[6] 'There is positively nothing to do here', complained Berlin's legation secretary in 1835. 'I am always at Potsdam shooting wild ducks.'[7] Extracting useful intelligence from such sources could be a trial. 'Tell us now and then', Palmerston mildly wrote to a minister in Naples (who also happened to be his brother) who failed to report on anything beyond the movements of the royal family, 'what the Neapolitan government think or mean to do about the affairs of the world – Spain, Greece, Italy, Morocco; what is the internal state of the country, as to commerce, finance, army, etc. We hear of a war between Naples and Morocco: is it true, and what is it about?'[8]

If the efficiency of Palmerston's operations in Europe was questionable, how much greater was the scope for things going wrong between London and China, where cultural and political barriers rendered most kinds of entente cordiale implausible, where linguistic competence was scarce, where official instructions – travelling in the pre-telegraphic 1830s by opium clipper, steamer, sidewheeler and camel or donkey litter – lagged months behind events. As Elliot endured the Canton summer of 1839, his dispatches moved towards his minister in Downing Street with distressing slowness: it took five months for his account of the blockade and request for military back-up to land on Palmerston's desk. It would take another six months for Palmerston's decision to send a fleet to return to Elliot.[9]

The Foreign Office was only one of the British government's problems. As domestic discontent mounted through the poor harvests, industrial depression and growing unemployment of the 1830s, the public lost confidence in the Whigs. When the administration refused to look at the Chartists' radical petitions – which demanded universal male suffrage, secret ballots, equal electoral districts, annual elections and the abolition of the property requirement for MPs – violence erupted. In Birmingham, the Bullring riots of summer 1839 left the city looking, in the Duke of Wellington's description, as if it had been 'taken by storm'.[10] On 7 May, the prime minister was forced to resign after winning a debate by only five votes, leaving the Tories, under Robert Peel, to assemble a government. When the young Queen

Victoria refused to have her favourite Whig ladies of the bedchamber replaced by a cohort of female Tories, Peel resigned, leaving Victoria to invite her beloved Melbourne, the Whig prime minister, to form his government once more. The Bedchamber Crisis left the Whigs looking not only unpopular, but also unconstitutional – dependent on the whims of a girl queen. Morally righteous in opposition, the Tories refused to support anything the Whigs did; the radical elements in Parliament – sensing the Whigs depended on their cooperation for survival – pushed hard for political reforms. It was an uncomfortable summer for the government in which Palmerston served.

Bad times at home were accompanied by troubles abroad. In the course of 1839, rebellions broke out in Ireland, Jamaica and Canada, forcing the government to suspend the constitution in both the last two territories. In Egypt and Afghanistan, both France (which was also busy in Mexico and Argentina, harassing British merchant vessels and blockading British investments) and Russia were meddling with access routes to India. In the early months of 1839, India's governor-general, Lord Auckland, dispatched a 10,000-strong British army across the Indus and up the mountainous valleys towards Kabul, to replace the Afghan ruler (rumoured to be friendly to the Russians) with a weak exile called Shah Shuja. The awful finale of the expedition – a retreat back to India in which only one Briton survived out of the 16,500 who began it – was still three years off, but the mere idea of the war was already horrifying politicians in London, who blamed Palmerston for picking an expensive fight, for underestimating the difficulties, for sexing up the case against Russian ambitions by heavily editing a collection of field dispatches on Afghanistan. Just like the Qing thousands of miles away, the British were anxious to count the cost of all these rebellions and wars: in 1837, the country achieved a budget deficit of more than £2 million; by 1840, plans to subsidize the new Penny Post had enlarged it further.[11]

'Parliamentary business', concluded the radical Lord Brougham on 23 August 1839, 'was instructed to the hands of men utterly imbecile and incapable'.[12] The diarist and amateur cricketer Charles Greville was especially unkind about Palmerston:

Palmerston, the most enigmatical of Ministers, who is detested by the Corps diplomatique, abhorred in his own office, unpopular in the H. of Commons, liked by nobody, abused by everybody, still reigns in his little kingdom of the Foreign Office, and is impervious to any sense of shame from the obloquy that has been cast upon him, and apparently not troubling himself about the affairs of the government generally, which he leaves it to others to defend and uphold as they best may.[13]

The triumphalist commentators of high British imperialism would later emphasize the contrasts between mid-nineteenth-century Britain and China: the one modern and progressive, the other antiquated and regressive; the one Christian, the other heathen; the one open, the other isolationist. In reality, both country's leaders – if they had been able to observe each other's situations – would have found much common ground.

The missive containing the news from China had settled first on the desk of Lord Auckland on 25 May 1839, as he sheltered from the Calcutta heat at the foothills of the Himalayas. 'Yesterday', he wrote to John Cam Hobhouse, President of the Board of Control in London, 'was Her Majesty's birthday, and all that are white in Simla dined with me in our most beautiful valley . . . there were cheers for the Queen, and never was loyalty better displayed that it has been in the Himalayas.' But, he continued, as if irked by the tactlessness of the unfortunate Indian *dak* (postal) runner who had toiled at speed through the worst of the summer heat, 'as I was about to finish my letter, the news from China came in, and here is a new source of trouble of anxiety'.[14] He decided to stay put; Calcutta was so unreasonably warm at this time of year – in any case, he needed to be close at hand for news from Afghanistan. 'The decision must be with you in England', he informed Hobhouse a week or two later, sitting himself comfortably on the fence.[15] 'As regards India,' he went on nonchalantly, 'we must for the present look upon the opium revenue as annihilated . . . but as you know, I have always great confidence in the growing resources of India and I would still look cheeringly at our financial prospects.' Not so 'upon the prospects of a war with China, for I see its embarrassments, and I do not see its end'. Hobhouse, after he received Auckland's letter in mid-September, was inclined to agree: 'Doubtless, you must give up the cultivation of the poppy, and substitute an unprofitable export duty for your present monopoly.'[16] Let the two million go, then – time for Britain to cleanse itself of the murk of opium money.

Neither would Palmerston commit himself on the China question. When William Jardine steamed into London in September, a conversation with the Foreign Secretary was high on his list of priorities. He soon found the political establishment – in contrast, perhaps, with the pliability of Canton society – surprisingly unyielding. 'We have heard nothing from H. M. ministers reporting their intention,' he replied to Matheson, on hearing the news of his partner's expulsion from Canton, 'nor have I seen Lord Palmerston . . . In his conversation with Mr Smith [Jardine-Matheson's London agent, and an MP] he led him to believe that as far as his own sentiments went, he was convinced some measures ought to be taken of the gross insult and robbery; but would not commit himself further.' The snubbed Jardine buried himself in merchant committee meetings, in petitions, in meeting Liverpool and Manchester deputations – but was still unable to suppress his irritation. The events of the Canton spring, he complained, are 'very little understood here, and many people are for doing nothing; they, very foolishly, mix up the insult and violence with the illicit trade, and are for remaining quiet, pocketing the insult, and refusing to pay for the opium.' Finally, on 27 September, an appointment with Palmerston was won. To try Jardine's patience a little more, the Pumicestone (a nickname bequeathed to the foreign secretary by diplomats he had rubbed up the wrong way) kept him waiting for two hours, before extracting as much practical information as possible (about the lie of the Chinese coast, the likely size of a force needed to hold key ports) in exchange for no promises. 'No direct avowal [was] made of a determination to coerce', a disappointed Jardine reported back to Matheson afterwards. 'The conference ended in his Lordship retaining the charts and saying they were to hold a Cabinet counsel Monday next . . . All this is unsatisfactory enough but we must await silently.'[17]

On 30 September, eight members of the government (including Palmerston) sat down to an extended Cabinet crisis meeting in Windsor Castle. China, however, was so far from the top of the agenda that the assembled worthies did not get near it that day. Instead, discussion was devoted to the attempt by the ruler of Egypt, Mehemet Ali, to take over Syria. 'The Turkish question', Palmerston informed his prime minister, 'is one of more extensive Interest and Importance to England than any other'.[18] The following day, the ministers at last gathered once more to think about what to do with China. Unfortunately, the best of the group's energies seem to have been used up the previous day; at one point in the conversation, Hobhouse grew so impatient that he picked up his hat, in readiness to go. The weariness of the assembled company seems to have pared the debate down to its logistics. With barely a sideways glance at the question of the morality of war, exhausted ministers concentrated on two key questions: Can it be done? And who will pay?

Buoyed by his meeting with Jardine, Palmerston was all for talking up the ease of the expedition: 'a small squadron of one line of battle ship, two frigates and some small armed vessels with two or three steamers might blockade the whole coast of China from the river of Pekin down to the Canton coast.' As Melbourne and Hobhouse doubted whether it would indeed be so straightforward, the debate moved on to the issue of who was going to pay for the confiscated opium. Those present really didn't mind – as long as it wasn't the government: the Chancellor, Francis Baring, was keen to clarify that *he* didn't have the money. Suppose the Chinese were to foot the bill? Palmerston suggested. This met with applause from the young, excitable Thomas Macaulay, attending his first Cabinet meeting. (His recent four-year stint in India spoke loudly of his special feeling for Asian sensibilities: between 1834 and 1838, he had instituted an anglophone colonial education system to create 'a class of persons, Indian in blood and colour, but English in taste, in opinion, in morals and in intellect.' For, after all, 'a single shelf of a good European library is worth the whole native literature of India and Arabia.'[19]) From here, the conversation veered away from the tricky question of extorting drug money at gunpoint, and towards the simpler, more stirring issue of patriotism: the main thing, believed Hobhouse, was 'obtaining redress for the outrage on Elliot, which we all agree was indispensable for the national honour'.[20] Treacherous natives, Macaulay felt, needed a firm stance – and perhaps he now wore his Cabinet colleagues down with an early rehearsal of the pro-war speech he would deliver in Parliament the following April.

> The moment at which [Elliot] landed he was surrounded by his countrymen in an agony of despair at their situation, but the first step which he took was to order the flag of Great Britain to be taken from the boat and to be planted in the balcony . . . It was natural that they should look with confidence on the victorious flag which was hoisted over them, which reminded them that they belonged to a country unaccustomed to defeat, to submission, or to shame . . . that made the Bey of Algiers humble himself to her insulted consul; that revenged the horrors of the black hole on the fields of Plessey; that had not degenerated since her great Protector vowed that he would make the name of Englishman as respected as ever had been the name of Roman citizen.[21]

'If he was always so powerful in talking, no business would be done', whispered one member of his captive Windsor audience.[22] 'I thought he spoke too much', agreed Hobhouse, in his diary. As much as anything, there seems to have been a sense that it was time for this beleaguered government to take a stance on something – anything. Spineless! the opposition had howled repeatedly as Palmerston did little to protect British interests and honour in either Mexico or Argentina in late 1838 – even after Britons had been fired upon by French men-of-war. Perhaps the Cabinet fancied its chances best against China (where, unlike in Syria, Afghanistan, Mexico or Argentina, there was no chance of confronting the French or Russians). 'The charges made against us of idleness', Hobhouse remarked to Macaulay, once the decision to send a squadron had been taken, 'could hardly be sustained . . . we had resolved upon . . . a war with the master of one-third of the human race.'[23] A habitual critic of Palmerston's ideas, Lord Holland, was unable to engage sufficiently with the subject of China to be present, his only opinion on the matter being that the cousin of his dining companion Gilbert Elliot-Murray-Kynymound, Lord Minto and First Lord of the Admiralty (Charles Elliot) needed a hand.[24]

But the Cabinet was still far from enthusiastic. Unconvinced that a small force would really be sufficient, the prime minister was all for

deferring to the indecisive Lord Auckland in India, thereby procrastinating for another six months. The business of fighting a war for
opium, worried the Chancellor, was going to be a 'bother in the H of
C'. The East India Company, far from enjoying the prospect of 'China
opened', refused to offer a 'positive opinion' of the decision (though
they cheered up when told that the government, and not the
Honourable Company, would be footing the bill).[25] Palmerston,
meanwhile, had no intention of pandering to Britain's opium
interests. Not a penny of the £2 million needed to cover the costs
of the destroyed opium would be advanced by H.M. Government –
it would all come, in good time, from the Chinese. When Jardine
and his representatives persisted in trying to extract at least a faint
commitment for compensation out of the government, their communications were tersely inscribed by FO clerks: 'returned by Lord P.
without observation'.[26]

In early November, Palmerston instructed Auckland to prepare
forces for China – though not with excessive haste. For war – even for
something as precious as the national honour – must not disrupt the
trading season. Hostilities, it was hoped, would be tucked neatly into
the window offered by the close of trading in March, and its reopening
in September 1840. Finally, then, the Governor-General prepared to
return to Calcutta and concentrate on things Chinese.

Palmerston's plan suffered from one inconvenient oversight: a failure
to consult Parliament on the issue. To the intense annoyance of his
opponents, he kept Elliot's dispatches locked up in the FO for as long
as he possibly could. But however hard he worked to keep the full
picture out of the public domain, there was no preventing information
– from merchant and missionary witnesses, from the Canton and
Indian English-language press – seeping out into the nation's newspapers. 'We have employed W. P. Freshfield, the solicitor, to look
into the nature of our claims [against] H. M. government and to
engage the Times newpaper [sic] to write in favour of them', wrote
William Jardine to Matheson in late October 1839, 'but I have not
heard what he has done.'[27] Not very much, one might conclude from
glancing through the paper's coverage of the China question as the

winter of 1839 turned into the spring of 1840. True, it gave space to a sprinkling of polite but firm requests from representatives of the opium lobby that the British government honour Charles Elliot's promise of compensation, backed by subtle reminders of the British government's own complicity. 'Your petitioners', wheedled one such example of the genre, 'have been deprived of property to a very large extent . . . they have the fullest confidence in the well known justice of the British government . . . that they will duly indemnify them.' So much confidence, in fact, that almost in the next breath they found it necessary to remind all concerned that 'the trade in opium has been encouraged and promoted by the Indian Government under the express sanction and authority lately of the British Government and Parliament, and with the full knowledge . . . that the trade in it was confined to China, and was contraband and illegal . . . it has proved a source of immense profit to the Indian Government, netting to them a revenue, during the last twenty years, of from half a million sterling annually, to latterly two millions sterling per annum.'[28] 'It is certain', one private correspondent huffed and puffed at the end of November, 'that our trade will never be on a proper footing until we teach these people to respect us, and the present seems a fitting opportunity.'[29]

More frequently, though, the paper (a pro-Tory, and therefore anti-Whig, organ) deplored the situation. 'Seldom', thundered *The Times* of 13 August 1839, as the earliest reports of trouble in Canton arrived in England, 'have we had to record events in which our trading interests, and our honour as a great and civilised country, have been brought so deeply into question as in this instance.' Over the following months, rather than publicize James Matheson's view that 'during 21 years that I have passed almost entirely in China, I can conscientiously declare that I have never seen a native in the least bestialised by opium smoking', *The Times* chose to serialize the Reverend Algernon Thelwall's *The Iniquities of the Opium Trade with China*, a 178-page diatribe against a business that 'brought the greatest dishonour on the British flag'.[30] No sympathy was expressed for either the actions of Charles Elliot (who, one editorial diagnosed, 'seems to have fed on a diet of brimstone'), or the imprisoned merchant community (who suffered no privation beyond obtaining 'a closer acquaintance with certain culinary processes than they could formerly claim').[31] 'Our sin', the 23 October issue observed, 'in growing and encouraging the trade in opium is, indeed, one of the darkest that ever invoked the wrath of the Most High God upon a people.'[32] 'England,' the *Leeds Mercury* concurred, 'is degraded not only in the eyes of the Chinese, but of the civilized world, and from this intolerable situation there is no honourable mode of escape.'[33]

On Christmas Day 1839, *The Times* could barely contain itself while discussing a pro-war pamphlet (whose recommendations on the China question almost precisely anticipated the stipulations of the 1842 Treaty of Nanjing). 'Most of our readers who have turned their attention to the disputes now pending with China must have been surprised and amused at many of the projects for settling these disputes which have from time to time been started ... We think, however, that the plan which we are about to lay before the public will at once be found the most astonishing and entertaining of the whole.' The editorialist then set out the pamphlet's vision: compensation for the opium and for the insult of the blockade; a commercial treaty; the cession of Lantao (the island just west of Hong Kong, on which the territory's airport now rests). 'It is meant as a joke, of course – a burlesque'.[34]

As Palmerston's secret instructions for war made their way towards India, things continued to get worse for the government. Between 3 and 4 November 1839, a 7,000-strong army of Welsh miners and labourers (carrying pikes, pistols, guns and heavy bludgeons, and led by a local magistrate) attacked a town prison. The twenty-five-minute battle with the authorities left twenty dead, and another fifty wounded. Five days later, the prime minister's attempt to give a toast at the Lord Mayor's annual feast was lost in a 'volley of hisses, hootings and groaning, never before dealt out to any political character, even the most reckless.' After repeated failures to quiet their audience, Melbourne and Palmerston returned to their seats 'to the tune of the Rogues' March'.[35]

Through this trouble, the government responded to questions about China – were they really going to fight? – with impressive coolness. On 24 January, the opposition requested that the Foreign Office produce the Blue Book of Elliot's *Correspondence Relating to*

China, and would repeat their demand every few days through February and early March. Every few days, Palmerston would fend them off with 'just a few more days' or 'early next week'. On 6 February, in the House of Lords, a Tory peer stood up and asked the prime minister if he had anything to say about China; not a thing, he airily replied. Later in that session, a disquisition on the state of the navy alluded directly to the four-ship squadron 'now said to be being fitted out for active service in China.'[36]

On 11 March, the papers from Paris picked up on a story from a Brittany broadsheet, *L'Armoricain*, that a French frigate was on its way to the Chinese seas to observe the prospective British expedition. The next day, the news erupted from the good ship *Volcano* that mild Lord Auckland had 'DECLARED WAR AGAINST CHINA', with 40,000 tons of shipping and 16,000 men.[37] *The Times* immediately foresaw a scramble by Britain's many enemies (Russia, Persia, France, the United States, Afghanistan, Burma, Nepal) to profit from Britannia's inevitable troubles in the China war. 'There is not an enemy to England on earth who will not seize the moment when she seems to be embroiled inextricably with any one foe, to wring from her some injurious or humiliating concession . . . the victory most essential to [Britain] is an *early* triumph over her internal enemy' – namely, Melbourne and his feckless government.[38] That same day, the future prime minister, Robert Peel, asked Palmerston when he might be kind enough to 'bring down any message to Parliament announcing the intention of her Majesty to resort to "hostilities"' in China. Through repeated questions, Palmerston insisted that 'the proposed operations' were 'communications', not hostilities. 'We suppose', concluded *The Times*, 'if the town of Canton were blown to atoms, the noble lord would call it an explanatory declaration.'[39]

As Palmerston (variously described as 'shifty', 'shuffling', 'slippery', 'brazen', 'offensive', 'cheating', 'the reverse of great') continued to wriggle out of questions through March and the start of April, the newspapers intensified their attacks. 'The reckless negligence and gross incapacity of the Queen's Ministers in their management of the relations of this country with foreign Powers have darkened the face of the whole world, as regards the British empire . . . It is the case of a lawless and accursed traffick, to be bolstered up by a flagitious and murderous war . . . [hurl] these execrable Ministers . . . from their places.'[40] The *Charter* (the mouthpiece of the Chartists) accused 'Mr. Opium Elliot' of behaving 'like [a thief and bully] gloating over the prospects of . . . bloodshed, famine . . . and multiform distress and misery.'[41]

On 7 April 1840, the Tories brought a vote of no-confidence (already the second of the year) against the government's handling of the China question in the House of Commons. The 115,922-word debate (not counting the heckles and cheers) meandered across three spring nights. The Tory side made many lengthy points about Palmerston's diplomatic errors: notably, his failure to give proper instructions or useful powers to Charles Elliot, or to control the illegal opium trade. Macaulay fought back with his 'unaccustomed to defeat, to submission or to shame' speech. It took the honourable members a whole day to move on to the question of moral culpability, but the young William Gladstone attacked 'this infamous and atrocious traffic' as soon as his chance arose:

> a war more unjust in its origin, a war more calculated in its progress to cover this country with permanent disgrace, I do not know, and I have not read of . . . under the auspices of the noble Lord, [our] flag is hoisted to protect an infamous contraband traffic, and if it were never to be hoisted except as it is now hoisted on the coast of China, we should recoil from its sight with horror, and should never again feel our hearts thrill, as they now thrill with emotion, when it floats proudly and magnificently on the breeze.

But eventually the opposition were perhaps brought low by verbal fatigue. Palmerston's speech on the final day, the famously crotchety Earl Grey allowed, was 'much to my surprise . . . most admirable.' The oratorical virtues on 9 April that served him best were probably relative brevity – his speech weighed in at just over 8,000 words, little more than half the length of the Tory opener – and pragmatism. How could he have given Elliot more powers, he asked the House, without opening this remote posting up to abuses? No, the key task was to protect 'the honour of the British flag and the dignity of the British Crown' and to secure the long-term prospects of trade with China. 'If the same indignities', he summarized, 'which had been heaped upon British subjects in China, from the time of Lord Napier's expedition down to the present period, were to be persevered in, unresisted and unredressed, it would be impossible to suppose that ... any British merchant could, with any regard to his safety or his self-respect, continue his commercial operations in these parts.' Just as it had done six months earlier in Windsor, a mix of exhaustion, crude economics and patriotic vanity somehow saw the Whigs through one of their most serious crises.

The mood of the chamber at the end of the three days' debate is probably best captured by the final sentence of the final speech – an attempted response by the Tory James Graham to Palmerston.

> If the House would permit him, he should like to follow the noble Lord through the various parts of his speech. The hon. Baronet was interrupted by loud cries of 'Divide, divide' ... The right hon. Baronet again attempted to address the House, but his voice was completely drowned in the shouts of 'Divide, divide, divide,' and he at length gave way, and resumed his seat.
> Ayes 262; Noes 271: Majority 9.[42]

Twelve more votes had leached away from the Whigs' twenty-one majority of two months previously. But it was enough to keep Lord Auckland's gunboats on their original course.

In the interests of historical completeness, we should probably record also the explanation for the final British decision offered in a couple of near-contemporary Chinese accounts. While Parliament and the Queen apparently both wanted to set off a 'border disturbance ... the merchants were against it, as it would increase taxes – so for several days Parliament was undecided ... In the end, an order was given to decide the matter by drawing lots at the shrine of the God of the Earth – three lots were in favour of war, and so they determined to call in the soldiers.'[43]

Chapter Seven

SWEET-TALK AND SEA-SLUG

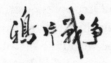

On 4 July 1840, mandarins strolling about the cliffs of the boat-shaped island of Zhoushan saw a fleet of foreign vessels approach. Though they were puzzled at first, the island's sub-prefect remembered, 'the explanation soon occurred to them and they guffawed with joy. Obviously, the ships had assembled here because of the cessation of trade at Canton. "Dinghai [the island's main town] will become a great trading centre," they said, "and we shall all make more and more money out of them day by day." '[1]

Zhoushan lay off the empire's most prosperous, south-eastern coastline: a few hundred miles east of the wealthy cities of Suzhou and Hangzhou. Since the Macartney embassy had visited the island in 1793, England's travelling painters had sketched Zhoushan as a land of orientalist fantasy – steep limestone cliffs, mist-shawled green vales, ornamental temples embellished with curlicued dragons, all dotted with decorous, parasol-clutching mandarins. The source of its wealth in the mid-nineteenth century was an open secret: illicit foreign trade – in all likelihood, opium. 'Before the hostilities,' Zhoushan's sub-prefect frankly confided in a court report, 'whenever a foreign ship arrived everyone from the Commandant, the Prefect and sub-Prefect down to chair-carriers and office lackeys all took bribes from the foreigners . . . the greater the number of ships, the greater the amount taken in bribes . . . their only fear was that numbers should decline.'[2]

But this was no merchant fleet: it was the force dispatched by Palmerston to punish 'the outrages which have been committed

by the Chinese upon British subjects, and upon the Queen's officer'
and to bring Britain's relations with the Qing empire onto 'a definite and secure footing'.[3] The campaign strategy was to bypass Canton
and make instead for the empire's centre of food distribution on the
south-east coast: the point at which the capital's grain supply set off
from Nanjing, via the Grand Canal, up to Beijing. Back in September
1839, the foreign secretary had listened closely to Jardine's advice on
how to subdue the Qing. Occupy Zhoushan and blockade the eastern
seaboard, the opium baron had recommended, then press on to the
capital to make Britain's demands.

There was no firing on 4 July. The British fleet (consisting of
twenty-two warships and twenty-seven transports, carrying 3,600
Scottish, Irish and Indian infantry) came in to a harbour where a
dozen brightly painted war junks, each with a crew of around fifty,
were already anchored.[4] A Captain Fletcher and Lord Jocelyn – Elliot's
military secretary – were dispatched onto the Qing commander's
vessel (identifiable by the three tigers' heads painted onto its stern)
to state English terms: the island should surrender within six hours,
or face the consequences. The admiral's crew complained of the
unfairness of being made to suffer for a quarrel manufactured by the
Cantonese. 'Those are the people you should make war on, and not
upon us who never injured you; we see your strength, and know that
opposition will be madness, but we must perform our duty if we fall
in so doing.'[5]

It was a sleepless night for the locals. As the British forces gazed
out from their ships over the island, its slopes bobbed with lanterns
slung over carrying poles – lighting the work of building and arming
makeshift embankments. By eight the next morning, all was as ready
as it was ever going to be and fifteen British ships lined up opposite
a file of Qing war junks. The British held their fire until 2.30, hoping
the Chinese would reconsider the offer of unconditional surrender –
but then, Jocelyn recalled, the broadsides began: 'the crashing of
timber, falling houses, and groans of men resounded from the shore
. . . When the smoke cleared away a mass of ruin presented itself to
the eye . . . crowds were visible in the distance flying in all directions.'[6] The British had fired for nine whole minutes.

When the British disembarked onto the empty shoreline, they
were greeted only by 'a few dead bodies, bows and arrows, broken

spears and guns'.[7] (The admiral's leg had been carried off by a round shot; he died a few days later, in the nearby port city of Ningbo.) Within two hours a Madras artillery regiment had trained four guns on Dinghai; by ten o'clock that evening, its inhabitants had run away; the Governor had drowned himself in a small pool. The following morning, the British flag fluttered over the city walls. The signs of flight (nearly a million people had deserted the island) were all over the city: half-smoked pipes, cups of untasted tea, abandoned pots of make-up.[8] In time, though, the island would quietly take its revenge. As they sweated out their makeshift occupation, British troops would be struck down in their thousands by malaria and dysentery. Zhou-shan would become a great British graveyard: 5,329 soldiers were admitted to the military hospital, resulting in 448 deaths.[9]

Nine minutes. This grotesque discrepancy in military strength between the British and the Qing would be replayed again and again through the two years of the war. Although it would later become a source of complacency to the British, at the time it provoked surprise as well as self-satisfaction. Back in the autumn of 1839, even Palmerston had initially doubted that the Qing forces would be as easily defeated as Jardine and others predicted. Sir John Barrow, second secretary at the Admiralty, veteran of the failed 1793 embassy to China, and certainly no sinophile, thought Jardine's contempt for Qing capacities 'extraordinary'.[10] Qing China was after all no tribal power but one of the world's great conquest empires.

How, exactly, could its armies have atrophied so drastically by 1840? The problems with the Qing military can be broken down into three main categories: materiel and defences; organization; and indi-vidual quality of troops.[11]

In all areas of equipment – weaponry, forts and most critically ships – the Qing equipment lagged behind that of the British. The most fundamental distinction between Qing and British armaments was that by 1840, the British had long moved into the era of firepower, while parts of the Qing army hung on to the bows, swords, spears and rattan shields that had served them well through the expansion of the seventeenth and eighteenth centuries.[12] In 1840, those Qing soldiers lucky enough to be issued a firearm found themselves still saddled with one of the musket's earliest incarnations, the matchlock: a muzzle-loading weapon developed in the mid-fifteenth century, with a chamber (the 'serpentine') near the flashpan into which a slow, smouldering match was dropped. Its main drawbacks were obvious: it was very hard to keep the match alight over extended periods of fighting, the match easily betrayed a soldier's location and the smoke generated by the musket obscured the target after a couple of shots. British regiments, by contrast, were supplied with more advanced models: either the flintlock (in which the smouldering match of the matchlock was replaced by a hammer-held flint) or, better still, the breech-loading percussion-lock.

Qing cannon also suffered from basic deficiencies, often lacking, for example, sighting devices and installations that enabled them to swivel in pursuit of a mobile enemy. Elderly cannon were rarely retired in a timely fashion, but rather left out – over centuries, perhaps – in all weathers to rust from neglect. (In 1836, a scornful Western observer of the guns at Canton called them 'old and honey-combed'.[13]) The quality of gunpowder was low, too, with industrial standards lagging some way behind those of nineteenth-century Britain. 'They opened their wretched wall-pieces,' sniffed Jocelyn of the short battle for Dinghai, 'which, from their construction, can neither traverse nor be depressed, and which, being charged with a bad description of powder, did no damage to the force.'[14]

Perhaps the Qing's greatest weakness was its warships. When, in early 1841, the hostilities shifted south, to Canton, Qing ships and forts would be crushed by the world's very first all-iron war steamer: the *Nemesis*. But the Qing navy could not compete with Britain's older, copper-plate-hulled wooden warships either, whose design had been perfected over two centuries' crisscrossing the globe on merchant voyages and in naval wars with France, Spain and Holland. Due to the situations in which they often found themselves – ranging far from any land-based back-up – such ships had to be self-contained fighting units, carrying as many as 120 guns. Qing war junks, by contrast, had a more cautious role to play. They were patrol vessels, carrying around ten guns, with no independent capacity for war-making. They were merely auxiliaries to the coast's primary defences – the granite forts that guarded the river that led up to Canton. These ships were, the same scornful observer of 1836 declared, 'large, unwieldy looking masses of timber . . . painted red and black, with large goggle eyes in the bows . . . useless, save in the smoothest water . . . To convey to the mind of a stranger the ridiculous excess of the inutility of the naval establishment of China would . . . be impossible.'[15] The Qing's inability to mount a naval attack robbed them of any kind of offensive advantage against the British; all they could do was man their forts and wait, nervously, for the enemy to pick its own time and place.

What of the forts themselves? A popular Chinese saying likened the bases guarding the riverways up to Canton to 'locks of gold and passes of steel. It's hard to pass through them – harder still to get out again'. These stone forts were among the largest in the empire, protected by walls some 230 yards wide and 5 yards high, and studded with up to sixty cannon. But their flaws were obvious. First, they were roofless – any well-directed shell could easily wreak havoc. And strategically, the forts were designed to cope only with attacks from the sea (preferably from pirates with no ambitions for territorial conquest and inferior firing power); little provision had been made for assaults from the land. As for their general state of repair near Canton, our observer from 1836 pronounced it 'the very worst imaginable'.[16]

But why did the Qing fail to capitalize on their numerical superiority over the British? Theoretically, the dynasty commanded the largest standing army (800,000-strong) in the world at the time – 114 times more numerous than the 7,000-strong British force dispatched to China. In reality, however, most of these 800,000 soldiers were scattered through the empire, far too busy with domestic peace-keeping duties (suppressing bandits or rebels; carrying out disaster relief; guarding prisons; policing smugglers) to be spared for the quarrel with the British. In August 1840, when the British fleet glided up to Tianjin, to hand Palmerston's official letter of complaint to the emperor, the imperial representative reported that a mere 600 of the 2,400 soldiers theoretically on the rolls could be mustered for immediate service. Almost every province of the empire had to contribute reinforcements to boost local forces: in the course of the war, some 51,000 soldiers found themselves in transit around the country, headed for the southern or eastern coasts. But they moved too slowly to be useful: troops from a neighbouring province took thirty to forty days to reach the front line (about the same amount of time it took the British to fetch reinforcements from India); those further away took ninety or more. In June 1840, the British fleet took only thirty-five days to sail up and capture Dinghai; the following year, the Qing took five months to rally a counter-offensive against the island – five months in which the British rested and reorganized, while reinforcements straggled in from distant corners of the empire. (By the time the last batches arrived, the Treaty of Nanjing was already being toasted in cherry brandy.)

Military discipline was another problem for the Qing. British accounts of Opium War engagements were scattered with admissions that forts were adequately planned, placed and supplied, and would have cost the invaders many lives to capture – if only the Qing troops had fought, and not fled. The conquest of the empire had been achieved by creating a hereditary military: an elite minority of Manchu, Mongolian and Chinese Bannermen at the top, with the professional Chinese Green Standard Army (about three times the size) taking on basic garrison duties through the country. For the Bannermen, the state provided a stipend of rice, cash and land, in return for army service. But by the middle decades of the eighteenth century, the Banners were suffering from price rises just like everyone else in the empire – the level of stipends had been set in the early years of the conquest, long before the inflation of the Qianlong period set in. When handouts failed to keep up with inflation, or even shrank, soldiers protested, went on strike, ran away or took civilian jobs. As the nineteenth century approached, the system was rotten with corruption: superiors squeezed inferiors in exchange for the promise of promotion, while families concealed deaths (and invented births) to maintain stipends.

Equipment budgets and military esprit de corps were the principal casualties of the fiscal deficit. Towards the end of the eighteenth century, musketry and artillery practice were phased out across many garrisons, because ammunition was too dear. One of the east-coast garrisons in 1795 requested permission from the Board of War to cancel the spring artillery practice, for fear that the noise would disturb the well-being of profitable silk worms; so much grazing land had been sold or rented out that the number of horses dwindled to almost nothing. In the Canton garrison, half-naked Manchus on drill practice were observed dragging rusty swords and elderly bows about.[17] 'The life of the Bannermen,' recalled the twentieth-century novelist Lao She (son of a Manchu soldier killed in the Allied Powers' 1900 war on the Boxer Rebellion),

> apart from consuming the grain and spending the silver supplied by the Chinese, was completely immersed, day to day, in the life of the arts ... everybody knew how to sing arias from the classical opera, play the one-stringed accompaniment, perform drum-songs, and chant the popular tunes of the day. They raised fish, birds, dogs, plants and flowers, and held cricket fights ... No longer capable of defending the empire's frontiers ... they became obsessed with their pets ... My father never fought or argued with anyone in his life: he was the gentlest soul you ever met.[18]

Repeatedly during the war, Qing armies of thousands would be routed by a few hundred, or even a few dozen well-disciplined British troops with functioning artillery and battle-plans.[19]

During the Opium War, Qing politicians of the pro- and anti-war faction could agree on only one thing: that their army was hopeless. Travelling east from Canton to Zhejiang in 1841, Lin Zexu bluntly analysed the reasons for the army's lack of interest in fighting the British. 'The most coveted positions in the Guangdong garrisons were in the naval fleet, where one per cent of salaries was drawn from the grain and silver stipend, and the rest from opium-smugglers' bribes. Once we banned opium, ninety-nine per cent of the navy's income went up in smoke. How could we expect them to resist the English rebels?'[20] 'Our soldiers cheat everyone', echoed Qiying, the emperor's chief negotiator at the close of the war. 'They refuse to pay full prices, gather in brothels and gambling dens, corrupt the sons of good families and handle stolen goods.'[21]

Beyond these technical military difficulties, though, lay a more severe flaw in the Qing war effort: a lack of interest in admitting that any kind of serious incident – let alone a war – with the British was happening at all.

*

At pains to show themselves to be civilized, the British tried hard to inform their adversaries of their demands before they pulverized them in battle. Through July, the fleet made several unsuccessful attempts to deliver Lord Palmerston's letter to the Chinese emperor at various points along the eastern coast. The first took place on 2 July, two days before the fleet reduced Zhoushan's defences to rubble, when one of the fleet's translators (a clerk in the pay of Jardine-Matheson), Robert Thom, was ordered to make for the island of Xiamen and find someone in authority to receive the document. Greeted successively by threatening noises, furious howls of 'No!', an arrow that he dodged by hurling himself to the deck, bullets and cannonfire, he eventually gave up on the idea.[22] (As usual, English and Chinese accounts of the encounter diverged. Jocelyn reported that the Chinese were given, in return for their welcome, a 'severe chastisement' (two and a half hours of broadsides); the local governor-general Deng Tingzhen claimed that, under his leadership, a large British warship was sunk.[23] As the war developed, the practice of fictionalizing battle reports – begun with Lin Zexu's version of the skirmish of November 1839 – would introduce serious cracks into the Qing chain of command. By 1841, the emperor had lost, with a good deal of justification, all trust in provincial dispatches, requesting independent verifications from a veteran official that he, in turn, threatened to check 'in other places'.[24])

Eight days later, with business at Dinghai concluded, Charles Elliot, accompanied by the expedition's admiral, his cousin George, tried the same thing at the port of Zhenhai, opposite Zhoushan on the mainland. The morning after accepting the letter, the local official returned it, reporting that he did not dare forward it to Beijing.[25] Charles Elliot now opted for direct communication with the Qing government and headed for Tianjin, a couple of hours south of the capital.

Neither of the first military engagements left the Qing government any better informed about what was going on. Deng Tingzhen, who had had ample experience of the British in Canton as Lin's second-in-command through the collisions of 1839, remained insistent that these were crafty but unthreatening opium vessels, until he heard, on 18 July, that these 'smugglers' had occupied Zhoushan.[26] And even if Daoguang's representatives in Canton – where the British fleet had first appeared – had instantly realized what was going on, the slowness of the imperial mail would have taken the immediacy out of their reports. It took thirty to thirty-five days for communications to travel from Canton to Beijing; a more urgent, express service promised a delivery time of sixteen to twenty days.[27] On the one hand, officials' memorials to the centre were saturated in self-abasing rhetoric: 'I' was translated into 'Your slave'; civil servants did not 'report', but rather 'submitted, respectfully kneeling'. On the other, distance and pressure of work enabled far-flung, overworked officials to stall or even actively mislead their overworked sovereign.

In the middle of July, Daoguang received a reassuring report from Lin Zexu in Canton, dispatched in June – a few days after the British fleet of some twenty warships had sailed into Macao. Lin's letter informed him that although some new ships had arrived, they were probably just opium ships: 'there is really nothing they can do'.[28] With a few cheering reports of how secret operatives had burnt thirty-six vessels and killed countless English (uncorroborated in British accounts), Lin signed off. 'I couldn't be more delighted', the emperor noted in vermilion.[29]

Three days later, on 20 July, a surprising, and less encouraging piece of news came in from the east coast: 3–4,000 English had taken Zhoushan. The furious emperor now sacked the officials supposedly in charge of the island, and replaced them with Yu Buyun (a veteran of the Central Asian jihad of the 1820s, whose main contribution to the war effort would be to run, fast, from the British in October 1841). Two days later Daoguang ordered the coastal provinces to strengthen their defences against these 'profit-seeking opium-smugglers'.[30] But by 26 July, after ordering several thousand reinforcements to the coast, he was starting to feel more relaxed: 'What does it matter that these rebellious foreigners have caused trouble in [Zhoushan]? Our troops have gathered to exterminate them – their annihilation is imminent.'[31] On 3 August, Daoguang received a memorial of 3 July from Lin Zexu in Canton (who had seemingly not thought it urgent enough to merit the expense of express delivery) telling him that more English ships had arrived; and that he had heard the fleet might be headed north, to Zhoushan then Tianjin. The emperor now gave Qishan, the governor-general of the province that included Beijing and Tianjin, basic instructions: 'If the English get to Tianjin and are reverently obedient in behaviour and speech, tell them that trade, according to imperial regulations, takes place only at Canton' – neither commerce nor communications was permitted in the north. If, by contrast, they seemed unruly, Qishan should exterminate them in battle.[32] Daoguang still assumed that, even though this particular flavour of foreigners had more firepower than average opium-smugglers, their ambitions were mercantile, and that promises of trade would keep them quiet.

Over the next few days, as the British fleet sailed towards the soupy waters of the Beihe River (leading westwards from the north-east coast, towards Tianjin and the capital), perplexing reports continued to drift towards Beijing: Deng Tingzhen's account of the encounter at Xiamen was followed by a report of the British attempt at Zhenhai to deliver a letter from some bogus-sounding English 'minister'. (Meantime, Lin was still dashing off confident reports from Canton. 'These foreign ships', he wrote in late July, 'only have confidence when they are in open waters on the high seas, where they can manoeuvre at will. Once inside a river-mouth, they are like fish in a cauldron; they can at once be captured and destroyed.'[33]) By 9 August, Daoguang was so confused about what these mysterious foreigners wanted that he was prepared to correspond directly with them. 'If they want to hand over a letter,' he told Qishan down at Tianjin, 'just send it on to me, whether it's in Chinese or in a foreign language.'[34]

11 August 1840 dawned quietly over the arid flats of Tanggu, the port nearest to Tianjin. So quietly, in fact, that as Charles Elliot and his fleet approached, he may have wondered if he had taken a wrong turning. Finally, though, some human activity was detected: an official boat about a mile ahead. As Elliot approached and moored, some satin-booted bureaucrats squelched through the yellow mud (to ensure the British came no further), took possession of Palmerston's letter and promised to hand it up the imperial hierarchy to Qishan, the province's governor-general, who would decide whether or not to pass it on to the emperor.

Qishan had responded to Daoguang's order to exterminate the

British in three ways: by deputing a military subordinate to strengthen defences to the north of Tianjin; by personally inspecting the Tianjin garrison and ordering local officials to check that their cannon were working; and by arming local militia. His orders seem to have been so discreetly dispatched that they did not reach the garrisons in question until the British sailed up. 'On each side of the entrance to the river,' noted one lieutenant, 'there was an old and dilapidated fort, fast falling to decay . . . Numerous workmen were seen busy repairing these forts and throwing up entrenchments in all directions'.[35] When they arrived, the British had the strong sense they were unexpected guests.

But guests they were – and *not*, Qishan and his establishment were at pains to imply, intruders, invaders or conquerors. On 13 August, as Qishan pondered whether or not to pass Palmerston's letter on, he hospitably dispatched to them 'a liberal supply of bullocks, sheep and poultry' – of which the crews, long starved of fresh food, could not help being glad.[36] On 15 August, he had another bulletin for them, delivered by a captain of the imperial guards: he would be sending the letter on to the court. But a reply would take time – ten days. Amuse yourselves until the 25th, he advised.[37]

In the Chinese narrative of the Opium War, you might expect the line between heroes and villains to be a clear one: honourably resisting servants of the Chinese empire on the one hand, wicked British on the other. The curious thing, though, is how much of the venom in the Chinese version of these events has been reserved for characters on their own side: and in particular, for the perceived corruption, indecision and incompetence of the Qing court. For much of the past century and a half, the Chinese have been more inclined to blame their then-rulers than the British for what went wrong. In this they have been helped, of course, by the fact that the Qing were a foreign dynasty. And few representatives of the government have been demonized quite as thoroughly as Qishan. Like the leaders of the British war effort, he is accused of harbouring a long-range conspiracy against China: of scheming to undermine Lin Zexu's anti-opium campaign; of selling the country out to British bribes; of dismantling defences and disbanding reinforcements to sabotage resistance. Qishan's crime, in China's historical imagination, is many times more heinous than that of any of the British, for he betrayed his own country. After his arrest in spring 1841, while Canton's defences fell to Britain's gunboats, he would be condemned as a 'treacherous minister'. In Maoist school textbooks, Qishan was not just Qishan: he was 'Shameless Capitulationist-Robber Qishan'.[38]

An improbable traitor, he was born a Manchu marquis in 1790: the seventh-generation descendant of Enggeder, one of Nurhaci's own trusted lieutenants (who in turn claimed to be descended from Genghis Khan). After winning in 1808 a coveted appointment to the Board of Punishments 'in recognition of his ancestors' services', Qishan spent the next thirty-odd years moving from one choice assignment to another. He achieved his first governorship in 1819, his second in 1821. In 1831, he became Governor-General of Zhili, the wealthy and almost always quiet capital region. Admittedly, this brief curriculum vitae leaves out less auspicious aspects of his career. In 1820, he lost his first governorship for failing to control the flooding Yellow River. In 1827, he was sacked from Jiangsu after making an extraordinary hash of repairing grain transport routes up to the capital. Again and again, though, he was saved by the emperor's personal intervention. Unlike Lin Zexu, he was a man who had by 1840 made many mistakes, but had somehow swaggered through them (accumulating, in the process, a spectacular personal fortune), thanks to imperial favour. He was someone with experience and connections, happy to volunteer for large tasks, fully expecting that (if and when things went wrong), Banner immunity would get him out of trouble.

This was a man too profitably embedded in the system that had made him to betray it. In 1841, when the emperor finally turned against him after the winter's negotiations broke down, his confiscated estate was rumoured to be spectacular: ten million silver dollars, three hundred and forty houses, and so on. What, practical historians have asked, could the British have offered to motivate him to betray the Qing?[39] Qishan failed to foil the British not because he had been bought by them, but because he was deeply puzzled by them. 'I have humbly investigated the hundred cunning tricks of the English', he told the emperor in autumn 1840, when asked what they were doing so far north. 'If all they want is to trade, then why do these rebellious foreigners not know that for our sacred emperor, the empire is like

one family? All they need to do is beg for trade in Guangdong –
why have they come so far, to Tianjin? If they wish earnestly to beg
for imperial favours, why have they brazenly occupied a town in the
south-east?'[40]

On 19 August, the emperor finally found time to read Palmerston's letter. It proved a typically busy Wednesday for him, with
critical decisions to be made on repairing defences in the north-east
(some 1,500 miles from Canton, the focus of conflict with the British)
and pension allocations for Banner widows.[41] And although he
claimed to have given the missive a 'particularly careful reading',
he seems to have skipped the inconvenient details of British demands
for money, land and consuls, and focused on the letter's complaints
against Lin Zexu: their quarrel, he concluded, was with an impolitic
imperial servant, not with the system as a whole.[42] Make a public
example of Lin, he quickly concluded, and the problem would go
away.

The next day, he gave instructions to Qishan on how to 'tame the
foreigners'.[43] Their grievances against Lin were to be investigated;
every other demand was ignored or dismissed.[44] The details would be
worked out face to face in a meeting with his representative, Qishan.
'The great emperor oversees the earth and seas – there is no place that
he does not regard with equal benevolence. If foreigners should have
the slightest grievance about their trade with us, we will immediately
investigate and punish those at fault accordingly ... The British
admiral should return south, and wait patiently for the matter to be
dealt with.'[45]

Imperial tradition gave the emperor two options for handling
rebels against the Qing imperium (and 'rebels' (*ni*) is how the English
were identified in almost every contemporary Chinese source on the
conflict): extermination (*jiao*), or soothing (*fu*). (In China's First
National Archives, just inside the western gate to the Forbidden
City, Daoguang's military memorials from the Opium War are filed
inside the 'Archive for Seizure and Extermination'.[46]) By choosing, in
1840, to 'tame' or 'soothe' the British, Daoguang was consciously
following a policy that, since the Han dynasty, had been known as
the 'loose rein' – controlling wayward foreigners with benevolence, to
avoid the unnecessary and expensive unpleasantness of a war. But to
the emperor, soothing was not an admission of weakness or surrender.

It was another form of control, albeit a paternalistic one. 'The English', he later analysed, 'are like whales and crocodiles in the sea, they have no fixed abode. Even if we stiffened our defences all along the coast, we would not annihilate them. What would be the good in exhausting our state coffers in such a hopeless cause? Luckily, they only want to trade and to have their grievances addressed – which gives me an opportunity to deal with them.'[47]

On 30 August, Qishan – dressed with restrained good taste in a blue silk robe, white satin boots and a straw cap trailing a fine peacock's feather – applied himself to soothing Elliot, in a yellow silk-lined marquee thrown up under the shadow of the Tianjin forts. His tactic was reciprocity: to offer the British so many gifts, compliments and professions of friendship that they would feel too guilty to make war; to disarm them with a full-blown charm offensive. He probably did not know that Elliot's first personal encounter with Chinese officialdom, back in 1834, had taken the form of two heavy blows over the head. But Qishan's affectionate manner seemed designed to confound the Briton's low expectations of dealings with the Qing bureaucracy. In his account of the meeting, Elliot – accustomed to being undermined by Palmerston, snarked at by opium-smugglers and lectured by Lin Zexu – almost purred to find such tender understanding in his Qing negotiator. A 'perfectly unaffected and quiet' Qishan received him, he remembered, 'with great courtesy'. Qishan agreed with all the British complaints against Lin Zexu, and occasionally looked 'obviously powerfully impressed' by Elliot's reasoning. He was, Elliot gushed, 'one of the very foremost men in this country.'[48]

While Qishan was working on Elliot, the British retinue was being lavishly banqueted in a mass of smaller, surrounding tents: with 'excellent beef and mutton,' remembered one lieutenant, 'birds'-nest soup, sea-slugs, and ragouts of comestibles, whose variety and number gave an air of novelty and curiosity to the entertainment.'[49] In later communications, Qishan turned his attentions to Charles' cousin George, acclaiming him for his 'eminent and masculine talent, and clear perception of reason'.[50] Qishan's reports back to the emperor, by contrast, were far less complimentary, suggesting that the English 'seemed to be showing remorse' at their base actions, and that if they were to attack on land, they would be able to do nothing except 'fire their guns'.[51] (The British visitors to Tianjin took a different view. Their bird's-nest soup finished, Elliot's retinue on 30 August began to look around them, at the impromptu defences that had been thrown up in the last few days, and found them 'extremely paltry . . . quite ludicrous. With two six-pounders and a couple of hundred marines they might have been ours at any moment.'[52])

Elliot got very little out of his six-hour conference, beyond flattery and the admission that Lin had misbehaved (an admission that Qishan would have relished, as he seems to have considered Lin an ambitious troublemaker implicated in the Manchu's 1827 humiliation over the waterworks fiasco in Jiangsu). Despite promising nothing, Qishan allowed Elliot to imagine that a satisfactory settlement was possible. While asserting that for the emperor to pay for the opium was neither 'reasonable nor just', he hinted that Daoguang might change his mind. 'Further time was necessary for deliberation', Qishan havered. 'His Imperial Majesty had already resolved to send a commissioner to Canton . . . proof that the dispositions of the Court were gracious and peaceful.'[53] Elliot confessed to Palmerston how awkward he would have felt putting uncivilized pressure on Qishan: how could he do so 'without creating the ill will of the Governor, with whom the Plenipotentiaries expected to have to treat' in Canton?[54] Qishan, in short, stalled him with sweet-talk and sea-slug. And after brief consideration, the two Elliots agreed to return to Canton.

Both the emperor and Qishan were elated at their skill in managing the British. 'To expend a few words and a little paper', declared Daoguang, 'is far better than dispatching 100,000 troops . . . You've carried out my orders down to the last detail, through many twists and turns, while keeping to the proper forms. We could not be more delighted.'[55] Qishan may have been less elated to hear that his reward was another, even more awkward assignment: to take over from Lin Zexu as special Imperial Commissioner to Canton, and complete the negotiation between two sides who − after a month and a half of talks − had managed to agree on nothing.

On 23 October, Daoguang received a request from the Governor-General of Zhejiang and Fujian for 150,000 ounces of silver, to cover the cost of future military operations on the south-east coast. 'What for?' the emperor barked back. 'When [the foreigners] came to Tianjin to hand over their letter, they struck me as perfectly respectful and submissive. I've sent my great minister to Canton to sort the whole matter out. Within a few days, the armies can be demobilized. You say the foreigners are running wild? Where, I ask you, where?'[56] 'Thus to all appearance', agreed Lord Jocelyn in his journal, 'does this Chinese war, if so it may be termed, seem drawing to a close.'[57]

Chapter Eight

QISHAN'S DOWNFALL

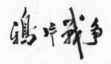

It took Qishan almost two months – fifty-six days – to saunter south to Canton. True, this was four days less than his predecessor, Lin Zexu, had taken in the early days of 1839. But back then, the empire had only had a drug problem. This time, the country was – or at least was meant to be – at war. Zhoushan, one of the empire's richest and most strategically important islands, had been stormed and its garrison routed, and the representatives of the British sovereign had come within easy firing distance of the capital province and demanded talks with the emperor's representative. But this was no great cause for concern, Qishan reassured Daoguang. 'Our Emperor has innumerable great problems to consider every day', he soothed him. 'Certainly it is not worthwhile to bother His mind with such petty business. Also, to put up coastal defences for years would entail heavy expenses and waste immense power of men . . . I will make them return to Canton willingly to wait for our solution of the question.'[1]

One of his many pauses took place in the north-eastern province of Shandong, where he made an acquisition he hoped would prove useful: one Bao Peng, a forty-seven-year-old chancer from near Macao, whom Qishan hired as translator and adviser in his upcoming talks with the British. After a varied and lucrative career down in Canton as an unlicensed comprador to the Americans and British, and as an opium-supplier to the well-to-do Cantonese, this Bao Peng had grown 'frightened of complications' when a Chinese interpreter employed by the English threatened to denounce him to Lin Zexu. In March 1839, therefore, he had decided to disappear north, taking refuge in the house of a local song-writer.[2] Perhaps keen to be rid of this dubious character, Bao Peng's host recommended his linguistic and diplomatic services to the passing Qishan, who took him on without, it seems, asking any awkward questions about his background, imagining him to be a most useful commodity: an English-speaker uncorrupted by Canton trading society. Bao Peng claimed to have been learning English since childhood; in practice, his competence seems to have gone no further than pidgin. Both British and Chinese observers portray him as a clown: Wei Yuan, a Qing contemporary and sharp commentator on the war, called him 'the pet boy of the traitor Dent' (the British merchant who had graced the very top of Lin's 'Most Wanted' list of British opium-smugglers, and whose arrest had been one of the basic demands of the March 1839 crackdown) and the 'slave' of Elliot, who sent him out as his 'eyes and ears'.[3] 'He professed much regard for the English,' remarked one British lieutenant, 'but, like all his countrymen, he was a most intolerable liar.' Former English associates were unable to contain their amusement at seeing their errand boy grandiosely reinvent himself as a government worthy, in his 'winter cap with a brass button', robe of 'rich puce-coloured satin' and thick-soled black satin boots. 'You thinkee my one smallo man?' he spluttered on a visit to his old master Dent in Macao, while being ribbed for his new airs. 'No! My largo man, my have catchee peace, my have catchee war my hand, suppose I opee he, makee peace, suppose I shuttee he, must make fight.'[4] Of course, Bao Peng's command of English was far superior to the non-existent Chinese-language skills of the English troops, whose inability to communicate verbally with local populations had already been, and would continue to be, the cause of much unnecessary suffering. Through the war, many Qing forces would fight desperately to the end or simply commit suicide rather than submit to the mercies of these aliens, while the British shouted incomprehensibly at them to surrender and live. Nonetheless, it boded ill for the negotiations ahead that this swaggering fugitive from justice should have been promoted to such a position of responsibility. After Bao's appointment, Wei Yuan commented, Elliot contracted 'a greater contempt for China's resources in men than ever.'[5]

Bao Peng, this opium-smuggler turned imperial diplomat, offered a particularly colourful example of Chinese collaboration with the British, but he was only one of many who betrayed the Qing by helping the empire's attackers: not out of conscious ideological choice, but simply because they needed to make a living, and the British were employers like any other. According to both English and Chinese sources, locals defected back and forth between the two sides depending on which offered them the most reliable source of income. After the opium trade dried up in the late 1830s, those who had drawn a living from transporting, unpacking, supplying and peddling were recruited (at the wage of six dollars a month) into anti-British defence militias – a strategy that Lin Zexu described as 'fighting traitors with traitors, poison with poison'.[6] When these bands were disbanded in late 1840 as part of the 'soothing' process, their members quickly changed sides again. 'Once they found themselves unemployed,' recalled one Cantonese observer, 'they took to wandering up and down the coast. The foreigners relied on two of their dastardly leaders, who incited others to go over too ... Without this help, the British would not have known anything – this was how Charles Elliot found out how slack the defences leading up to Canton were.'[7] When the British fleet returned to the south, seasoned Cantonese boatmen offered their services to the British, with all the importunate matter-of-factness of taxi drivers touting for trade outside a railway station. 'How four-piece ship no wanchee pilot', one local navigator shook his head, on being rejected.[8] Everywhere the British went, they were dependent on local willingness to provide them with fresh food and water. When the Elliots returned south in late November 1840, and docked their fleet on the eastern side of the mouth of the river up to Canton, a floating Chinese township kept them well supplied with fresh food, even at the risk of persecution by officials.[9] When the names of this impromptu comprador community were taken down by a group of police spies, the businessmen besieged and set fire to the police boat. 'These poor wretches were literally roasted alive, their persecutors preventing their escape with long bamboos', recalled an English lieutenant. 'What a most extraordinary nation this is! ... They will trade with you at one spot, while you are fighting, killing and destroying them at another!'[10]

*

Charles Elliot and company reached Macao on 20 November. Qishan arrived perhaps only a couple of days later, but did not announce himself officially until 29 November. For well over a month, they exchanged around ten communications, generally polite but without resolving anything. Qishan, as at Tianjin, was keen to defuse as much minor unpleasantness as he could without addressing any of the major British demands. On 5 August, a young Englishman called Vincent Stanton, who had abandoned a half-finished degree at Cambridge to tutor a family of English children on Macao, had (while out swimming) been seized and imprisoned by Qing soldiers. On 10 December, Qishan had him released from his manacles, taken to his own mansion and fattened up for a day or two, then handed back to the English community. Five million dollars would be paid for the destroyed opium: 'seeing that the honourable Plenipotentiary has shown in all things respectful and compliant conduct . . . the Minister has constrained himself to devise means for arranging this matter'. Punishment of Lin Zexu was curt and quick: on 13 October, Lin discovered he had lost his job to his second-in-command.[11] The old British demand to abandon unequal Chinese usages in diplomatic communications was also easily dealt with: 'it may be assented to', Qishan wrote blandly on 11 December. But on anything bigger, agreement was impossible: the 'request to grant territory' (Hong Kong) was 'inconsistent with reason'; or, he later clarified, 'really opposed to all that is reasonable'.[12] In any case, no settlement, no resumption of trade, was possible while the British were still occupying Zhoushan. From the remote safety of frozen Beijing, Daoguang offered little constructive support: 'Judging from your report,' he snapped at Qishan, 'the foreigners are outrageous and not amenable to reason . . . After prolonged negotiation has made them weary and exhausted, we can suddenly attack, and thereby subdue them.'[13]

The intriguing thing about this correspondence is – particularly given Elliot's subsequent reputation as arch-imperialist among Chinese historians – how very far and free the plenipotentiary wandered from his foreign secretary's original instructions. Through the diplomatic tennis of December 1840 ('no-gotiating', frustrated opium traders in India called it), Elliot politely dropped almost all of Palmerston's demands (for the opening of five mainland ports, consular representation, extra-territoriality and so on). True, Elliot was not afraid to menace as well as concede: to remind Qishan of 'the inexpediency of delay, where such large forces are assembled.'[14] But compared to the harsh stipulations of the final 1842 Nanjing Treaty, Elliot's terms were mild.

Perhaps because he had been so long in China, he seems to have never believed he would get what Palmerston was asking for.[15] But even if he could have managed it, Elliot did not think it good for the long term of Sino-British relations that the Qing should be brought so uncompromisingly to their knees: 'negotiation', he believed,

> supported by the mere appearance of formidable force, would at once place the trade at Canton upon a vastly improved footing, [then] we might probably get permission to trade at one or two other ports . . . if I can secure so much without a blow, it will better become me to incur the responsibility of departing from the letter of my instructions, than to cast upon the country the burden of a distant war for the sake of a balance of concessions pretty surely within our grasp . . . by a quiet improvement of opportunities . . . we shall have avoided the protraction of hostilities, with its certain consequences of deep hatred.[16]

But even Elliot could get impatient. On Boxing Day – after the regiments had marked the holiday with roast beef and plum pudding – he issued an unseasonal threat to resume hostilities at noon on 28 December, if there had been no decent response to British demands for new trading posts by then. On 7 January, after a few more days' stalling from Qishan, the British fleet started up the river. This time, the plan was to strike a very 'definite blow' to the site of so many British frustrations of the past half-century: the approach to Canton – the Bogue – where the South China Sea began to narrow into the Pearl River.

This is how the Bogue would have looked early on 7 January 1841. Taikoktow and Chuanbi, two rocky, fortified islands some three miles apart, guarded the western and eastern banks of the Pearl River. Just north of them sat a second line of watchposts on the islands of Wangtong and Anunghoy, again solidly defended with mudworks and granite forts full of guns and men. To ensnare aggressors, a double lacing of large, chained wooden rafts blocked the passage between Anunghoy and Wangtong. A third set of defences rested on the green, stony cliffs of Tiger Island, another mile or so to the north-west. Further up, as the channel towards Canton narrowed and wound through low-lying paddy fields, lay yet more forts and guns.

This threefold defensive scheme was the brainchild of Canton's sextuagenarian admiral (and, according to one source, descendant of the Chinese god of war), Guan Tianpei. After decades of unexceptional army service, Guan had soared to imperial favour in 1826, when he successfully guided 1,254 imperial grain-supply boats along China's east coast from the mouth of the Yangtze and safely into dock in Tianjin. Still remembering with admiration Guan's rice-herding talents, the emperor had turned to him in 1834 to tighten Canton's defences after the Napier fiasco. By 1841, the admiral had had six long years in Canton to reflect on deficiencies in the Qing defences. Any weaknesses (in weaponry, fortifications, discipline) could, he concluded, be solved not by improving their quality, but by increasing their quantity. For six years, then, Guan toiled on building up a network of granite forts, each with the same drawbacks: their cannon were badly cast and immobile, and supplied by poor-quality powder, while their circular walls exposed the forts' defenders to bombardment from above. Finally, he gave them all optimistic names: the Forts of Eternal Peace, of Consolidated Security, and of Suppressing, Over-Aweing and Quelling Those From Afar.

The backbone of the Qing strategy was defence – any hope of making in the open sea a successful naval assault on the British ships was long dead. 'If I were to order the fleet to gather its strength and meet them in battle out in the ocean,' Lin Zexu warned Daoguang in early 1840, 'victory would not be guaranteed. The waves are too big, and the wind too changeable.'[17] But both Lin and Guan were full of ideas for water-borne guerrilla warfare. One plan was to hire thousands of locals to form teams of desperadoes that would approach on small boats and hurl flaming jars of oil or stink-pots at the British, or leap onto the warships and massacre the crews in hand-to-hand fighting. Another scheme was to build fleets of skiffs, heaped with dry grass and gunpowder. In the heat of battle, fearless irregulars would row them out, link them together with iron chains, nail them to the side of British boats, set fire to them, then escape.

Unfortunately, much of this strategizing was wishful thinking. Even if they had had the nerve to try, these militia teams would have found it practically impossible to get within stinkpot-hurling or nailing distance of Britain's cannonading fleet; the idea of scrambling up from small fishing junks (that lacked modern, elevated guns) into the towering British warships, meanwhile, was unlikely. For a while, Lin had planned to use masters of Daoist breathing techniques, who claimed to be able to walk on riverbeds for up to ten hours at a time, to dive down and drill holes in British ships. After repeated rehearsals, it was discovered they were good only for bobbing about in the shallows. Yet Lin still kept them on the payroll: 'every water-brave we keep in our pay', he reflected, 'means one less ruffian in the pay of the English.'[18]

As he built his forts, Guan overlooked one more dangerous possibility: that the British would allow themselves to be distracted from thoughts of their ultimate destination – Canton – and directly attack the forts *themselves*. Guan was convinced that the British would be too fixated on reaching the prize of Canton to concentrate their guns on his beloved granite fortifications, and that as the fleet hurried towards the city they would trip over the defensive chains of rafts and be annihilated by nearby Qing cannon. The exact opposite occurred: as the British set about systematically destroying each of the forts they passed, Guan's structures were exposed as poorly designed, isolated, exposed units, from which his terrified soldiers ran as fast as they could.[19]

Early on the morning of 7 January, three British steamers set off towards the Bogue, planning to land some 1,400 marines, infantry and artillery on Taikoktow and Chuanbi. While the marines set up artillery to storm the rear of the forts, they were covered by steamer fire. Twenty-five minutes after the fleet had begun to shell the highest fort on Chuanbi (on the eastern bank of the estuary), the British flag fluttered over its walls, the Qing guns stopped and the forts' defenders scattered in panic. It was a more brutal affair on the island's next promontory, where a pincer movement by the British trapped the Qing garrison inside the fort. Expecting a fight to the death, the

Qing soldiers were mowed down by gunfire, threw themselves off the fort's cliff and into the water below, or attempted futile resistance. The fort's commander, one Chen Liansheng, fought until 'every part of his skin was perforated with the gunfire that rained down on him', while his son, maddened with grief, fell soon afterwards.[20] The scenes inside the forts – their brain-spattered walls, their 'blent, blackened, smouldering, stinking' human remains – struck the conquering British as terrible. 'A frightful scene of slaughter ensued', recalled one lieutenant's memoir, in a section triumphantly entitled 'Small Loss of the British': in one spot, the bodies of 'the slain were found literally three and four deep'.[21] 'The sea was quite blackened with corpses', described an army doctor.[22] Many wounded Qing soldiers were burned alive when, falling to the ground with their matchlock guns, their matches set fire to the packages of gunpowder that they carried strapped to the chests and waists of their cotton-padded uniforms.

The decisive weapon of destruction on 7 January was the brand new, 184-by-29-foot iron steamer named the *Nemesis*, secretly commissioned for the war with China. Her journey east had begun badly: in early 1840, she had almost failed to make it past Land's End, when, 'the weather being hazy and the night dark, she struck heavily on a rock', springing a leak that, without judicious application of the hand pump, might well have sunk her.[23] For some eight months after this inauspicious start and despite constant anxiety about fuel (she guzzled eleven tons of coal a day), she had been piloted towards China (past slavers, hippopotamuses, cannibals and plagues of locusts) by her veteran captain, William Hall. Eventually, in the last week of November, she had made it to Macao, still in time to take part in what Hall hopefully described as the 'brilliant operations' to come in the Gulf of Canton. And once her difficult journey was complete, her resilient iron sides, her accuracy of fire and her shallow draught proved indispensable to the British war effort as she weaved through the densely fortified waterways of the Canton basin. Her impact was psychological as well as military: in her first engagement at Chuanbi her captain proudly observed 'the astonishment of the Chinese . . . unacquainted with this engine of destruction.'[24] As the Qing's plans were confounded, again and again, by this extraordinary new machine of war – able to tow warships upriver on frustratingly still days, to barge into improbably shallow waters – the apparently supernatural powers of the *Nemesis* spread panic and bewilderment.

With the forts on the western side of the Bogue similarly secured and reduced to ruins, the *Nemesis* – watched by the marines in possession of Chuanbi – set about annihilating Guan Tianpei's fleet of war junks, which had hung back just north of Chuanbi in waters that, their commanders judged, were not deep enough to allow the British hulls to approach. While one of the wooden British sloops, the *Larne*, cut off any escape route around the back of the island, the *Nemesis* brought its Congreve rockets into range. Almost the instant after the first shot, Captain Hall remembered, one of the junks 'blew up with a terrific explosion, launching into eternity every soul on board, and pouring forth its blaze like a mighty rush of fire from a volcano . . . The smoke, and flame, and thunder of the explosion, with . . . portions of dissevered bodies scattering as they fell, were enough to strike with awe . . . the stoutest heart that looked upon it.'[25] Both sides momentarily paused at the shock of it – the rocket must, presumably, have struck the ship's powder stores. The crews of the other junks then fled onland, leaving the vessels to drift towards shore, where they were destroyed, in time for lunch, by British cannon.

The day's accountancy was as follows. On the Qing side, an hour and a half's fighting had left some 280 dead and 462 wounded. The English suffered thirty-eight wounded, but no deaths. A hundred and seventy-three Qing guns were removed or spiked; eleven war junks were destroyed. The *Nemesis* had received a little damage on her paddle-box.[26]

The British fleet drew breath and fell to a fitful sleep, anticipating further exercise the following day. But as 8 January dawned calm and bright and the fleet sailed up to Guan's next layer of defences – Anunghoy and Wangtong – a small boat, skiffed by an elderly woman, approached. 'Let us resume talks,' went Admiral Guan's message.

From the fact that the Qing had waved the white flag, and from the horrific carnage that their guns had wrought, Charles Elliot may have assumed that his violence had – in the rough pedagogic language of Victorian imperialism – instructed his Qing interlocutors about the true nature of their British adversary, informing them that the empire's forts were helpless before British firepower and discipline. He would have been wrong. Over the coming months, years and decades, explanations for the early failure of Canton's defence focused not on British strength, but on domestic conspiracy theories. The forts had fallen, it was quickly decided, because of a fifth column in the Qing ranks – led by Qishan. And the source of most of the rumours was his old antagonist, Lin Zexu.

Hearing back in October 1840 of his dismissal, Lin had responded mildly enough: 'the Emperor's will must be done.'[27] On the face of it, he had passed the following months in Canton tranquilly: banqueting civil-service examiners, decorating pillars with couplets, rearranging his book collection. But it could not have been an easy time, as this former paragon of the imperial government waited for a hostile rival to complete an investigation into his conduct of the 'border disturbance' with the British. Qishan's report – finished around early December – was predictably critical, rounding particularly on Lin's failure to make good his original promise to give the British proper compensation for their opium.[28]

But as the negotiations started to go as badly for Qishan as they had for Lin, Lin turned on his vulnerable successor. In a series of persuasive letters to well-placed sympathizers, Lin fought back against Qishan's accusations that it was his mishandling of the British in 1839 that had caused all the trouble. On the contrary, it was Qishan who had deliberately wrecked everything. Lin was convinced that the British fleet, on arriving in June 1840, had been so intimidated by his own infallible defences of Canton – the fireboats ready to be nailed to British warships, the martial-arts divers ready to drill holes in hulls – that they had sailed off to make trouble at Zhoushan; he refused to accept that the British plan had been, from the start, to bypass Canton and put pressure on Beijing at the Yangtze and at Tianjin. 'These rebellious foreigners did not dare before [now] to venture an attack because our defences were then tight, and our unity of spirit made us as impregnable as a rampart', Lin wrote. 'But Qishan turned our arrangements upside down, broke our morale, sabotaged our soldiers' spirit, stiffened the [enemy's] resolve, and brought insult to our military prestige.'[29] Qishan was, in sum, a treacherous appeaser, accused of demobilizing militia, of refusing Guan Tianpei much-needed reinforcements and funds, and of spreading fear-mongering rumours about the hopeless condition of Qing defences.

Lin's campaign struck home: around the middle of February 1841, an intemperate fellow official called Yuqian (who later that year would oversee the complete collapse of Qing defences in the south-east) impeached Qishan to the emperor. After the shock of early defeat against the British, Lin's efforts to shift the blame away from himself and the empire's military inadequacy, and towards Qishan, were wonderfully consoling to his peers. If only we had stood and fought properly without traitors in our midst, they repeated to anyone who would listen, the foreigners would not have stood a chance. As Canton's defences crumbled through January, then February, March, April and May, a conspiracy theory was the perfect salve for the Chinese empire's amour-propre. By blaming everything on Qishan and his diplomatic approach to the British, the empire's uncompromising Confucians pushed damagingly for more war. All that was needed against flintlock guns and the *Nemesis*, their analysis implied, was Lin Zexu's heroic spirit of resistance.

It is true that Qishan had few illusions about the possibility of victory against the British, and made no secret of the fact. In late January, he dispatched to the emperor his own views of the military situation, expressing extreme contempt for 'the utter uselessness of our marines.'[30] The Qing weapons were badly cast, he argued; the forts were vulnerable to blockade; the naval crews were so prone to seasickness that they needed bribing even to stay at their posts. Worst of all, the loyalty of the local population was highly questionable: 'I have found, through careful examination, the main characteristics of the people of Canton to be falsehood, ingratitude and greed . . . [They] are used to mixing daily with the foreigners, and regard them like brothers.'[31]

But for all his pessimism, he knew that there was no way he could refuse to back up the forts if it came to a fight, and to this end he diverted some 8,000 reinforcements into them between late December and early January. Forts designed to be manned by sixty soldiers now contained, on average, around 320. Qishan himself reported to the throne on the eve of war that 'the forts are full up.'[32]

His congestion of the fortifications probably made the panic and slaughter on 7 January even worse than it would otherwise have been. Qishan set aside, moreover, 11,000 dollars to bribe the men to stay and fight. His enemies also rumoured that he had demobilized Lin's fearless militia, who then immediately went over to the British and led the attack on the Canton forts. 'After the guns of the fleet bombarded the forts from the front,' analysed Wei Yuan, 'about 2,000 Chinese traitors scaled the hills and attacked them in the rear ... far outnumbering the garrison of 600 men.'[33] 'I heard that after Qishan arrived in Guangdong', agreed his impeacher, Yuqian, 'he disbanded the braves ... They were then used by traitors ... that's why [the forts] fell.'[34] Although the British received help with piloting and supplies from entrepreneurial locals, English accounts make no mention of a whole army of turncoats, and it is hard to imagine that they would not have done, if it had occurred. Since Napier, the British had liked to describe war as liberating the grateful Chinese people from the yoke of Tartar tyranny. The defection of 2,000 locals in one of the key early engagements, therefore, would have been an extraordinary public-relations victory to be advertised wherever possible. Canton's forts fell because they were no match for British firepower; the rumours about Qishan were most likely rumours – nothing more.

By 21 January, Qishan had two intriguing documents lying before him. The first was Elliot's new draft treaty, demanding Hong Kong, six million dollars, equal diplomatic communications and the reopening of the Canton trade just after the Chinese New Year; the Qing empire would have Zhoushan back in exchange. The second was Daoguang's response to Qishan's late-December memorials describing the British terms. Now the emperor seemed actually to be paying attention to what the British were asking for. Even though the draft treaty was still many times milder than the final 1842 version would turn out to be, Daoguang found 'the demands of the rebellious foreigners totally excessive ... it's time to dispatch a punitive mission to suppress them ... If they try to hand over any more communications, you are not permitted to receive them ... My mind is made

1. The foreign factories at Canton in the early nineteenth century.

2. The riverfront at Canton in the mid-nineteenth century.

3. A Canton merchant's house drawn in the mid-nineteenth century.

4. The harbour of Hong Kong in the early 1840s.

5. The Daoguang emperor, the Manchu Qing ruler on the throne
during the Opium War.

Papaver Somniferum.

Poppy _ White or Opium

6. Opium poppy.

7. An opium poppy pod with incisions. Raw opium is seeping through the cuts.

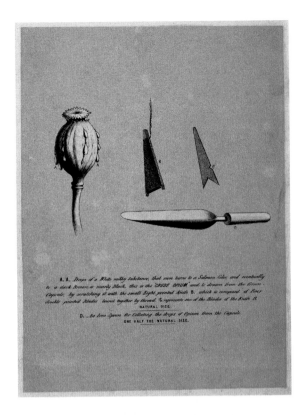

8. Opium being prepared in an Indian drying room.

9. A mid-nineteenth-century British sketch of a Chinese opium den.

10. Fleet of opium clippers.

11. The *Streatham* (right) and the *Red Rover* (left) near Calcutta.
The *Streatham* was an East India Company ship, while the *Red Rover* was
one of the earliest opium clippers, purpose-built to run between
India and the China coast.

12. Ball of opium, approximately 10cm in diameter. To smoke it,
a pea-sized ball of the drug would be heated then inserted into
the hole on the roof of the opium pipe's bowl.

13. Opium pipe.

少穆公遺像

14. Karl Gützlaff – Pomeranian missionary, interpreter for opium-smugglers, Opium War spymaster for the British – in Chinese dress.

15. Lin Zexu, the imperial commissioner who reached Canton in spring 1839 to wage war on opium.

16. Charles Elliot, the British superintendent of trade (and later wartime plenipotentiary) to China whose clash with Lin Zexu would trigger the Opium War.

17. A Chinese painting of Lin Zexu's destruction of the opium at Humen in 1839.

18. John Henry Temple, third Viscount Palmerston (1784–1865),
prime minister 1855–65 (oil on canvas by John Partridge, 1850).
As foreign secretary in 1839, Palmerston oversaw Britain's
decision to go to war with China.

19. Qing archer.

20. A Qing military official.

21. A Chinese junk.

22. Sketch of a temple on Zhoushan, the picturesque, prosperous island on China's east coast occupied by the British during the Opium War.

23. Guan Tianpei, the sexagenarian admiral who built up Canton's defences in the 1830s and perished among them in the British assault of 1841.

24. The *Nemesis*, the world's first all-iron steamer, destroying Chinese ships.

25. The British capture of Dinghai, the main town on Zhoushan, in summer 1840.

up, there will be no wavering at all.'[35] Qishan's position was now impossible. Elliot had demonstrated that he could ask for exactly what he wanted; the emperor had emphasized that he would not give it. Beyond tut-tutting at Elliot for his 'precipitation', there was nothing much Qishan could do, except play for time (while Guan Tianpei tried to patch the Bogue's defences back together) and lie to the emperor.

Not only did he disregard the emperor's orders to refuse British letters, on 27 January Qishan invited Elliot to an enormous placatory banquet on the bank of the Pearl River — their first face-to-face meeting in almost five months. As befitted a man in dire diplomatic straits, Qishan did not cut corners. At around nine o'clock in the morning, Elliot arrived (on board the *Nemesis*), accompanied by around twenty-five officers, fifty-six soldiers and sixteen drumming and piccolo-tooting musicians. The atmosphere was more village fete than parley: the riverways were crammed with brightly coloured official boats, the path up to the conference marquee strewn with bunting. While Elliot's party fell upon a 'sumptuous and tedious, though not unpalatable' buffet breakfast of shark's-fin and birds'-nest soup, mutton and wine, what Elliot called a 'complimentary and friendly conversation' with Qishan took place in an inner chamber draped with yellow silk.[36] (According to another British account, far too much cherry brandy was consumed for any sensible business to be done.) Later, to Daoguang, Qishan almost denied the meeting had happened at all. He had happened to bump into Elliot, he explained, while checking on the city's defences, and offered his retinue some 'light refreshments', as they had missed their breakfast.[37]

Although the situation was hopeless, Qishan still had to try to muddle through: fussing over expressions in Elliot's draft treaty, waiting to hear if the British had left Zhoushan, rallying the Qing forces (through early February, the second tier of Canton's defensive forts were strengthened with new cannon).[38] On 13 February, another couple of communications awaited Qishan in Canton. The first was an imperial edict informing him that he had been replaced by the emperor's cousin, Yishan (newly invested as the 'Rebel-Suppressing General'), and a veteran of the 1830s Xinjiang wars called Yang Fang, both of whom would shortly arrive to 'annihilate the foreigners'. The second was yet another nagging request from Charles Elliot to sign his draft treaty of 21 January – a document they had been discussing for the past six months.[39] On 20 February, after a week's silence from Qishan, Elliot sent a back-up copy for his urgent consideration. When Qishan asked for another ten days to consider it, war was declared once more.

On 25 February, the British began battering Canton's remaining two lines of defence. The Qing did their best to maintain a good show: on the fortress island of Anunghoy, a single band of soldiers was set to marching around the same hill, changing their clothes after each circuit to give the impression of infinite forces. But by half-past one the following day, undaunted British troops were spilling out of the *Nemesis* onto the islands of Wangtung and Anunghoy, and the Qing forts were haemorrhaging their defenders. Although around 1,000 men surrendered to be taken prisoner alive, many died fleeing in panic down the hillsides, or along the beaches below the forts. By the evening, the *Nemesis* could be spared for more humanitarian tasks, such as fishing escaped Chinese soldiers out of the water. (Several of these terrified individuals, sure that the *Nemesis* wanted them only to carry out further torture or mutilation, drowned by holding themselves under the water.[40])

But in all, the resistance was less desperate and more pragmatic than it had been six weeks before. The tone was set early on by the officers directing operations on Wangtong, who locked their rank and file inside the forts to prevent them from running away, then fled in small boats as soon as the firing began. As a result, their abandoned subordinates fired their cannon at their departing superiors, rather than at the British.[41] In another fort, the local Cantonese soldiers were the first to flee, swiftly followed by reinforcements from Hunan. When the stampede bottlenecked at a bridge, panic forced those lining the bank into the water, while those behind used their comrades' heads as stepping stones – none of those forced under the water survived.[42]

By 27 February, the forts of Eternal Peace, of Consolidated Security, of Suppressing, of Over-Aweing and of Quelling Those From Afar had all fallen – as had Guan Tianpei, the man who had spent the last six years building them up. Before the assault began, he had made valiant efforts to hold his subordinates' nerve, pawning his own clothes to bribe them with a couple of dollars apiece. But they began to run as soon as the firing began. As Guan drew his sword to prevent their exit, a bullet hit him in the chest.[43] Besides Guan, the British claimed six hundred Chinese lives, and the capture of some 460 cannon. Five British were wounded. As with 7 January, officials blamed the defeats on fifth-columnists: on turncoat opium-smugglers hired by Elliot, on Chinese traitors who explained the secret waterways of the Canton River to the British. The truth was, most likely, less elaborate: the Qing guns could not swivel to direct their fire at the British ships or infantry; and the gunners ran away.

Over the next three weeks, the British forces pushed up the riverlets and waterways that led to the city, splashing through paddy fields, burning forts, observed and sometimes assisted by locals, who stepped forward willingly to remove obstructions such as wooden piles driven into the river or to offer their services as pilots.[44] In the engagements of January to March, the *Chinese Repository* estimated, the Qing had lost more than 2,000 men; the British had suffered one dead of his wounds, and three killed by their own weapons.[45] By 18 March, Elliot was back where the conflict had started – at the factories on the southern edge of Canton. Almost two years previously, he had left the city a beleaguered, unpopular civil servant; now he glided magisterially in to dock on the deck of the *Nemesis*. 'In a few moments', recalled the steamer's captain, 'the British flag was displayed with three cheers, and . . . Canton lay completely at our mercy'.[46]

But Qishan was not there to witness Elliot's triumph. As this diplomatic and military fiasco took shape, Daoguang did the only thing that he could to make himself feel better: he blamed everything on his commissioner. On 13 March, Qishan had left the city – wreathed in chains, his property confiscated by the state – for the capital, to await trial for treason. He was accompanied by Bao Peng, whose luck had finally run out. Ever the survivor, Qishan would live to make a comeback, and a good one. After weeks of being interrogated about the bribes he was supposed to have taken from Elliot and about his treacherous destruction of Canton's defences, he was condemned to death. But in time, Daoguang commuted this to

banishment; then fully reinstated his old friend in 1842, releasing
him to enjoy senior appointments in practically all corners of the
empire except (probably to his great relief) for Canton, until his death
in 1854. The less well-connected Bao Peng was not so fortunate. In
March 1841, he was put on trial alongside his master: although
charges of spying for the British could not be made to stick, he was
convicted of acting as an unlicensed comprador and condemned to
serve out his days as a slave in remote, freezing Xinjiang, the harsh
frontier zone to which Lin Zexu was also exiled. The British heard
even worse rumours: that Bao had been sentenced to death by 10,000
cuts, his family executed, his village demolished and the countryside
up to a twenty-mile radius laid waste.[47]

Chapter Nine

THE SIEGE OF CANTON

When Yang Fang – one of the emperor's new appointments of February 1841 – first reached Canton in early March, a well-informed local called Liang Tingnan remembered that 'he was cheered and cheered, everywhere he went'.[1] And in some respects, Yang did not seem a bad choice to take over from the disgraced Qishan. He had an impressive record in quashing rebellions on the empire's frontiers. Having joined the Qing army aged fifteen, he had made a career out of keeping in check the many domestic threats to the Qing imperium: insurgent minorities in the south, the White Lotus rebels in the north-west, mutinous garrisons. His finest hour had come in 1828, when he had captured Jehangir, the Central Asian chieftain who had declared a jihad against the Qing three years previously, and dispatched him in chains back to Beijing for execution 'by a thousand cuts'. For this feat, the delighted Daoguang named him the Marquis of Resolute Bravery (third degree), and showered him with decorations and honours: the Purple Whip, the Double-Petalled Flower Feather, coral thumb-rings, the right to ride a horse around the Forbidden City; that kind of thing.[2] On the minus side, however, Yang Fang was going to turn seventy-one that year, had retired for reasons of poor health in 1835 and had no experience of dealing with Europeans. He was also so deaf that he had to communicate with his colleagues in writing.

Yang Fang's first assessment of the situation after entering Canton gives an idea of his fitness for purpose. 'The foreigners' cannon', he announced, 'always strike us, but ours cannot strike them back. We

live on solid ground, while the foreigners float back and forth on the
waves. We are the hosts, they are the guests – why have they been so
successful against us? They must be making use of the dark arts.'
Fortunately, he had a counter-attack in mind. Every ten households,
Liang Tingnan recalled, 'was to collect together all the women's
chamber-pots they could find, place them on wooden rafts, and send
them out to defend the city.'[3] It's hard to know exactly how Yang
Fang judged the military capabilities of chamber-pots, but perhaps,
given the low status of women in Confucian society, their toilet-
buckets seemed to Yang Fang quite the most potent weapon of
destruction available against the supernatural force of the British
guns.

Whatever he intended by it, Yang's strategy indicates that this
was a man who had reached the front line of the war without much
of a plan. Liang Tingnan's tones are too bland to identify irony with
much certainty, but another local did not bother restraining his
mockery of the city's new general. 'All day long,' he remembered, 'all
Yang Fang did was buy watches and other foreign goods, then at
night he bought the services of pretty boys for his entertainment . . .
He didn't have any plan to speak of. His best idea was to buy up the
city's toilet buckets to defend us against the foreigners' cannon, then
to make straw effigies, carry out Daoist rites and supplicate the ghosts
and spirits.'[4] Soon enough, Yang showed what he had in mind with
the chamber-pots, at an assault planned for one of the forts a few
miles short of Canton. 'The idea was', Liang explained, 'that when
they heard cannon shot, rafts would be lined up in the water, with
the chamber-pots blocking the robbers' way, then soldiers, crouched
behind them, would spring out to attack.' But as soon as he saw
the foreigners' banners, 'Yang Fang's deputy fled and everyone else
followed suit . . . When Yang Fang saw for himself how fiercely the
foreigners were advancing, he drove his soldiers back into the city.'[5]
Safely back behind Canton's walls, Yang Fang consoled himself by
tying up his weak-kneed deputy; he would have beheaded him, too,
if the other senior officers had not persuaded him to be merciful.

Yang Fang's secret weapons notwithstanding, through early
March the British advanced up the inner waterways of the Pearl
River, capturing forts, camps and hundreds of cannon, and destroy-
ing dozens of war junks – all with only a handful of warships. The

suggestion made by a local official's messenger to the commander of
a British schooner on 9 March, at a fort just five miles shy of Canton,
probably sums up the Qing appetite for war at that point. 'My chin-
chin, you no fire plum, my do all same pigeon, that no can do; my
can fire six piece gun no plum got, save Emperor's face then makee
walkee.'[6] (An approximate translation: Greetings! We can't just not
shoot at each other, even if we'd rather not. Suppose I fire six blanks
to save the emperor's face then run away?) The stalwart British
commander dismissed the errand-boy with a kick, calling his master
'a mighty big coward.'

On 18 March, once he had rehoisted the British colours above the
white factory walls a little to the south-west of Canton, Elliot
informed Yang Fang by letter that the British troops would not be
withdrawn until trade was resumed, and that a Qing response was
required by return. He was given it by 20 March: 'the merchants of
all nations alike are permitted to trade . . . as usual; there shall be no
hindrance or obstruction made, nor any trouble created'.[7] The river,
the *Chinese Repository* reported, was 'again crowded with passers to and
fro, and the foreign factories showed signs of becoming again what
they formerly were.' Chinese merchants who had fled crept back;
shops and warehouses reopened. 'The high officers of the English
nation', cajoled Elliot in a public notice to the 'quiet and industrious
people of Canton', have shown that 'they cherish the people of
Canton'. The emperor's men, for their part, enjoined the locals to go
quietly but energetically about their usual business.[8] The Canton
trade, once resumed, would continue all the way through the worst
of the following year's hostilities along the east coast.

It was just like old times. It would have been easy to forget that
a war was supposed to be occurring. Everything seemed determined
to return to normal – including the opium trade. Even while the
fighting was still ongoing, soldiers, officials and militiamen were
shuttling back and forth, noted Liang Tingnan with interest, often
selling the 'foreign smoke'. The opium made its way into the Canton
estuary on steamers (travelling in the lee of warships) which then
met, by prearrangement, Cantonese skiffs that would pull up alongside and offload as much opium as they could during the confusion of
battle. One commander, Liang claimed, 'fired blanks. While the sky
was dark with smoke and flames, and the guns blazing, a long stream

of smugglers rowed quickly off. By the time the smoke had cleared, the opium had been spirited away.'⁹ Tea was moving out of the city at a great rate, too: by the final third of May, more than half a million pounds a day was passing out of the river.

It was a strange state of affairs for the emperor's men to be observing. Around 9 February, Yang Fang had received imperial orders to 'destroy the foreigners'; and yet here he was, a month later, looking on while they busily bought tea, just as they had done every winter season since at least 1760.¹⁰ Once he had exhausted his military strategies, he fell back on another, more basic technique for persuading the emperor that he was working very hard at destroying the enemy: lying to him.

He began on 6 March, the day after he arrived in Canton, informing the emperor that nothing more worrying than British 'patrol-boats' were drifting about. 'You put my mind at rest', wrote the emperor, receiving the memorial on 21 March, a day after Yang Fang had agreed to let the British trade again. Yang wrote again on 12 March, transforming the rout at Wuyong (in which panicked soldiers had stampeded their comrades to death) into a victory in which the British casualties – at four hundred and sixteen – were far higher than the Qing's, and following which 'the hearts of the people were much calmed . . . the army and people's courage grew and we can look to the future without worry.'¹¹ Daoguang now informed his Cabinet that Yang Fang was a military genius: 'Day and night . . . I await news of your victory . . . Who could be better for the job than my Marquis Yang Fang? My happiness is beyond expression!'¹²

By 17 March, though, even Yang Fang seems to have gone too far, when he dressed up a British attempt the day before to offer a ceasefire as a great Qing victory. 'When two of the large warships, a steamer and a dozen sampans tried to charge up the river . . . a hundred of our unflinching cannon fired in unison.' Having lost two ships and countless men, the English 'fled in terror, no longer daring to advance.' Although the emperor was lavish in his praise ('How brilliant you are – an astonishing victory'), he was finding it increasingly hard to understand why Yang Fang did not strike a final, decisive blow. 'Yang Fang's victory', he now wrote to the Rebel-Suppressing General Yishan, 'shows that Canton has nothing to fear . . . you must hurry to find a way to cut off the foreigners' retreat and ruthlessly exterminate them, to impress upon them how mighty we are.'[13]

On 18 March, Yang Fang's fictions caught up with him, when Charles Elliot actually reached Canton and demanded trade, in exchange for guaranteeing the safety of the city. By this point, however, Yang had no choice but to continue with his fabrications. The British, he reported to the throne on 22 March, had turned up in Canton begging for trade. 'They no longer dare harbour unruly designs,' Yang Fang explained, 'and only hope for the old system to resume.' Daoguang, unfortunately, was unmollified even by such invented humility: 'the request to restart trade', he declared, 'is an evil plot by the rebels . . . to make us relax our military vigilance . . . Cut off their exit route, round them all up and storm Hong Kong.'[14] By 3 April, Yang Fang had admitted to Daoguang that he had effectively authorized trade. Daoguang was furious: 'If we settle this thing with trade, why are we bothering fighting?' he demanded.[15] Yang Fang now secretly dispatched the Prefect of Canton to tell Elliot that he would be informed when and if the emperor demanded more war, so that the two sides could amicably arrange a half-hearted battle somewhere safely out of the city.[16] Too late: on 23 April, the emperor announced that he was dismissing Yang Fang – but that he could stay on in Canton to see if he could redeem himself. The Son of Heaven had realized, perhaps, that he was running out of personnel options.

Yang Fang was in any case officially subordinate to Yishan, whom the emperor had named 'Rebel-Suppressing General' back on 30 January. What, exactly, had his superior been suppressing these past two months?

In appointing Yishan, Daoguang may have hoped to have found someone desperate to prove himself. He was the great-great-grandson of Yinti, one of the several sons of Kangxi cast aside in 1722 by his

fourth son, Yinzhen, in the latter's campaign to become the Yongzheng emperor. That year, the omnicompetent Kangxi had died,
failing to name an heir. By 1723, Yongzheng had pushed and
manoeuvred his way onto the throne; three of his brothers died in
prison in mysterious circumstances soon afterwards. Although, by
simply surviving, Yinti fared better than several of his brothers, he
spent much of his adult life effectively under house arrest – keeping
a dull, lonely vigil over his dead parents, at the Imperial Tombs. Had
the succession struggle worked out differently back in 1722, then,
Yishan would not have found himself, as an adult, a jobbing fourth-
grade Imperial Clansman but rather a potential emperor. Perhaps
irked by the fantasy of what might have been, he seemed less ready
than some of his fellow well-born Manchus to loll back on the cushion
of Banner privilege. By 1840, he had endured some fifteen years in
the wind-swept deserts of the north-west, overseeing the colonization
of almost 30,000 acres of mountainous land.[17] Although he clambered
his way up to a military governorship, it must have felt like exile:
both then and now, Xinjiang was the empire's wild western gulag.
As he toiled out on this remote frontier, his mind must (at least
occasionally) have wandered back to Beijing and to the comfortable
sinecures enjoyed by fellow Manchu aristocrats such as Qishan.

Perhaps, by 1841, he was weary of dutiful service and felt that
his new, grandiloquent appointment was his opportunity to enjoy
himself in the more agreeable climates of China proper. A fortnight
after his appointment came through, he at last gathered together,
with great noise and fanfare, a more than fifty-strong retinue. On
16 February, he slowly set out south. 'I had the good fortune', wrote
a Russian diplomat resident in the capital at the time, 'to witness his
extraordinary departure.

> The General was being carried, while some of his retinue
> travelled in carriages, others on horseback . . . some had bows,
> others arrows, some carried bed mats, pillows and the like. In
> Russia, if a man has received orders to carry out an expedition,
> he just gallops off, but this is not how things are here.[18]

En route, Yishan seems to have had similar difficulty in drumming up any real sense of urgency. He arrived in the province of
Guangdong after forty-six days' travel (heavy rain, according to him,

made the roads difficult) – yet he hung back for another week and a half just inside the province's border, claiming that he was waiting for the new governor-general to arrive, so they could move onto the city together.[19] (Once arrived, this newcomer – one Qi Gong – was at pains to dampen hopes that he might be of much use: 'Don't expect too much from me', he assured Yishan. 'I haven't the talent for this job.'[20]) In the end, Yishan's journey down to Canton took him fifty-seven days – one day longer than it had Qishan, about four times as long as express couriers would take and roughly the same length of time that a new British plenipotentiary, Henry Pottinger, would spend travelling to China from London that summer.[21] If he travelled slowly enough, Yishan seems to have hoped, the whole problem would go away.

There is an obvious explanation for Yishan's lack of interest in reaching Canton: he did not know what to do, any better than did Yang Fang or Qi Gong. Daoguang's orders were clear: Yishan was to 'single-mindedly exterminate the foreigners . . . If you have the words "reopen trade" still in mind then you are completely betraying the purpose of your mission.'[22] Yet by the time he arrived, all the defences south of Canton had fallen, and trade was flourishing. It was fairly clear that 'extermination' of the British was impossible. At the very best, Yishan concluded after lengthy consultation with local worthies, Canton could resist through defence: the British could be 'coaxed out of the river with fine words' then the (failed) forts rebuilt and remanned.[23] But how were the British to be 'coaxed out' except by the promise of trade concessions, which the emperor had expressly forbidden? The only truly effective solution to the problem – the construction of a navy that could stand up to British ships – was impossible in the short term. The image of Qishan's departure back to Beijing in manacles must have haunted Yishan and Yang Fang, as they tried to persuade the emperor to allow trade. Daoguang was having none of it, his vermilion scrawls over his representatives' memoranda raging at any suggestion of compromise or delay: 'We only know one word: "Attack!" . . . We are angry in the extreme! . . . It is imperative that not a single rebel sail should escape . . . Tremble! . . . We only await the news of victory with the greatest impatience.'[24]

The usually parsimonious emperor had decided that now was not the time for half-measures: he was going to throw money and men at the problem. Accordingly, in the first three months of 1841, he had ordered some 17,000 troops from seven different provinces to converge on Canton, and voted three million ounces of silver to finance the recovery of Hong Kong. Surely, he thought, simple force of numbers would triumph. Theoretically, the few thousand British troops off the south coast should be swallowed up by official troops and by patriotic local populations. Daoguang's expectations were built, however, on a simple misassumption: that his subjects viewed the conflict as a war between the Qing 'us' and the British 'them' – that they unanimously desired revenge for 'the great numbers of our soldiers killed by these rebels'.[25]

Things did not look so straightforward on the ground, where many of those involved in the defence of Canton eyed each other with suspicion, and often violent hatred. The fight for the city – across the sweltering month of May 1841 – would turn out to be a vicious, even cannibalistic civil rout. The tone was set by the leadership, who seem to have suffered from extreme distaste for the civilians they were ostensibly protecting from British depredations. In their reports, the imperial commissioners were careful to emphasize the unreliability of the locals: partly because they genuinely distrusted them, and partly because it was always useful to have a scapegoat at the ready, in case the emperor accused them of failure. (Disdain for local populations was not restricted to Canton. That March, Yuqian, the sabre-rattling governor who would lead a hopeless defence against the British later in the year on the south-east coast, described local volunteers all the way up and down the south coast as 'bandits . . . To use them against the foreigners would be to use poison against poison. If they are wounded or killed, there will be no regret; thus there will be no injury to Heavenly prestige and, at the same time, a local evil can be removed.'[26])

Around 16 March, Yang Fang wrote to the emperor of the eight great difficulties in defending Canton, including the facts that the Qing navy had been wiped out, that the British had the run of the river up to Canton, and, tellingly, that the courage of the province's soldiers had been destroyed, and that the place was crawling with traitors. But using troops from other provinces was no solution, either: they were not familiar with the city and its suburbs. (Yang Fang admitted that, as an outsider, he had the same problem, and had not had time to investigate for himself the lie of the land around the city.) Neither were the Cantonese to be relied on: 90 per cent of them had already fled, while many of whose who stayed behind did so to 'burn and plunder'.[27] A week after Yang Fang arrived in Canton, he rode out from his headquarters through the narrow, congested city streets. 'Suddenly,' he reported to the emperor, 'a Chinese traitor seized my left arm and almost unhorsed me ... Your slave immediately ordered that his head be hung up and exposed – by killing one man, to strike fear into the hearts of the populace.'[28] Another contemporary account seems to tell a different story: that the unfortunate man was a hapless hauler who had got in the way of Yang Fang's retinue while eating a bowl of porridge and was immediately beheaded for his error.[29] On 8 May, a Cantonese man who had offered an opinion on the conflict was paraded through the streets as a traitor, stripped to the waist, both ears pierced with small flags, while being struck with a rattan whip to the beating of a gong.[30]

Almost as soon as Yishan arrived in the city, he made the following diagnosis of the situation: 'The trouble lies within, not without, because every merchant has got rich through the foreigners, and even the lowest orders make their livings from them. All the merchants and people who live near the coast are fluent in the foreigners' language. The craftier of their number are spies, and know everything that is going on around the government offices, and are quick to pass it on.' The going rate for information, he reported, was twenty dollars – for which locals were so avid that they regularly fabricated reports for the foreigners. All the losses of January through to March were, he argued, down to treachery and cowardice – 'and that is why I say we need to defend more against the people than against the pirates.'[31] As Yang Fang and Yishan procrastinated about war through April, they busied themselves instead putting up threatening notices about the dangers of collaboration, 'to curb the traitors' hearts'.[32] Yishan's feelings were fully reciprocated by the Cantonese. 'Yishan had no interest', one local writer commented acidly, 'in logistics, battle-plans, the lie of the land, about strategies for victory and defence, for subduing the enemy and resisting foreign aggression – and neither did he have anything to contribute. The only thing he was good for was buying watches and woollens, and giving or attending great banquets.'[33]

There was, quite likely, a deal of truth in official suspicions about the loyalty of the Cantonese, whose interests were financial rather than patriotic. Howqua, the richest of the merchants, was happy to inform his old British friends of recent developments on their return to the Canton factories at the beginning of March: about Qishan's dismissal, about the appointment of Yishan and Yang Fang, and so on. 'The locals', Liang Tingnan pronounced, 'were perfectly used to the foreigners ... and in any case were unable to understand complicated things. Feeling that the whole business would not hurt them, they quietly sympathized with Elliot.'[34] As British trade operations in Hong Kong prospered at surprising speed through the autumn and winter of 1841, the island's newly founded *Gazette* remarked complacently that well-to-do Cantonese merchants were already flocking towards the free-trade port. 'What do we care for this so-called war?' the message seemed to go. 'There's money to be made.'

The usual dysfunctions in the Qing military machine made matters worse. Through the spring, Daoguang's 17,000 troops straggled into town late, underfed, underpaid, undertrained, underequipped – or not at all. 'The imperial troops that have arrived', Yang Fang told the emperor, 'are all unaccustomed to naval warfare.'[35] There was no doubt in Yang Fang's mind that this ill-treated ragbag would go over to the highest bidder: 'there has long been the rumour', he reported to the emperor concerning the fall of the Canton estuary forts in February and March, 'that our marine forces received three hundred dollars for each unloaded cannon shot.'[36] 'As for our fleets,' ran Yishan's analysis, 'in the past they all made money out of protecting the opium trade. As for our soldiers, they cared only that the rebellious foreigners should be victorious and that the prohibition on opium should be relaxed.'[37] Over half the province's cannons 'have been scattered and lost and, except for the defence of the city, are inadequate for offence or defence ... No reply has been received about those sent from Hunan and Guangxi. The saltpetre sent for has not reached Canton either. We are burning with anxiety.'[38]

Daoguang's men tried delaying. They tried lying. They even tried to angle for the emperor's sympathy: 'The sores on your slave's legs have again broken out,' Yang Fang wrote on 28 April, 'but he does not dare on this account to evade any of his responsibilities.'[39] In the end, they tried fighting.

Despite the unfavourable impression that locals had of Yishan's military capabilities, he did have a plan of sorts. His idea was to launch a surprise water attack on the light British fleet stationed near the city: to organize assault teams who, supported by land artillery, would rush at the British ships by night on skiffs, fireboats and rafts loaded with flammable materials. Useful materials were being stockpiled on the southern edge of the city: fire arrows, fireballs, exploding poison cannon, poison fireballs and so on.[40]

There were a number of flaws in this scheme, most of them arising from the unreliability of the Qing forces, and logistical problems in getting men and materiel together. Because Yishan was so distrustful of the local soldiers, he insisted on using amphibious commandos from Fujian and Zhejiang – of whom, as the day of the planned attack drew near, perhaps fewer than 1,000 had arrived. In the event, their numbers were hastily boosted by 700 last-minute, probably clueless extras from Sichuan and Canton. But this top-secret plan's greatest drawback was that it was not top secret.

For one thing, the Qing had long been transparently preparing for war. 'Edict after edict was hurled against the British', remembered a British lieutenant. '"Exterminate the rebels! Exterminate the rebels!"' [41] By April, the *Chinese Repository* estimated that some 50,000 soldiers were gathered in or around Canton: 'Not one fourth of these', its correspondent added, 'are fit to bear arms. Many of them are wandering as vagrants about the suburbs. Even those on guard at the gates of the city appear unarmed.'[42] Another British captain stationed on the factory front exercised his brain by counting the daily shiploads of reinforcements that passed by on their way into Canton, while jittery civilians travelled in the opposite direction.[43] Forts and batteries were being rebuilt; 36,000 local militia had been recruited.[44] Yang Fang sent Elliot letters that he might or might not have supposed to be subtle: telling him that vast numbers of battle-hardened soldiers had arrived, that the British were hopelessly outnumbered, that peaceful negotiation was the only option. 'Cast not aside the words of an old man, but open your heart and let your bowels of kindness be seen.'[45] On the morning before Yishan's nocturnal stealth attack was launched (21 May) Elliot exhorted all British and American merchants to leave the factories for their own safety; yet again, one of his loyal Cantonese informants must have come good for him.

By midnight on 21 May, the factories were almost deserted, beyond a handful of profit-fixated American merchants. As the traders scattered, the rest of the British fleet moved up from Hong Kong and Macao, stationing themselves in a long snake between Canton and the entrance to the Bogue. Four warships, and the *Nemesis*, were anchored nearest the factories. 'Everything was buried', recalled one captain, 'in the most profound silence' until several junks – tied together in twos and threes – were observed being set alight, then sent drifting towards the British boats.[46] A fleet of other junks and rafts followed, stuffed with oil-soaked cotton. Soon, Chinese soldiers were swarming through the water towards the warships – perhaps intending to drill holes in the hulls. A neat 'shear with the helm' enabled the foremost ship to dodge the fire junks, while a touch of artillery put the attackers off. Firing from Chinese batteries hidden amid Canton's houses, though, proved more of a problem for warships trapped (on an airless Canton summer night) in one of the Pearl River's narrow channels. The only thing that saved them was darkness and an ebb tide: in nine minutes, just before fireboats could approach to inciner-ate the warships, the *Nemesis* had chugged to the rescue to answer the fire from the city. (Though there was a very bad moment when a lit rocket became stuck in its firing tube, threatening to explode on board, until Captain Hall calmly reached down and dislodged it, badly burning his hand.) As the Qing counter-offensive started to go wrong, the panic on the faces of the crews of the fifty-odd fireboats was illuminated by their burning cargoes; many jumped ship and drowned, or were caught by British musket-fire. By dawn, the batteries had been silenced and destroyed, and their firers put to flight. The tide now turned, dragging the remaining fireboats back towards the city, whose wooden southern suburbs burst into flames.

With hindsight, it was no surprise that the Qing attack failed. Yishan – perhaps suffering from imperial pressure, perhaps (as one contemporary Chinese account has it) 'yielding to a desire for glory' – had ordered a secret attack that seems to have taken his own side more by surprise than the enemy. He informed Yang Fang only *after* the soldiers had actually left the city for the river – possibly fearing that Yang, who may well have had high hopes that he could bamboozle the emperor indefinitely with mere talk of preparing for war, would force him to cancel the idea.[47] (The moment that Yang belatedly learnt of the plan, he is said to have stamped and sworn, declaring that 'we're bound to lose'.)

Pausing only to celebrate Queen Victoria's birthday with a high-noon salute on 24 May, the 2,393-strong British force cleared the river to the south of the city of functioning forts, and made its way to the west of Canton. By dawn on the 25th, all had been landed just off a creek around two miles north-west of the city. The entire force – a good number of them diarrhoea-stricken – began to tramp over rice-fields and burial grounds, dragging with them their four 12-pounder howitzers, four 9-pounder guns, two 6-pounder field-guns, three mortars and two 62-pounder rockets to their objective: Yuexiushan (the Mountain of Transcendent Excellence) – a moderate hill, a few hundred feet high, in the centre of the northern edge of the city wall. The men straggled at their peril: one camp follower, slowed by his burden of provisions, but nevertheless no more than 500 feet ahead of the next company, was found the day after lying by the roadside, headless.[48]

By 10 a.m. on 25 May, the hill and a new collection of optimistically named fortifications (the Forts of Extreme Protection and of Extreme Security, and the Tower that Suppresses the Oceans) were in British hands (the 49th and 18th Regiments participating in a strictly disciplined race as to which would scramble up the hill to claim the forts first), with their Qing defenders scrambling down the hillsides firing tiny rockets to mask their retreat in smoke.

After an uncomfortable (those lucky enough to sleep did so in scratch bivouacs) and busy night (fifteen pieces of artillery had to be dragged up the hill and set up by nightfall), 26 May dawned more quietly. British guns now pointed at Canton from its southern, water-bound approaches, and from the hills to the north. Perched up on their hill, the British at last had a little time to study the city before them, with its six miles of walls – twenty-five-feet high, twenty feet thick – now purged of any activity beyond the waving of white flags, and its gates spilling civilians out into the countryside.

To anyone with a sense of Sino-Western trading history, this was a moment to savour. For almost a century, European merchants' exclusion from Canton had been emblematic of so many of their frustrations with the Chinese empire. 'Now', observed Liang Tingnan, spying the British on the hill with their telescopes, 'they could see everything that was going on.'[49] For the first time, Britons could stare into this once secluded city: over its two square miles of narrow granite streets, lead-blue brick houses, mud hovels and temples. To the north and south of the city, twin pagodas rose up, reminding onlookers of the masts of a junk. 'That one of the first cities of the Chinese empire,' a British army dispatch put it with characteristic-ally clipped reserve, 'whose population of 1,203,004, defended by 40,000 soldiers, in and without the walls, whose defences had been now a whole year in preparation; strong in its natural position, and approachable only by an intricate and uncertain navigation, near 400 miles inland, should have in 3 days fallen before a force of not more than 3,500 effective men, soldiers, royal marines and seamen, I trust will be considered a circumstance gratifying and creditable to the national feeling, and to Her Majesty's arms.'[50]

Strictly speaking, Daoguang had wasted his three million ounces of silver; but, at fifteen dead and a hundred and twelve injured, the British had incurred their heaviest losses yet.

By 26 May, the city – and its defenders – were in spectacular disarray. The British bombardment alone had done terrible damage. 'The cannon did not fall silent for a single moment', wrote Liang Tingnan. 'When night fell, the fires burned as bright as day ... Neither officials nor soldiers dared come out to help – all you could hear was the noise of burning and death.'[51] But the Qing armies were almost as destructive. Discipline had fallen to pieces as soon as the first assault had failed on the night of 21 May, and the troops had taken out their disappointment by thoroughly plundering and destroying the foreign factories. Soon, 7–8,000 of the rank-and-file soldiers from other provinces fell back inside the city gates. In the meantime, all those who could do so travelled in the opposite direction, with such reckless panic that women and children were trampled underfoot. In the chaos, non-Cantonese soldiers – from far-away corners of the empire, finding themselves in a strange city, probably not understanding the local dialect, and seeming almost as terrifyingly foreign to local populations as the British themselves – were isolated from their own regiments and officers, and crammed into tents fifteen at a time. As a result, morale collapsed: 'they broke and fled', recorded Wei Yuan, 'indulged in mutual recriminations, began to complain about their pay [and] looted just as they liked.'[52] The officers were similarly undisciplined, scattering into abandoned civilian houses, leaving their commanders clueless as to their whereabouts. 'You never saw them except on payday,' remembered Liang Tingnan.[53]

Commanders either refused outright to leave the city to fight, or strenuously dissuaded others from doing so. 'I'll get them!' roared old Yang Fang, preparing to lead a 2,000-strong column out of the northern gate to do battle until his colleagues forcibly prevented him. At one point during these desperate days, Yishan was importuned by a handful of labourers who wanted to know what, precisely, he was planning to do to save the city. He responded by having their leaders immediately beheaded.[54] 'Innumerable bodies strewed the streets', observed one resident. 'All discipline was gone, and the roads were filled with clamour and confusion. Everywhere, I saw plunder and murder. Thousands of our soldiers ran away, having loaded themselves with stolen goods, then pretended they had lost their way pursuing the enemy.'[55] When the British started to fire on the commanders' former headquarters, Liang Tingnan scornfully remarked that 'the fleas had already jumped'.[56]

As banditry spread through the province as a whole, the threat of civil war loomed over the city. Tensions were particularly bad between the Hunanese reinforcements – concentrated around the east gate – and local fighters. Many of the Hunanese had apparently passed the time by sleeping with female lepers, who gave the disease to them – the folk belief was that if a woman could pass the affliction on to a man, she would recover and be able to get married. Another folk belief told that eating the flesh of a child would cure the sickness and so, allegedly, some stole and cooked children in their camp. Outraged local soldiers then went on a murderous rampage against the Hunanese child-eaters. 'The bodies were piled high on the drill-ground', remembered Liang Tingnan.[57] 'Traitors! Traitors!' screamed local militiamen, chasing back inside the city any victims who tried

to escape.[58] An uncorroborated British account reports that some
imperial troops ate the flesh of irregulars from Hubei.[59]

Sifang Fort – the Fort From Which All Directions Can Be Viewed –
is a pleasant spot to visit these days, nestling in the centre of the 230
acres of Yuexiu Park, a surprisingly beautiful oasis of green within
contemporary Canton's grubby concrete sprawl. Heading along the
park's broad pedestrian avenues carpeted with fallen tropical blossoms,
towards the dull red walls of the Tower for Suppressing the Seas, you
could easily miss the turning towards the old fort – now a small,
discreetly signposted arena – from which the British and their guns
looked down over Canton.

It was a less comfortable place in 1841: an exposed mound just
beyond the old walls of the city, ideal for catching the worst of the
Canton summer sun. Canton's climate is bearable between about
October and April; by May, it has long ceased to be reasonable, even
to those in appropriately loose, cool clothing. Imagine the sufferings
of the British troops, then, in their heavy uniforms: the long-sleeved,
stiffly tailored frock jackets constructed out of dense, heat-retaining
wool; the cap's steeply inclined peak more useful for channelling
sweat than for casting shade. On 30 May, one British major collapsed
and died of a heatstroke.

At first light on Wednesday 26 May, Elliot – stationed to the
south of the city, where the attacks of 21 May had started – had
a message couriered to the land forces: the British had made their
point by trapping the city to north and south, and he did not want
the troops to enter Canton. 'The protection of the people of Canton,
and the encouragement of their good will towards us, are perhaps
our chief political duties in this country.'[60] (If he knew anything
about what was raging inside the city, his instructions would have
been motivated as much by self-preservation as by paternalism
towards the Cantonese. British troops had been vulnerable enough
to assassins while crossing the open land north-west of the city on
25 May; the narrow, crooked streets of a city overrun by warring
troops and civilians would have been lethal.) Nonetheless, all the way
through the heavy rain of 26 May, the British commander on the

hill, Major-General Hugh Gough, set up his artillery for an assault the following day – he had little faith in the promise of yet more negotiations.

Thursday morning dawned: the guns, Gough instructed, would start at seven, and the infantry an hour later. The men 'were ripe for it', one lieutenant recalled.[61] But just as the show was about to begin, a British officer was spotted blundering his way up towards the command. He would have been there earlier, he breathlessly explained, but had lost his way at ten o'clock the previous evening and ended up sleeping in the rice fields. Elliot and the Chinese commissioners, he revealed, had come to terms: a six-million-dollar ransom was to be extracted for the city, along with the promise that the commissioners and their non-Cantonese troops would be at least sixty miles from Canton within six days – leaving the city without banners *or* music, Elliot had specified. The Mountain of Transcendent Excellence was promptly renamed 'Truce Hill', but the military men's mood was far from conciliatory. 'You have placed us in a most critical situation', Gough wrote privately to Elliot. 'My men of all arms are dreadfully harassed, my communications with the rear continually threatened and escorts attacked.'[62] 'I protest', the senior naval officer on the hill put it more pithily.[63]

On 29 May some of the men decided to make the best of their unexpected furlough and went off on a ramble through the nearby countryside. And like the inquisitive Victorians that they were, they found much of interest in temples and catacombs in a small hamlet not far from the city wall. On wandering inside, they opened up – purely in the interests of science – a few of the coffins, and noted that the features of the embalmed bodies 'presented a dried and shrivelled appearance; and there was a strong pungent aromatic smell perceptible on raising the lid'.[64] Their exploration at an end, they returned to camp and, it being evening, probably had dinner and fell asleep.

On the morning of the 30th, the British account continues, Gough's attention was called to a 5,000-strong line of peasant fighters, armed with spears, shields and swords, gathered behind the British camp on the hill. At 1 p.m., a detachment set out to scatter them before night fell. But after about three miles of pursuit, a spectacular rainstorm broke, unleashing a downpour so torrential that it obscured objects even a few yards away, and in which guns became useless and the path back was lost, with the surrounding paddy fields merging into 'one vast sheet of water'.[65] Seeing that the British muskets had stopped working, the peasant soldiers started jabbing at their enemy with spears. The rearmost soldier was run through and his body quickly dismembered, but otherwise only a major's coat suffered an injury – frayed by a three-pronged weapon.

When the detachments reconvened, however, one company was discovered to be missing, and a rescue mission of marines dispatched. Through the darkness and heavy rain, and after a long and tiring trek, the absent company was found, drawn into a square formation in a sodden rice-field, one private dead and fifteen other men wounded, and surrounded by Chinese fighters who were being kept at a distance by the occasional shot produced out of a hastily cleaned and dried musket. Nonetheless, the Chinese scattered in their thousands as the rescue party approached (giving the 'flying and cowardly enemy a farewell volley', snorted one lieutenant), and the British survivors were back in camp by 9 p.m.[66]

The following day, the locals were out in force again – perhaps 25,000 of them, drawn from maybe eighty or ninety nearby villages, arranged over the conical hills north of the city – but a brisk intervention with Canton's authorities by Major-General Gough (communicating that if the Chinese forces were not persuaded to retreat, the city would be attacked and every neighbouring village razed) ensured that peace prevailed once more. Eventually, out rushed Canton's prefect, Yu Baochun, to inform the gathered militia that 'since peace has been signed . . . you must let the foreigners go.'[67] On 1 June, the ransom paid, the British left Truce Hill, in far more comfort than they had arrived, for Canton's authorities hospitably provided 800 coolies to drag the guns back to the ships.[68]

The Chinese and British versions of just about every engagement in the Opium War contain perplexing divergences and discrepancies – but perhaps none quite as striking as accounts of the events of 29–31 May 1841. As sketched out by a British lieutenant above, these events were merely a gentle excursion turned moderately sour, the slightly bothersome tail-end to the British humiliation of Canton

— the whole engagement is too trivial even to merit a name. In China, by contrast, every schoolchild still knows these events as 'The Sanyuanli People's Anti-British Struggle', or as Sanyuanli for short — after one of the villages from which the thousands of peasant soldiers were drawn. Most of the British versions were purpose-fully coy, or even silent about the motivation behind local fury. One important reason, of course, was the desecration of ancestral burial places; the British had also been vigorously 'foraging' (looting) for days. Much worse, local women had been raped — a fact obscurely referred to by the *Chinese Repository* as 'doings of which it is a shame even to speak'.[69] To the demoralized people of Canton, the incident was instantly mythologized as a triumph: as the spontaneous rising of righteous patriots against the invaders, voluminously commemorated in placards, poems and essays. Each retelling of the story added new, eye-widening details: about how the British howls had filled the mountains and valleys, about how they had kowtowed for mercy, about how the 'tiger-troops marshalled in lines' had 'roared like thunder':

A thousand, ten thousand, come together in an instant.
Because of our virtue, we are angry, and anger has produced
courage.
The locals have united their strength to drive the enemy away.
Every family's fields and cottages need to be protected.
Everyone is inflamed; our passions do not need rallying with
drums.
Women are as brave as men,
Wielding hoes and rakes as weapons.
Teams of multi-coloured banners
Line the mountains and valleys all around.
The foreigners blanch as soon as they see us
. . .
With our hearts united, Heaven lends its help
Sending sudden rain from a clear sky,
To leave the fierce foreigners' guns useless.
They stumble and tumble through the muddy fields.
. . .
Their ugly chieftain stands in the middle of them all
With his elephant skin armour covering his body.

But one jab of a spear pierces his barbarian throat
...
They want to flee, but have no wings,
How easy it is to destroy these villains.[70]

Otherwise objective contemporary chroniclers of the war suddenly
lost their heads when it came to describing the skirmishes near
Sanyuanli at the end of May 1841. Casualty lists soared: to 200, then
300 British dead, creating a total of almost 750 casualties (the British
themselves reported five dead and twenty-three wounded). Liang
Tingnan and others confidently declared that Gordon Bremer (a
British commander who had sailed for India at the end of March to
fetch reinforcements) was among the fallen: 'a fat, swaggering brute'
with 'a head as big as a bucket'.[71] If only the ordinary people had
been allowed to fight, went the subtext to it all, the British (and
their terrifying technology) could have been annihilated. The key role
played by chance – the sudden downpour disabling the relatively
primitive muskets with which the 37th were equipped – was overlooked, or interpreted as a sign of Heaven's favour for the uprising.
Much later, to Marxist historians, it became the perfect prototype of
the spontaneous People's War against Imperialism that justified the
Chinese Communists' rise to power.[72] Today, the rice-field in which
the missing company of the 37th Regiment was trapped has been
long obliterated by Canton's explosive post-Mao building boom, and
the original village of Sanyuanli has become another drab suburb in
another drably developing Chinese city, crowded with concrete apartment blocks weeping grubby streaks of air-conditioner fluid. But
amid it all, there remains a huge, phallic, pale stone 'Anti-British
Monument' reminding all passers-by that 'The Memory of the Martyrs
Sacrificed in the Anti-Imperialist British Invasion Struggle Will Live
Forever!'.

But on closer inspection, this episode exposes the fault-lines,
and not the patriotic cohesion, of the Chinese empire. The warriors
of Sanyuanli and its vicinity might have been fired by fury at the
British, but this was a fury that scorned the rest of Chinese society
– and especially the government. 'We do not need official troops, nor
the help of the state', proclaimed one of the notices generated by the
militia. 'We shall hack, we shall kill, we shall destroy all of you. If

you ask others to calm us, we shall not heed them. We shall do our best to flay off your skins and eat your flesh. Let it be now known that we shall massacre you with cruel ferocity.'[73] Such vitriol would have sent a chill up official spines: if successful, how long would it be before the villagers' vigilantism was turned on the Qing itself?

For Cantonese involved in the fighting of late May 1841 would never forget that while the peasant militias gathered hungry for a second day of battle with the British on the hills and rice-fields outside the city, it was a representative of *their own government* (the prefect of Canton, Yu Baochun) who came to the rescue of the British: 'We do not understand', protested one song, 'why our great net should be opened / And the fish inside, gasping for breath, be allowed to escape? / [Our officials] are like the traitors of antiquity who compromised with the tribes from the north.'[74] Why, in other words, was such a good opportunity wasted? Placards celebrating local valour often devoted more space to denouncing the raping and looting carried out by government officials and forces than British wickedness: 'They're the worst kind of devils: better to die at the hands of the British than at those of the government soldiers.'[75] 'How loathsome', exclaimed a traveller crossing central China who heard the story of Yu Baochun's negotiations, 'that we failed to drum everyone up to joyfully exterminate this army of villains . . . *We* made a mess of frontier affairs *ourselves*. Utterly, utterly odious!'[76] When it came actually to handing over the ransom, the official appointed to do it (again, the luckless Yu Baochun) was so afraid of the consequences for his own safety that he met Elliot secretly and in disguise. But he was vilified all the same. Three months after the fighting, as he arrived in a sedan chair to preside over a local session of the provincial examinations, candidates hurled their inkstones at him: 'We have spent our lives studying the sacred books of the sages. We all know what integrity, righteousness and honour are. We will not sit exams adjudicated by a traitor!'[77]

But if Beijing's officials did not trust the people of Guangdong, and vice versa, neither did the people of Guangdong trust each other. The paranoid obsession that the country was being sold out by 'Chinese traitors' increased through the tense first half of 1841: by the time of the Sanyuanli incident, villagers were hunting supposed fifth-columnists in their own ranks more vigorously than they were pursuing British invaders, with more than 1,200 murdered in the area. One of many who regretted the lost opportunity of 29–30 May felt that while the villagers had the British on the back foot, Elliot should have been taken hostage, to be exchanged not for money, or for unconditional evacuation of occupied forts, but for a Chinese traitor.[78] Treachery rather than foreign aggression, many thought, was the real cancer eating at the empire. Through the summer of 1841, patriotic resistance became a front for the pursuit of vendettas.

And although Sanyuanli's poems and placards officially pro-claimed their anti-British passions, if we pare the motives for the mobilization of late May down to their essentials, the villagers of Sanyuanli rallied to very specific local grievances (raping, pillaging, grave-desecration) rather than to abstract patriotism. If things were otherwise, why did the whole of Guangdong province not rise up against the British, rather than only the villages immediately affected by foreign looters and rapists? It's not surprising that most well-informed, educated Beijingers – thousands of miles from the conflict – remained oblivious to it. More startling, perhaps, is how impossible it is to speak confidently, even, of consistent patriotic, anti-British feeling across the theatre of war – the waterlogged villages and islands of southern China. By the winter of 1841, Daoguang had at last come round to the idea of using Cantonese forces to put pressure on the British in Hong Kong. Yishan was discouraging: they had, he told the emperor, 'no stomach' for a new coastal confrontation.[79] But an eventful boat-trip made by Charles Elliot only six weeks after Sanyuanli shows even more clearly how unconcerned locals were by foreign invasion.[80]

On 20 July, Charles Elliot and General Bremer, newly returned from India with reinforcements, set off from Macao for the British base in Hong Kong. Their timing was bad: by about half-past ten on the following day, a typhoon had washed two of the crew into the sea and blown the ship terrifyingly close to the granite cliff of an unknown island. By the afternoon, the weather had got even worse: the main mast had fallen and surviving crew and passengers found themselves washed up on another (again unidentifiable) island. After they had recovered from their battered ship some food, a tarpaulin and eight much-needed bottles of gin, and spent an appalling night perched on rain-lashed rocks, the whole party – about a dozen of them – set off to find some local assistance. Soon enough, Elliot encountered two Chinese men and recognized one, to his delight, as a boatman from Macao who agreed to take them back there for 1,000 dollars, when the weather improved.

The members of the party were then forced to march, relieved of their arms and all clothing except for their Victorian underpants, over three hills and spent a nervous twenty-four hours in a shed. By the time the sea had calmed, at 8 a.m. on 23 July, the price for the passage back had gone up to 3,300 dollars. Quickly assenting, Elliot and Bremer lay down in the boat and were covered by mats; and all set off. Just as the two Britons were finishing a lunchtime bowl of rice around 2 p.m., their pilot suddenly pushed them back down to the bottom of the boat, quickly covering them over with mats again – moments before an official boat glided by, asking the Chinese crew if they'd come across any shipwrecks of late. No, no, they chirped; and the official passed on. After another couple of hours, Macao was sighted – and the adventurers flagged down a Portuguese lorcha, which took them safely into port. The travellers were unconventionally dressed: before embarking for Macao, their Chinese boatmen had issued Bremer with a 'blue worsted sailor's frock', and Elliot with a Manila hat and a pair of stripy trousers. But they were back safely, to enjoy a hearty meal and a good night's rest. There had been bad times, for sure: uncertainty, discomfort and unpleasantness (at one point, one of the Macao boatmen had expressed a strong interest in removing the ear of Bremer's black servant). But at no point does it seem to have crossed the minds of Elliot and Bremer's Chinese escorts to hand them over to the government, although they knew perfectly well who their passengers were.[81]

Treachery, the Qing might have called it, had they heard about it. But actively to betray a country or cause requires some strength of feeling – a conscious decision (based on calculations of profit or loss, or ideology) to defect to another's side. In many of the war's Chinese bystanders – including Elliot's boatmen – it is difficult to diagnose any degree of partisanship. The Qing had tried various methods to get the locals to rally to the empire against these violent aliens. It had demonized opium as a foreign poison; it had organized villagers and fishermen into ad-hoc defence squads; it could allow the ravages of war to speak for themselves. Most importantly of all, it had tried financial incentives: offering 100,000 dollars for the capture of Elliot; 50,000 for Bremer; 20,000 for a cutter; 200 for a white soldier and 50 for an Indian.[82] Nothing had worked. Elliot's boatmen – based at Macao, just seventy miles down the coast from Canton – were too apathetic about the war even to find out how to profit from it: the 3,300 dollars they charged to bring the British crew back was less than a fiftieth of the money they could have made, *if* they had bothered to pay any attention to the government's ransom notices.

With the city secured, there was nothing left for Daoguang's servants to do but to tell him what had happened – which is exactly what they did not do. Yishan's first wave of lies (dispatched on 23 May) told stirringly of how the Qing army went on the assault on the night of 21 May, of how its soldiers 'hid in the water, then made for the enemy's hulls'. As the fires on board raged (consuming two large warships, four large sampans, several small sampans and a dozen skiffs), 'the cries of the rebellious foreigners could be heard for miles around . . . Countless rebels were killed by cannonfire, or were drowned.' According to Yishan, on 22 May (a day on which, according to Captain Hall, the crew of the *Nemesis* was busily engaged spiking cannon and cutting off – as trophies – the queues of defeated Qing soldiers), the *Nemesis* was forced into retreat, with hardly any Qing injuries to report. 'Excellent . . . tremendous . . . wonderful', scribbled the vermilion brush.[83]

Like Yang Fang before him, Yishan's lies became more fluent with practice, and his version of the peace negotiations of 26–27 May (during which, within twenty-four hours, he crumbled before all Elliot's demands, pledging to 'take full responsibility' for making good his promises; and during which Yang Fang had chatted over the city wall with Hugh Gough, and even thrown down some golden bangles at him as a token of his esteem[84]) was a masterpiece. Although it admitted that the British had (through the timely help of hundreds of Chinese traitors) taken the forts to the north of the city, the rest of the account was almost an exact inversion of what actually happened.[85]

The foreigners outside the walls waved at us, as if they had something to say ... Apparently, they wanted to petition me with their grievances. 'How could our Generalissimo possibly agree to see you?' my general roared. 'His only orders are to make war.' The foreign officers immediately removed their hats and made an obeisance ... Apparently, because the English hadn't been allowed to trade and their goods haven't been allowed to move freely in and out of the city, they were facing bankruptcy ... so they had come to beg the General to communicate sincerely to the Great Emperor that he should take mercy on them, permitting trade and ordering the Hong merchants to make good their debts. Then they would immediately leave the river ... and not make any more trouble.[86]

The whole plan was risky: Yishan was trying to disguise the ransom paid after the defeat as the debts owed by insolvent Hong merchants to the British. Amazingly, it worked. 'The nature of these foreigners', Daoguang sighed on 18 June, after receiving this account, 'is like that of dogs and sheep. It isn't worth trying to bargain or reason with them ... Now they've taken their hats off and bowed, begging for imperial mercy ... I forgive you.'[87] As for the debts, the Hong merchants would cover those. On 30 June, Yishan received imperial authorization, and promptly reported to Daoguang the British response: 'Their commanders were overjoyed, removing their hats and prostrating themselves with emotion, crying out that they would never dare make trouble in the province again.'[88] When, two weeks later, the emperor received this happy confirmation, he ordered the demobilization of the forces he had so expensively convened over the past six months.[89] Everyone was delighted: Yishan's work won him the coveted Order of the White Jade Feather, and promotion or rewards for 554 of his subordinates, while Daoguang could reduce military spending, believing the foreigners had been chastised. And no one needed to feel any financial pain apart from those wretched traitors, the Hong merchants.

What was entirely lost on Daoguang – because Yishan had deliberately not told him, and he lacked the time or energy to corroborate his servant's version of events – was that this new peace applied only to Guangdong. Twice, on both 5 June and 15 July, Elliot emphasized to Yishan that 'the struggle between the two countries is not yet resolved and we still have grievances to settle with the emperor ... we will continue to fight until everything is settled. But we will withdraw our troops from Guangdong ... this province need not fear further injury.'[90] To Daoguang, though, this was no national conflict – it was a trade dispute local to the south. And surely now it was at last at an end; or so he must have thought.

Chapter Ten

THE UNENGLISHED ENGLISHMAN

As Charles Elliot scrambled on shore to Macao, having narrowly escaped a trip to Beijing that would have ended in a slow and painful execution, a surprise awaited him: a reunion with a long-lost brother, Ned, who (in the way of things in the South China Sea) had turned up at Macao en route to Singapore from Sydney. But there was more news. An officer came up and told him the latest from England: Elliot had been recalled, and his successor, Sir Henry Pottinger, was expected any day. 'To be cast ashore at Sanchuen, and find [oneself] adrift at Macao', Elliot is supposed to have responded (struggling, in his Manila hat and striped trousers, to hang on to what dignity he could), 'was more than a man had a right to expect in one week, be he Plenipotentiary or be he not.' After a decent meal and a rest, a line from Dryden came to him: 'Slack all thy sails, for thou art wrecked ashore.'[1] Fresh back from a near-death experience, having spent the last six months leading (often from the very front line of battle) a campaign up the waterlogged maze of the Canton River delta with a price of 100,000 dollars on his head, Elliot now found himself thrown to one side by the country for which he had sacrificed personal safety, profit and family life.

It was perhaps the dismissal of Charles Elliot that marked the true turning point in this war: from here on, the campaign would be more about gunboats than diplomacy. True enough, back in the spring of 1839, Elliot had brayed as loudly as anyone for an instructive war that would 'teach' China to fall in line with civilized European trading norms. But once he'd got his war, he spent a curious amount of time avoiding it: calling regular pauses for talks, for trading, for elaborate negotiating banquets. Violence, he actually believed, was to be minimized at all costs. He was fighting, he argued, 'a just and necessary war; but it is not to be forgotten that the acts of the Chinese authorities which made it so ... [were] preceded by serious errors on the part of British subjects.'[2]

But with Elliot gone, so was any spirit of self-critical compromise. He was replaced by no-nonsense hardliners: professional men of the British army and navy who were there to do a military job – to subdue the Qing empire as expediently as possible – or by representatives of a chauvinistic new breed of rulers of British India. Gone was any sense that sympathy or familiarity with Qing customs or sensibilities might, in the long-term, more effectively open the empire to trade with Europe. No, the Chinese empire wanted blasting into line. 'The body social of the Chinese', one missionary expressed the sentiment well, 'is too inert, too lifeless, for the whole body to be affected by a rap on the heel; it must be on the head.'[3] It was, perhaps, with respect to China that the Victorians began whole-heartedly to embrace attributes that we now think of stereotypically Victorian: a strident patriotism that shouted about the civilizing missions of Christianity and Free Trade, while trampling over other political, economic and cultural visions. Sino-Western relations are still paying the price of the Opium War's quick fix today.

The case against Elliot had started building back in October 1840, when his cousin, Lord Auckland, began agitating – a whole two years before Britain would be finished talking, fighting and ratifying in China – about how long operations were taking. 'I do not like the state of things there, for while all of good result is uncertain, it seems at least to be sure that your ships will be wearing and incurring danger and my fine regiments will be wasting and breaking down on Zhoushan, and a year of expense will have passed, and for all military objects, we may be much weaker than we were some months ago.'[4] While Elliot's cousin George remained on the expedition, the latter carried much of the blame. 'The admiral has made a shocking mess of China', commented Auckland's merciless sister, Emily. '[T]he force and the ships and the money have all been wasted, leaving things just as they were a year ago.'[5] But once George had abandoned the campaign in December 1840 – pleading ill health – all recriminations fell on Charles: for pulling his punches, for being too tender with the Chinese, for allowing himself to be put off, fooled and generally humbugged over and over again. 'The Chinese have bamboozled us,' wrote one London diarist, 'that is the plain truth.'[6]

On 8 April, details of the treaty that Elliot had thrashed out with Qishan on 20 January reached Britain. No sooner had *The Times* rejoiced in the 'Successful Termination of the Affair in China', though, than the disappointed complaints began.[7] 'I am very mad with it all', grouched Auckland from India.[8] Queen Victoria, in a letter to her uncle King Leopold of the Belgians (whose son would later be infamous for his appalling colonization of the Congo), stamped her little foot at the whole affair. 'The Chinese business vexes us much, and Palmerston is deeply mortified at it. *All* we wanted might have been got, if it had not been for the unaccountably strange conduct of Charles Elliot . . . who completely disobeyed his instructions and *tried* to get the *lowest* terms he could.'[9] A letter from a disgusted resident of Macao went into more detail: 'Regarding the terms of Captain Elliot's treaty with the Chinese, I have not temper to speak. He had the Chinese at his feet, and might have done what he wished; and what has he got? A few paltry dollars and a barren island . . . The Chinese are already chuckling, and say they have got the best of it. It makes me quite sick to think of it.'[10] The Chinese, it would seem, had not been terrorized and humiliated nearly enough.

On 20 April, Palmerston sent Elliot a tetchy two-columned document comparing his original instructions with what his pleni-potentiary had actually achieved. He had failed to use occupied territories to extract solid concessions concerning indemnities and extraterritorial rights for British citizens; to agree reasonable tariffs and duties on British imports; to negotiate on terms of diplomatic equality; to open northern ports; to force the Qing to abolish the infuriating monopoly of the Hong merchants. Finally, he had failed to ensure that whatever unsatisfactory agreement he reached was even ratified by the Qing. 'You seem', Palmerston concluded, 'to have considered that my instructions were waste paper . . . and that you were at full liberty to deal with the interests of your country according to your own fancy.'[11] A fortnight later he felt, if anything, even more peeved. 'Her Majesty's Government', he wrote on 3 May to Elliot, 'do not approve of the manner in which, in your negotiations with the Chinese Commissioner, you have departed from the instructions with which you have been furnished . . . her Majesty has determined to place the conduct of her affairs in China in the hands of another Plenipotentiary . . . on the arrival of whom . . . you will accordingly return home at your earliest convenience.'[12]

To this was added the hostility of the British trading community, who were almost united in their ingratitude to Elliot. In their very interests, in March 1840, Elliot had stopped the fighting to allow the season's tea to be shuttled out of Canton, thereby enraging his military commanders, his foreign secretary, his sovereign and the British press. 'Here we are at the island of Hong-Kong', wrote Hugh Gough in April, 'in the most delicious state of uncertainty . . . You are aware the trade is open. Captain Elliot only thinks and dreams of this, as if its being so was the sole object of the frightful outlay of money expended and expending.'[13] (Elliot took a different view of budgetary matters. He estimated that in the two years up to August 1841, his policy of restraint had maintained a trade of more than ten million pounds, generating eight million pounds' worth of customs duties for Her Majesty's Treasury, while the expedition itself had cost a mere half-million pounds.[14]) But were the men of money grateful? Not a bit of it: they set about writing letters to influential London and Indian newspapers concerning 'the indignation and disgust which Charles Elliot's proceedings have excited amongst all classes of British subjects both in India and in China. Not only has he neglected the just claims of private individuals, but he has sacrificed the honour of his country.'[15] They had clearly never forgiven Elliot for making his disgust for the opium trade so *very* obvious before the war. The only trader with a touch of tenderness for Elliot was, improbably, James Matheson, who found it hard to forget that Elliot had, through the manoeuvres of January, agreed to a temporary ceasefire that conveniently allowed a million and a half pounds of Jardine–Matheson tea out of the river and on to London. When Matheson's rivals threatened to petition London with complaints about Elliot's handling of events, he told Jardine to 'pay liberally any lawyer or other qualified person who will defend him in the newspapers.'[16]

By the time that Elliot returned to England from China, in November 1841, public opinion had been poisoned further by the dyspeptic dispatches of Major-General Hugh Gough who – all the while cohabiting cordially with Elliot in Macao and Hong Kong – had written with 'grievous mortification and disappointment' of Elliot's refusal to let him rape and pillage Canton.[17] That winter, everything that Elliot had done was publicly dismissed, demonized or, at best, mocked. The journalist George Wingrove Cooke – who would send poison-pen reports from the front line of a second China war in 1857 – sneered at this 'gallant, wrong-headed little man' unable to understand the basic political and military principle that 'omelettes' were not to be made without 'breaking eggs'.[18] On reporting a rumour that Qishan was to be sawn in half for his role in the reviled treaty, *The Times* commented that 'Elliot's head, trunk, and limbs should be made into a thousand cylindrical sections, as a warning to all his family.'[19] (For years after the war, Qishan believed Elliot had indeed been beheaded by his Queen. 'A dreadful fate, that of poor Elut', he is supposed to have told a French visitor to north-west China in 1846. 'He was a good man.'[20])

For Elliot, the balance of accounts after he left China probably looked something like this. Since sailing east in 1834, he had sacrificed all possibility of normal family life through separations from his children and often his wife. He had been poorly paid: even though his salary was increased from £800 to £3,000 a year when he was appointed plenipotentiary, this was half what was offered to his successor. When he returned to England under a cloud, he had to petition and pester to be paid the rest of his salary and expenses, and to secure himself a pension. Eventually he was handed a governorship in what he termed a 'den of villains, misery, murder & musquitoes' (Texas) as his only future way of earning a living.[21] 'No man', he summarized, 'can rob me of the signal distinction of being about the worst treated public officer of my day.'[22]

But Elliot remained determined to show that he was not bothered, and concentrated on holding his head high at society dinner parties and dances. 'Very amusing with his accounts of China', recorded the diarist Charles Greville a couple of weeks after Elliot's arrival in London. 'He seems . . . animated, energetic, & vivacious, clever, eager, high-spirited & gay.' At a 'grand fancy ball' given by the Queen, he appeared in 'a superb Chinese costume as Commissioner Lin'.[23] What sustained him through this thoroughly awful press? The conviction, perhaps, that he had been right.

Elliot's moderate China policy – despite all the stops and starts it had brought to the war (at the height of the Canton crisis in April 1841, Gough called him 'whimsical as a shuttlecock') – had a careful scheme behind it. For Elliot was fundamentally pessimistic about what could reasonably be achieved in China, preferring to measure success not by the criterion of how much could be won, but rather by that of how much mischief had been prevented. 'The least that is necessary for your purposes in China is best,' he mused, after the signing of the tough Treaty of Nanjing in 1842, 'and those purposes, or that purpose, is the security of your trade. A safe seat for your commerce is all you require in China, and all you can have without damage to yourselves . . . Avoid political combinations as much as possible, and endeavour rather to link yourselves to the people and system of China (wonderfully pliant) than force them into your Pall Mall fashions and usage.'[24] Free trade secured by Hong Kong, then, would slowly but surely solve all Britain's problems with China: winning over local populations by appealing to their pocket-books and letting the Chinese quest for profit slowly open the rest of the country.

Defending himself against the charge of excessive tenderness towards the Chinese, he riposted that this 'was a war in which there was little room for military glory . . . success must be attended with the slaughter of an almost defenceless and helpless people, and a people which . . . was friendly to the British nation.'[25] At times, this belief verged on the paternalistically imperialist, as he daydreamed optimistically about the love and respect that the Cantonese could reasonably feel for people who were, at best, money-grubbing foreign traders, and at worst, terrifying invaders. The people of Canton, he wrote in April 1841, 'so dependent upon Foreign Trade, have been pushed by the Court to the verge of endurance, and when we had happily placed ourselves in a situation of mastery over Canton, it at once became manifest that the local government had no choice between immediate exclusion [of British merchants] with the hearty dissent of the masses of the people . . . or an immediate, direct, and formal disregard of the Emperor's will.'[26] In blasting his way up to

Canton in the *Nemesis*, Elliot felt he was absolutely acting in the best interests of the local Chinese.

For all this self-delusion, Elliot did think it important not to humiliate the Chinese utterly. The British should demand recompense for what they had lost in the destruction of the opium – but anything more would be counterproductive. Much better for the long-term to bank good will than hard cash. Therefore, to finish the war on the terms negotiated with Qishan in January 1841 was quite sufficient. Six million dollars would do for the opium and the costs of the expedition so far. The Hong debts did not need pressing: such was the easy, informal understanding between British and Cantonese merchants before the war that, Elliot believed, the whole business was best resolved privately. Crucially, Britain had raised the flag on Hong Kong, with its exceptional harbour, and usefully close but safely distant position from the mainland, which (Elliot confidently predicted) would become 'within a very few years one of the most important, and perhaps the most interesting possession of the British Crown'.[27]

There was plenty of common sense behind Elliot's policy of moderation. No particular military genius was required to work out, given the state of things inside Canton in late May, what would have happened if the British had stormed its gates. At best, occupying the city would have tied up soldiers needed for operations elsewhere. At worst, Elliot predicted 'the disappearance of the municipal authorities and the police, the flight of the respectable inhabitants, the sacking of the town by the rabble, its certain desolation, its not improbable destruction by fire, and our own hurried departure from the ruins.'[28] The army was furious to have been denied a chance of plunder, but Elliot was sure that if the city had been taken, the six-million-dollar ransom that he successfully extracted would have swiftly melted away: 'The Chinese rabble are expert looters.'[29] His gentle influence was celebrated in Canton: 'Elliot! Elliot!' one Briton said he heard boomeranging around the walls on 26 May while rumours of a ceasefire comforted the terrified city, 'as if he had been their protecting joss'.[30]

Ultimately, though, Elliot's policies won him few friends on either side of the conflict. 'Everybody wonders what will be the next news', wrote Emily Eden on 12 April 1841. 'Probably, he will prevent Sir Gordon Bremer from taking Canton, for fear it should hurt the feelings of the Chinese, and the Emperor will probably send down orders that our sailors are to wear long tails and broad hats, wink their eyes, and fan themselves, and Charles Elliot will try to teach them. I don't think my national pride ever was so much hurt.'[31] 'Much travel', Elliot himself admitted, 'has pretty nearly unEnglished me, and the generous treatment I have received in [Britain] has not kept alive so much of my prejudice as to prevent me looking at things there much as a foreigner might do.'[32] And of course in China today, he remains the arch-villain of the conflict: the enemy of oppressed colonial peoples everywhere.

But in early 1841, there was still a chance that a moderate line would prevail. In January, even the petulant Queen Victoria could accept that there was a moral high ground to be gained by restraint: 'it will be a source of much gratification to me', she remarked, opening Parliament on 26 January, 'if [the Qing] Government shall be induced, by its own sense of justice, to bring these matters to a speedy settlement by an amicable arrangement.'[33] Up to this point, there was more than one way to define 'national pride'. Back in March 1840, when the war in prospect had been so bitterly criticized in several of the country's newspapers, there were many who felt that the national honour was committing suicide by even contemplating conflict with China on such grounds. But even after the decision to go to war had been taken, professional men of war were still capable of taking a relatively nuanced view of the effects of violence: 'the object was to gain our point by firmness and determination,' wrote the campaign's military secretary in 1841, 'but they do not imply rapine and bloodshed . . . war, undertaken against a nation so puerile in that art, would better deserve the name of murder, and could certainly add no laurels to British valour.'[34]

On the eve of Elliot's recall, on 2 May 1841, the views of the Prime Minister, Lord Melbourne, were out of step with those of his infuriated foreign secretary. 'Palmerston is, or was, for disavowing Elliot and the treaty . . . I have grave doubts of this. The treaty as it stands saves our honour and produces all the necessary moral effect. To renew the war would keep the whole thing alive, which it is of the utmost importance to close [and] the Chinese will be convinced that we never meant to observe that or any other treaty.'[35]

'POISON UNPAID FOR', an Irish newspaper mocked those disappointed at Elliot's January treaty. 'The war with China is, for the present, over. No more European money, or Oriental blood, is to be expended this year in the promotion of immorality, and the extension of colonial empire.'[36] The Whigs were, Chartist papers declared, 'ruffian-poisoners'.[37]

But some time between the outraged lampooning of the proposed 'Opium War' in April 1840 and the summer of 1841, many British – their politicians, parts of their press, Queen Victoria herself – seem to have shed their moral uncertainties. They now fixated on extracting what they felt was due to them (without consideration of any point of view except their own, uniquely civilized one), cheering any feats of 'gallant' modern violence that furthered these ends. Seeing off a new admiral of the China expedition in May 1841, the Lord of the Admiralty looked forward to meeting him next, 'somewhat richer than you are now, some three years hence, when you will return to us . . . loaded with the spoils of China.'[38] An underlying cause of this change seems to have been economic, as much as particularly political or sinophobe: the cavernous budget deficit that the Whig administration had generated. Two arguments had allowed the proposal for war with China to squeeze its way past Parliament: that it would be quick, easy and cheap; and that, once it was done, it would secure all-important revenues from the China trade. When reports from the front claimed swift 'brilliant successes' in Zhoushan and Tianjin, and that the Elliots had been 'received with distinction' by the emperor, public opinion for the government's war just about held out: 'Such are the great results,' smugly declared the government, 'accomplished by means of little wars.'[39] While the dispatches were full of success, *The Times* preached mercy: if only Britain's war party could remember that although the Chinese 'have tails on the top of their heads, and round faces, and no whiskers, yet really are not made of paste or earthenware, but have life and flesh and nerves and sensations, and a sense of justice, and that they who kill 100 Chinese kill 100 men . . . we might perhaps hear a little more about Chinese peace and contentment, harmless dispositions . . . and difficulties of understanding the necessities of foreign nations, and less about stagnation of intellect, dogged unsociability, servility and idleness.'[40] But when reports about the fleet's withdrawal from north China and about

Elliot's moderate treaty with Qishan revealed in early 1841 that the
plenipotentiary had agreed that only six million dollars of British
costs would be covered while a quarter of the thousands of men on
Zhoushan had died of sickness there, or were unfit for service, the
whole business became an embarrassingly 'unsuccessful' contest. If
there was one thing worse than an 'inglorious', 'immoral', or 'disgraceful' campaign, it was an 'ineffectual' one. 'The expense incurred
by the country in maintaining that drivelling expedition has been
enormous', *The Times* now declared. It was 'an insult to our military
prowess . . . a foul scandal to our diplomatic arrangements.'[41] 'Without going into any defence of our hostile demonstration against
China,' reasoned a correspondent in April 1841, 'we had declared war
against her . . . and it was necessary to prosecute it to a successful
termination.' He thought Elliot's decision to protect the 'defenceless
and helpless people of Canton' frankly weak-kneed. 'It was impossible
to make any distinction between the people and her government,
or to forego any measure that could distress both.'[42] This theory of
civilized warfare went thus: the harsher the British were, the sooner
the war would end, the better for the Chinese. 'Something approaching to absolute terror must be inflicted', opined one of the armchair
strategists of 1841, 'before arrogancy so great, and self-confidence
so deeply-rooted, can be expected to give way . . . There is now,
unhappily, but slight apparent chance of terminating this affair
without the infliction of some fearful specimen of the horrors of
war.'[43] Far from humanizing the Chinese, newspapers now turned
them into fairy-tale cartoons: the emperor became 'the embroidered
doll'; his officials 'flurried petticoats'; while the granite fortifications
in which hundreds of soldiers had been gunned down or burnt alive
were 'gingerbread forts'.[44]

For sure, it was Palmerston and the rest of his 'miserable Cabinet'
– rather than the unwitting Qing empire – that such public opinion
really meant to round upon. 'Can anything be more degrading to
British arms than a Whig expedition like this?' asked *The Times*,
while the Conservatives mocked the Chancellor for 'sitting on an
empty chest, fishing for a budget.'[45] Knowing this, though, would
not have brought much comfort to those subjects of the empire who
felt the heat of British impatience between 1840 and 1842. By the
close of hostilities with Canton, when Elliot estimated that around

5,000 Qing soldiers had lost their lives, the British troops were growing increasingly inured to large-scale slaughter of the Chinese, and impatient at their plenipotentiary's regular hoisting of the white flag. Back in 1839, a novice sailor had fervently hoped he would never see battle again, after the two-hour Battle of Kowloon. On 8 January 1840 (while the British command tried to instruct the Chinese in 'the different usages of civilised warfare'[46]) an army surgeon commented that 'the appearance of [the] flag of truce was very disheartening to all who, flushed with the success of yesterday, and not satisfied with the quantity of human bloodshed, were eager to dip their hands more deeply into it.' The next day, a group of sailors were dispatched to pile Chinese dead – around 200 of them – into a pit. 'The road to gloary', ran a board they fixed over it.[47]

And so it was that, in early summer 1841, Elliot was recalled and replaced by Henry Pottinger, a fifty-one-year-old veteran of the British Indian Army and intelligence services with a luxuriant moustache and a determination not to 'allow himself to be humbugged', as the Canton press introduced him to the foreign community out there: 'A better man you could not have', they added.[48] (Accompanying him was a new admiral, William Parker, who so reviled tobacco that he wouldn't let any of his sailors touch the stuff on board. Heaven only knows what opinion he had of opium.) So far in China, one commentary wearily announced, 'every succeeding negotiation has only served to show the faithless and reckless character of the Celestial Government [while] our humanity has only passed for cowardice.'[49] Pedagogical imperialism was the new fashion for the campaign. 'At present,' considered another editorial, 'Sir Henry is teaching them the A, B, C of international and maritime law. No doubt his pupils are by no means over docile; but still, by seeing the enterprising character of British commerce, and the amazing powers of steam navigation, as well as the overpowering equipments of our naval and military forces, the probability is that a conviction of their prodigious inferiority may at last dispose them to be . . . more deferential to strangers . . . redounding ultimately to the common benefit of mankind.'[50] The appointment of Pottinger was one of Palmerston's last acts as foreign secretary, before he was ousted in the summer's general election. The Conservatives – who had argued so verbosely against the war – swept into power on a wave of criticism of the campaign's meekness; and therefore committed to prosecuting it with new ruthlessness.

In a depressing way, the hardliners were right. The emperor, as it turned out, would not authorize true plenipotentiaries, with authority to negotiate and settle on his behalf, until – a year later – the British had reduced key garrisons along the east coast to rubble, and were preparing to do the same to the empire's second city. By this point, Britons would be shooting disarmed, fleeing Chinese soldiers 'as coolly as if they were crows, and bayoneting to death those who fell wounded'.[51] The common benefit to all mankind, indeed.

Chapter Eleven

XIAMEN AND ZHOUSHAN

Between the last days of August and the beginning of September 1841, Daoguang could contemplate another thick and rather confusing bundle of correspondence. It began on 23 August, when he received a message from the Governor of Zhejiang reporting a rumour that the British ships were on their way north and were intending to attack Zhoushan again. Would it therefore be all right, the governor asked deferentially, to ignore His Majesty's command of 28 July to withdraw the soldiers garrisoning the coastal defences? Daoguang's response was characteristically parsimonious. 'Get on with demobilizing the soldiers, to save on supply costs.'[1]

On 5 September, a little more information arrived – a memorial from Yishan, the hero of Canton, composed on 23 August. A new English leader had arrived, apparently: just a new superintendent of trade, probably, by the name of Pu Ding Cha. Although Yishan had sent the Prefect of Canton (the ill-treated Yu Baochun) over to Macao on 15 August to meet him, this Pu Ding Cha had already sailed north 'to beg for ports'. Yu Baochun had sternly informed his deputy, a certain Ma Gong, that now – thanks to the emperor's benevolence – the old trade system could be restored and that Pu Ding Cha had no business going north to make further demands. Ma Gong, therefore, should hurry after him as fast as he could to stop him. The Englishman had, apparently, nodded repeatedly at the sagacity of the plan and promised to do his best, but observed with regret that since setting out, Pottinger had been sped on by fast southerly winds and he might already have arrived. Still smarting at his dismissal (Ma

Gong had told Yu), Elliot had taken revenge by concealing from Pu
Ding Cha the fact that Yishan and the emperor had permitted the
old trade to restart down in Canton, thereby fooling his successor into
setting off up the coast to make new trouble.[2]

What could it all mean?

Probably that, as usual, Daoguang's most trusted subordinates
had been systematically misleading him. On 27 August (nine days
before Yishan's memorandum reached Daoguang), a whole new island,
Xiamen, on the east coast, had fallen to British guns, under the
leadership of the new plenipotentiary, Sir Henry Pottinger. Daoguang
would find out about it only on 13 September. By 5 September (the
day that the emperor read Yishan's report), the British were leaving
Xiamen to occupy Zhoushan, and two new ports on the mainland.

This is perhaps what really happened. On 10 August, Pottinger
had sailed into Macao. On 12 August, he announced to the fledgling
colony of Hong Kong that 'the slightest infraction [by the Qing] will
lead to an instant renewal of active Hostilities . . . such an event is
. . . highly probable, from the well understood perfidy and bad faith
of the Provincial officers themselves.'[3] The next day, he dispatched
his secretary, Malcolm (Yishan's Ma Gong), to Canton to carry letters
to the authorities there, explicitly outlining his purposes in sailing
to China: that he was fully invested, by the British government, to
negotiate for the terms stipulated in Palmerston's first letter to the
Emperor of China, and that until those terms were met, the British
fleet would continue to make war further north. Worst of all,
Pottinger wanted the Canton authorities to report *all of this* to the
emperor in Beijing.[4]

At this, Yishan may well have panicked – for Pottinger's
announcement threatened to blow his earlier tissue of lies to pieces.
On 18 August, he had sent his subordinate, Yu Baochun, to Macao
to have emergency words with Pottinger. But in a deliberate parrot-
ing of the Qing haughtiness that had so infuriated earlier British
envoys, Pottinger flatly refused to see any Chinese official who was
not authorized (as he was) to negotiate on behalf of his country's ruler.
Bravo, applauded British expatriates and officers, who took a childish
glee in the snub. 'Alas how are the mighty fallen!' crowed the captain
of the *Nemesis*. In Pottinger, he rejoiced, the British at last had a man
who acted 'with an intimate knowledge of the Oriental character'.[5]

On 21 August – seven days after Yishan claimed – the fleet had left for Xiamen, the bustling, prosperous port island off the coast of Fujian. Yishan, yet again, had lied virtuosically to the emperor: about who Pottinger was, about the 'submissiveness' of the British, about the reason for the fleet's departure north. Yet again, thanks to the best efforts of his representatives, Daoguang was no closer to understanding who the British were and what they wanted.

If Elliot's accusers carped that all his years in the east had 'orientalized' him – leaving him too soft on indigenous sensibilities – probably the reverse could be said for his successor to the China job. By background, the two men were not so very different. Pottinger began his career with establishment credentials every bit as impeccable as Charles Elliot's. The Pottingers were an old Anglo-Irish family, who claimed direct descent from Alfred the Great's grandfather. Through much of the eighteenth century, the clan was well established at Ballymacarrett in a mansion they had grandiloquently dubbed Mountpottinger. But by the birth of Henry in 1789, the family's fortunes were looking a little shakier: most of the holding at Ballymacarrett had to be sold off in 1782; in 1811, Mountpottinger also had to be relinquished, eight years after Henry – along with four of his brothers – had left to seek fame and fortune in India.

Once in India, Henry proved himself a faithful servant of often dubious British interests and ambitions. Throwing himself into the patriotic adventure of the early Great Game, he was dispatched to Baluchistan and Sind, the Indian kingdoms that gave onto Afghanistan, and therefore the buffer zone between British, French and Russian imperial interests, to explore and survey these regions with an eye for political opportunity. Out there, he made himself very useful, filling his reports with statistics, geographical information and scornful generalizations about the 'Oriental character'. The tribes of the Sind he found 'avaricious, full of deceit, cruel, ungrateful and strangers to veracity', while the local women were 'usually ugly'. As for the Persians, he noted, 'good faith, generosity and gratitude are alike unknown to them'. With a strong-minded consciousness of the national dignity that he would showcase in China, he refused to rise to show respect to the emissary of a local ruler.[6] By the late 1830s, while Britain's first war against Afghanistan brewed, a chance to strengthen the British position presented itself. As an honourable climax to Pottinger's India stint, in early 1839 the governor-general charged him with turning the tribal rulers of the Sind into taxable subjects, to help finance Britain's ventures in Afghanistan; by 1 February, a Bengal army had secured the British just that. Pottinger's only dissatisfaction with the agreement he had authored was its lack of honesty, for the final treaty paradoxically claimed to leave the Sind 'in separate independence under British protection'. 'It would be better', argued Pottinger, 'at once to take possession by force, than leave it nominally with the Ameers, and yet deal with it as our own. One line is explicit and dignified and cannot be misunderstood; the other I conceive to be unbecoming to our power, and it must lead to constant heartburnings and bickering, if not to a rupture of all friendly relations.'[7] Fine, steal their sovereignty, he seemed to be arguing; but unless we are clear and open about it, the natives will be unhappy. By the time he reached China, Pottinger was, in a pretty fair recent summary by a Chinese historian, 'an old hand at colonial invasion activities in eastern countries'.[8]

Despite Yishan's valiant attempts to stifle all embarrassing intelligence, when the British fleet was sighted advancing up the east coast, the man in charge of Fujian province, Yan Botao, did not panic. For months, like most Qing officials involved in the fighting with Britain, he had been largely disregarding his emperor's orders – and especially those directing him to dismantle defences in Xiamen.

Before the trouble with the British had blown up, the island's defences had been negligible. To the south, the 'Big Fort' had been manned by a grand total of twenty-five regulars. Another thirty kept an eye on the north-west, from the 'Fort of the Lofty Peak'. Service on the 'Yellow Burial Place Fort' – from which a single soldier surveyed the south-east approach to the island – was presumably reserved for misanthropes. But in the early stages of the war, almost

3,000 extra soldiers and militia had been drafted in. When Yan Botao reached the island in early 1841, he added a mile-long granite wall along the south coast and sank into it 100 cannon. New forts were built to east and west, and filled with extra soldiers and cannon. By the end of the process (which consumed one and a half million ounces of Qing silver) the cliffs of Xiamen swarmed with some 15,000 men under arms, and more than 400 new cannon. 'If the foreigners are determined to die,' Yan boasted to the emperor, 'we will be left with no choice but to attack them all the more fiercely. We won't let a single one of their ships or men survive; we will express Heaven's condemnation and rejoice the hearts of all men.'[9]

Around 1.30 p.m. on 26 August, the British artillery assault began. A couple of hours later, the Nemesis approached the beach and disgorged its infantry, who scrambled up Yan Botao's famous wall on each other's shoulders. Once the attackers were on the wall (the first act, naturally, being to fly the flag), most of its defenders (some of them dressed as tigers, in yellow uniforms with black spots and stripes, and tiger-head helmets) fired a couple of shots then exited. One cliff-face fort was taken by a single officer rushing up the hill and through its open gate, discharging every firearm he had on him at the forty or fifty soldiers he found there, 'lolling and smoking [opium, presumably] between their guns.'[10] Without hanging around long enough to notice his lack of reinforcements, the fort's defenders rushed out of the opposite gate and back down the hill.

That evening, the British troops camped out on the cliffs; the next day they simply entered the island's abandoned city (one of the country's richest ports), with little to do except resist the temptation of abandoned vats of rice liquor and to tut-tut at the rapacity of Chinese robbers, who had already thoroughly looted it (its bullion had been ingeniously smuggled out inside hollowed logs). How extraordinary, the captain of the Nemesis exclaimed, that the massive bombardment and occupation of the island should lead to a general collapse in law and order. The only protection that locals had to look for 'from the violence and plundering of their own rabble,' Captain Hall remarked, 'was from the presence of our own troops'.[11]

In other words, it was an Opium War battle like any other. Inside the walled city, watching the disaster unfold on 26 August, Yan did the only thing that a man in that situation could reasonably have done. He burst into tears and ran away.

But for Pottinger, Xiamen was just a diversion – it was not even part of Palmerston's instructions. Zhoushan was the island he was supposed to be retaking.

This time, though, Daoguang was confident he had the man to keep things in hand: Yuqian, a fiery Mongol whom he had appointed in February 1841 his third Imperial Commissioner against the British. Yuqian had a good deal in common with an earlier, ill-fated incumbent of the job, Lin Zexu – indeed, the two men were firm friends. Both had worked their way up the examination system then landed, through reputations for strict, impartial application of the empire's laws, a series of senior posts: Yuqian had been appointed governor-general along the rich east-coast provinces of Jiangsu, Jiangxi and Anhui in 1840. But while Lin – a man of humble beginnings made good – exemplified the workings of the Qing imperial meritocracy, Yuqian was a member of the steppe aristocracy, born into Genghis Khan's very own clan, the Borjigit (and therefore descended originally from the coupling of a Blue Wolf and Fallow Deer). Yuqian personified the cosmopolitan ideal desired by the great Qing emperors Kangxi, Yongzheng and Qianlong: a pure-blooded descendant of nomadic warriors who excelled also in Confucian culture. But there was a flaw in the Qing's grand ambition to create omnicompetent scholar-soldiers. It was supposed that just because Yuqian possessed an exceptional military pedigree (both great-grandfather and grandfather had fought valiantly for the conquest of Xinjiang in the Mongol Bordered Yellow Banner – the former committing suicide after suffering defeat), this expertise would flow naturally into him, even though his own life had been spent mastering China's elaborate literary traditions. In practice, against the British, it turned out that his ancestors' skill-set would prove harder to tap into.

Like Lin, Yuqian was full of self-confidence. Within a few weeks of his receiving his Imperial Commission, he had impeached two fellow officials for advocating compromise with Britain (Qishan and a genial, elderly imperial relative called Yilibu). Both wound up on trial in Beijing: the former sentenced to beheading, the latter to banishment. Yuqian had only hatred for the importunate British and contempt for anyone who dared to suggest that they could not be 'utterly exterminated'. All this, of course, was exactly what Daoguang wanted to hear: he wanted certainty – and this was a particularly trouble-free form of it. For Yuqian blamed all the defeats and failures of the war so far not on inconveniently large, long-term causes that would take years to remedy, but on something far simpler: on a failure of nerve. The problem with a traitor like Qishan was that he had 'panicked' and 'fallen into the traps of the rebellious robbers': as a result of his 'soothing', the rebellious robbers had been feasted and gifted like honoured guests, and had their every whim and request attended to. 'These days', Yuqian pronounced, 'our ministers are all mediocre and cowardly . . . The English are simply treacherous merchants . . . There was no need for Qishan to talk them up as he did, enabling them to bend the country to their will.'[12]

Thus Yuqian's medicine for the ills of Qing China was simply for the people in charge to stiffen their upper lips and get on with vanquishing the British. He was unable to forget the chastening statistic that in the fall of Zhoushan the previous year, only twenty-six Qing soldiers had perished; the rest had run away before they could come to any harm. 'The nations of the West', he wrote, with wonderful élan (given that he had never set eyes on the British army or navy), 'know nothing but material profit. They have no other skill than trade . . . no culture, law or education. Nor does England have enough power to capture cities or seize territory in other countries.' Inconveniently, he admitted, they did have very large, powerful ships that made victory against them at sea impossible. Therefore, he concluded with assurance, the Qing must fight them on land, for the enemy 'cannot use fists or swords. Moreover, their waist is stiff and their legs are straight. The latter, further bound with cloth, can scarcely stretch at will. Once fallen down, they cannot stand up again.'[13] After he was appointed to defend the east coast in February 1841, Yuqian would get an opportunity to test this strategy.

The six months he spent in Jiangsu preparing for the British only strengthened his assumptions. Three days before he arrived on 27 February, the British had voluntarily evacuated Zhoushan, under Charles Elliot's orders, to fulfil the January treaty with Qishan.

Joyfully concluding that the British were terrified of him, Yuqian proceeded by executing four locals accused of working for the British occupiers the previous year (as compradors or informants), sending their severed heads on a public tour of the island, to educate the rest of the population in the perils of treachery. He dug up a hundred of the English who had died of fever or dysentery, chopped up their bodies then threw them into the sea. And in March 1841, he captured an English captain who had mistakenly landed on Zhoushan with supplies for the already departed forces. The man, Stead, was tied up and publicly sliced to death, his head displayed to the masses. A few months later, an English captain and Indian sailor from an opium boat were taken prisoner. The captain, while still alive, had his arms and back flayed (Yuqian had the skin fashioned into reins for his horse), then was sliced to death. The Indian was treated more mercifully, his head being flayed (and, again, displayed to the masses) only after it had been removed from his body.[14] In the mood to be militant, Daoguang approvingly waved these decisions through: 'You did the right thing', he scribbled on the memorial recounting Stead's death. 'Admirable fixity of purpose', he wrote of the business with the reins.[15]

There was little new about the way Yuqian prepared for a British assault: three miles of thick mud walls, up to sixty feet wide and thirteen feet high, were built along the exposed southern coast of the island. And once the hard work of construction had been done, and 5,600 soldiers and militia stationed there, Yuqian could indulge in the traditional pastime of giving hopeful names to his fortifications. Two gates set into the wall were dubbed 'Stable Governance' and 'Long-term Peace'; a fort on top of a hill in the middle of the earthworks became 'The Fort That Terrifies Those From Afar'.

Yuqian was even more pleased with himself than usual. 'The British threat is now completely under control', he crowed to Daoguang. 'If the foreigners were to dare approach the coast, or try to get on land, to exterminate the lot of them would be an easy matter – not one of the robbers' ships would return home.'[16] As he still believed that the British could not fight on land, most of the island's troops were concentrated around the south coast; the British, he was sure, would never make their way past his defences. The island's much larger, mountainous interior was merely scattered with a few barracks and look-out posts. Neither did he have a realistic sense of the power of the British ships and artillery. 'Our cannon can hit the British,' he groundlessly reassured the emperor, 'but their cannon cannot hit us!'[17] Well-informed Chinese historians, by contrast, were sceptical about Yuqian's military talents: 'He was hot-headed', sniffed Wei Yuan, 'and totally ignorant of warfare . . . nothing was done at all, let alone anything sensible.'[18] The biographer of the *Nemesis* saved a strong Victorian insult for Yuqian's earthworks, finding them 'unscientifically constructed'.[19]

In Yuqian's reports, the struggle for Zhoushan in October 1841 was an epic six-day battle, in which a 5,000-strong Chinese army, despite bravely damaging and repulsing the English ships and 'killing countless foreign bandits', was eventually defeated by massively superior English forces – of 10,000, 20,000, perhaps even 30,000 soldiers.[20] In English accounts, the whole affair is far less effortful and far more clinical: after five days of reconnaissance (involving the odd skirmish, the odd exchange of fire), a fleet of seven warships and four steamers began to pound the Chinese coast in the time-honoured fashion at dawn on 1 October. Obstructed by nothing other than some unhelpful tides, the *Nemesis* landed the infantry, who – protected by the steamer's fire – clambered up the hills behind the earthworks and, after some fairly energetic hand-to-hand fighting, occupied the forts there. Once the coastal defences had been cleared, the troops climbed up the hill that overlooked the city of Dinghai, admired the view, set up their guns and began firing on the city. Then the Chinese scattered out of the north gate and into the island's interior. By 2 p.m., with 'three British cheers . . . the British flag at last proudly floated over the fallen city.'[21] The English reported two dead, and twenty-seven, or perhaps twenty-eight wounded; they estimated that 'many' of the 5,000-odd Qing forces perished. 'The inhabitants of [Dinghai]', observed one British lieutenant complacently, 'quickly recognised their old friends, and appeared very happy at seeing them return. Before three days had elapsed a good market was established, and everything went on as quietly as if we had never abandoned the place.'[22]

*

For the time being, Yuqian was too busy to brood over this catastrophe. For Pottinger was already moving on to his next target, before the winter closed in: to Zhenhai, Yuqian's own headquarters and the citadel that guarded the river approach to the final British objective of 1841, the large port city of Ningbo. Yuqian had not taken nearly as much trouble defending Zhenhai as he had Dinghai, for he thought its natural position made it impregnable. On either bank perched a fort; across the mouth of the river stretched about a mile of muddy shallows – the very thing for snaring deep-bottomed British gunboats, Yuqian had thought to himself on his arrival earlier that year. And if the invaders were forced to attack in smaller boats, or to land, they could easily be picked off by the fort's batteries. Just to cover himself, though, in June Yuqian had added a smattering of new forts around the crags guarding the entrance to the river. 'No need to panic', he wrote to Daoguang.[23]

Yuqian's main concern remained the courage of his men – if he could secure that, he thought, all would be well. As the start of hostilities approached, he considered only a quarter of his 4,000-strong garrison to be trustworthy. On hearing that the British were gathering to attack Zhenhai, therefore, he summoned his officials to a pre-battle sacrifice and libation. 'The rebellious caitiffs are running counter to the Covenants of Heaven', he swore before them. 'They won out in Guangdong and Fujian because we were not prepared . . . You must fight to the death . . . Our orders are to punish . . . if anyone dares take a foreigner's letter to Zhenhai, they will be executed according to earthly laws, then killed again by the spirits in the darkness of the afterlife.'[24] Yuqian's rousing speech, unfortunately, failed to stir one key member of his staff: his chief commander, Yu Buyun, another old warhorse who had fought alongside Yang Fang against Jehangir's jihad. Refusing to kneel to take this solemn, warlike vow, Yu now told his superior that he was not, on reflection, in favour of fighting, supporting his point of view with a personal list of mitigating circumstances: his wife was unwell, he had no son, his foot hurt. 'We should put the British on a loose rein', he argued – in other words, negotiate and offer concessions. Yuqian was having none of it. 'If you want to retreat to Ningbo,' he hissed at Yu, 'you can make your own explanations to the emperor. If Zhenhai falls, I fall with it!'[25]

While the Qing struggled to contain their disarray, the British advanced on a carefully arranged battle-plan. At daylight on 10 October, two battleships, a frigate and three sloops moved into position near the north and south banks of the river-mouth, and began pounding all the forts in sight. Such was the power of the British guns, the ships could halt safely out of range of Qing cannon along the shoreline and still obliterate the forts over the city. By a quarter past eleven, landing parties protected by this fire had scrambled onto the bank and up to the fort on the hills overlooking the city of Zhenhai, and the Union flag was flapping over its walls. Nothing now stood between British guns and the city itself, beyond a set of enclosing walls twenty-six feet high. A few volleys scattered the last of the defenders and the walls were scaled to the east, while Chinese civilians and soldiers fled out of the western gate. Yu Buyun (who had been entrusted with holding the heights on the northern bank) ordered his men not to fire their guns, hung out a white flag of surrender, then bolted down the hill, his men following not far behind. When Yuqian spotted this – from his vantage point on the eastern edge of the city walls – he let loose some of the city's cannon on his fleeing subordinates (who are said to have responded by detouring out of range round the far side of the mountain).

Meanwhile, Major-General Gough was seeing off – with clinical brutality – a 5,000-strong force on the southern bank. Gough divided his army of 2,000 into three parts: the left and right flanks advanced, unseen, under cover of rising ground, leaving only the central third visible. Once the Qing soldiers had been lured out into range to meet this reduced force, a tremendous fire from the concealed left and right wings erupted. After a few moments of utter confusion 'at what appeared to them a most wonderful increase of force', reported a British lieutenant, 'they gazed around in stupid and motionless amazement' then tried to flee, tripping over the bodies of the dead and dying. Many tried to escape upriver but the rifle fire was too good for them. Soon, the water was running red.[26] One and a half thousand Qing soldiers perished, ran one estimate; at most, sixteen British were killed and a few wounded. Civilians, inevitably, suffered too. The lieutenant also noticed a family of four children struck down by a single shot, their grief-stricken father torn between embracing their bodies and trying to drown himself. 'The unavoidable miseries of war', he laconically observed.[27] By 2 p.m., the battle was at an end.

Yuqian now came down from the city walls, kowtowed towards Beijing in the far north-west and tried to kill himself. Even this, though, he did not manage successfully, choosing to drown himself in a small stone-edged pond. He was easily fished out by his retinue, resuscitated and rushed west out of the city. At some point along the way, he seems to have taken poison (probably opium); he died the following day. In death, as in life, Yuqian was the ideal Confucian warrior super-hero: killing himself rather than submit to his enemies. But his suicide made the final collapse of Qing resistance inevitable, as chaos now spread through the ranks. As Yuqian was rushed inland towards Ningbo, his retinue swelled with hundreds of bodyguards, soldiers and other hangers-on looking for an excuse – any excuse – to escape the carnage at Zhenhai. The roads out of the city were choked also with civilians. 'As they trampled one another,' recalled Yu Buyun, 'the sounds of weeping were everywhere, while evil bandits took the opportunity to rally their gangs and go out on plundering missions.'[28]

On 13 October, four steamers and four warships under the command of Admiral Parker sailed fifteen miles upriver to the province's second city, Ningbo. Arriving at 2 p.m., they found the city completely ungarrisoned: its defenders, including Yu Buyun, had long fled. A report Yu wrote a week later was full of grand talk about his gallant struggles with the enemy, in the course of which his right leg had been partly crushed by an enemy shell: 'he must have fallen and hurt his leg in his anxiety to run away', one Chinese historian has acidly speculated.[29] The British ships anchored against the city walls, the troops hopped out, and by 3 p.m., without a shot being fired, the band of the 18th (Royal Irish) was playing 'God Save the Queen' along the walls of the city.

With yet another city lost, all the emperor could do was find someone to blame. Daoguang's first instinct on hearing of the fall of Zhenhai on 18 October (the conflict with the British was now considered sufficiently troublesome to justify the expense of top-speed couriers between Beijing and the theatres of war) had been to punish Yuqian. But when news of his suicide reached Beijing a few days later, the emperor decided instead to heap him with posthumous honours (canonization, hereditary ranks for his descendants, a temple erected to his memory in Zhenhai once the war was finally over) and elaborate funereal sacrifices. 'He did not disgrace himself before his fellows', Daoguang commented approvingly.[30] So Yu Buyun replaced him as scapegoat-in-chief, eventually losing his head on Chinese New Year's Eve, 1843.

Still the notion persisted that if only the Qing had not been betrayed from within – again – the battle could have been won. Liang Tingnan saved some of his strongest vitriol for Yu Buyun: 'He was the first to run away,' he wrote, 'from one bolt-hole to another, and led others to follow his bad example. And then he slandered others to deflect blame from himself.'[31] 'The dastardly Yu Buyun', agreed Wei Yuan, 'reported to the Emperor that poor Yuqian had been the first to flee, and spread a report that the foreigners had attacked Ningbo in order to avenge the death of the white foreigner, whose head had been stuck on a pole during the summer by Yuqian.'[32] And despite thousands more deaths, the emperor still had little more idea about what the British wanted by it all – whether the attacks on Zhoushan and Zhenhai were about trade, vengeance for the execution of their countrymen, or something else altogether.

Chapter Twelve

A WINTER IN SUZHOU

There is no record of the exact whereabouts of Daoguang's nephew Yijing, or of what he was doing, when he was informed on 18 October 1841 that the emperor had a new assignment for him. Perhaps he was in his study, practising his excellent calligraphy, or dashing off one of the eleventh-century-style ink-blob paintings at which he was so proficient. Or he may have been reviewing, as Commander of the Beijing Constabulary, patrol rosters for the coming winter. Then again, he was possibly considering – like the diligent Director of the Imperial Gardens and Hunting Parks that he was – whether the bonsai needed an extra pruning before the frosts set in. All this he was to abandon straightaway, for he was now the Awe-Inspiring General, under imperial orders to depart immediately for Zhejiang, to direct the counter-assault against British-occupied territories, and bring Zhoushan, Zhenhai and Ningbo back into the embrace of the empire.

It was a decision that would probably have taken most people by surprise (including Yijing himself), in part for the speed at which it was made. Daoguang had only received news of Yuqian's death that very day, and for the emperor to bypass his usual working parties, consultations and multiple changes of mind was unusual. But it was unexpected principally because Yijing would have seemed such an unlikely choice. Only fifty years old in 1841, he at least had youth to recommend him, relative to a Guan Tianpei or a Yang Fang. But he did not have much else – and certainly no track record as a competent war-maker. Up to this point in his career, Yijing had lived to the full the closeted, privileged life of the senior Imperial Clansman: advancing quickly and easily through the Special (simplified) Examinations for Sons of Princes, and into a succession of low-risk, high-ranking official posts – of which the Imperial Gardens directorship was probably one of the most comfortable.

After the war was over, even Daoguang amid his recriminations would recognize the sheer wrong-headedness of giving his nephew the task of exterminating the foreigners. Refraining from executing Yijing for overseeing the disasters of spring 1842, he would – almost unprecedentedly – blame himself for having chosen someone with such flimsy military experience to direct operations against the British.

Yijing began well enough, managing to leave Beijing less than two weeks after receiving his new appointment, and reaching the rich, picturesque canal-city of Yangzhou a mere eighteen days later. After this prompt start, though, he paused, 200 miles further south-east, in equally lovely Suzhou. And there he stayed for the next two months. Suzhou during the Qing dynasty was a fine place to pass a winter (or spring, summer and autumn): a serene maze of canals, villas and elaborate gardens, peopled by over-educated pleasure-seekers dining, drinking, listening to operas, cultivating their rock gardens and honing their poetry-writing skills. 'Mangtachwan', a secret agent working for Henry Pottinger, helpfully summarized in late December 1841 what he felt that the British needed to know about their new adversary: 'Yijing, imperial nephew and Commandant of Peking . . . Generalissimo and first Imperial High Commissioner for the Affairs of Zhejiang, is a man of pleasure, fond of ease, presents and bribes and a real courtier. He has not made up his mind what course to pursue.'[1]

Yijing's style was a bewildering change from that of Yuqian's. While Yuqian forced his reluctant underlings to swear solemn vows to resist unto death or face the wrath of the spirits, the Awe-Inspiring General (to begin with at least) could not even make up his mind whether or not to fight the British. 'Just after the general had left the capital,' remembered one of his camp aides, 'he wavered between whether to soothe or to make war. After hearing about how ineffective recent attempts to offer amnesty to the rebels had been, though, he feared they were damaging to the country's prestige, and pledged to fight.'[2]

But how to fight? That was another question altogether, requiring an entirely different, and far more extensive decision-making process. To that end, after arriving in Suzhou, the new general had a wooden box placed outside the camp gates, into which volunteers could drop proposals – a total of some 400 were received and 144 new advisers acquired, who promptly began swaggering about the place calling themselves Junior Commissioners. (When war finally seemed to be drawing close, the box of suggestions disappeared at their orders, in case any uncomfortable comparisons were made between suggestions and actions.) Yijing's aides were far more eager to enjoy Suzhou than to make war, drinking, whoring, extorting and banqueting their way through the winter. A piece of doggerel doing the rounds gives a sense of popular esteem for the morals of the military machine that had descended upon the south-east. 'The prostitutes of Hangzhou brag the loudest / Next year, they say they'll all give birth to little Junior Commissioners. / After them come the prostitutes of Shaoxing. / Next year, they'll have little soldiers. / Pity the poor weeping whores of Ningbo. / Next year, they'll all have little foreign devils.'[3]

The amiable Yijing offered wonderful profiteering opportunities to the unscrupulous. When accused by one of his subordinates of fecklessness, he frankly admitted that he had not a clue what was being spent on the campaign.[4] His filing system was extraordinary: communications were passed to his secretaries, who promptly put them in an attic where, in the way of things stashed in attics, they tended to get lost. Any documents that survived were donated at the end of the campaign as scrap paper to an old friend. When it came to putting together the official report on the counter-assault, the extant financial records were found to be so compromisingly fraudulent (the auditor 'knew full well that the emperor must not get to hear of any of it') that they were all thrown away, the accounts fabricated from scratch and the silence of those in the know secured with bribes.[5] One disreputable character by the name of E Yun (described by fellow officials as 'an inveterate scoundrel – there was no act of malfeasance below him') – won himself a slice of the budget by talking the gullible Yijing round. Through 1842, E Yun pocketed at least 12,000 ounces of silver nominally to hire, feed and reward local militia to whom he failed to give any training and who ran away on 1 April.[6] The situation begs the question of what kind of political and social community Qing China was, that a bloody struggle against foreign invaders should for so many become an unmissable opportunity to fleece the government and to dispatch ignorant, untrained members of the populace to almost certain deaths. 'The whole system of Chinese policy', noted Pottinger in late November 1841, 'shows that whatever may be the feelings of the emperor towards his subjects, the mandarins and all the government officers are indifferent to their affairs, further than suits their own purposes.'[7]

Yijing's best excuse for not moving was that he was waiting for reinforcements drawn from all over China to make up a 12,000-strong force to be unleashed against the British. By the second week of February, almost all of them had arrived. Whether they were actually worth waiting for seems less certain. Many were exhausted, having travelled hundreds of miles to reach the theatre of war. The journey had taken its toll on discipline, too, and on local populations who — according to Qing convention — were expected to supply the troops as they passed through. 'The soldiers stole doors as litters,' remembered one account, 'and forced the people to porter them, four civilians to one soldier. They entered the camp on their backs.'[8] (This comfortable style of military travel was copied, a century later, by Mao and other Communist leaders on their Long March up to the north-west in 1935.)

And of course this combined force — drafted in from eight different provinces (400 men from Henan, 600 from Nanyang, 1,000 from Shaanxi, 1,000 from Gansu, 800 from Ningxia, 800 from Guizhou, and so on) — would again suffer from the regional fragmentation that had ended so badly in Canton. Even senior officers refused to take orders from Yijing's central command. The new arrivals — drafted in to replace Zhejiang soldiers who had bolted in September and October the previous year — were unfamiliar with the climate and territory in which they would be fighting. 'They got ill from being in a new place,' remembered one camp aide, 'and wanted to go home.'[9] The accumulation of so many soldiers — without family or local attachments to restrain them — edged the province towards civil war. 'Generally speaking,' observed the captain of the *Nemesis*, 'the collecting of any considerable body of troops together in any particular province or locality in China, so far from strengthening the hands of the authorities, is more likely to occasion disturbance among the inhabitants . . . Little confidence being placed in their regular soldiers . . . the people were now called upon by the authorities to collect their brave men from all the villages and hamlets along the coast . . . in most instances, these bodies of uncontrolled patriots became a scourge to their own neighbourhood'.[10] A sleep-deprived British officer in Ningbo grouched about the nocturnal clatter of the city's ad-hoc local police force, who struggled to intimidate would-be robbers by knocking two pieces of bamboo together while out on patrol.[11]

In mid-February, a Chinese spy reported to the British, 'the troops were in a state of mutiny for want of pay and proper provisions . . . the heavy exactions of the Mandarins have driven the people . . . to a revolt, and a considerable force under Manchu officers have been detached to quell this insurrection.' The army was formidably large, revealed another spy, but its principal strength consisted in 'bands of robbers who are relentless ruffians and live by open plunder.'[12] After getting lost while out on patrol, soldiers from west China were mistaken for Europeans and attacked by another Qing division – three were killed in the clash.

Theoretically, though, by early February (a mere three and something months after he had left Beijing), Yijing had under his command the best sort of army he could hope for. Truly, he now had no reason for not getting on with the war. The attack had originally been scheduled for 9 February, and all was ready by then: the battle-plan worked out, the troops in place. More importantly, Yijing was aesthetically prepared for triumph. After months of painstaking work, the camp painter had produced a prophetic painting entitled 'All Goes According to Plan'. Keen also to mobilize the many literary talents among his staff, Yijing had held a competition to solicit the most elegant and stirring announcement of victory. 'Never had such prose been seen in over a thousand years!' sighed a camp aide. Nothing, it seemed, had been left to chance; all that was left was to 'count the days and wait for news of victory'.[13]

9 February, however, came and went. A council of war was held,

at which the other officers urged him to fix a time for the assault:
'I shall let you know as soon as I have determined on a day', Yijing
stalled them.[14] (The Awe-Inspiring General, another spy told the
British a few days later, was willing to bribe them to leave Ningbo
and 'to take the credit of having driven us from that city'.[15])
Something was clearly troubling Yijing – perhaps the gods were not
smiling on the venture. On the following day (New Year's Day),
therefore, he took himself to a nearby temple of the God of War to
pray for victory, and check that the spirits were happy with everything. The lot that he drew informed him that

> If men with the heads of tigers do not greet you
> Your security cannot be guaranteed.[16]

On 13 February, one of the final units arrived: some 700
Sichuanese aborigines, decked out in their traditional tiger-skin
tunics, their heads crowned with tiger-heads and claws, and trailing
tails. This, an overjoyed Yijing decided, was the oracle's sign: he
must launch his attack at the Hour of the Tiger (between 3 and
5 a.m.), on the Day of the Tiger in the Month of the Tiger
(10 March) in the Year of the Tiger (1842) – a traditionally auspicious
date for Chinese warfare. It had worked in 589, for a general fighting
to reunite China after centuries of invasion by foreign tribes; it could
therefore work in 1842, also. As to who should lead the assault, it
did not really matter – as long as, again, he was born in the Year of
the Tiger.

On 6 March, then, Yijing finally began to move out his men, and
sent a 4,000-word memorial to the emperor, detailing his confident
master-plan for victory: 'I shall enforce discipline and sweep the
rebellious barbarians from the face of the earth. I shall cut off the
heads of Pottinger, Gough and Parker and present them to your
Majesty that they may be exhibited throughout the empire. Whilst
they are still alive, I shall eat their quivering flesh and sleep on their
skins. Thus my indignation will be vented, the laws of the country
vindicated, and the foreigners taught to look up with awe to the
glory of the Celestial Empire.'[17] (A little earlier in his warlike
preparations, according to counter-intelligence, he dispatched to the
British a spy disguised as a merchant 'to learn on what terms we were
disposed to treat'.[18] He also tried casting a tiger skull-bone into a

Dragon Pool, to persuade the dragon to swim up and attack the British.) 'Great success is inevitable', noted Daoguang at the bottom of it all.[19]

In the meantime, as they waited for reinforcements to arrive and the cold weather to pass, the British set about passing as healthy a winter as they could, amid the knee-deep snows of eastern China. The day would start early, with a cold bath to get the circulation going (a British habit that Liang Tingnan noted with some perplexity). Under-exercised officers set up racecourses with Chinese ponies, or stalked partridge. One of our military witnesses to the Opium War – Lieutenant J. Elliot Bingham – seems to have had a taste for musical theatre, when army business permitted. As he began his chapters on the manoeuvres of winter 1841 (for a published account that must have proved popular – by 1843, it was appearing in a second edition), he quoted as an epigraph a rousing chorus refrain from an 1825 classic of the London stage, Henry Bishop's *The Fall of Algiers*: 'England conquers but to save / And governs but to bless.'[20]

How natural it was that, as Bingham smugly reported, local populations who fell under British rule should be so 'perfectly contented with their new rulers, every kind of excess or plunder being rigidly prohibited.' How regrettable it was that the good, peace- and prosperity-loving burghers of Ningbo, Zhoushan and Zhenhai should have been so badly let down by their less virtuous countrymen: 'from the mandarins having forsaken their posts,' he observed, 'all government in the neighbouring districts was upset, and large bands of robbers were formed, by the lower orders of Chinese, who plundered in every direction.'[21] The curious thing about the British occupation of parts of eastern China through the winter of 1841–42, though, is how many members of the local population responded by staying peaceably put and by supplying the English not only with goods or services, but with crucial military information about the Qing counter-offensive.

Soon after the city fell, Karl Gützlaff – that useful clergyman – was installed as magistrate for the occupation regime in Ningbo, single-handedly dealing out summary justice to local petitioners, who knew him by his Chinese name of Guo Shili or, more familiarly, as Daddy Guo. 'He has no scribes to assist him,' ran a piece of commemorative doggerel about his legal talents,

Although he consults no paperwork,
No one has ever settled court business as quickly as Daddy
    Guo.
From the court floor,
A cry of complaint is heard . . .
Without a word, Daddy Guo takes up his stick and waddles off.
In just another moment, he returns, dragging a felon to be tied
    up before the table of judgement.
He bares the criminal's back and gives him fifty lashes.[22]

When Gützlaff was not keeping the peace, he was directing an extensive network of Chinese spies – variously identified as 'Li', 'Mangtachwan', 'Blundell', 'Norris' – that he had begun cultivating as early as 1832, on his first illegal interpreting missions up the east China coast in the pay of the East India Company and opium-smugglers. The Foreign Office archives of the campaign are stuffed with their invaluable intelligence: frank personality profiles of the Qing leaders ('void of talents and too old for his situation', 'the most arrant coward'), military budgets, grain supply routes, numbers of soldiers in various garrisons, troop morale, divisions in the ranks.[23] 'Yijing's soldiers are not to be depended upon,' went one report, 'and they will likely run away, on the very first onset; nor do the Mandarins at present place much reliance upon their army. When the Tartar General at Hangzhou was requested to draw off his forces to defend the approaches to the city, he planted a hundred-odd guards around his camp and said: "with these, I shall protect myself against friends and foes, and if you (the commissioners) insist upon my moving from this spot, I shall point these guns at the city." '[24] Other collaborators went further, offering suggestions for strategy, and military help against oppressive local authorities. 'My ambition', wrote one fifth-columnist to Gützlaff, 'is to lead forth an auxiliary Chinese Army when you advance upon Shaoxing and Hangzhou. There are many brave men who will join your forces . . . Yuqian, the commissioner, deceived us. Your success against this cruel man shows the protection of Heaven . . . Yours is the day: and by obtaining such fortune, it is evident that you will be able to end the war [on your own terms].'[25] Through his agents, Gützlaff even learnt of the disguise (white quills) to be worn by Chinese agents infiltrating Ningbo and Zhenhai before the counter-attack on the cities began.[26]

What kind of men were they, to betray the great Qing empire to a Pomeranian preacher? Some were desperate rebels, clearly doing it for the money alone: making up stories where necessary, serving happily as double agents to maximize their profits. Others again were more respectable. One of Gützlaff's first collaborators was a frustrated examination candidate who swore to serve Gützlaff 'like a horse or dog' if only he would pay for him to travel to Beijing to take the civil-service examinations.[27] Another was a physician who sat in teahouses picking up scraps of information for which he got paid a dollar or two apiece – one of which choice titbits turned out to be the correct date of Yijing's counter-offensive. Another was apparently well-connected enough (being excellent friends with the lieutenant-governor of Zhejiang) to escape punishment on being exposed as a spy.[28]

Clearly troubled by the epidemic of espionage that had broken out, the Qing authorities tried hard to woo back local populations. By the winter of 1841, the problem was seen as so severe that simple cash rewards would no longer work. Anyone who distinguished himself in guerrilla attacks against the English, ran one edict, 'will be reported to the Emperor and ennobled . . . Traitors who betray our martial preparations shall be seized, decapitated and their heads exposed . . . do not allow yourselves to be beguiled by [the foreigners'] wiles, but meet stratagem with stratagem . . . Come the spring, and our great army will have assembled with refreshed vigour and destructive guns, and we shall then with the rapidity of lightning, sweep them away from the face of the Earth. In the meanwhile, return to your homes and keep our plans secret.'[29] (Naturally, this confidential edict was obtained, translated and lovingly archived by Gützlaff.) On 5 February, Gützlaff noted that 'authentic information was received that a chosen band of Robbers had left Hangzhou for Ningbo with the object of taking away the lives of Pottinger, Parker and Gough, in which case they are to be promoted to the ranks of officers, to receive a donation of 10,000 taels of silver, and to have the choice of the greatest beauties in the empire.'[30]

But the British still felt constantly under menace from local populations who – given the slightest opportunity – would kidnap, mutilate and murder foreigners who wandered more than a safe distance from camp. Of the garrison stationed at Ningbo, perhaps forty-two were carried off during the winter, several of them killed, with others kept as hostages until the following summer of negotiations. A captured private was found tied up in a bag: 'a large walnut, with hair wound round it, had been forced into his mouth, the sides of which were cut to admit it. He was quite dead.'[31] The business was 'repugnant to the feelings of civilized nations', commented one British lieutenant.[32] As the occupation went on, relations deteriorated to the extent that it became unsafe for soldiers to walk alone through the narrow streets of occupied Ningbo.

None of this was particularly surprising, given that the British occupiers seem to have viewed local Chinese principally as sources of raw material (labour, food, clothing), their sole test of worth being how readily, cheaply and efficiently they produced these things. And if goods were not voluntarily surrendered for ready money, recalled one matter-of-fact lieutenant, 'we were obliged to have recourse to the plan of taking a few respectable inhabitants and detaining them as hostages . . . till a fresh supply of bullocks was brought in.'[33]

For all the pragmatism of some collaborators, there could be little affection between the two sides, with British aggression and Chinese humiliation begetting resentment and hostility. A field officer's account of his wanderings through the streets of Ningbo nicely expresses the spiral of contempt. 'While in one of the shops in the suburbs one of the crowd that followed us threw some orange peel, which struck my cap . . . Another day I was insulted again . . . I avenged myself by a few blows with the flat of the sword.' Because of his adversary's padded winter clothes, he regretted, 'I might as well have beaten a pillow. I have always carried a good stick since then, to break the noddle of the next Chinaman who shall trespass on my dignity. They are a most insolent race.'[34] If the Chinese, he later mused, 'look grave, we say, "See the sulky villain." If, on the other hand, they smile, we exclaim, "Oh, the hypocrites" . . . In addition to this, some of the soldiers . . . if no officer is by, purchase things at their own prices, and beat and ill-treat [them]. Is it wonderful they do not exactly *love* us?'[35]

And in spite of the success of the British military manoeuvres in the autumn of 1841, Pottinger was making no diplomatic progress towards bringing the war to an end. Without enough troops to press on with the campaign, and without any official response to their demands to treat with a plenipotentiary, the British were stuck in their occupied cities, their 3,000 men fragmented into penny-packet garrisons. Through the winter of 1841–42, Pottinger sent two official letters to his Qing counterparts – neither was acknowledged as received because the Qing camp had failed to procure a qualified translator to mediate. The Awe-Inspiring General's Cantonese interpreter turned out only to understand spoken, not written English.[36]

Yijing's plan in early March was to storm simultaneously all three of the territories occupied by the British in Zhejiang: Ningbo, Zhenhai and Zhoushan. Some 36,000 men were to hurl themselves at the western and southern gates of Ningbo; 15,000 were to rush Zhenhai, a dozen miles downriver; another 10,000 were to cross the sea to Zhoushan. (To back up the 12,000-strong professional army, Yijing had supposedly hired around 90,000 peasant militia.) The true numbers available looked very different. Many of the soldiers officially on the campaign's registers were simply not ready to take part in the attack. A quarter of the 12,000 sent to Zhejiang were immediately diverted into garrison and defence duties on arrival: Yijing judged half the 2,000 troops from nearby Jiangxi to be unfit for battle, for example, and set them to guarding granaries instead. When it came to positioning troops for the assault, Yijing moved out a total of only around 8,000 for the attacks on Ningbo and Zhenhai.[37]

However historically auspicious the Tiger Day of the Tiger Month may have been, it was a terrible time to make war in south-east China. The early days of March are when the knee-deep snow and ice of winter turn into slush. And as bad luck would have it, 10 March 1842 had been preceded by days of rain. 'The roads and paths were deep in mud', remembered one of Yijing's subordinates, as men, carts and cannon slogged into their positions. 'More than half our porters deserted before their job was done.'[38] The army advanced through an eerily emptied countryside: alienated locals had run away with all their provisions, leaving the under-supplied troops without access to food. Cold, wet and hungry, they waited for the attack.

Astonishingly, Yijing's chronic indecisiveness almost worked in his favour. By 9 March, the British had received so many intelligence reports about the imminent start of the counter-attack that they had ceased to believe any of them. A successful surprise assault on Ningbo, therefore, was still possible. The three-mile-long walls around the city were too long to maintain a tight sentry patrol – particularly at the dead of night. But in the dark hours of the morning of 10 March 1842, just enough mistakes were committed by Qing forces to bring the British into a state of tolerable readiness.

After a couple of gunshots along the river at 12.30 a.m., and a botched attempt to launch fire-rafts at the ships moored on the river outside the city, the British garrison was under arms. At 4 a.m., a solitary Chinese figure approached the west gate, holding in his raised hand a lit torch. The British sentry told him, in some version of the local dialect, to go away; he carried on his way towards the gate. With a single musket shot, the Chinese man was dead, but the south and west gates were now rushed from within and without. The attackers to the south pushed swiftly up towards the city's central marketplace, where they were driven back by British gunfire. The battle was more prolonged at the west gate, where a force of around 140 British troops faced off the greater portion of the Ningbo assault squad – probably at least 3,000 Chinese soldiers. For hours, the fighting was hand-to-hand, with desperate British soldiers hacking lumps of stone out of the city walls to hurl down at their attackers. As dawn arrived, though, a single howitzer – set up twenty yards from the Qing force – saved the occupiers. Squeezed into a narrow, straight street, the mass of attacking divisions provided a continuing supply of new targets for the new gun. The effect was 'terrific', observed one campaign-hardened officer of the awful scene. 'The enemy's rear, not aware of the miserable fate which was being dealt out to their comrades in the front, continued to press the mass forward, so as to force fresh victims upon the mound of dead and dying'. By the time the howitzer fell silent – after only three rounds – there was a 'writhing and shrieking hecatomb' closely packed for 'fully fifteen yards'.[39]

At the front of this pile lay the bodies of the Sichuanese aboriginal fighters. Although they were dead-shots at 100 paces, they had brought only long knives on the assault. Yijing had ordered that muskets and cannon should be used as little as possible, to reduce civilian casualties; the non-Chinese-speaking aborigines had misunderstood this as an order to bring no guns at all. As British looters picked over their bodies, small purses containing six dollars were found on each – Yijing's reward to them for having arrived with their tiger-skin caps on 13 February to fulfil the prophecy. 'Bad luck to ye!' one Irish private cursed a corpse with a crushed skull, 'ye've bin an' spint one of 'em; here's only five.'[40] Five or six hundred Chinese troops were lost; no British deaths were reported.

The Qing were convinced that treachery had again brought them low. The English, reported Liang Tingnan, had 'enticed the Qing army into the city with the help of a Chinese traitor, while they exited by another gate.'[41] There was probably some truth in this. Yijing had placed extravagant amounts of trust in an equivocal individual called Lu Xinlan, a former canal-maintenance official and resident of Ningbo who had gone over to the British for (according to one estimate) half a silver dollar. During the winter of 1841–42, though, he had secretly written to Yijing, pledging that the people of Ningbo could be organized into dare-to-die ambush teams at the cost of 5,000 ounces of silver, and convincing the general that retaking the city would be 'as easy as turning over your hand'. 'Though only half of what he said had any basis in reality,' remarked one exasperated onlooker, 'Yijing reported it all to the emperor as if it were all reliable.'[42] None of Lu's guerrilla fighters materialized in the confused early hours of 10 March. (To be fair to him, he short-changed the British as ruthlessly as he did the Qing. Just before the attack on Ningbo, he convinced Gützlaff to give him 60,000 strings of copper cash to convert to silver in the nearby countryside. He was never seen again.)[43] A simultaneous attack on Zhenhai that morning was repulsed after a small boy slipped the British interpreter in the city a note warning the garrison to prepare for an attack.[44]

But incompetence was to blame as well as premeditated treason. Reinforcements from deep south China for the attack on Zhenhai got lost in the dark, and did not come within even seven miles of the city until lunchtime on the day after the attack had failed. (It was very windy and rainy, went the excuse.[45]) A messenger entrusted with top-secret information for Yijing about organizing Chinese resistance within Ningbo similarly lost his way. When he asked a passing postman for directions, he was misdirected north; the battle for Ningbo was long over by the time he at last straggled into camp.

It never seems to have occurred to the leadership to do anything but panic once things started to go wrong. As thousands ran from British guns in Ningbo and Zhenhai, Yijing's chief-of-staff fell asleep over his opium pipe and had to be carried off, catatonic, on a litter. Around 13 March, rumours spread of a second-wave attack on Ningbo. By the time the British had rallied for it, the Qing commander in question (Yu Buyun again) had reconsidered and was leading his troops in full retreat west. Yijing – who had, in any case, according to some estimates retained some 60 per cent of the best troops as a personal bodyguard – soon followed, running inland to Hangzhou, presumably pausing only to scoop up four tubs of rare orchids that he had received as a gift during the campaign, and that he had sworn always to take with him in his personal baggage. (He would later explain this flight to Daoguang as 'going to check on the defences of the hinterland'.[46]) By 6 April, Gützlaff's spies were telling him, 'the population have changed the title of Yijing to the "Retreating" instead of the Terror-Inspiring General', and 3,000 disgusted Qing troops were offering to go over to the British. 'Do not delay offensive operations', they advised the invaders. 'We are acquainted with all the roads, and shall be able to render you effective service. Being discontented with the Manchus, we make this offer from the heartfelt desire of serving your cause and not from a wish to acquire riches.'[47]

But at least some kind of attempt was made to retake Zhenhai and Ningbo. The same could not be said for Zhoushan. The soldiers that Yijing had selected to cross the sea to seize the island were from landlocked north China, and suffered too badly from seasickness to be of much use in a naval manoeuvre. Seaworthier fishermen from the coastline a little further north were drafted in at the last moment to navigate, but turned out to be timidly unfamiliar with the rocky outline of Zhoushan. The expedition was planned to commence at 4 a.m., but the tide was against the fleet; by the time it had turned, news of the debacles at Ningbo and Zhenhai had leaked out, and the crews apparently 'lost heart', and spent the next month 'cruising aimlessly up and down the coast, unable to muster the nerve for an attack'.[48]

The forces that survived the massacre at Ningbo – 8,000 Qing perhaps (many of them sumptuously dressed in the black and purple velvet of the imperial guard's uniform) – made a final stand just eighteen miles north of the city, amid a fluttering mass of tents and pennants in the hills that enveloped the small walled town of Ciqi. Despite the Qing army's advantages of height, the British – about 1,200 of them, supported as usual by field artillery – swarmed across rice-fields, and up and around the slopes on which the Qing soldiers were positioned. Surrounded on all sides by 'bayoneting and hewing' British forces, the hills and nearby fields were soon 'thickly covered with the bodies of the slain'.[49] Refusing to surrender, 500 Qing soldiers – the elite of the army – were said to have died on the battlefield alone. Including those cut down in the retreat (most of the fugitives were picked off by musket-fire, or by the *Nemesis*, waiting its moment in a nearby creek) the total probably rose to around 1,000; three Britons were killed and around twenty wounded. Perhaps 80 per cent of the Qing wounded died in agony: although one of the regional commanders had a 'metal-wound drug', there was no wine in the camp to mix it into an application. 'We sat by helpless, watching our comrades die', remembered one observer. 'Even now, the thought of it tortures me.'[50] (British observers claimed that many of the wounded who later died did so because they had taken too much opium to steady their nerves.[51]) By the end of all this carnage, the British rank-and-file were fully battle-drunk. In one paddy-field near Ciqi, two sailors and a soldier stood in an equilateral triangle whose sides were around fifty yards long, picking off helpless, barely armed or entirely disarmed Chinese soldiers with musket-fire. 'If we don't kill them now, Sir,' a fourth man told an appalled observer, 'they will fight us again, and we shall never finish the war.'[52]

As he ran, Yijing would have had plenty of time to decide how he was going to explain to the emperor what he had done with all his silver (by this point, the war had cost the empire around 30 million ounces of bullion) and his tens of thousands of men. Exaggeration and fabrication seemed the best option. Four or five hundred British soldiers had been killed, including their chief Palmerston, he triumphantly told his sovereign. But the British had fielded 17,000 (rather than their actual 2–3,000) men and Chinese saboteurs had burnt to the ground Qing camps (that had in reality been abandoned by fleeing officers).[53] The best tale of all was told of the battle for Zhoushan that never was. Yijing might have overlooked the fact that the flotilla had spent much of March and half of April floating up and down the coast trying to avoid attacking anything at all, had the fleet's commander, Zheng Tingchen, not been given 220,000 dollars of the campaign budget to cover his costs. This was a large sum of money for which to have nothing – not even a humiliating defeat – to show. Under threat of court martial from Yijing, therefore, Zheng obediently reported on 13 April a stunning naval victory over the English in which one large man-of-war and twenty-one smaller ships had been burnt by fire-rafts, and 200 English drowned and countless more burnt to death. (In later accounts of the engagement, these figures swelled to five men-of-war and to 600 drowned foreign sailors.) The alleged triumph (unsubstantiated in British accounts) was so welcome to Daoguang that it quickly won Yijing the coveted award of a double peacock's feather.[54] It was also so improbable that – embarrassingly for Yijing – Zhejiang's governor, Liu Yunke, openly challenged its veracity.[55] Pushed to defend the truth of it himself, Yijing lamely argued that 'so much time had passed, and so much water had gone under the bridge. If we were to prevent courageous men of action from getting timely rewards, I fear it would inevitably dampen morale . . . No further investigation required.'[56] To Yijing's relief, on 7 May the British voluntarily evacuated Ningbo to push on towards the Yangtze, an act that enabled Yijing to boast to his uncle that his forces had 'forced the British troops – terrified at the advance of the great Qing army – to retire.'[57] Finally, Gützlaff learnt from his secret agents, Yijing completed a report to the emperor 'in which he spoke in high praise of the victories obtained by the Imperial Troops at Ningbo, Zhenhai and Ciqi. Liu Yunke alone refused to sign such a tissue of falsehoods, but the joint commissioners and Yijing put their seals to it and it was dispatched.'[58]

Yijing's punishment would come in time – in the form of Daoguang's inability to decide what to do with him. Months after the final peace treaty had been signed, in December 1842, Yijing would be summoned to Beijing to await judgement of his conduct of the war; about two weeks later, he was ordered instead to remain in the south, to prepare a financial report on the campaign; within another couple of days, yet another command hauled him to the capital under arrest, on charges of wasting resources. His hangers-on now vanished – only a few members of his high-living entourage accompanied their disgraced, manacled Awe-Inspiring General on even the first 150 miles of his doleful return to the capital. Back in Beijing, he was first imprisoned to await execution; then saw his death sentence repealed, as Daoguang sank into a post-war crisis of self-doubt and declared himself responsible for the defeats. Eventually, Yijing was sent – like Lin Zexu and Bao Peng before him – to Xinjiang. In 1853, he died of malaria.[59]

Other survivors of the manoeuvres of spring 1841 were less fortunate. Before the assault on Ningbo, Yijing had made room in the budget to buy nineteen monkeys: the idea was to tie firecrackers to their backs then fling them onto English ships moored nearby. 'But the fact was,' a truth-telling observer pointed out, 'no one dared go near enough to the foreign ships to fling them on board.'[60] After the final rout at Ciqi, their keeper fled, leaving the attack-monkeys of Ningbo to starve slowly to death in his front lodge.

Chapter Thirteen

THE FIGHT FOR QING CHINA

As Captain Hall of the *Nemesis* approached the garrison port of Zhapu in the middle days of May 1842, he seems to have been overcome by pastoral rapture: at its 'rich, luxuriant, well-watered plain', its 'curiously-shaped blue-tiled roofs' and 'remarkable hills'. The whole panorama, he rhapsodized in conclusion, reminded him powerfully of 'the prettiest parts of Devonshire.'[1] Although Zhapu lacked the carp-filled lakes, pagodas, gardens and artfully landscaped hills of the provincial capital, Hangzhou, it had grown well-heeled on trade with Japan and Korea. Within the town's three-mile-long walls some 8,000 Manchu Banner families lived quietly in picturesque rows of whitewashed, bamboo-fenced houses.[2]

In 1645, the area had seen some of the most appalling massacres of the Manchu conquest. After the Qing armies' ten-day rampage through the beautiful, fallen city of Yangzhou, its canals and bridges were choked with the dead – more than 800,000 Chinese bodies, tradition told, had been cremated. (Though these pillaging forces also included ethnic Chinese soldiers under Manchu command, and local bandits.[3]) But with this punitive 'pacification' completed, the Manchus had more than made their peace with China's wealthiest region. As elsewhere in the empire, the new dynasty scattered Banner garrisons along the coast, to establish pockets of Manchu authority over the majority Chinese population. Theoretically, in a town such as Zhapu, the Manchus were divided from the Chinese by an internal wall sectioning the garrison off in a northern corner of the city. In reality, the Bannermen of Zhapu, like all the east-coast garrisons,

209

quickly absorbed the comforts of the region. The first generation to settle there after 1644 had been sons of Nurhaci's warrior elites: tough, loyal archers of the north-east. By 1689, when the Kangxi emperor noted a peaceful coexistence between Bannermen and locals, this most civilized of Chinese landscapes had tamed its conquerors. Even the climate seemed designed to subdue the Manchus: their homeland's bitter winters (where temperatures sank to around minus twenty) and cool summers were now replaced with almost frost-free winters and indolent summer heat. The vigorous emperors of the high Qing – especially Kangxi and Qianlong – were themselves seduced by the charms of the east coast. There, they built pavilions from which to admire the moon; they composed odes to the beauty of Hangzhou's famous West Lake; Qianlong was said to be particularly fond of the haircuts that he received in Yangzhou. And for the times when they were unable to visit the area in person, they set their craftsmen to creating exquisite replicas of east-coast palaces in their summer capital at Chengde.

Soon, the east-coast Bannermen began losing interest in war. The softening process began with their commanders. The Zhejiang garrisons became rest-homes for the over-privileged and well-connected, or for those reaching the end of long, distinguished careers: commissions there were a reward for officers who had overworked themselves for decades in far less congenial parts of the empire (Mongolia, Xinjiang, Yunnan). Further down the hierarchy, there was an economic explanation for the decline of the martial spirit in rank-and-file Manchu Bannermen. As inflation steadily devalued the state's handouts of silver and rice, Bannermen faced two options: to sink quietly into poverty; or to develop sidelines – tea-houses, noodle-carts, banditry. Whichever option a Bannerman took, military efficiency was badly affected. But the poverty in the south-east – where there were so many pleasurable ways to while away idle hours – was at least genteel. Surrounded by their wives and children, scraping by on state handouts, Bannermen dabbled in local history, poured out poetry and paintings inspired by nearby landscapes, honed their calligraphy, flew kites, grew melons, tended their fish, caged birds, praying mantises and dogs, and gossiped over tea and pastries. Men were not stationed at Zhapu and its neighbouring garrisons, it seemed, to do anything so uncivilized as to fight.

The whole situation was a good deal too pleasant for the emperor's liking. 'Local customs have corrupted their manners', ran one garrison inspector's verdict, while Qianlong fretted about how the Manchu's warlike 'old way' (*fe doro*) was being lost in sinicization. 'These people are useless', he raged. 'They disgust me more than I can say.'[4] Nineteenth-century emperors like Jiaqing and Daoguang gave up hopes of a martial recovery; they were anxious only to prevent their Manchu brethren from participating too obviously in the black market, opium-smuggling and extortion.[5]

In July 1840, when the British fleet had tried out a few of its cannon on Zhapu, killing six Bannermen, local commanders had (while, as usual, reassuring the court that 'our troops advanced, fought bravely, and drove the British out of Zhapu') reported on alarming holes in Zhapu's defences – specifically concerning the lack of weapons and forts.[6] The sense of anxiety only grew through the autumn and winter of 1841, as Xiamen, Zhoushan, Ningbo, Zhenhai – all the coastal garrisons directly south of Zhapu – had fallen before British ships and guns. By 17 May 1842, when the British fleet (increased to around 10,000 by reinforcements from India) sailed into view, Zhapu's chance to prove its faithfulness to the *fe doro* had arrived.[7]

On 18 May, 820 British troops landed on Zhapu's beach and launched themselves at the batteries on the hills around the city. As usual, the Qing soldiers were dislodged. But here the similarities to earlier engagements in the war ended. One battle-weary British officer ought to have been prepared for what lay ahead when he encountered an unwounded Bannerman sheltering behind one of the many tombs scattered over the hills and prevented one of his rank-and-file from shooting him. 'The ungrateful fellow,' recalled the outraged Briton, 'instead of being pleased at his escape, deliberately began to cut his throat with a short sword, or knife. I did not interfere with his occupation, but waited to see if he were in earnest; and he was, for he effectually killed himself.'[8]

As the British pushed on towards the town, the last remaining Manchu defenders outside its walls – almost 300 of them – made a final stand inside the dark maze of shrines, halls and courts that made up the Temple of Heavenly Respect on top of one of the hills only a mile from the city. And this position they held, shooting dead any attackers who attempted to rush the building. Irritated by losing at least a handful of men to Banner gunfire, the British decided to blow the temple up. As monks spilled out of the grounds and into the nearby woods, a bag of powder was attached to the side of the building and set alight, bringing the roof down over its defenders. With the fire spreading through the building, organized resistance collapsed, while those inside tried to remove their padded cotton tunics and powder bags before they caught fire. After the flames subsided, the dead and wounded were found grotesquely huddled together: mutilated, charred, disfigured. Only 43 of the original 276 lived long enough to be taken prisoner – the British secured the few survivors by knotting their queues together, as if they were tying bunches of rats by their tails. When one Manchu stood up, as if resurrected, from the pile of dead and drew his rusty sword, he refused to make a dash for it but instead began hacking at his own throat.[9]

As the gates to the undefended city now fell, there was little left for the rest of the Manchu garrison but to sacrifice itself in exemplary fashion. 'When they could no longer fight,' witnessed the captain of the Nemesis, 'they could die ... Many ... were with difficulty prevented from cutting their throats, which they did with apparent indifference.'[10] One elderly wounded officer was carried from the fighting by the British: 'I want no mercy', he told them. 'I came here to fight for my emperor ... if you wish to gain my gratitude, and can be generous, write to my revered sovereign, and say I fell in the front, fighting to the last.'[11] But this was not the worst of it. Terrified by the idea of what the British might do to them in captivity, Manchu families destroyed themselves: mothers hanging their children or drowning them in wells; husbands doing the same to their wives, before falling on their own swords. If fathers allowed their children to flee, they were carefully instructed to 'beg for death' on encountering a British soldier. If fathers were not there to help, whole families took poison, and were later found dead with distended throats and black lips.

In terms of sheer horror, if not in scale, the scenes rivalled those of the massacre at Yangzhou two centuries previously. 'Cruel', 'revolt-

ing', 'barbarous', cried British eyewitnesses on finding yards, alley-
ways and wells piled with the dead. If only the Qing soldiers had
surrendered, they sighed, they would have known the mercy of the
British. Contemporary Chinese sources told a revealingly different
story: of civilians being shot in cold blood by British soldiers on
failing to produce acceptable documentation, of women being cut
down by the British, still cursing them as they fell. Inland, women
were divided for rape between the invaders (the prettiest reserved for
the white British, the rest for the Indians).[12]

His day's work over, the captain of the *Nemesis* returned to
appreciating the bucolic delights of the countryside, sighing over 'one
of the richest and most beautifully cultivated spots in the world', its
loveliness only slightly marred by the 'dead bodies floating along the
canals'.[13]

Around halfway through 1841, Granville Loch, a Royal Navy captain
just past his thirtieth birthday, returned to England from a tour in
the Mediterranean, swiftly wearied of his furlough and looked about
for something to do. At that point, a recklessly adventurous Briton
might have aspired to rush into the disaster unfolding in Afghanistan. By late November 1841, the British garrison that had swept
all before it two years earlier surrendered to an Afghan uprising and
began a dreadful winter retreat that would be survived only by a
Scottish doctor with a broken sword. 'It is impossible', declared *The
Times*, 'to view [our contest with China] with the same exciting
interest that attaches to the terrible realities of our Affghan [sic]
warfare.'[14] But the Chinese operation had its own particular glamour.
Just imagine, Loch exulted to himself: 'entering as invaders into the
heart of an immense empire, where we are looked upon as "barbarians
from beyond the civilised world."'[15] With this thought, he extracted
his commission from the Admiralty and boarded a fast ship east,
speeding past the palms, the sago plants and the eighty-foot poison
trees of the 'lazy tropical races', past the nutmeg, pineapples, tigers,
canoe-capsizing alligators, drumming fish and shrieking dugongs of
Java, Malaysia and Singapore, to reach south China in early June.[16]
There, after around ten days scrambling over the peaks of Hong Kong

and buying substandard scraps of chinaware from sharp Macao tradesmen, Loch travelled up the east coast to rejoin the expedition for its
final advance up the Yangtze: to be united – just after the horrors
of Zhapu – with this 'small but gallant force' and its 'glorious spirit
of enterprise'.[17]

The memoir that he left is a useful lens through which to view
the closing months of the campaign. Loch tried hard – like the good
son of empire that he was – to remain a cheery patriot, and dis-
passionately scientific Victorian observer of China's anthropological
and biological novelties. Yet still the horrors of war show through.
He remarked on country 'flat as Kent or Essex beside the Thames',
smothered with roses, 'the tulip, the tallow, the mulberry', of flushing
a pheasant or two out of the wild honeysuckle, moments after passing
half-burnt tents hung with smouldering corpses, or wounded men
'dying without assistance in sight of thousands'.[18] Arriving in time to
witness the fleet's acquisition of Shanghai on 19 June, he ambled
about the tea-houses, gardens and temples of the town, tut-tutting
about the rapacity of Chinese looters, 'passing, like a string of
busy ants, in a continuous line . . . They will bear', he observed knowl-
edgeably, 'thumping, kicking, and maltreating in every way, but
will most pertinaciously hold to their bundles.'[19] Meanwhile, he
recounted, the army messed luxuriously in the apartments of the
absent well-to-do: swathed in plunder (fur-lined cloaks of the finest
silks and satins), stoking cooking-fires with exquisite ornaments and
curios, bellowing the flames with embroidered fans.

After Shanghai, the fleet turned a corner west, to begin its journey
up the Yangtze towards Nanjing, the ancient capital that controlled
the movement of grain ships up to Beijing. Heavy rain slowed the
approach to Zhenjiang (the final Qing garrison blocking the way on
to Nanjing) and Loch passed the time exploring – like an overgrown
character out of *Swallows and Amazons* – bulrush-tangled creeks,
hiking through the soaked countryside and rambling to deserted
temples. One of his stomps up a hillside was enlivened by an
encounter with a withered, opium-addicted soldier, whom his companion high-spiritedly dragged up the slope 'by his pigtail'.[20]

On 17 July, the high, square walls of Zhenjiang finally loomed
up out of the river's rusty granite cliffs. A red-and-yellow flag flew

from its gate, but no other sign of life was apparent: to Loch, it already resembled 'a city of the dead'.[21]

For days, as rumours of the British approach swirled inland, Zhenjiang had been in a state of civil war analogous to that endured by Canton a year earlier. This time, though, the nature of the conflict was a little more straightforward. Down south, the Cantonese had been pitted against the Hunanese, the countryside against the city, villages against villages. In Zhenjiang, the fight was a simple standoff between the Manchu authorities and the local population.

The man in command of the garrison was Hai Ling, a Manchu veteran who had won his posting to mild Zhejiang after long tours of service in the north-east, and whom well-informed contemporary observers of the events of 1842 judged 'an imbecile'.[22] By the first week or so of July, a combination of anxiety (at waiting for the British) and frustration (at being denied the men and money he needed to defend the citadel) seems to have unhinged him. Back in 1841, he had set about patching up the crumbling garrison walls, but had been refused funds for extra forces or new cannon. He had then suggested the cheaper expediency of hiring local 'water braves' to patrol the mouth of the river on the approach to the city. Zhejiang's Governor-General, Niu Jian, unfortunately, firmly believed that the British would never attack so deep into the Yangtze because it was too narrow (he was also convinced that the British steamers were powered by oxen) and responded to Hai Ling's requests by impeaching the Manchu for scaremongering. By July 1842, Niu had a fine pedigree in underestimating the British threat. 'Though the rebellious foreigners speak of ravaging inland,' he had written to the emperor a month previously, 'it's just empty bluster. I have the situation perfectly under control – they are not going to attack.'[23] And even if they did, he concluded, 'they'll be hopelessly outnumbered. What difficulty will there be in killing them all?'[24] He quickly changed his mind during his first military encounter with the British on 16 June at Wusong, a 175-cannon garrison guarding the mouth of the Yangtze. 'As soon as the foreigners blasted their way into the city,'

Liang Tingnan remembered, 'Niu Jian turned white and ran away.'[25] Deprived of reinforcements, enraged by obstructions from incompetent civilians, Hai Ling deteriorated (a Zhenjiang diarist called Zhu Shiyun recorded) into a 'very excited state', and decided to turn his energies to the only measure that lay within his power: persecuting traitors – real or imagined – in the population under his control at Zhenjiang.[26]

By the middle of July, Hai Ling was in sole charge of the city. His bureaucratic tormentor, Niu Jian, had arrived on a whirlwind tour of the place on 13 July, during which he claimed credit for having organized a 150-vessel fireboat attack that British accounts failed to mention. (A contemporary piece of Foreign Office intelligence alleged that Niu's master-plan was to place potent, poisoned vats of the local liquor, samshoo, in the path of the British army.[27]) 'I don't know what he was doing here', a candid local remarked of Niu's visit.[28] With the British only twenty miles away, Niu dashed off a quick proclamation, reassuring the city that no British warships were approaching and that there was nothing to worry about: 'Misleading reports have been spread by a certain captain, who has already been cashiered. The ships in question are merchantmen – it's impossible they'll come far upriver. Go to bed and sleep in perfect security.'[29] On 14 July, and doubtless little regretted by Hai Ling, Niu rushed on to Nanjing, whose walls were presumably thicker than Zhenjiang's. By this point, it must have seemed to Hai Ling that only he and a garrison of around 3,300 Bannermen stood between the approaching British. 'Leave me alone', he told his associate commanders, 'to defend the city'.[30] 'A brilliant plan has been made,' he informed the townspeople, 'which assures us of complete victory; there is no reason to panic and stampede.'[31]

It soon became clear what his 'brilliant plan' was. In these last, panic-stricken days, he 'made no preparations', Zhu Shiyun recalled, 'collected no stores for defence and made no attempt to organise a volunteer force.' For he was far too busy killing civilians. 'It was only at the four gates that Hai Ling had cannon actually pointing outwards', remembered Zhu. 'Inside the city his whole activity consisted in arresting passers-by day and night, on suspicion of their being traitors. Whenever women or children saw Manchu soldiers, they fled in terror; upon which the soldiers ran after them and killed them, announcing to Hai Ling that they had disposed of traitors, for which he rewarded them.'[32] 'False rumours of spies swirled around the city', remembered Liang Tingnan, 'and every house was searched; people were killed on the flimsiest of suspicions – everyone was terrified, no one had any idea how the city was to be defended.'[33]

On 17 July, when the British started cannonading the town, Hai Ling responded by repeating that Zhenjiang 'contains nothing but traitors' and pointing a massive cannon down into the citadel, from a hill just beyond its walls. The commander was little more beloved by his troops. Because by mid-July the city had been sealed off for several days (to prevent the exodus of 'traitors'), the soldiers detailed to defend it were hungry and restive. On 20 July, on the eve of the storming of the walls, the Qing troops were paraded briefly outside the citadel, in the hope that the British ships – which had anchored nearby – would be intimidated by the sight of them. If they had taken a close enough look, the British would have spotted their adversaries gnawing on uncooked aubergines – the best thing they had had to eat in five days. By that evening, the starving soldiers stationed outside the gates were 'threatening to open fire, storm the city, capture General Hai Ling and eat him raw'.[34]

Given this painful prelude to hostilities, some parts of the population may have actually begun to yearn for liberation by the British. After the assault, the story circulated that the 'foreigners had originally intended to attack the city on 22 July. But when their commander-in-chief heard the news that Hai Ling was about to slaughter the inhabitants, he ordered an immediate attack forbidding the use of cannon, for fear of inflicting heavy casualties on the townspeople . . . When they entered the city in strength, they did not wantonly kill a single person, and let anyone who wanted to leave the city.'[35]

On 21 July, a day so hot that seventeen British sailors and marines would die from sunstroke, Pottinger's transports landed some 7,000 men on the southern bank of the Yangtze, just north of Zhenjiang.[36] The 2,700 Qing soldiers outside the city vanished. The two other commanders whom Hai Ling had told to leave everything to him had taken his words to heart, directing operations on the hills outside the city from sedan chairs set under some nearby palm trees. After the British were undeterred by several rounds of fire, though, they sprang into action, fleeing south for the safety and shade of a nearby town. 'At which', observed Zhu Shiyun, 'all their men broke into a general stampede up hill and down dale, to the great amusement of the foreigners.'[37]

After this easy early success, Zhenjiang's western gate fell quickly, reduced to splinters by British sappers. By midday, British soldiers were on the western rim of the city walls and their greatest problem so far had been heatstroke. Things looked different at the northern gate. By a temple on top of a small wooded hill north of the city, three scaling ladders were propped against the city wall and a mixed English and Indian force began to ascend. But here, the Manchus stood and fought. A moderate Banner force – of around 1,500 – dug in for the next hour and a half: bayoneting, sword-fighting, wrestling the British on the walls to drag their enemies and themselves to their deaths. Chinese civilians outside the city watched while purple flames 'flounced out as though there were some demon in their midst, plying a bellows'.[38]

Securing the walls, then, was a brutal business; taking the city was appalling. As the British reeled from the unexpected resistance, surviving Bannermen hurried back to the Manchu quarter to destroy themselves and their families. The blood of even the doughty captain of the *Nemesis* 'ran cold', as he recalled a Manchu soldier found hacking at his wife's throat with a rusty sword, having already thrown his children into a well to drown. (The British shot him and recovered the woman and children. When the wife came to from her ordeal, she had only invective for her saviours.[39]) Groups of fourteen, even twenty bodies were found hanging from rafters in single houses, while most of those taken prisoner later succeeded in starving themselves to death.

Some of the most shocked responses came from those newest to the China campaign. As Granville Loch toured the walls beneath the gentler afternoon sun, he looked down over 'old men, women, and children, cutting each other's throats, and drowning themselves by the dozen; and no one either attempting or apparently showing any inclination to save the poor wretches, nor in fact regarding them with any more notice than they would a dead horse carried through the streets of London to the kennel.' A wander through the quietened, cooling city at dusk, with the fragrance of flowers hanging over its neatly pretty houses, revealed unforgettable horror.

> We entered an open court strewed with rich stuffs and covered with clotted blood; and upon the steps leading to the 'hall of ancestors' there were two bodies of youthful Tartars, cold and stiff, much alike, apparently brothers . . . Stepping over these bodies, we . . . met, face to face, three women seated, a mother and two daughters; and at their feet lay two bodies of elderly men, with their throats cut from ear to ear . . . the hardest heart of the oldest man who ever lived a life of rapine and slaughter could not have gazed on this scene of woe unmoved . . . The expression of cold unutterable despair depicted on the mother's face changed to the violent workings of scorn and hate, which at last burst forth in a paroxysm of invective, afterwards in floods of tears . . . her gestures spoke of her misery – of her hate, and (I doubt not) her revenge.

After failing to make clear that her best option was to confide herself to his protection, he did the best he could for her: preventing his men from bayoneting the last man alive. Astounded by the desperate courage of the Manchu soldiers, he offered them – in death – the greatest compliment a British officer in 1842 could offer a non-European: 'If drilled under English officers, they would prove equal, if not superior, to the Sepoys.'[40]

Amid the wreckage of the city, Hai Ling perished. According to one version, when he decided that all was lost he returned home, built a pyre of his official papers, sat himself in the middle of it and burned to death. When the scene was discovered by a British interpreter, only a charred skull and a few leg bones were left. Another account claims that he hanged himself (after first dispatching his wife and children). Others doubted the suicide story altogether, alleging instead that he was murdered by his own men. Despite vigorous attempts after his death to canonize him as a patriotic war hero, in the style of a Lin Zexu or a Yuqian, popular memory in China has never been comfortable with this hagiography and he is generally commemorated (more accurately) as an unhinged military dictator.

Loch returned to his ship that evening, after taking one last look at the city from its walls. As the British moved on, Zhenjiang no longer merely resembled a city of the dead: 'The moon was up, and shone with clear and tranquil light upon the silent town, lying like an amphitheatre at our feet; so still, so smiling . . . in sad mockery of the misery and despair of its concealed and wretched inhabitants.'[41] 'I am sick at heart of war', wrote General Gough who, only a year before, had railed so at Elliot's refusal to allow him to set his guns on the civilians of Canton.[42]

Just as at Zhapu a month of so earlier, or at Sanyuanli the previous year, the only effective opposition to the British in the Opium War fought not for patriotism or even profit, but for their own women and children. As they died inside the city, the Bannermen may have wondered why no reinforcements from the camps to the west of the city were coming to their aid. These troops from western and central China had fled south at the first exchange of fire with Britain – this was not their fight. The casualty statistics for the day tell the story well enough. 30 per cent of the garrison's resident Banner troops died on 21 July, while only 1.6 per cent of the Chinese reinforcements from Hubei, Sichuan, Henan and Jiangxi lost their lives.[43] The war was, British observers now noted, 'a Manchu and not a Chinese affair.'[44] And once the Manchus were laid low by the British, their persecuted Chinese subjects took vengeful advantage of their disarray. After Zhapu, British intelligence officers observed, 'the Chinese populace fell upon the helpless families [of Manchu soldiers], committed every enormity and carried off every moveable article worth taking.'[45] (Reprisal, perhaps, for the Qing army's own brutality against civilian Chinese populations in previous decades' suppressions of religious rebellions – which had left tens of thousands dead.[46]) In Zhapu, at least two separate accounts claimed, the Manchus had so badly antagonized Chinese soldiers that the latter became fifth-columnists for the British: 'As the Manchu garrison had been in the habit of calling the Chinese disloyal, the Fujian braves sided with the enemy and set fire to the town. The foreigners then scrambled in over the wall'.[47]

Even as desperate struggles went on inside and around the city, many of those removed from the front line carried on with their lives, apparently unconcerned about what might be happening to their compatriots a few hundred yards away. To reach the city, Granville

Loch and his column – under and returning fire – had to cross a village in easy sight of Zhenjiang. Far from escaping the theatre of war, its inhabitants were standing, spectating, in the streets, 'coolly employed eating their bowls of rice . . . although they were viewing a contest between foreigners and their fellow-countrymen, and in danger themselves, from their position, of being shot'.[48]

For once, British and Chinese appraisals of the battle for Zhenjiang converged: this was a disastrous defeat for the Qing that left the way to Nanjing wide open to the British. All the same, the British, suffering their greatest losses in a single engagement of the war to date (39 dead, 130 injured and 3 missing), readily admitted the surprising ferocity of the Manchu resistance. Yet both sides still found plenty else to disagree about – and particularly over the question of looting. 'The strictest orders', remembered the captain of the Nemesis, 'were given to prevent the pillage of the town . . . and also to arrest the proceedings of the Chinese rabble, who in this as in other instances, were the worst enemies of their own countrymen.'[49] But as soon as it fell, the city became an open-air Aladdin's cave: a sea of porcelain, bronzes, satins, silks, embroideries and wax-encased balls of opium (the last were found stockpiled in government buildings). Granville Loch fudged British involvement in the universal rape and pillage: 'Less villainy was perpetrated than could reasonably have been expected.'[50] Zhu Shiyun's diary of the days that followed the city's fall was less roundabout: 'The foreign devils are seizing people, cutting off their queues and conscripting them . . . For days on end great numbers of women in the city have been raped or carried off.'[51] The town's occupiers sacrilegiously gouged down into the foundations of an iron pagoda, clumsily trying to uproot it as a souvenir; they viciously beat (dismembered, according to one account) a Chinese who tried to buy stolen goods off them with a counterfeit coin. Black magic was at work, panicked civilians whispered to each other: hundreds of Chinese were being kidnapped by the British, and drugged with a strange and terrible potion that robbed them of the power of speech and turned them into Indian 'black devil' soldiers.[52]

Their business at Zhenjiang concluded, the British fleet sailed on, satisfied at a point well made. 'Terrible' though the business was, concluded Captain Hall from the deck of the Nemesis, the defeat would undoubtedly 'produce in the mind of the Emperor . . . a

conviction that a speedy peace . . . was preferable to a continuance
of the war.'[53] By the first week of August, he and his comrades
had turned a last bend in the Yangtze. The long walls of Nanjing,
studded with triangular, Lamaist yak-hair pennants and scarlet-
uniformed Manchu guards, snaked before them. 'The energy of British
character', proclaimed Lieutenant Bingham, 'under the blessing of the
Almighty, had placed, without an accident, a fleet of seventy sail . . .
in the heart of the Celestial Empire!'[54]

Chapter Fourteen

THE TREATY OF NANJING

In April 1842, a seventy-one-year-old Manchu called Yilibu received some terrible news. His distant relative, the emperor, had revoked his sentence of banishment to the Great Wall fortress town of Zhangjiakou and decided to post him to beautiful Zhejiang. In the normal run of things, such a change of fortune – a transfer from the bleak Sino-Mongolian frontier to the balmy south-east – would have been cause for rejoicing. Not in 1842, though. Yilibu was old and ill, weakened by his military exile in the north. He had already suffered enough for this war: in the summer of 1841, he had spent two painful months on trial in Beijing, for his handling of the British occupation of Zhoushan through the winter of 1840.

On 3 April, he was summoned to the Yuanmingyuan (the Summer Palace) for an audience with the emperor. This was an opportunity for the emperor to interrogate in person someone with first-hand experience of the British about their motives, their ambitions, their strengths and weaknesses. (Every other minister who had served in the war had either not been allowed to return to Beijing, or had done so in disgrace.) Two and a half years after this war was supposed to have started, Daoguang found himself still lacking the most basic information about his antagonists: where in fact, he wondered in a communication of May 1842, is England? Why are the English selling us opium? What are the Indians doing in their army? How is it they have a twenty-two-year-old woman for a queen? Is she married? Has Elliot really gone home?[1] Yilibu was ready for Daoguang's questions: he planned, he told one of his aides that day, to make a detailed report about what he knew of handling the British. But as soon as Yilibu had announced his arrival, for unexplained reasons Daoguang changed his mind – he would not see his elderly kinsman after all. Yilibu was allowed to kowtow to the gate of the Second Palace, then on 15 April permitted to leave for Zhejiang through the Gate of Upright Openness, in the southern stretch of the city wall.

Daoguang had wasted his best chance to hear a frank account of the British and the war. From here on, it would be business as usual, with his 'slaves' obfuscating and lying as hard as they could, at a safe remove from their sovereign, to bring this border disturbance to an end.

Until 1842, any official servant who implicitly (by ignoring imperial orders to 'exterminate' the foreigners) or explicitly (by pointing out the weaknesses of the Qing army and the strengths of the British) acknowledged British military superiority had risked, at best, dismissal and more likely interrogation and punishment (exile, and possibly death). As a result, Daoguang's nervous servants had spent the last two years diligently deluding him about the nature of the British threat and demands. But the more misinformed the emperor was, the less likely a solution became. Daoguang's furious impatience with those who failed to resolve the conflict in accordance with his expectations caused his most experienced, talented officials to view an imperial commission to the front line of the war with dread. Two years after the war had begun, the days when a Lin Zexu or a Qishan – expecting a quick resolution followed by promotion – would step confidently up to the mark were long gone. By 1841 Daoguang had run out of qualified individuals; there can be no other explanation for his appointment of the incompetent Yijing as Awe-Inspiring General. As the British edged towards Nanjing, devastating Zhapu and Zhenjiang en route, neither the emperor nor his representatives in the south-east could even lay their hands on a copy of Lord Palmerston's original letter outlining the terms for peace. Millions of ounces of silver had been squandered on a war whose cause Qing officials could no longer remember – if indeed they had ever understood it.

But at least by spring 1842, no one in the theatre of war itself was suggesting any more that the British could be 'exterminated'. 'Annihilate them', the Governor of Zhejiang, Liu Yunke, had cried only a year earlier. But once Zhenhai had fallen, and Yuqian's moribund body had been rushed out of the citadel, Liu took a different view. The army was crushed by defeat, he now wrote to the emperor, and the costs of war were crippling. The British cannon were too fierce, their soldiers too expert at fighting on land and at sea; the Chinese people – scourged by Qing armies – were easily bribed into collaboration with the enemy.[2] 'I have examined the methods employed since ancient times for controlling and taming distant foreigners,' Liu analysed, 'and I have found only fighting, defending and soothing. In the present war, neither fighting nor defending has worked; and we are not allowed to soothe. My own stupidity and lack of talent leaves me without a plan and unable to act.'[3] In case, though, the emperor should mistake this diagnosis as an offer of help, Liu swiftly begged for sick leave. Since a recent posting in Sichuan, he complained, his arthritis had been troubling him badly. 'My tongue gets number by the day, there is an indentation along the right side of my back, my left ear is blocked, and my memory is awful.'[4] (Liu's ailments seem to have cleared up once other unfortunates had been appointed to negotiate the final peace treaty with the British.)

Instead, Liu recommended that the emperor dispatch the septuagenarian Yilibu, another imperial clansman, this time of the Red-Girdled Yellow Banner, whose finest hour had come twenty-three years previously when he had captured some Burmese bandits on the south-western edge of the empire. Liu was mistakenly convinced that the British were now fighting not for opium, for trade or for national honour, but to take revenge for Yuqian's flaying of the English prisoners. As Yuqian's predecessor managing the British presence on the east coast between 1840 and 1841, Yilibu had distinguished himself as an altogether more mollifying presence than the angry Mongolian. Instructed by the emperor to retake British-occupied Zhoushan by force, he had responded by wining and dining the English prisoners that his army had acquired, and by procrastinating his offensive. He could not possibly attack straight away, one memorial to the emperor said, the reinforcements had not arrived; neither had the cannon, said another. He was waiting for the English 'to relax fatally out of self-confidence', reported the next, and so on it went, until (to Yilibu's relief) the English voluntarily evacuated the island in March 1841 to fulfil the stipulations of Charles Elliot's stillborn agreement with Qishan.[5]

Liu's change of opinion reached the emperor at the Yuanmingyuan on 28 March 1842, just three days after Daoguang had received reports from the Awe-Inspiring Yijing of the failure of the Qing's spring offensive. ('My anger and hatred are inexpressible', commented the vermilion brush.[6]) Liu's memorials – with their talk of bankrupting war costs, untrustworthy civilians, banditry, the capital's food supply in peril – began to move Daoguang towards the idea of negotiating. He made two new appointments to handle matters in the south-east, Yilibu and an old drinking and riding friend, the Manchu aristocrat Qiying (whom he now declared Grand Commissioner for the Frontier), and issued his most confusing order yet: his new commanders must 'first exterminate, then soothe' the English.[7]

Qiying and Yilibu reached Hangzhou on 9 May. Their plans for bringing the war to an end were immediately sabotaged by the hopeless Yijing who – piqued by the arrival of his replacements – fired off a series of false reports of naval victories. 'Their plans are exhausted, their ingenuity used up', he informed his emperor.[8] Convinced, again, that victory lay within his grasp, on 25 May Daoguang wrote severely to Qiying and Yilibu, denouncing their defeatist memorials and ordering Yilibu to return to the capital, unless he could make himself useful in Zhejiang 'annihilating the foreigners'.[9] But it took twelve days for a dispatch from Beijing to get a response from Hangzhou – quite long enough to give Daoguang's servants the freedom to start going about things as they saw fit: to sue for peace. On 17 May, as the British evacuated Ningbo to move on to Zhapu, Qiying sent Yilibu on ahead 'to investigate the situation and find a way to implement the Loose Rein; to disseminate the awesomeness of Heaven and demonstrate great righteousness.'[10]

Yilibu's first appeal to the British is worth quoting at length for its demonstration of the gulf in understanding between the two sides. All this war, he wrote, 'is indeed disturbing the celestial harmony and it is of great importance to put a stop to this business, lest heaven be provoked to wrath and celestial punishments follow. Your honourable country desires trade, the Celestial Empire wishes to receive the duties thereon, and neither of us is anxious to harass soldiers, and spend the revenues.'[11] 'We ponder', his equally bemused subordinates reasoned,

> with veneration upon the Great Emperor's cherishing tenderness towards foreigners, and utmost justice in all his dealings. He thereby causes the whole world to participate in his favour, and to enjoy his protection, for the promotion of civilisation . . . and the full enjoyment of lasting benefits. But the English foreigners have now for two years . . . on account of the investigation in the opium traffic, discarded their obedience and been incessantly fighting, commencing in Guangdong, and proceeding to Fujian, and from thence to Zhejiang. What can possibly be their intention?

In travelling so far to China, the British 'all owe their lives . . . to the supreme Heaven, and every one of them has a parent and a wife and a family, whoever is wounded or falls in battle becomes a demon in a foreign land, and causes his father and mother great anxiety and renders his family destitute, at which the Great Ministers feel the deepest concern.'[12] Demonstrating his own shaky grasp of British motivations and demands, Yilibu hoped to disarm his foreign adversaries with two concessions. The first was to let them trade again. Trade? Henry Pottinger might have queried in response. The British had been *trading* since March 1841 at Canton, with full authorization from Yishan. By now, they wanted far more than trade. Yilibu's second trump card was to offer to return Britons kidnapped during the winter at Ningbo – like Liu Yunke, he was convinced that the British were holding the east coast ransom merely to recover prisoners. As he chased after Pottinger's fleet, then, he dragged the British captives with him, looking for an opportunity to use them to his advantage.[13]

Even if all this might have swayed the British, Yilibu was too late to save Zhapu: by the time he had got close enough to the British to hand over this letter, hundreds of the town's defenders were scorched corpses. And by the time he had actually reached the massacred garrison, the British had moved on yet again, and there was no one to receive the prisoners. When he eventually received Yilibu's letter, Major-General Gough wrote back that he and his plenipotentiary would discuss only the conditions stipulated in the letters already submitted, with the emperor's own plenipotentiaries. As soon as he read this reply, Yilibu probably panicked: what conditions, what letters was Gough referring to? Who had them: the emperor? Qishan? And what was a plenipotentiary? The emperor of China was the Son of Heaven – he could not invest his celestial powers in someone else.[14] Even sicklier and more exhausted than he had been a month before, Yilibu simply dispatched the prisoners to the base-camp that the British were keeping a little north of Shanghai, along with financial compensation for their ordeal (fifteen dollars for each Indian soldier, thirty for each native British) and the following vague communication: 'Everything you mention can be easily settled; once we have a protocol for arranging the overall discussions, we will memorialize the emperor and set down some rules.'[15] Back in 1839, British politicians and merchants had argued that Qing pomposity and inflexibility had forced them to the battlefield. Two years of war had illuminated the chaotic realities of Qing diplomacy, with the highest-ranking servants of the dynasty scrabbling to offer the British vague, informal quick fixes, as they lied shamelessly to their emperor.

Meanwhile, Qiying misled the emperor with fraudulent reports about how 'grateful' and 'submissive' the foreigners were: 'they only want to trade ... With the flames of rebellion raging,' he wrote of the fall of Zhapu, 'we find ourselves between the twin difficulties of attacking and defending and do not dare lightly exterminate them ... we can only try and maintain calm, and use all our efforts to find an opportunity to handle things.'[16] Qiying's clever attempts at disinformation were, it turned out, futile. Around 26 May, the emperor received full details of what had happened at Zhapu and instructed Qiying to return to the Loose Rein. Daoguang's shocked bewilderment on hearing about the Banner massacre was obvious: 'You mentioned', he asked Qiying, 'that [one of your officers] reported that the foreigners don't want war, they only want trade ... Tell me the truth.'[17] To Yijing, he wrote: 'You reported you were just waiting for an opportunity to exterminate them . . . Have you really got a grip on the situation?'[18]

In mid-June, the British replied to Yilibu's request that they withdraw troops with a note congratulating him on his promotion ('we had understood he was strangled', a surprised Pottinger mused in a dispatch to the foreign secretary) but reminding him that 'there will be no stop to the war until a Plenipotentiary is nominated.'[19] Qiying tried to bluff his way through the difficulty, claiming that he was, indeed, plenipotentiary. 'If we do not treat one another with sincerity,' he added brazenly, 'we shall certainly meet with the punishments of Heaven.'[20] Pottinger refused to believe him until he produced further credentials. While Yilibu continued with his fuzzy moral reproaches (by acting thus, he scolded the British, they 'must incur the wrath of supreme heaven, and must range their names with ill odor on the page of history'), Qiying tried to persuade the emperor to invest him and Yilibu with the required authority.[21] 'If the foreigners are willing to withdraw their soldiers, earnestly ask for trade and beg again to meet with Yilibu and myself, I wish to agree to their request.' 'Impossible', scrawled the unreasonable vermilion brush through June and July, having changed its mind yet again about the possibility of military victory. 'The recipients of this letter must only exterminate, without wavering.'[22] 'The celestial mind', as Qiying remarked to Yilibu around this time, 'has a great tendency to change.'[23] (To the emperor himself, Qiying wrote that his 'heart was almost broken' with the emotion of feeling the emperor's trust in him.[24])

On 27 July, however, the news of the massacre at Zhenjiang reached Daoguang, along with an almost hysterical memorial from Niu Jian, in Nanjing. 'The emergency is inexpressibly serious, please think of something quickly to save us all!'[25] And just like that, Daoguang conceded the whole idea of plenipotentiary power: 'Act as circumstances require', he wrote back to Qiying. 'Sort things out quickly and expediently – do not waver.'[26] He at least remembered to put the authorization in the fastest post. It reached Qiying on 1 August – three days before the first British ship anchored just outside Nanjing.

So Qiying and Yilibu could do as they liked – they were 'act-as-circumstances-require' plenipotentiaries. And the emperor's men decided to use their freedom to the full – for, knowing Daoguang as they did, how long would it last?

The first thing they did – without informing the emperor, of course – was to put the negotiations in the hands of someone completely uncommissioned: a household aide of Yilibu's called Zhang Xi.

This was an individual of such obscurity that we have almost no sources on him beyond an unreliable biography (that claims he was seven feet tall and very handsome) pinned onto the end of the detailed diary that he wrote describing his role in the Nanjing negotiations, and a scattering of comments from British participants and observers (some of which contradict his diary and biography). Zhang Xi, in short, was a stock figure of the late-Qing landscape: one of the millions of Chinese men who had failed to pass the civil-service examinations but who managed to scrape a living as advisers to legitimate employees of the state. While administrative budgets failed to keep up with population rise, those lucky enough to land official postings had no choice but to hire (by using their own salaries, or by creating new taxes) personal secretaries or local enforcers. Zhang Xi's own career rose and fell with that of his master, Yilibu, whom he had followed faithfully for years – even into exile in Zhangjiakou – while fainter-hearted hangers-on had abandoned him.

Back in Beijing in early April, Yilibu had asked Zhang Xi to come with him to the south-east, to help bring the war to an end. This, however, was a test of loyalty too far, and Zhang Xi pleaded ill health. 'A sudden fever took hold of me and my old illness broke out again.' Taking to his bed, he claimed he was unable to get up – and certainly not well enough to face the 'cold winds' of Zhejiang's mild spring and roasting summer.[27] But eventually, Yilibu's urgings became too pressing: 'You must have long recovered from your illness', he begged in May. 'You must not hesitate or delay . . . Don't disappoint my earnest expectation!'[28]

On 13 July, Zhang Xi left the north for the south-east. On 5 August, his journey slowed by bandits, refugees and British blockades, he at last caught up with the two imperial agents, Qiying and

Yilibu, at Wuxi, a few dozen miles from Nanjing. Yilibu had barely had time to dash off a poem of joy at being reunited with his beloved aide, when bad news came in: 'a large number of ships containing disobedient foreigners have reached Nanjing and have decided to bombard the city on August 7.'[29] Yilibu and Qiying made a quick decision to send the exhausted Zhang Xi ahead through the night, to persuade the British to hold their fire. After pulling on a convincing costume – a robe of silk gauze and a hat of Qing office, crowned by a button that indicated high official rank – Zhang Xi travelled by boat, by horse and, for the last thirty miles, on foot, to arrive just in time: on 7 August.

With a fine display of diplomatic sangfroid, Zhang Xi flipped through a calendar and told the city's harried governors that they had nothing to worry about: the British would not fire today – it was a Sunday. 'I dare not tell a lie,' Zhang Xi replied, when Niu Jian quizzed him as to whether this was reliably correct.[30] (It was in fact a Monday.) In reality, the British did not deliver their promised attack that day because they were still waiting for the rest of the fleet to arrive. As they prepared themselves, the British were also skilfully delayed by a time-consuming stream of civil servants: white-buttoned and brass-buttoned officials, bearing letters offering vague promises to negotiate and insultingly small ransoms, sweetmeats, fresh tea and pieces of silk. Although none of this would deflect the British from their intended course of action, receiving and processing these communications at least bought the Qing a little time.

Yilibu – without Qiying – staggered into the city the following day, suffering badly from heatstroke. Almost his first act was to send Zhang Xi onto Pottinger's ship, the *Cornwallis*, with another letter. He was given a respectful reception by Pottinger, his omnicompetent Chief of Secret Police, Karl Gützlaff, and two other senior interpreters. It was all very simple, said one of the translators, John Morrison. 'If you can act according to our public notice and our repeated communications, then the matter may be concluded.'[31] Here, the discussion hit an impasse – for Zhang Xi (unsurprisingly, as he had only joined the campaign the previous day, and neither Yilibu nor Qiying had bothered to brief him before they sent him off to the front line) did not actually know what was in these documents. Fortunately, he was willing to admit this and the British, ever-patient, explained again what they wanted: a ransom for the city, indemnities for the opium and the war, the opening of ports, and so on.

At this moment, Zhang Xi's negotiating style began to verge on the undiplomatic. Hearing for the first time what the British required for peace, he 'felt a hundred turmoils in his stomach ... If I were given the seal of a great general,' he informed his nonplussed interlocutors, 'I should, first of all, arrest you, cut your bodies into ten thousand pieces, grind your bones, and spread the ashes as revenge for the victims – the soldiers and the people – in order to quench the anger of the whole empire.'[32] He then spat (several times) and went red in the face, further re-emphasizing his point by beating the desk, spitting on the deck again and denouncing his interlocutors some more.[33] The sepoy bodyguard outside the cabin now barred the door with their swords, blocking Zhang Xi from his escort of four other officials.

As dusk approached, Zhang Xi at last took his leave. The British said they would temporarily delay the bombardment of Nanjing, in exchange for three million dollars (ten times the sum originally offered by Niu Jian). On returning to Yilibu that evening, Zhang Xi seems to have completely forgotten his original brief – to negotiate for peace – and decided instead that more war was in order. 'We should appease the foreigners with negotiations,' he argued, 'while preparing stealth attacks.' He then outlined a detailed strategy for annihilating the British with fireboats (the same fireboats that had failed in at least half a dozen other key engagements), a strategy that, he revealed, he had also explained in depth to Pottinger (who immediately took extra precautions to guard against such an attack). Finally, he burst into tears.[34] Niu Jian was unconvinced: 'Let's not play with the tiger's beard', he observed.[35]

The British continued landing their troops; they aimed four howitzers (the weapon that, after three rounds, had done such awful work on the Sichuanese at the battle of Ningbo) at the city walls. Niu Jian went on claiming that Nanjing was far too poor to pay three million dollars. At around midnight on 10 August, the British promised the attack would begin in the morning. After Qiying finally reached the city on 11 August, Yilibu quickly scrawled a note for Zhang Xi to deliver to the British: 'All these conditions, about the cost of the opium, the opening of ports and diplomatic equality, can be settled.'[36] An oral pledge, moreover, was made to pay the three million; a conference was promised for the following day.

On 12 August, Zhang Xi had his third meeting with the British, this time at a small temple just beyond the north-west corner of the city walls. Again, the British laid out their demands; Yilibu and Qiying were to respond within twenty-four hours, and produce the official documents confirming their status as plenipotentiaries. So as to avoid any further confusion, the British translators carefully wrote down their terms.

When the meeting drew to an end at around seven in the evening, Zhang Xi returned to report back to Qiying, Yilibu and Niu Jian inside the city, who were busy making themselves comfortable inside the Western Flowery Hall of the governor-general's offices. 'There's no hurry,' Qiying expansively told him, 'let's take our time.' Zhang Xi must have given his superiors an outline of what the British wanted, but both his report and their response suggest a general lack of focus from all four men. Zhang's diary rejoices over the fact that – through, he claimed, his personal skill and charm – he had succeeded in bargaining the total indemnity down from 30 to 21 million dollars (British sources corroborate no such bargaining process). But the finer points – indeed, all the treaty's other clauses (Hong Kong, the amnestying of Chinese who collaborated with the British, the setting of regular transit duties, the opening of five treaty ports and consular rights within those ports) – Zhang Xi seems to have largely ignored. In his diary, he gave far more space to describing the brass incense braziers in the temple at which they had met than to inscribing the actual terms of the treaty (which he did not even note down in full). Qiying and Yilibu seemed even less interested in what had transpired: 'they did not look at the demands,' Zhang Xi told his diary, 'but immediately ordered them to be sent to their subordinates, who themselves quickly put them aside.' With the ceasefire agreed, both the emperor's representatives had great difficulty in taking the matter at all seriously. Yilibu, Zhang Xi remembered, 'became very relaxed. He kindly instructed me just to clear up with them the future customs duties and forbid any more merchants' debts, but definitely not to promise an ounce of silver in compensation, and I should not even discuss with them the issue of examining the imperial edict [authorizing Yilibu and Qiying as plenipotentiaries] or of stamping anything with the imperial seal.' In other words, Zhang Xi was to fob them off with a couple of minor, unratified concessions. His verdict delivered, Yilibu then closed his eyes.[37]

13 August dawned – the day on which Zhang Xi was supposed to give the British a considered answer to their demands. Regrettably, the barely examined list was still with the secretary to whom Qiying and Yilibu had handed it unread and who, on merely glancing at it, had found it 'very problematic' then filed it away somewhere.[38] That morning, an errand boy sent to recover the piece of paper discovered the secretary had gone out to visit friends and had not yet come back. As the diplomatic deadline drew dangerously close, not only had the plenipotentiaries failed to agree upon, or even read, the British demands; they had also lost them. Zhang Xi worried that the British would not take it well: they were, after all, expecting to see the imperial commissioners' official investiture and agreement to their draft treaty. He shared his worries with the officers who were to accompany him to the meeting: 'The city is in peril', he told them. 'Its position is as precarious as a mound of eggs.' His peers were sanguine about how the British would react: 'Just talk slowly, and stop worrying.'[39]

The British arrived at the temple at midday and immediately asked to see the imperial edict confirming Yilibu and Qiying as plenipotentiaries. Zhang Xi's excuse was passable: his masters, he explained, had sent it off for the Awe-Inspiring Yijing to inspect, and he had not yet returned it. And when would that be? the British translator asked. 'Maybe today, maybe tomorrow,' Zhang Xi vaguely replied. 'Who can tell?' The British then wanted to know if Qiying had agreed to their document of demands; Zhang Xi admitted that he had come out without this piece of paper also. The British now lost their collective temper ('they felt unhappy', observed Zhang Xi) and accused their interlocutors of insincerity, of 'cheating them in every way'. They said they would start firing at the city at daybreak unless there was a more satisfactory response, and went back to their ships.[40]

'The three excellencies were amazed,' Zhang Xi drily recorded on his return to the city, 'and had no idea what to do.' (At this painful audience, one of Zhang Xi's peers whispered to him what he surely already knew: that Qiying had not listened to much of what he had said the day before.) As the city descended into panic, the negotiators began to squabble. Why had Zhang Xi said the edict was with Yijing, Qiying wanted to know. 'What,' an exasperated Zhang Xi responded, 'would you prefer I said? You gave me no instructions.' (Qiying gave no reply.) Those present considered their options: to stand and fight, or to read the treaty and negotiate. 'If I die for my country,' Yilibu pondered aloud, 'then a special temple will be consecrated to my memory. You will all be honoured with autumn sacrifices for a thousand years to come.' One of Zhang Xi's fellow negotiators answered with a full and frank account of the foreigners' ferocity: 'If their demands are not complied with,' he argued, 'woe and disaster will come at once.' Qiying maintained an eloquent silence.[41] The emperor's representatives decided to ask the secretary for the document containing the British demands. The scribe looked blank until Zhang Xi reminded him that they were referring to the piece of paper that he had deemed 'problematic' the previous day. Eventually, the document was recovered and after a quick conference, all the main items were accepted.

Around midnight (with about three hours until the promised assault would begin), Zhang Xi rushed out of the city, and by five in the morning – as the sky paled into dawn – had presented the agreed treaty to the foreigners on board their ship. After breakfast, the British processed back to the temple at which the previous day's unhappy meeting had taken place. While Zhang Xi waited (his five viscera, he remembered, were burning with sorrow), his colleagues urged him to keep a sense of proportion. After all, the Han Dynasty used to send 5,000 pounds of gold to keep the Mongolians from raiding the north – paying unruly foreigners to keep the peace was nothing new. 'The loss was small, the thing saved was great . . . You should not feel so badly in your heart.'[42] Granville Loch mistook the sorrow on Zhang Xi's face for disappointment at the appearance of the British. Their shirts and breeches were clean enough but had not known an iron for weeks, Loch regretted; their coats were tired and worn. The Qing party, by contrast, 'rustled in embroidered silks and flowered muslin of a design and beauty of texture worthy even to deck the forms of our own fair dames.'[43] The British were ushered courteously into a spacious, high-ceilinged wooden hall, and were begged to make themselves comfortable in vast ebony chairs around a long, rectangular table. Outside, a handful of policemen – distinguished by scarlet conical hats, each topped with a bright rooster feather – kept an inquisitive crowd at a distance with the help of cow-hide whips.

Both sides' accreditations were examined, with particular attention paid by the British to the emperor's edict investing Qiying and Yilibu as plenipotentiaries. The mystical object was ceremoniously produced, remembered Loch, from 'a little shabby yellow box badly made and worse painted'. An official 'carried the roll of yellow silk in both his hands and proceeded – his eyes reverentially fixed upon it – with slow and solemn steps towards the table ... I was greatly amused watching the anxious and horrified faces of the various Chinese when Mr Morrison touched the commission'. Loch assumed this was down to the intense respect that all Chinese had for the Imperial Word, and to disgust at the idea of such a sacred object being polluted by alien hands.[44] His diagnosis was probably some way off the mark. For the edict was almost certainly a forgery, cobbled together in panic the previous evening.[45] Major Malcolm, the secretary of the British legation, proudly displayed to the Qing representatives his Royal Patent, inscribed on a square of duck-egg-blue card and embellished by Queen Victoria's Great Seal of the Realm. Perhaps the closest equivalent that Qiying and Yilibu possessed was the emperor's scratchy 27 July memorandum, admitting that they could 'Act as circumstances require'. The Qing unease at seeing the British examine their concoction so closely probably sprang not from a horror of lese-majesty, but rather from fear of their deception being discovered and the British storming out of the negotiating room and back to their howitzers. That evening, after it was all over, Zhang Xi vomited (repeatedly) with sunstroke, and perhaps stress.

But once a skeleton treaty had been agreed that day in the temple's grounds, pleasantness prevailed. The most senior Chinese officer present at the conference on 14 August 'laughingly remarked that the conditions were hard, but, after all, were only what they would have demanded under similar circumstances ... a war between nations might be likened to a game of chance, in which the loser must pay the winner.'[46] On 19 August, the plenipotentiaries at last encountered each other in person; in almost three years of violence, the British had only had two meetings with an imperial official of any decisive rank (both between Charles Elliot and Qishan). The band played, the drums beat, the cannon saluted, Zhang Xi's hand was shaken many times, as Yilibu and Qiying – clumsy in thick Manchu boots more suited to striding over the frozen wastelands of the north than to hopping onto a British steamer in the dog days of a south-eastern summer – boarded Pottinger's ship (the messes brightened with 'articles of choice taste [the men] had picked up on their perambulations'), and talked about nothing very much at all. Qiying, Loch guessed, thought it beneath him to show too much interest; Yilibu was unwell, as usual; and Niu Jian was apparently too busy enjoying the cherry brandy to produce anything but the occasional 'smack of satisfaction'. After bowing deeply to a portrait of Queen Victoria, they left (Loch recalled) 'highly pleased at their reception.'[47] A return visit was paid by the British to the Imperial Commissioners' apartments on 24 August. Beneath a canopy of decorated lanterns and on floors carpeted with crimson drugget, tables groaned with food, speeches were made, hurdy-gurdies clattered. In the shade of a willow tree to one side of the hall, two mandarins (under instructions from Qiying) tried to engage John Morrison in an intimate chat away from the clamour of penny-trumpets and drums, in the hope of renegotiating one of the treaty's clauses. Sharply responding that this was no place to talk official business, Morrison stalked off.[48]

On 26 August, Pottinger returned – in a vast sedan chair with green stripes – for another banquet, in which 'numerous patties of minced meat, pork, arrow root, vermicelli soup, with meat in it, pig's ear soup, and other strange dishes, were served in succession ... as a *coup de grace*, Ke-ying insisted upon Sir Henry opening his mouth while he with great dexterity shot into it several immense sugar-plums. I shall never forget Sir Henry's face of determined resignation after he found remonstrances were of no avail; nor the figure of Ke-ying, as he stood planted before him, in the attitude of a short-sighted old lady threading a needle, poising the *bonne bouche* between his finger and thumb preparatory to his successful throw.'[49] Only after this force-feeding was completed did the Qing – hoping, perhaps, that the British had been stuffed to the point of insensibility – start to discuss the treaty. The basic demands were quickly cleared: twenty-one million dollars' indemnity, the opening of five ports to trade, British right of residence and the setting of tariffs there, the abolition of the Hong monopoly. Yet again ignoring Daoguang's orders (this time to take care 'to make such arrangements as shall cut off for ever all causes of war, and leave nothing incomplete or liable to doubt'), Qiying and Yilibu wanted to finish the business as quickly as possible.[50] 'The Imperial commissioners', Pottinger observed, 'declared their readiness to sign and seal the Treaty at once, and without further explanation.'[51] 'None of the critical examination into phrases or expressions', Loch recalled, 'so keenly canvassed and suspiciously viewed by European diplomatists, occupied a moment of their attention. All their anxiety, which was too powerful to be concealed, was centred upon the one main object – our immediate departure'.[52]

On this occasion, Pottinger finally raised the question of the ostensible cause of the war: opium. Both Qiying and Yilibu refused point-blank to have the issue written in any official way into the treaty; though they agreed to informal discussion. Why, they wanted to know, did Great Britain so unfairly allow the opium poppy to be cultivated in India, then imported into China? China's opium problem, Pottinger insisted, had nothing to do with Britain, and everything to do with Chinese weakness for the drug. 'If your people are virtuous, they will desist from the evil practice; and if your officers are incorruptible, and obey their orders, no opium can enter your country. The discouragement of the growth of the poppy in our territories rests principally with you'. He now had another smooth suggestion. 'Would it not, therefore, be better at once to legalise its importation, and . . . thereby greatly limit the facilities which now exist for smuggling?' The emperor, Qiying and Yilibu insisted, would never hear of it.[53]

As Pottinger finally came away from this five-hour meeting, he remembered that 'Qiying cordially embraced me in his arms, according to the Tartar usage, and desired one of the gentlemen interpreters to explain to me that he and his colleagues were satisfied that I was a good and just man. This expression their Excellencies significantly confirmed by pointing to their breasts, and then to Heaven. They stood till I was mounted and rode away.'[54]

Meanwhile, Qiying concentrated on spinning the outcome of the negotiations to the emperor. 'Although the demands of the foreigners are indeed rapacious, yet they are little more than a desire for ports and for the privilege of trade. There are no dark schemes in them', he comforted Daoguang, while editing out key stipulations, such as the abolition of the Hong monopoly.[55] They had become 'very polite and obedient.'[56] 'How depressed and discontented I was to read your memorial', the emperor wrote back. 'I can only hate myself and feel ashamed that things have reached this point.'[57] But he might as well have saved his vermilion ink for things he could actually do something about. Weary with it all, over the last days of August, he steadily capitulated to the British demands. His first offer to magnanimously 'lend' Hong Kong lapsed into a full cession of the island; he stopped resisting the idea of a war indemnity, only querying how the money was to be raised.[58] Daoguang's final discontented queries reached Nanjing on 7 September – ten days after Qiying, Yilibu and Niu Jian had signed and sealed the treaty in red lead paint and with a great agate stamp drawn from a yellow silk box.

As 29 August – the day on which the treaty was to be signed – dawned, relations between the two sides were not yet so cordial for every drop of diplomatic mistrust to evaporate. Four copies of the treaty were prepared, in Chinese and English, bound with ribbon to prevent (as Loch explained) any of the sheets being removed by 'these slippery gentlemen to blind the eyes of their Imperial master.'[59] The emperor's men paled when the British began a twenty-one-gun salute to honour the Queen's birthday; Qiying was convinced that the British planned to take him prisoner.[60]

Yilibu was almost too ill to attend the treaty's grand closing ceremonies. At the meeting on 26 August, he had accepted a British offer of medicine to treat his ringworm and dispatched Zhang Xi to pick up the prescription. Although Zhang Xi hinted darkly that the medicine itself had made his master ill, the British told a different story: that Zhang Xi ('a notorious drunkard', alleged Loch) drank far too much in the British ship's gunroom, lost the label that went with the medicine, and told Yilibu to swallow at a gulp three days' supply. ('The foreigners', Zhang Xi's biographer confusingly counters, 'especially esteemed his great capacity for drinking.'[61]) As a result, Yilibu had to be carried to and from Pottinger's ship, the *Cornwallis*, and spent the whole ceremony reclined on a sofa. With remarkable civility, he thanked the doctor in person for the dose, 'and trusted that the cure would be as certain as the remedy was violent.'[62]

In sum, though, Loch concluded that 'It was a glorious spectacle for all who saw it . . . under the walls of their ancient capital, in the cabin of a British 74, the first treaty China was ever forced to make was signed by three of her highest nobles under England's flag.'[63] The treaty, Zhang Xi remarked, would 'serve as an eternal document of confidence and trust . . . After the seals had been stamped, all felt very happy.'[64] The gun salutes must have been loud enough to drown out the cries of an infuriated Qing general inside the city who, on hearing that the peace negotiations had been successfully concluded, screamed that Niu Jian was an 'instigator of calamity' – his beard is said to have stood on end with fury.[65] After all this time, expenditure and slaughter, everything the British had wanted was signed away in a handful of meetings.

As the British ships weighed anchor and drifted back south through early October, Qiying was jubilant: 'Everything difficult can become easy . . . To rescue thousands and millions of lives in Jiangsu and Zhejiang is a great saving . . . our offspring must be prosperous and great in the future.' 'The root of disaster has probably been planted, and the poison will flow ceaselessly', Yilibu worried.[66] 'You have let me down, and the empire', sulked Daoguang at the two of them when a copy of the actual treaty reached him on 6 September – he relieved his feelings by arresting Niu Jian, for failing to strengthen defences along the Yangtze in time.[67] Zhang Xi simply rejoiced to return home 'with his body still intact . . . How enjoyable and fortunate this is!'[68]

Chapter Fifteen

PEACE AND WAR

What a 'great and glorious thing' the China war had been, letters to the editor of *The Times* reflected as 1842 drew to an end and the news from Nanjing sailed in over the Channel: 'Perhaps no circumstance in the history of Great Britain ever gave such universal satisfaction to all classes of society in this country.'[1] And although, of course, it added 'increased lustre . . . to the glory of the British empire', it was (even a French newspaper concurred) 'equally beneficial to the subjects and interests of both England and China', opening 'a new continent to the increasing activity of all Europeans'.[2] 'Was not the fire of London in 1666 a good?' *The Times* concluded rhetorically. 'Did it not lead to immense improvement? . . . The answer must be in the affirmative.'[3] The lower-brow pictorial press delighted itself with triumphantly scornful images: of the *Nemesis* effortlessly smashing Chinese ships into fireballs, of fat, bored Chinese soldiers lolling by ancient cannon mounted on tree-stumps. 'A large family of the human race,' exulted the *Illustrated London News*, 'which for centuries has been isolated from the rest, is now about to enter with them into mutual intercourse. Vast hordes of populations, breaking through the ignorance and superstition which has for ages enveloped them, will now come out into the open day, and enjoy the freedom of a more expanded civilization, and enter upon prospects immeasurably grander.'[4]

In 1845, a harmless wax effigy of the fearsome Lin Zexu was installed in Madame Tussaud's. Six years later, other Chinese relics – including an entire war junk – were dragged back to England for the curious public to gasp at in the Great Exhibition. In a surely

Chinese artillery men.

choreographed stunt, at the Exhibition's opening ceremony a Chinese man – in full mandarin dress – charged out of the crowd and kowtowed to the Queen. One of the visitors to Crystal Palace, Charles Dickens, took the opportunity to sneer at the comic fragility of China (this 'glory of yellow jaundice'), comparing 'the greatness of English results' with 'the extraordinary littleness of the Chinese ... Consider the materials employed at the great Teacup Works of Kiang-tiht-Chin (or Tight-Chin) ... the laboriously carved ivory balls of the flowery Empire, ball within ball and circle within circle, which have made no advance and been of no earthly use for thousands of years.' The war junk on display struck him as a 'ridiculous abortion', a 'floating toyshop', a symbol of 'the waste and desert of time' represented by millennia of Chinese civilization.[5]

Despite the ambivalence that the conflict had generated before and during the Opium War, the fact of victory convinced many that Britain had been right: that the war had performed a necessary and relatively bloodless service to world civilization by opening China. And once expectations (of opportunities for trade, conversion and travel) had been inflated by the Treaty of Nanjing, merchants, missionaries and diplomats set about manoeuvring for yet more concessions and advantages – and if necessary, for a second war to achieve them. For others, though, the war remained an embarrassment, generating guilty repentance. The very term 'Opium War' – satirically coined through the debates of early 1840 to draw attention to the 'misdeeds' in China of the 'disgraceful' Whig government – expressed this bad conscience. To Victorian Britain – a nation that prided itself on its sense of Christian superiority over the non-Europeans that it conquered – the name brought discomfort. The British, it announced, had fought a war to push an addictive, illegal narcotic on the Chinese population. It was, one strand of opinion held, 'the most disgraceful war in our history . . . we lost about 69 men, and killed between 20,000 and 25,000 Chinese. There is no honour to be gained in a war like that.'[6] 'No man', a speech-maker declared in 1858, 'with a spark of morality in his composition . . . has dared to justify that war.'[7] During the Second World War, both the Nazis and the Japanese government would try to discredit the Allies by reminding their subject populations (including Chinese civilians, whom Japanese soldiers killed in their millions between 1937 and 1945) of Britain's past aggression against China.[8]

But war guilt can also have the opposite effect, leading to ever more militant acts of self-justification. Once blood has been spilt in dubious circumstances, those involved often try to brazen it out: first, through blaming the injured party for forcing them to act thus; and second, through affirming the validity of their violence by persisting with it. Through the nineteenth century, this pattern of response seems to have governed the behaviour of many of the most influential opinion-makers on China in countries like Britain – for the most part traders, diplomats, missionaries; later on, journalists and scholars. These groups rejected the idea of empathizing with the Chinese empire, publicizing instead the insufferable sins of the Chinese that had necessitated the first war (their pride, their xenophobia, their resistance to change, their heathen cruelty and immorality), all of which could only be subdued by yet more punitive violence.

As sinology became an academic discipline in the course of the nineteenth century, the West's earliest scholars of China – men, one would imagine, who felt a particular sympathy for Chinese culture – sprang mainly from the impatient ranks of those who believed that

China needed to be 'opened' by the West. Thomas Wade, first Professor of Chinese at the University of Cambridge, had been chief negotiator at the close of the second Opium War. He had complained furiously to the head of the Qing government when he discovered that the characters for 'Great Britain' were insufficiently elevated in a Beijing newspaper, and in the early 1890s barged into a debate at the Cambridge Union to spend an hour rebutting a speaker who had suggested that the first Anglo-Chinese War had been anything to do with opium.[9] When, consequently, some Chinese politicians and civilians responded to Britain's strident 'civilizing' overtures with growing resentment, the British merely felt all their allegations of Chinese xenophobia had been confirmed, and seized upon this hostility as a rationale for further war.

If we were to pick just one British individual to illustrate how the expectations, assumptions and bad feeling begun by the first Opium War built up to later conflicts, we should probably settle on Harry Parkes: outstanding sinophone, bullying sinophobe and architect of the second Anglo-Chinese war of 1856–60 – one of the men, his authorized biographer summarized, 'who made the Indian Empire and planted the colonies of England over the face of the globe.'[10]

Harry Parkes makes his first appearance (as a slight fourteen-year-old boy with blonde hair and bright blue eyes) in Sino-Western relations in August 1842, at the negotiations for the Treaty of Nanjing. Parkes had been abandoned to the China trade young. Orphaned at five, he had begun his education conventionally enough, but a twist of fate – a cousin had married Karl Gützlaff – gave his older sisters the idea of dispatching him to China in 1841, at the age of thirteen. On reaching Macao on 8 October, he was promptly apprenticed to John Morrison, one of the most senior British translators. 'We are sadly in want of interpreters', observed Morrison, who would die of overwork two years later, just as his father Robert (the first Protestant missionary to China) had done before him in 1834, 'and the moment he can speak a little Chinese we shall be right glad to have his services.'[11]

The following May, Morrison headed for the south-east to help with the negotiations at Nanjing, and took his apprentice with him.

It must have been a fine adventure for a high-spirited boy: extracting oxen from local farmers, seizing Chinese junks and fast-talking his way onto Pottinger's ship to attend the final ceremony (where he gained a taste for shark's fin soup). The closing engagements of this long, strange war catapulted Harry – son of a Wolverhampton ironmaster – into intimate contact with Britain's colonial elite. Pottinger quickly took a shine to him, inviting him to drop into dinner 'just whenever he pleased'. 'He is my boy and must come', the plenipotentiary laughed when someone objected to someone so junior being present at key diplomatic encounters.[12]

After two more years' apprenticeship in east and south China, the sixteen-year-old Harry was deemed competent for his first job: interpreter to the British consuls at the new treaty ports in Fujian. For years, he swaggered about these places defending British dignity in tasselled, braided, violet-cushioned sedan chairs of blue silk, all the while denouncing the natives (including, no doubt, the carriers who transported him in his silken thrones) as 'a most obstreperous race'.[13] He was devastated to discover, returning briefly to England in 1850, that he was expected to heave his belongings about with 'no coolies to help'. By the eve of the outbreak of the second Opium War in 1856, his time in China had given him an excellent knowledge of the Chinese language (and also Tibetan and Manchu), but minimal sympathy for the Chinese themselves. He had 'taken their measure and knew precisely how and where to plant the blow when blows were needed . . . The only way to gain respect in China is to *command* it.'[14]

While Parkes made his way, fourteen years passed: fourteen eventful but not particularly happy years for relations between the Qing empire and the foreign traders on its coasts. In Hong Kong, brick and stone warehouses replaced the wooden shacks that lined the northern shorefront; opium poured into the new storage space. By January 1842 – even though the China trade had been hit by the interruption of the war – the place bustled with facilities: with roads, barracks, hospitals, hotels, tailors, brothels, cookshops, opium dens, banqueting houses, a newspaper, a casino with a damp Venetian facade, theatres and a performing orang-utan called Gertrude, on daily display to the public between midday and one o'clock, 'taking her dinner, sitting on a chair at a table, using spoons, knives and forks, wiping her mouth with a towel [. . .] she will open a bottle of wine and drink to the health of the spectators, she will after smoke a cigar'.[15]

The trading community in Shanghai developed quickly too. Barely two months after the cherry brandy had been drunk over the Treaty of Nanjing, the new British consul had picked a site for a foreign concession amid the swamps surrounding the old Chinese town, to contain eleven traders' houses, two Protestant missions and a Union Jack. To general rejoicing, the concession's first sewer was laid down in 1852, by which point the settlement had swollen to 200 commercial ventures: banks, builders, publishers, steamship agents, watchmakers and shopkeepers alongside, naturally, opium trading houses. Shanghailanders were devoted to living well. A typical nineteenth-century dinner, a manual entitled *Shanghai Hygiene: Or, Hints for the Preservation of Health in China* disapprovingly described, began 'with rich soup, and a glass of sherry; then one or two side dishes with champagne; then some beef, mutton, or fowls and bacon, with more champagne, or beer; then rice and curry and ham; afterwards game; then pudding, pastry, jelly, custard, or blancmange, and more champagne; then cheese and salad, and bread and butter, and a glass of port wine; then in many cases, oranges, figs, raisins, and walnuts . . . with two or three glasses of claret or some other wine.' A moderate, health-preserving breakfast, advised the author, should consist merely of 'a mutton chop, fresh eggs, curry and bread-and-butter, with coffee or tea, or claret and water.'[16]

But beyond the dining table, things were going a little less well for those expecting an expansion of trade after 1842. The Treaty of Nanjing had promised much but achieved little. Manchester industrialists fretted that the Chinese seemed uninterested in buying the pianos and knives and forks that British merchants shipped to Hong Kong for the China market. As a commercial centre, the island was still seen as a poor second-best to Canton, the old foreign-trade centre of the empire. And although the Treaty of Nanjing had supposedly authorized foreigners to live in the city, relations between the British and Cantonese remained difficult.

The cause of the trouble lay in one of the Opium War's many failures of communication. Despite the precautions that Pottinger had taken to avoid diplomatic trickery over the final Treaty – binding the documents together with ribbons to prevent light-fingered mandarins from pulling out pages they suspected their emperor might find objectionable – a discrepancy between the Chinese and English versions of the agreement somehow remained. Article II in the English version promised permanent residency to the British and their families in the new treaty ports; the Chinese version allowed foreigners into the cities only 'temporarily' – for the duration of the trading season.[17] Over the following decade and a half, this slip would sour into a casus belli.

Canton's aversion to letting the British in was understandable. The city's half-million population had relatively little enthusiasm for welcoming the same group of foreigners whose guns had held them to a humiliating ransom across the final, sultry week of May 1841; the same group of foreigners who had soon after embarked on a spree of rape and grave-robbery in the surrounding countryside. Treaty or no treaty, they did not want to live among the British – it was enough to have a few hundred of them squeezed into the factory space to the south of the city. The emperor's men, meanwhile, did not dare force the issue. Since 1842, any official suspected of secret negotiations with the British feared for his personal safety. 'The moment the entry question is raised,' the imperial commissioner to Canton wrote in 1849, 'popular anger soars to the point of wanting to eat the Britons' flesh and sleep on their skin. Persuasion is useless.'[18] If the government buckled to British demands, civil war would result.

In many parts of south China, civil war was already in progress, with ethnic minorities fighting the opening engagements of the Taiping Rebellion – the fifteen-year revolt that would swallow up much of east China, leave tens of millions dead and almost end the Qing dynasty. The explosion of the Taipings was bound up with the growth of the Western presence in China. On the one hand, their ideology was based on a puritanical, authoritarian reading of Christianity gleaned from contact with Canton missionaries and their tracts. On the other, Taiping leaders reviled another noted Western import: opium. Those caught consuming the stuff were quickly beheaded, if they were lucky; if they were less lucky, they were first 'savagely beaten with one thousand blows' and given a final supper of sticky rice. The Taiping hatred of opium was also an expression of their passionate anti-Manchuism – a force in Chinese society that had only grown since the Opium War. The Qing, Taiping rulers believed, had deliberately encouraged addiction in order to enslave the Chinese. '[T]he Manchus have poisoned the body and soul of our nation', one Taiping leader analysed. 'Each year fifty million taels worth of opium is consumed ... In every matter they have violated our moral principles and each rule is designed to dominate our people ... The common people have been trapped and are sinking farther down in great danger.'[19] The destructive tensions between Manchus and Chinese present during the first Opium War properly unhinged the empire in the 1850s. To the Xianfeng emperor (1831–61), Dao-guang's harassed successor who took the throne in 1850, the ongoing British trouble was a sideshow, relative to the Taiping Rebellion.

Some British dimly understood that violence had not, and would not win Chinese hearts and minds – even men like Palmerston and Pottinger were irked by their fellow countrymen's bad behaviour in China, the former expressing his irritation at those who 'amuse themselves by kicking over fruit-stalls and by making foot-balls of the Chinese'.[20] But such scruples were pushed aside by outrage that the Chinese had not respected the letter of the Nanjing Treaty. Local Cantonese unwillingness to let the British into the city became shorthand for something much larger and more sinister: for the unreasonable xenophobia of the Chinese, and for 'the invincible repugnance with which the Treaty was held'.[21] The result was a vicious circle of antipathy. Every time the British pushed for entry to the city, they provoked a reaction from the population in Canton. Every clash with the Cantonese, in turn, convinced them yet more deeply of the existence of a grand, empire-wide conspiracy against them – though, according to foreign accounts of the time, the Cantonese people in normal circumstances managed to coexist quite peaceably with foreigners. 'Should a foreigner get into a disturbance in the street,' observed an American who lived in the foreign quarter of the city between 1825 and 1844, 'it was generally safe to say that it was through his own fault.'[22]

In autumn 1842, the Qing negotiators had come to a vague agreement with Pottinger that, at some point, the British would be allowed into the city. But as time passed, relations did not much improve. Three months after the Treaty of Nanjing, an Indian soldier's argument with a local fruit-seller escalated into a fatal stabbing and the burning, by a Cantonese mob, of the foreign factories outside the gates. In 1845, the British pushed the issue of entry into the city again, this time forming pistol-waving gangs who attempted to force the gates of the city. When Qiying, unlucky enough to have been appointed (after his handling of matters in Nanjing) Imperial Commissioner to Canton, tried to stick notices around the city urging the Cantonese to rethink their intransigence about the question of British entry to the city, locals responded by ripping them up and announcing on their own placards that the foreigners would be massacred as soon as they passed through the gate: 'The English are born and grow up in wicked and noxious villages beyond the pale of civilization, have wolfish hearts and brutish faces, the looks of the tiger and the suspicion of the fox.'[23] In 1846, another row with another fruit-seller sparked off a melee (in which three Chinese were shot dead). The British responded in the time-honoured fashion, with a gunboat storming of the forts guarding the riverway up to Canton. In December 1847, six Britons hiking a little to the west of Canton were killed by villagers on whom they had perhaps first opened fire. On it went, with the British demanding right of residence, and Cantonese opposition (cursings, stoning, robberies, chasings, mutilations, murders) padding out a multi-volume series of parliamentary Blue Books entitled Insults in China.

In the minds of men like Harry Parkes, Canton became the 'headquarters of fanaticism, arrogance, and duplicity – the focus of the anti-foreign feeling in China.'[24] It had to be humiliated and penetrated, warmongers argued: it was futile negotiating with this murderous mob as they had no intention of observing the terms of Nanjing – they had to be beaten out of their superiority complex. The sole aim of the Chinese authorities, concluded the British government's men in Canton in 1852, was 'to impede and resist the access of foreigners' and to 'inflame the people of Canton against us.'[25] 'If we permit', concluded Palmerston (who by 1855 would be prime minister), 'the Chinese to resume, as they will no doubt be always endeavouring to do, their former tone of superiority, we shall very soon be compelled to come to blows with them again.'[26] ('These half-civilised Governments', he had commented darkly a couple of years earlier, 'all require a Dressing every eight or ten years to keep them in order.'[27]) The precedent of the Opium War hung over it all: the idea that the Chinese simply must be forced. Although the Treaty of Nanjing had been 'a wise and solid foundation . . . a Treaty, unsupported by guns, is waste paper.'[28]

Although Palmerston and his consuls tried hard to manufacture an ethical justification for war, the main cause of British discontent was economic; and opium was once more implicated. Since four new ports had been opened to British commerce in 1842, it had been assumed that purchases of British manufacturers ought to quintuple. But by 1848, official exports to China were actually less than in 1843, while British consumers remained as hooked on tea and silk as ever (sales of tea more than doubled between 1842 and 1856; silk imports increased more than twentyfold).[29] A return to the bad old days of trade deficit resulted: in 1854, Britain found its balance of payments to China more than £8 million in the red (rising to £9 million in 1857). Reducing exports from China was no solution – they contributed too much to import duty in Britain, and to the costs of the Royal Navy. Palmerston decided the problem was caused by the limitations of the Nanjing Treaty, and that the Chinese interior – not just checkpoints along the coast – had to be opened to free trade. 'I clearly see', he told British consuls in China, as they pushed (fruitlessly and illegally) to revise the treaty, 'that the time is fast coming when we shall be obliged to strike another blow in China.' He left it to *The Times* to give a moral sheen to the quest for profit. Britain, the newspaper proclaimed, must 'enforce the right of civilised nations to free commerce and communications with every part of this vast territory'; it was no good 'treating with such a power as if it belonged to the enlightened communities of Europe.'[30]

Opium was apparently the only thing saving the British balance of payments from ruin. Although pianos and cutlery did not appeal to Chinese consumers through the 1840s and 1850s, drugs still did. As Palmerston candidly admitted in March 1857, 'At present the nature of our commerce with the Chinese is such that we can pay for our purchases only partly in goods; the rest we must pay in opium and in silver.'[31] 'The fumes of opium', one British missionary, a Reverend Smith, remembered as he sailed into Zhoushan in 1845 'wafted on the breeze, [infecting] the whole atmosphere around.' Business on board Shanghai opium ships, he later observed, was 'painfully animated.'[32] Through the 1840s, the *Chinese Repository* estimated that profits from the opium trade would leap from $33.6 million to $42 million, between 1845 and 1847 alone.[33] However loudly England's politicians and merchants bellowed about the civilizing mission of Free Trade, the fact remained that into the 1850s and beyond, opium sales in China (produced under British monopoly in India) underwrote much of the British empire: they funded the Raj (by 1856, opium revenue represented almost 22 per cent of British India's total revenue), they generated the silver for Britain to trade along the Indian Ocean, and in China they bought tea and silk.[34] To some extent, they kept the world economy moving: after British bills bought American cotton, American traders used these bills to buy tea in Canton; the Cantonese then swapped them for Indian opium.[35] Acknowledging the economic importance of its opium monopoly, in 1843 the British annexed a new slice of west India, the Sind, at least in part to hike up transit fees on opium grown outside British Bengal, thereby helping to make production of the drug beyond British-controlled territories unprofitable.[36] Through the 1840s and 1850s, after Pottinger had failed to legalize opium in 1842, British politicians remained nervous of a repeat of the 1839 campaign against the drug (which would jeopardize British profit margins), and pestered (without result) the Qing government to lift the official prohibition on the trade.

In 1856, Harry Parkes – newly appointed acting consul in Canton – barged into this vexed situation. Long before his appointment, Parkes had been convinced that entry to Canton was at the centre of the China problem – and had told Palmerston as much while on a brief trip home in 1850. In 1856, on another visit to Britain, he had enjoyed a second private interview with the prime minister in which he may well have been directly encouraged to find a pretext on which to force the question. Parkes was more than ready to generate some excitement, for the boredom of his new posting seemed expressly designed to infuriate him. There was nothing for him to do, except draft reports on coolie emigration, marry romancing expatriates and take walks around the hills nearby to work up an appetite for excessive colonial dinners. (Parkes was a maniac for fresh air: on a whirlwind grand tour around Europe in 1850, he yomped across the Alps for six days at the rate of twenty-six miles a day.)

On 8 October 1856, his opportunity arrived, provided by the Chinese governor of the province, Ye Mingchen, who committed the strategic error of requisitioning in Canton a Chinese pirate ship (of Chinese ownership, Chinese-crewed) by the name of the *Arrow* that was – allegedly – registered in Hong Kong and flying the British flag.[37] (Ye was a busy man, responsible for fighting the fires of the Taiping Rebellion in China's anarchic southern provinces, and the piratical *Arrow* was a part of the general climate of violent lawlessness pervading the south. As guardian of public order – through the 1850s he executed tens of thousands of local rebels – Ye was sensibly suspicious of the ship's activities.) Hearing of this 'outrage', Consul Parkes immediately rushed onto the scene to rescue the Chinese pirates, as if they were fine, upstanding British citizens. In the fray, he was struck. That same day, his cheek and pride still stinging, he dispatched a furious letter to Ye, informing him that unless reparation was rapidly forthcoming the British would be calling in the Commodore of H.M. Navy in the China seas: 'An insult so publicly committed must be equally publicly atoned.' The seizure of the ship, Parkes explained to the Governor of Hong Kong, Sir John Bowring, was 'a declaration on Ye's part that he will respect neither British flag nor British register.'[38] Over the next three days Parkes took a variety of unreliable, embellished testimonies from Western observers of the affray: most notably, from the boat's twenty-one-year-old Irish master, one Thomas Kennedy, who – it slowly emerged – had been making the vessel available as a floating warehouse for stolen goods. Chinese witnesses, in the meantime, upheld that the flag had not been flying, as did the only independent witness (a Portuguese sailor). Another interesting fact surfaced: both Parkes and Governor Bowring knew that the *Arrow*'s register at Hong Kong had expired on 27 September, so even if it had been flying the Union Jack, it would have had no legal right to do so.[39]

Casting aside such legalistic detail, on 11 October Parkes informed Bowring that 'it is only by active measures on our part that . . . reparation can be obtained . . . for so gross an insult.'[40] Luckily for Parkes, Bowring – a learned, fractious Englishman with a fine command of Latin and an ignorant impatience with China – was delighted to seize the pretext to threaten Canton's authorities. The Hong Kong governorship had rescued him from a string of business failures, and since arriving in 1852 he had been desperate to secure his reputation with a grand diplomatic success. He was convinced that gaining entry into Canton was his ticket into the history books – to the degree that an uncomprehending House of Lords dismissed him as a monomaniac.[41] Through October, both men deliberately, cynically and illegally warmongered to vent their dissatisfactions with China and the post-1842 status quo. 'Cannot we use the opportunity and carry the City question?' Bowring secretly wrote to Parkes on 16 October. 'If so, I will come up with the whole fleet.'[42] When Ye offered to return most of the sailors, Parkes refused them and instead drew up a plan for obliterating Canton's forts, while demanding to enter the city. 'Want of personal access', he wrote in the middle of the crisis, 'has been the occasion of the present trouble.' The business with the *Arrow*, he more or less admitted, was a smoke-screen.[43]

On 16 October, hostilities were opened when Parkes ordered the capture of a Chinese warship. On 29 October, British guns broke through the city wall and set about destroying Ye's government offices. By 3 November, British forces were shelling the old southern city, and Britain was again at war with the Qing empire. Through December and January, regular British bombardment turned the southern stretches of the city into 'one mass of smoke', with Chinese firefighters working frenetically under showers of 'shot and shell and Minié balls'.[44] 'We are so strong and so right,' Bowring rejoiced. 'We must write a bright page in our history.'[45]

Back in Britain, however, opinion was deeply divided at the turn events had taken in China. On hearing of the storming of Canton and the loss of civilian life in November 1856, the inhabitants of Manchester wrote to the Queen of their 'feelings of shame and indignation'.[46] The *Daily News* concurred: 'a more rash, overbearing and tyrannical exercise of power has rarely been recorded than that upon which it now becomes our painful duty to comment.'[47] The *Morning Post* disagreed: 'As far as past years teach us anything on the subject, there seems no way of reaching the heart of China but by the sword.' And China had so much to gain from being forcibly opened: Britain's merchants, missionaries and travellers would bring with them the 'seeds of civil advancement' – steam, gas, printing presses, schools, churches, railways, the House of Commons. 'Right or wrong,' the paper concluded pragmatically, 'we are in the quarrel, and there is nothing but to go on with it ... To yield to [such savages] were to imperil all our interests, not only in the East, but in every part of the world.'[48] 'The plain English of it is,' *Punch* summarized in a parodic rewriting of Bowring's letters to Parkes, 'that we haven't a legal leg to stand upon, so I have ordered up [the Admiral] and the big guns.'[49]

A sense of horror spread to both Houses, where the question of war with China was debated in March 1857. The Lords found Parkes' behaviour 'grotesque', and Bowring's 'unworthy ... of a great and civilised country.'[50] Pursuing such a war, they added, 'will cast disgrace upon our name and our flag, and will bring ruin upon our trade with [China].'[51] In the Commons, attacks from the Tory opposition were fully to be expected. A more serious problem for the government was that plenty of its own people were appalled by Palmerston's plans to fight: the Under-Secretary to the Colonies, Frederick Rogers, declared the business 'one of the great iniquities of our time', and Sir John Bowring 'a fool'.[52] A vote of no confidence in the government, on the grounds that its representatives in Canton had indulged in unjustified violence against China, was tabled by the Liberal Free-Trade and Peace Campaigner Richard Cobden. 'The Government of England', he told the House, are 'bullies to the weak and cowards to the strong.' 'In dealing with nations less civilized than ourselves', concurred the Conservative Edward Bulwer-Lytton, 'it is by lofty truth and forbearing humanity that the genius of commerce contrasts the ambition of conquerors.'[53]

The question of opium entered the debate on the very first day: he had been told, remarked a former chief justice at Bombay, 'that they ought to shut their eyes to this ... but he asserted that it had all to do with the question, for it had produced those deep feelings of hostility to the English merchants and the English Government on the part of the Chinese, and a reciprocal feeling of animosity on the part of the English, so as satisfactorily to account for the truculent sentiments displayed by nearly all the British residents in China.'[54] Palmerston – tired, septuagenarian and gout-ridden – tried to set patriotic pulses racing by denouncing Governor Ye as an 'inhuman monster', who had executed 70,000 Chinese in the last year alone. If we do not fight, he argued, we will be committing our countrymen in China 'to the mercy of these barbarians'.[55] He made little impression on his audience. 'Very dull in the first part,' the diarist Charles Greville pronounced his speech, 'very bow-wow in the second'.[56]

After four long days of debate, the government was defeated: the House had decided that the government proposed 'by force to increase our commercial relations with the East' – and that this was not acceptable.[57] Cobden's motion was carried by sixteen votes, doing, acclaimed Gladstone, 'more honour to the House of Commons than any [division] I ever remember.'[58] Among the rebels was Sir Francis Baring – seventeen years earlier, the Chancellor of the Exchequer who had financed the Opium War. Back in 1840, the confusion of motives that had built up to war with China – greed, opium, opportunism – had come within a whisker of bringing down the government. In 1857, it actually did.

But as soon as the administration had been unseated by bad conscience over affairs in China, Palmerston fought back by bombarding voters with self-justifications. While the fallen government prepared to fight what became known as the 'Chinese election' of spring 1857, its supporters waged a xenophobic scare campaign, bombarding pictorials with shocking propaganda images of Chinese tortures and executions, of 'disjointing, chipping to pieces, tearing the body asunder by pullies, skinning alive etc.' 'Really the whole civilised world', went one commentary, 'ought to combine together . . . to teach these wretches the common principles of humanity.'[59] The commercial community rallied about Palmerston, for 'upholding the honour of Great Britain . . . in a determination to protect the lives and property of British subjects, peaceably engaged in commercial intercourse with China.'[60] The war party's rhetorical strategy was simple: to repeat loudly that violence against China was honourable and inevitable until, in the popular imagination, it became so. The focus of debate about the war was adeptly shifted from a nice point of international law to emotional questions of patriotism and national interest.

The Protestant missionary lobby – shedding crocodile tears – also quickly joined the Palmerstonians: 'We weep over the miseries let loose on [the Chinese]; but we cannot shut our eyes to the fact, that nothing but the strong arm of foreign power can soon open the field for the entrance of the Gospel. If "pride goeth before destruction, and a haughty spirit before a fall", then it was inevitable that chastisement from some power would sooner or later result.'[61] For the missionaries, like the merchants, were disappointed with the results of 1842; they, too, wanted the great Chinese hinterland opened up to them: to be able to live, travel, build schools and churches wherever they liked – a privilege due 'to the honour of Great Britain, to the great principles of liberty, and above all to the interests of Christianity.'[62]

Not that Palmerston needed others to speak for him. He slandered the Chinese wherever he could: at diplomatic dinners thrown by the Lord Mayor, at constituency addresses, in newspaper articles (the 'Chinese election' was the first in British history in which the prime minister personally addressed the entire British nation in print) and in blatant lies. Claiming fictitiously that the heads of 'respectable British merchants' had been displayed 'on the walls of Canton', he labelled Ye 'an insolent barbarian [who] had violated the British flag [and] broken the engagements of treaties . . . and planned . . . murder, assassinations, and poisons' of British subjects. The politically informed wrote of their contempt for Palmerston's 'electioneering claptrap'.[63] But the public seemed to like it. Palmerston's actions, *The Times* applauded, were 'spirited', 'wise' and 'British'.[64] And after 7 April 1857, when the votes were counted, Cobden and other key members of the peace party were out, rejected by the electorate as 'un-English'; Palmerston was back in. Despite the distaste of the Houses of Commons and Lords, the great British electorate had returned the warmongers on a platform of jingoistic sinophobia. Palmerston was free to fight the China war that, less than a month earlier, Parliament had denounced. 'Almost for the first time in our history', mourned Earl Grey, 'we were engaged in a war which had not been formally made known to their Lordships by a Message from the Crown, and which Parliament had not been called upon to consider up to the moment when a large force was being despatched from this country.'[65] The last time this had occurred had probably been the first Opium War.

Britain's finest legal minds had debated through the winter of

1856–57 for nothing. Since September 1856, the British had been in secret negotiations with potential allies (the French, the Americans, the Russians), planning a joint operation to China. By 27 November, the principles of cooperation with the French had been established.[66] By early February 1857 (again, as with the first Opium War, weeks before the question was actually debated in the Houses of Commons or Lords), the Cabinet had already sent instructions east. Its representatives in India were to dispatch forces to China to coerce the country into revising the old treaty. China's hinterland (not just its treaty ports) was to be opened to British enterprise; an extra dispatch (stamped 'secret and confidential') ordered that opium was to be legalized.[67] On 10 March, seven days after the war vote was lost, it was announced that Lord Elgin – a former governor of Jamaica and Canada – had been appointed plenipotentiary to the expedition.

'Our position is certainly an embarrassing one,' even Parkes, the mastermind of the imbroglio, admitted, 'but it is one from which we cannot recede, and it is only by maintaining it and working on the fears of the people that we can be successful or escape defeat which would be most injurious to our interests.' War, in other words, would have to do again. Or as *Punch* satirically ventriloquized Bowring a second time, 'we have gone too far to recede. Tell [the admiral] to blaze away . . . My heart bleeds for these infatuated Chinese.'[68]

Once the expensive decision to fight had been taken, it took on a compelling logic of its own. From time to time, members of parliament would haul themselves to their feet to denounce this 'miserable war' (a war, moreover, that threatened to distract Britain from the far more serious business of the Indian Mutiny).[69] But the voices of doubt were drowned out by the politicians, businessmen and pressmen who had claimed the moral high ground for the conflict. *The Times* demonstrated the importance it attached to the war by appointing, for the first time, a Special Correspondent to China, George Wingrove Cooke. 'It is [the Chinese merchants and mandarins] who have rendered all this necessary', he wrote from Canton amid showers of British rockets and crashing Chinese roofs. 'Even in the interest of the Chinese, Canton must fall.'[70] His letters from

China were – by wild popular acclaim – promptly reprinted in book-
form in 1858; by 1861, they had run to a fifth edition, almost every
page laced with venom towards the Chinese. 'Humanity, self-denial,
and that true courtesy which teaches Western nations that it is a
part of personal dignity to respect the feelings of others', he wrote
as Anglo-French guns mowed down thousands on a pretext invalid
in international law, 'is in China dead in fact, and alive only in
pantomime.'[71]

On 29 December 1857, Canton was shelled into submission while
its wooden and thatched roofs crackled into flames – an occurrence
that *The Times* reported (with 'great satisfaction') as being 'singularly
well planned and wholly successful', while sighing at the 'obstinate
determination' of the Chinese, which had left the Allied commanders
only the 'painful alternative of attacking Canton.'[72] The Chinese
suffered around 450 casualties, to some 130 British and French.[73]
Resistance was severely hobbled by domestic uprisings in nearby
Guangxi province, where government forces were battling for survival
(back in autumn 1856, rebels had shattered seventy Qing warships).
Governor Ye did not dare transfer reinforcements to Canton, for
fear of jeopardizing Qing prospects in the ongoing civil war.[74] On
5 January 1858, British redcoats and French bluejackets entered 'the
virgin city' (Cooke's vulgar phrase) along the Avenue of Benevolence
and Love, and occupied all government buildings (including a Tartar
palace carpeted with bat dung).[75] Harry Parkes took personal pleasure
in hunting down his old enemy, the governor, through the narrow
streets of the city: 'Ye was my game'.[76] Eventually, his prey was
sniffed out: 'a very fat man contemplating the achievement of getting
over the wall at the extreme rear of the yamun', Cooke reported. A
captain on hand 'took the fat gentleman round the waist, and the
coxswain twisted the august tail of the imperial commissioner round
his fist.'[77] In breach of diplomatic protocol, within a month Ye was
shipped off to exile in India (where he died, of sickness and ennui, a
year later). Perhaps his worst punishment was to be forced to travel
in the company of Cooke, who delighted readers back home with his
mocking descriptions of the fallen governor (of his scrawny queue,
inferior to the tail of 'the smallest porker in China', of his 'simial
expression', of his tar-black teeth). Worse still, Cooke went on,
'he spits, he smokes, he eructates, and he blows his nose with his

fingers.'[78] With Canton's top official in British captivity, the city
quickly subsided into anarchy (the British protested throughout that
the French were *much* worse plunderers than they were, with the
Chinese the worst of all). At the end of it all, Parkes (a man who
fervently wished to be 'free at least of Chinese, language and people,
of both of which I am heartily sick') was left warlord governor of the
place.[79]

That May, the Anglo-French fleet sailed north, destroyed the forts
that controlled access to Beijing and humiliated the Qing negotiators
into agreeing to the Treaty of Tianjin, securing Palmerston's demands
for treaty revision. But when Lord Elgin's brother, Frederick Bruce,
returned in June 1859 to ratify the document at Beijing, the Qing
government tried to prevent his entry to the capital by blocking
the riverway up from Tianjin. Bruce responded by opening fire on the
forts south of Beijing. To the obvious shock of the British and French,
the Qing fired back with focused accuracy (proving their willingness to study Western battle tactics): 519 British sailors and soldiers
died, 456 were wounded. The carnage was particularly bad among
the infantry landing parties, who sank clumsily into pits dug into the
riverbank that fronted the forts, then were easily picked off ('potted
like crows') by Qing snipers. 'I never saw nor could have dreamt of
such a smash', one participant wrote, describing survivors missing
arms and legs, while corpses left strewn over the bank were beheaded
by Qing soldiers. 'Our loss is awful.'[80] 'We must strike a signal blow,'
a letter to *The Times* dictated, 'and amply revenge our slaughtered
countrymen, who have fallen by one of the most deliberate acts of
treachery that history affords. Let us by all means, and without loss of
time, prepare and despatch an expedition . . . to recover our dimmed
prestige and teach these vain barbarians that they have grievously
misapprehended the power of the [British] nation . . . the name of
European will hereafter be a passport of fear, if it cannot be of love,
throughout their land.'[81] It was time to send Elgin back to complete
the job.

The China station was a posting that Elgin had not relished from the
start. Britain's policy as a whole he pronounced 'stupid'; the pretext

of the seizure of the *Arrow* 'wretched . . . embarrassing . . . a scandal.'[82]
'Can I do anything', he wondered, on reading of the Indian Mutiny,
'to prevent England from calling down on herself God's curse for
brutalities committed on another feeble Oriental race? Or are all my
exertions to result only in the extension of the area over which
Englishmen are to exhibit how hollow and superficial are both their
civilisation and their Christianity?'[83] In 1858, he was unable to
'reconcile to my sense of right' Palmerston's orders to legalize opium.
'Though I have been forced to act almost brutally I am China's friend
in almost all this', he told his diary.[84] 'Lord Elgin', Harry Parkes
revealingly concluded, 'I do not consider a great man'.[85] And now
Elgin found himself wrested from the quiet job of Postmaster-General
that he had been given in 1859 and sent back to China, with
Palmerston urging him to attack and occupy Beijing. 'The general
notion', Elgin disagreed, 'is that if we use the bludgeon freely enough
we can do anything in China. I hold the opposite view.'[86] Within
another year, however, the China war had desensitized him into
committing what would become, in late-twentieth-century China's
public-history industry, one of the flagship acts of imperialist aggression against China.

The war – in its closing months – was one of the first to be
recorded in photographs, by an Italian photographer of fortune, Felix
Beato, fresh from capturing on film the killing fields of the Indian
Mutiny. His extraordinary visual account begins in spring 1860
with the fleet massing off Hong Kong, its coastline fringed with pompous neo-classical government buildings and the palaces of opium
princes.[87] After a slow journey north, on 14 August, a vengeful assault
on the Tianjin forts commenced, in which Anglo-French guns
pounded Qing soldiers until the ground outside was strewn with
Qing dead and wounded. 'Every man had done the duty expected of
him by his country', vindicating 'the tarnished honour of our arms',
commented one of the expedition's translators, Robert Swinhoe.[88]
An expert natural historian, Swinhoe would distinguish (before his
death aged forty-one) new species of petrel and pheasant (both of
which would be named after him). Surveying the corpses of fallen
Qing soldiers at the end of the day's work, however, he found 'all
were alike ugly, with thick yellow skins; all alike dirty and odifer-
ous.'[89] As the dying groaned in agony, an ecstatic Beato fussed about

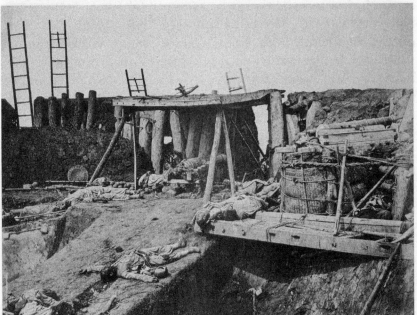

Felix Beato's 1860 photographs of the Anglo-French fleet at Hong Kong and of dead Qing soldiers in the forts near Beijing.

the carnage, pronouncing it 'beautiful' and insisting none of the corpses should be moved until he had captured them for posterity: strewn about the siege ladders and wooden posts of the forts, their heads lolling from dislocated necks.[90] 'I am very cheerful and with good reason', rejoiced Harry Parkes in a letter home (for Elgin had taken him along too, for his China expertise). 'We lost 201 men in killed and wounded . . . The enemy must have lost 1200 or probably 1500.'[91]

In the month that it took to arrange talks, the Qing decided to fight back with short-sighted duplicity: by kidnapping the thirty-strong negotiating party led by Parkes, then interrogating them (under torture) in Beijing's Board of Punishments. This provided yet more evidence of 'notorious Chinese treachery', of 'passive and mulish obstructiveness', of 'obstinate pride'.[92] The reluctant Elgin now had no reason to hold back from appropriately instructive punishment: 'the moral influence of our nation', observed one member of the expedition, 'is the mainstay upon which individuals ever must depend for protection.'[93] Winter was closing in; the Chinese empire had to be taught a short, sharp, painful lesson. Between late September and early October, British and French fought their way, through sand-dusted fields, cabbage gardens, woods, villages, imperial tombs and two garrisoned citadels, to the northern rim of Beijing. By this point, the armies were properly heartless: on their approach, they encountered a funeral procession led by a filial son taking his father's body back to the ancestral village. The coffin was thrown into a ditch, the mules confiscated.[94] As Beijing – its thick, high walls periodically interrupted by tiered gatehouses or overshadowed by the minarets of palaces – rose into view, British officers would have been portentously aware that they were the first Britons to reach the capital of the empire since the last, failed British embassy of 1816–17 (when the British ambassador had been expelled for refusing to kowtow to the emperor); and how circumstances had changed since then.

On 7 October, French forces (with the British only a little way behind) reached the emperor's beloved European-inspired Summer Palace (the Yuanmingyuan): some thirty-seven acres of pavilions, bridges, gardens and temples extending across the north-west of the city. There, after a brief engagement with twenty badly armed eunuchs, the gates were flung open, 'disclosing the sacred precincts of his Majesty's residence, to what a Chinaman would call the sacrilegious gaze of the barbarians.'[95] A treasure-house lay before the French army: 'a mine of wealth and of everything curious'.[96] The men of war, English observers remarked indulgently, behaved like 'grown-up schoolboys', 'suddenly told to take what they like in a pastry-cook's shop.'[97] Soldiers began running around in a temporary delirium of indiscriminate looting; objects too heavy to be removed were simply destroyed. The camp was a sea of the empire's best silks, with army cross-dressers dancing around in the gorgeous embroidered gowns of the emperor's concubines. Officers struggled in vain to rein in their rank and file; not even a dozen from each company responded to orders to 'fall in'.[98] 'My loot,' remembered one typically destructive colonel,

and I really thought I was in for a good thing, was a large silver stork, quite six feet high, and beautifully modelled. Having cut off his long neck and legs, and doubled up his wings by blows from a big stone, I and the men carried the mutilated body with much fatigue and difficulty down to my cart ... On arriving at camp, I sent it at once to the regimental gunsmith, who was also a goldsmith, that he might give me an idea of how much I might expect for my booty. His report was that the stork I had taken so much trouble over was not pure silver and therefore valueless ... As an experiment I cut a lump off one of the legs weighing a couple of pounds and threw it into the road. If it were of any value I knew it would have disappeared by morning. But when I went to look, although it had been moved, it was still lying in the road, so my hopes went down to zero ... After this the legs were thrown out in the road, then the head and neck, and finally the whole body that I had brought with so much care to camp, but no one would take even a little bit of the feast as a gift.[99]

Three days later, the soldiers forgot their madness and recovered their ranks, as they rearranged themselves into tidy lines before Beijing. But in the eyes of the pillagers, the sovereignty of the Qing would never quite recover from this desecration, as the imperial family's most beloved treasures slipped, with deliberate, humiliating carelessness, through the hands of soldiers and officers and into private and public collections across Europe, after briefly resurfacing in auction catalogues as 'curious altar ornaments', 'the Great Seal of State', 'a magnificent Incense Burner ... used as a stove in the Emperor's library'. Where they were put on public display, such as in London's Victoria and Albert Museum, they were proudly identified as originating 'from the Summer Palace of the Emperor of China'.[100] Revelling in the sacrilege of their actions, French and British soldiers had stood defiantly before the imperial throne, where 'so many princes and ambassadors ... had humbly prostrated themselves, according to the slave-like obeisance customary at the Chinese court'.[101] Many eye-witnesses to the looting admitted the treasures were dazzling: 'to depict all the splendours before our astonished eyes,' wrote one Frenchman, 'I should need to dissolve specimens of all known precious stones in liquid gold for ink, and to dip into it a diamond pen tipped with the fantasies of an oriental poet.'[102] Others, however, tried their best to continue humiliating the Qing in writing: 'there was nothing imposing in the *tout ensemble*', recalled one Briton. 'The artists and architects of China have failed to produce any great work'.[103] (He still scooped up a throne cushion as a souvenir.)

There was no more fight in the Qing – principally because they were simultaneously facing off a full-scale civil war triggered by widespread rural revolts. By the close of the 1850s, the Taiping Rebellion (from the deep south) and the Nian Rebellion (based in the east-central province of Anhui) had more or less taken control of the southern half of the empire and were threatening a northward push on the capital. Under pressure from both foreign invasion and domestic insurgents, the Xianfeng emperor had fled north of the Great Wall a full fortnight earlier and his brother, Prince Gong, had been left behind to tidy up the crisis. On 8 October, the prince had written to the British promising the return of the prisoners. Over the next few days, Parkes and nineteen European and sepoy soldiers were delivered back alive. The remaining hostages came back in coffins – they had been tortured to death, or had died from infected wounds in, one British officer observed, 'the most flagrant disregard to all international law. There is truly no term in our language which so essentially describes the Chinese rulers as the word barbarian ... The gloomiest page of history does not disclose any more melancholy tale than that told by one and all of those who returned.'[104] All that was left now for the Anglo-French forces to do was to decide on what Parkes termed 'exemplary punishment' for the Qing dynasty.[105]

On 18 October, 'as expiation of the foul crime of which the Chinese government had been guilty', what remained of the Summer Palace was burnt, 'to mark by a solemn act of retribution the horror and indignation with which we were inspired by the perpetration of a great crime.'[106] 'The world around looked dark with shadow', remembered one of the 5,000-odd British soldiers involved in the work. 'When we first entered the gardens they reminded one of those magic grounds described in fairy tales; we marched from them upon the 19th October, leaving them a dreary waste of ruined nothings.'[107] The 'crackling and rushing noise', remembered the naturalist Swinhoe, 'was appalling . . . the sun shining through the masses of smoke gave a sickly hue to every plant and tree, and the red flame gleaming on the faces of the troops engaged made them appear like demons glorying in the destruction of what they could not replace.'[108] But plenty of those in the Allied camp considered this reprisal gentle. 'There are people', the French plenipotentiary noted, 'who would like to burn Peking and to torture every Chinese mandarin.'[109]

The only photographic record of the Summer Palace was made by Felix Beato, who captured the Pavilion of the Spirit of Literature a handful of days before the palace's precincts were burnt, its curlicued gables towering over the gardens in melancholy sepia. By the time the flames had subsided, only blackened gables and charred pine trunks remained. 'It betokened to our minds a sad portent of this antiquated empire,' recalled Swinhoe, 'but . . . there is time yet for China to regenerate herself, and by cultivating friendly relations with foreign empires, learn [to] keep pace with the march of progress.'[110] 'A good work has been done', concluded a British army chaplain.[111] Two days later, that reluctant imperialist Lord Elgin – by this point, irascible with depression – was carried in a sedan chair borne 'by sixteen Chinamen dressed in royal crimson liveries' and accompanied by an army band playing 'God Save the Queen', to a treaty ratification ceremony. The new Treaty of Beijing quadrupled the indemnities agreed in 1858, as well as yielding everything for which politicians, merchants and missionaries had agitated between 1842 and 1856 – the right to establish an embassy in Beijing, freedom to travel, trade and work beyond the treaty ports, and the legalization of opium. To conclude the European triumph, Felix Beato strode forward to capture the agreement on film, while Prince Gong viewed the camera 'in a state of terror, pale as death'.[112]

Amid the smoke and victory, it was easy to forget that this was a war – a world war, pitting Britain, France, and at times the United States and Russia against the Chinese empire – that was provoked (in contravention of international law) by a young British alpha male, exploited by a cantankerous monomaniac and waged by a melancholy plenipotentiary who thought it 'wretched'.

Not everyone lost sight of the murky background to these dazzling triumphs, though. And it was the guilt of those with longer historical memories that ushered in the next, strange phase of the Opium War's afterlife.

Chapter Sixteen

THE YELLOW PERIL

In 1860, it still took a couple of months to reach Britain from China: time enough to think about what a person had seen and done there. For one such traveller, Henry Loch – former Bengal cavalryman, veteran of the Crimea, Cheshire Yeoman and private secretary to Lord Elgin – sailing into Dover on 27 December 1860, it was a triumphal progress. That September, Loch, alongside Harry Parkes, had been kidnapped, imprisoned and threatened with death by representatives of the Qing government – his experiences seemed to vindicate fully the need for force against the Chinese. As he travelled back, he was preceded and overtaken by dispatches that worked the country into a frenzy of anti-Chinese patriotism. According to the press, the fate of the hostages was 'anxiously discussed in every circle': the country was 'agonised' about this 'sensitive and thrilling topic', to read of Loch's 'ill usage at the hands of a cruel enemy who has not even the excuse of barbarism'.[1] By the time Loch docked, carrying with him the ratified treaty – an event celebrated by a cannon salute in London – he was a national hero, welcomed back onto British soil by hearty cheers and the mayor, who told him that 'the recital of his sufferings had excited the utmost sympathy and commiseration of his country-men [but] that these sufferings had induced the vigorous measures that had resulted in a glorious peace.'

A large number of ladies also turned out to greet the returning hero who, beneath his sizeable Victorian beard, 'appeared highly gratified' by his reception.[2] Queen Victoria and Prince Albert – delighted to be presented with plundered novelties from the emperor's

267

own bedroom (a jewel-encrusted, silk-tasselled cap, a jade-covered edition of Confucius's sayings and a fluffy Pekinese that some wag had christened Looty) – were both anxious to meet him. Loch himself had no doubt as to the significance of what he had experienced: the war and treaty just past 'happily concluded an event which was the commencement of a new era, not only in the history of the Empire of China, but of the world, by the introduction of four hundred millions of the human race into the family of civilized nations.'[3]

A British traveller of 1849, though, had reached different conclusions on the voyage home from China. He was not a disinterested observer of relations between the two countries over the past decade: his family – uncles, cousins, nephews – was steeped in the opium trade. He was not only a veteran of ten years' commercial service in China, but also a witness to the first Opium War – he had helped ensure that the conflict had not disrupted opium supply to China by overseeing the unloading of opium onto British-occupied Zhoushan in 1840.[4] His name was Donald Matheson, nephew of the more famous James. By 1849, his conscience had ordered him to abandon the clan business; within another eight years he would become a luminary of the newly founded Society for the Suppression of the Opium Trade (SSOT). After 1896, when his aunt Mary, James Matheson's widow, died and the family property passed to Donald, this guilt-ridden Presbyterian would get the opportunity to wage his personal war on the drug from the magnificent Gothic pile that Uncle James had paid for with opium profits.[5] His early 'China-opening' career and later dedication to the nineteenth-century anti-opium cause would exemplify the way in which the mercantile sinophobia and bad conscience of the first Opium War would conspire together to poison Sino-Western relations.

For decades after 1842, Britain failed to make up its mind about opium, and its effects on China. 'The ravages of opium we meet with here on every hand,' claimed an impassioned missionary in 1856, 'and the deterioration of the morals of the people we meet with generally, I cannot but ascribe, in great part, to the use of this ensnaring and destructive drug.'[6] 'Nowhere in China are the people so well off,' an observer of western China contradicted him in 1882, 'or so hardy, and nowhere do they smoke so much opium.'[7] 'Why, the slave trade was merciful compared with the opium trade', Karl Marx quoted a radical anti-opium pamphleteer in 1856. 'We did not destroy the bodies of the Africans . . . we did not debase their natures, corrupt their minds, nor destroy their souls.'[8] 'I would recommend the well-intentioned persons who have of late been raising such an outcry on the subject of opium', a botanist argued back, 'to reform their own [rum-sodden] countrymen . . . the Chinese are just as capable of taking care of themselves as their would-be guardians are.'[9]

Through the middle decades of the century, the British also went on liberally eating and drinking the drug. Until the 1868 Pharmacy Act (which limited opium sales to chemists'), grocers' catalogues were full of opium-enriched patent potions, listed next to jam and barley-sugar.[10] Opium consumption remained particularly high in the Fens, where shop counters stockpiled 3–4,000 vials of laudanum for Saturday nights.[11] It was used against pain, spasms, insomnia, to induce perspiration and reduce bronchial mucus, for diabetes, for melancholy, for overexcitement, for drunkenness; laudanum mixed with ox-gall served for earache, insanity, hysteria and toothache; with egg yolk, for piles.[12]

Commentators found it similarly difficult to agree on whether or not the events of 1839–42 had had anything to do with opium. Certainly not, argued one David Wells in a learned American journal of 1896: they all sprang from a 'deliberate insult' to foreigners in Canton. If 'England had not undertaken the task of teaching the Chinese this initiatory lesson, the government of the United States would sooner or later have had to have done it.'[13] Poppycock, rebutted a subsequent issue: 'the seizure of contraband opium . . . was the direct cause of the war . . . We (the British people) are responsible not only for supplying the Chinese with an enormous quantity of poison from India, but also for setting agoing its widespread cultivation in China.' The war was 'a national disgrace.'[14]

But as early as the 1880s, the tone of the opium debate in countries like Britain was changing – for Chinese use of the drug was rising at a disturbing rate. However hard some individuals disputed the accusation that the most recent Anglo-Chinese war had been connected with opium, discussion of how exactly it was to be legalized in China occupied six pages of Elgin's official correspondence with the Foreign Office. Despite efforts to conceal the fact, the treaty that concluded the second China war in 1860 had discreetly added opium to a list of legitimately dutiable goods. Although the tax on opium was supposedly prohibitive (thirty taels of silver per chest), Chinese imports steadily grew: from 75,822 chests in 1859, to 84,528 in 1879.[15] In Beijing, went one report from 1869, 'there are opium shops in almost every lane, and two or three in larger ones.'[16] Use now spread beyond the smart coastal cities to the countryside. 'Over the past thirty to forty years,' remarked one 1878 almanac, 'smokers have become as common in the remote countryside as they used to be in the cities. These days, a town spends more money on opium than it does on rice.'[17]

In response to this increase in opium-smoking, a British anti-opium lobby – offspring of the middle-class pressure-group politics that, in the first thirty years of the nineteenth century, had mobilized such vocal opposition to slavery – began to organize. It was all right, still, for respectable society to use the drug responsibly and creatively: 'Drops, you are darling!' Wilkie Collins hymned his bottle of laudanum. 'If I love nothing else, I love you!' He sipped his opium tincture all the way through the writing of *The Moonstone* (1868); when the novel was done, he claimed no memory of having written the thing. It was also acceptable for knowledgeable doctors to minister ever stronger, larger, more addictive doses (administered by the hypodermic syringe, invented in the 1850s) of synthetic opiates in the form of morphine (isolated from raw opium around 1805) or later of the miraculously potent Heroin (patented in 1895). But educated opinion was increasingly appalled by negligent labouring mothers who drugged their infants by day to keep them quiet with minders; by working-class users who abused opium syrups and pills as a stimulant cheaper than booze; and by the back-street grocers who supplied them.

To help establish its own credentials for defining, controlling and prescribing drugs, the medical profession now began to reclassify unregulated use of opium (of any kind – moderate or extravagant, regular or irregular) as a self-inflicted disease called addiction: a 'vice', a sign of 'moral bankruptcy' or 'moral insanity' that required expert policing.[18] The new theorists of drug use and addiction mixed their claims to scientific rigour with a language of ethical disapproval; self-prescribed consumption of opium was increasingly condemned out of hand in tones never applied to alcohol or tobacco. 'The familiar use of opium in any form', pronounced Sir Clifford Allbutt, inventor of the clinical thermometer, 'is to play with fire, and probably to catch fire.' 'Habitual use', lectured the President of the Royal College of Surgeons, 'is productive of the most pernicious consequences'. In 1908, the Secretary of the British Medical Association proposed that a drug habit should be classified as a form of mental disease, of 'moral infirmity', requiring some form of committal.[19]

The anti-opium lobby's disapproval took on a new racial dimension when it was directed against use of the drug in China (which had emerged, in recent decades, as undoubtedly the world's biggest opium market). Over the course of the nineteenth century, as Asia and Africa had fallen before Western science and industry, theorists of the European empires had sought convincing explanations for their supremacy, fixing the world into racial types distinguished by immutable characteristics – with the whites clearly at the top, and the 'yellows' and 'blacks' below. The conspicuous popularity of the drug amongst the Chinese became a symptom of the moral weakness and torpor of this alien, inexplicable race. The campaign that fought the opium trade in China was, therefore, a contradictory creature. On the one hand, it betokened a special sympathy for China and guilt about the role of the West (and especially Britain) in foisting the drug on the population. On the other, it could not conceal a certain disgust for the Chinese themselves. The opium trade produced a rationale for the Christian presence in China, turning the country into a depraved mass of opium sots to be disciplined and improved by salvation-hungry missionaries. 'I am profoundly convinced', declared the founder of the China Inland Mission, 'that the opium traffic is doing more evil in China in a week than Missions are doing good in a year.'[20] In other words, the Western presence in China had first created a problem then provided the service to solve it – the opium trade both generated and justified the civilizing mission.

In 1874, the new Society for the Suppression of the Opium Trade formally began its crusade. It divided into committees, it held essay competitions, it lobbied MPs, it threw petitions at the House of Commons, it paid bonuses to anti-opium medics to add science to the campaign. Above all, it published: a stream of tracts, pamphlets, books and a journal called the *Friend of China*, all chorusing the noxious nature of the drug ('Truly, it is an engine in Satan's hand') and of the trade itself (a 'great and grievous sin'). 'One of the fallacies put forth', argued an 1847 forerunner to the campaign, 'to palliate the enormity of this crime, is that the vice of opium smoking is not worse than that of gin drinking; but this is on a par with another fallacy, that if Englishmen did not supply the Chinese with opium, another nation would. How sunken must be the morals of an individual, when *crime is measured by crime!*'[21] Yet the anti-opium lobby's pronouncements were also underpinned by a horror of Chinese degeneracy. It oversimplified the dangers of opium use, refusing to distinguish between the great variety of types and patterns of Chinese smoking (medical, recreational, daily, frequent, occasional and so on). In the testimonies of anti-opium missionaries, opium use could only be 'bad, *utterly bad* . . . Morally – demoralizing, Physically – weakening, Socially – degrading'.[22]

In time, this 'deplorable' national addiction was presented as a defining characteristic of the Chinese race, corroborating the belief that they were 'immured in darkness . . . intrinsically an immoral and sensual nation . . . in a sleepy or dreaming state' (in contrast with the expansive vitality of Europeans).[23] 'The phlegmatic temperament and indolent habits of the Asiatic make him more liable to contract the habit', testified one China-based missionary, because of their 'love of pleasure and vice. The opium dens are moral sinks, and opium smoking is associated with gambling and gross sensual indulgence.' Opium, another missionary confidently reflected, 'is the judgment of God on a dishonest race.'[24] The hardy, extrovert race of Europeans would never take to it, claimed other analyses, because they preferred the fiery effects of alcohol and, in any case, it was too 'uncomfortable to lie down for any length of time wearing a pair of tight trousers and ordinary boots.'[25]

In time, then, the guilt that had originally generated the anti-opium movement morphed into denigrations of the 'Chinese national character'. This in turn opened the door to the comforting idea that China's yen for opium had, in fact, very little to do with British gunboats and profit margins, and everything to do with the base instincts of the Chinese themselves. One reverend reported that his anti-opium sermons in China were at times interrupted by the heckle, 'Who sells Opium?' 'My answer has been, I fear, not a very Christian answer: "Who smokes the Opium?" I have thus silenced them hundreds of times.'[26] A happy historical coincidence further lightened consciences about Britain's opium-trading activities in the late-nineteenth century. By the 1880s, Chinese domestic production of opium had begun to equal imports. At last, the British could point at statistics to prove that the Chinese were determined to poison themselves.

Even the most vigorous critics of Britain's opium-running activities in China were sinophobic. Donald Matheson, for example, refused to blame the British for the Opium War. A student of history, he remarked, would be misguided to assume hostilities sprang from the seizure of opium: the casus belli was 'one more deep-seated and more remote in point of time . . . the arrogant assumption of supremacy over the monarchs and people of other countries claimed by the Emperor of China for himself and for his subjects'.[27] 'In the beginning and the very origin of the quarrel we were distinctly in the wrong', admitted Justin McCarthy, SSOT's spokesman on Chinese history. At the same time, though, 'the whole principle of Chinese civilization . . . was . . . erroneous and unreasonable . . . As the thought of having to go a day unwashed would be to the educated Englishman of our age . . . so was the idea of innovation to the Chinese of that time . . . The one thing which China asked of European civilization and the thing called Modern Progress was to be let alone.'[28]

Yet a guilty terror of retribution for past iniquities lingered on. By the late-nineteenth century, this fear was decades old. In April 1840, only days after the Opium War vote had squeaked through Parliament, *The Times* had named it 'the mother of a brood of conflicts . . . so far as the colonial scepter of Great Britain waves . . . her reputed power . . . shall have offered provocation to . . . vengeance.'[29] An anti-opium agitator of 1847 had agreed: 'We stand convicted before the nations of the world, as well as before an Omniscient Deity from whom nothing can be hidden, as a government and people actively and legally engaged in the perpetration of murder and desolation, on a scale of such magnitude as to defy calculation . . . We are all involved in the guilt, and participants, even by our silence, in a sin [that] must ere long bring on us that Divine vengeance which though slow, is sure, and never invoked in vain!'[30] For if, as those who had fought and won the Opium Wars argued, the Chinese hated foreigners, it stood to reason that they would exact vengeance for the humiliations suffered at the hands of the West.

The puzzle was working out how exactly revenge would be taken. All that was clear was that it should be ingenious and horrible: for whatever the faults of the vice-laden Chinese as told by popular stereotype, China was also (in Victorian estimation) a proud, ancient civilization 'with a literature and laws and institutions of its own.'[31] If the Chinese were to be hated, they were also to be feared. Retribution, when it came, would be fully worthy of their elaborate capacity for treachery and cruelty (a capacity that had been abundantly confirmed by the British experience of fighting them in two Opium Wars).

In 1886, a forty-nine-year-old Scottish globetrotter called Constance Gordon Cumming thought that she had cracked the mystery: 'If . . . a taste for opium should once gain a footing in England, as it has already done in America, there may be reason to fear lest the poison which Britain has so assiduously cultivated for China, may eventually find its market amongst our own children – a retribution too terrible to contemplate, though one against the possibility of which it were well to guard.'[32] British bad conscience was merging with imperialist loathing for China: the outcome would be the 'Yellow Peril'.[33]

Through the 1890s, the popular boys' comic *Chums* devoted most of its pages to informing sons of the empire about stamp-collecting, rugby and famous swords of the Middle Ages, and to answering such key questions as 'Why do boys who have left school always have a great affection for masters who flog?' In late November 1892, though, its editors took a break from their standard repertoire to dispatch a '*Chums* Commissioner' to carry out a spot of contemporary London reportage by investigating 'the terrors of the opium den'. Guided by a knowledgeable clergyman, the journalist tramped through the 'foul alleys' of Stepney and Shadwell in search of 'the deadly juice', until the two men reached their destination: 'one of the most noted of the opium dens in the East-end'.

It was a dark, claustrophobic hole of a place, its twenty bunks occupied by prostrate, insensible bodies 'reaping their reward' from their 'fill of poison'. The *Chums* mission was greeted in pidgin English by a sinister, ingratiating Chinese proprietor with 'little pigs'-eyes' and 'decayed and discoloured teeth': 'Bring you friendey. No smokey pipey?' 'It will probably make me ill,' the indomitable commissioner thought, 'but it is as well to try things just as an experiment.' As soon as the pipe reached his lips, however, he 'began to choke. My throat seemed closed, my nostrils afire, my brain swam . . . my head was sinking into my body, while my legs were momentarily growing shorter . . . I was breathing blue flames – and then I suddenly regained my senses and was violently sick . . . Such was my experience on the occasion of my first and last visit to an opium den.'[34]

The message of the piece was not particularly subtle. It was a parable on the horrors of racial pollution: a lesson to British boys on the dangerous, degenerate presence of Chinese poison in the very heartland of the empire. What is more interesting, perhaps, is that by 1892 this dread had become sufficiently mainstream to permeate even the usually cheery, wholesome pages of children's comics. And to understand how this had come about requires a brief diversion into the paranoid world of European racial science in the second half of the nineteenth century.

Some racial theorists concluded fairly soon after the publication in 1859 of *The Origin of Species* that, in the general Darwinian struggle for survival, inferior races were bound to be extinguished by the (white) master-race (whose global domination was justified and maintained by its command of modern science). As one commentator put it, 'the weaker races are perishing off the face of the land from inherent inability to stand before the superior race.'[35] Belief in the rigidity of divisions between the world's races was reaffirmed by the 'unspeakable horrors' of the Indian Mutiny, in which Hindu sepoys – suspecting a mass British conspiracy to Christianize them – massacred British women and children, then were themselves (in far greater numbers) massacred by vengeful British troops. Uninterested in local explanations for this sudden eruption of Indian violence, many shocked readers of dispatches judged instead that it was simply proof of inveterate barbarity. 'One stands aghast', observed a shuddering John Bright, 'at the reflection that after a century of intercourse with

us, the natives of India suddenly exhibit themselves greater savages
than any of the North American Indians who have been brought into
contact with the white race.'[36]

But by the close of a nineteenth century that in many respects
appeared to have belonged to Great Britain, confidence was seeping
out of the imperial enterprise and its sense of racial triumphalism. As
the question of Irish Home Rule dominated debates of the 1880s, the
very principle of imperial unity seemed in doubt. Soon, opponents
of Ireland's independence were convinced, 'every subject race . . .
would know that we were no longer able to cope with resistance'.
The disastrous state of public health exposed by Boer War recruits,
and Britain's shrinking economy (between 1870 and 1906, its share
of global manufacturing capacity retracted from 32 per cent to 15 per
cent) further confirmed forebodings of decline.[37] 'The big smash is
coming one of these days', Kipling prophesied in 1897.[38]

The fear arose that current racial distinctions between populations
might not be immutable – for if all species changed and evolved
according to their environment, they might not only progress, but
also regress. Troubled fin-de-siècle theorists made an intellectual
industry out of degeneration fears, classifying a host of physical,
psychiatric and social disorders (hernias, goitres, pointed ears, phobias,
alcoholism, prostitution) as hereditary pathologies that were undermining European populations. Such thinking combined with growing
public hysteria about deviant social groups (criminals, the insane,
the poor, homosexuals, communists) to feed the idea that the white
races in countries like Britain and France might be in decline. And
if that were so, the outcome of the inevitable conflict between races
would be in doubt. 'Civilisation', speculated a Secretary of State for
India after 1905, 'is in real danger, near, sinister and terrible from
the uprising of Asiatic power, yellow, brown, and black against all
the forces of the West.'[39]

In the nineteenth-century hierarchy of races, the Chinese had
always been a little hard to place. To European minds, they had long
been more than simply inferior to the whites. Although back in the
eighteenth century, Linnaeus – the Swedish father of taxonomy – had
confidently classified the Chinese as *Homo/Monstrous*, on a level with
the Hottentots, many of his contemporaries had lauded the country
as a political, cultural and social utopia.[40] Even during the scornful

decades of the nineteenth century, China presented a challenge to Britain. It was a long-established, literate and sophisticated empire, albeit (in the dominant Victorian view) an underperforming one. By the early years of the twentieth century, Western anxieties were growing that this 'sleeping lion' seemed ready to turn on its former aggressors. As usual, the primary source of unease towards China was economic. One of the clauses of the 1860 Treaty of Beijing had forced the Qing emperor to legalize emigration of his subjects. By 1900, Chinese workers had begun to disperse through the global economy, forming sizeable communities of cheap labour: around 31,000 in Australia, 15,000 in British Columbia, 3,000 in New Zealand and 1,000 in Great Britain.

This seemed to turn the tables on British imperialism. For two decades up to the 1860s, British gunboats had been busy penetrating China. Now the Qing empire was striking back by infiltrating white society. Britain – transfixed by fear of decline – responded by viewing this diaspora as an unprecedented threat to 'Anglo-Saxon values'. The simple truth was that Chinese labourers in Australia, South Africa, America and Britain were quieter, harder-working, more reliable and more sober than their white counterparts. Given the practical superiority of Chinese populations, white workers therefore had little choice but to shift the grounds of attack: from a question of labour efficiency to one of a moral, racial clash between Asians and Anglo-Saxons. In the closing decades of the nineteenth century, a hate campaign against the Chinese flourished in Britain, the United States and settler societies such as South Africa and Australia, accompanied by draconian legislation restricting immigration.

Almost wherever Chinese communities went, they were accused of vice, violence and mutiny, of being a secretive, alien, xenophobic community that refused to integrate with Anglo-Saxon society. 'Colonies of Chinese' were 'being founded in all the chief ports of the British Isles', announced scaremongers. 'An imported horde of underpaid Chinese starvelings' threatened to take over 'the great traditions of the British sea dog.'[41] While suspicion and violence grew, relations inevitably deteriorated, neatly reinforcing earlier prejudices about the sinister exclusiveness of the Chinese. As police and judges began to assume that any violence in Chinese communities was Triad warfare, these communities tried to resolve disputes between themselves rather than throw themselves onto the unsympathetic mercies of the law courts. Meanwhile, Chinese immigrants who tried to assimilate – by learning English, by wearing European clothes, by marrying local women – were ridiculed, or suspected of trying to penetrate English society for invidious reasons.[42] Respectable middle-class magazines spread dread further up the social scale. In 'The Chinese in England: A Growing National Problem' (an article distributed liberally around the Home Office), one hack journalist warned of 'a vast and convulsive Armageddon to determine who is to be the master of the world, the white or yellow man.'[43]

The denouement of the Boxer Rebellion (quickly dubbed the 'Yellow Horror' by contemporary observers) seemed to vindicate the prophets of race war.[44] Until this point, the milder advocates of British imperialism – Charles Elliot's intellectual heirs – argued against blanket stereotyping of the Chinese. It was only the government that was anti-foreign, they argued; the ordinary, commercially minded people, by contrast, welcomed the British and their trade. The events of 1900 demolished that idea. Local violence against European missionaries in north-east China had steadily grown through the 1890s until around 1898 anti-Christian feeling coalesced into a secret society identified in foreign press reports as 'the Boxers' (for the style of martial arts that, its members claimed, rendered them invulnerable to bullets). In spring 1900, after thousands of these desperate, leaderless rebels converged on Beijing, a nervously wavering Qing government decided to support the movement.

On 20 June, Boxer groups began to lay siege to the foreign legations in the capital. While the Western press inaccurately reported that the entire foreign community in the capital had been massacred, a combined force of American, British, French, German, Japanese, Italian, Russian and Austrian troops stormed the city, having devastated in the process the countryside and towns they had passed through en route. By the end of the fifty-five-day siege of the legations in Beijing, some 200 foreigners had been killed across China in incidents of both popular and state-sanctioned violence (the most notorious being the execution of forty-four men, women and children in the north-west under orders from the local governor who had called them to his provincial headquarters with the promise of protection).

The Boxers – drawn substantially from the lowest ranks of society

– seemed to offer conclusive proof of the evil impulses of the Chinese race. It did not matter that local circumstances – famine, impoverishment, the imperialist scramble for north China and dubious missionary manoeuvres to seize land and protect 'Christian' bandits through the 1890s – made the Boxer explosion of anti-missionary violence explicable, if no less horrendous for those involved. Neither did it matter that, over the late-nineteenth and early twentieth centuries, Chinese immigrant populations in North America, Australia and Europe would suffer far more xenophobia than the Boxers meted out to Westerners through the 1890s. The debacle confirmed all the West's worst and oldest prejudices about China; press and publishing were flooded by missionary and military accounts of the horror and violence, which seemed to justify the unleashing of any kind of retributive humiliation on the Chinese people as a whole. In the aftermath of the rebellion, as thousands of foreign soldiers ravaged north China, anything Chinese was vulnerable to defilement. Every enclosed, sanctified space was to be blasted open in a great 'punitive picnic': villages and towns were razed; one of Beijing's city walls and a cemetery were dynamited to make way for a railway line; the vast white courtyards and vermilion pavilions of the Forbidden City were occupied for a memorial service for Queen Victoria. Privates played hockey around the dynasty's most sacred temples, picked over the private apartments of the emperor and empress, and lolled about on imperial thrones. Captured on Kodak Reloadables, their sacrilegious actions thrilled audiences at home.[45]

The populace was punished too, in beatings, bayoneting and mass public executions (often thronged by victorious crowds of soldiers, missionaries and photographers). In one particularly horrific incident, a man with suspected (though unproved) Boxer connections was first punched and kicked (by Americans); shot through the head (by a Frenchman); then had his skull 'stomped' in (by a Japanese soldier). Even so, the man survived for an hour longer, while his tormentors stood about, roaring with laughter at his death agonies.[46] '[W]here one real Boxer has been killed since the capture of Pekin,' observed the American commander of the Allied reign of terror, 'fifty harmless coolies or labourers on the farms, including not a few women and children, have been slain.'[47]

Western fear of China and the Chinese was given a keener edge by the modernizing reforms introduced by the Qing government after the Allied invasion of 1900. As the dynasty sent out embassies to study the political, technical, social and military institutions of the West and edged towards constitutional monarchy, journalistic hostility only intensified. China was, *The Times* concluded, 'a nation teeming with vitality . . . slowly modernised, then suddenly eager for expansion, perhaps for conquest, for world-power, if not for revenge for wrongs inflicted upon it by nearly every European power.'[48] When the Chinese empire refused to participate in the Western-dominated international system, it was attacked as an arrogant, xenophobic threat. When it began to play by Western rules (sending its subjects to work abroad, modernizing and Westernizing its armies, schools and government), it was accused of plotting to use Western technology against the West.

Back in Britain, and other Western countries in which Chinese labourers had settled, inchoate fears of the retributive Chinese 'invasion' coalesced in a dread of the Chinese opium den. For opium was the perfect instrument of degeneration: this Oriental poison subtly permeating Britain and its people with its vengeful smoke. Trying hard to forget recent Western readiness to provide opium to the Chinese, late Victorian and Edwardian journalists (including the *Chums* commissioner) portrayed the smoking establishments set up by Chinese immigrants in cities like London as vice-ridden head-quarters of Oriental iniquity. After an excursion in 1866, Charles Dickens provided one of the earliest templates for these accounts, filling pages with descriptions of bestial Asiatics piled on top of each other, of their 'livid, cadaverous, corpse-like' faces and 'stolid sheep-like ruminations'.[49] One contributor to *Strand Magazine* in 1891 found everything in the den that he visited similarly dreadful: the evil-looking proprietor with his 'parchment-coloured features', 'his small and cunning eyes . . . twisting and turning so horribly'; the filthy yellow walls; even the staircase was 'the most villainously treacherous . . . which it has ever been my lot to ascend'.[50] 'Oriental cunning and cruelty', observed another visitor to an opium establishment in 1904, 'was hall-marked on every countenance'.[51] 'A great many people', remarked a report of a Whitechapel den, 'despise the Chinese: they say they are untruthful, and sly, and cruel, and conceited, and very dirty . . . there is a good deal of truth in all this;

but then we must remember that they are heathens . . . the love of opium deadens a man's conscience and makes him ready to do any wicked deed.'[52]

The curious fact is that while panic about opium dens was taking hold – through the closing years of the nineteenth century – there were few Chinese in Britain as a whole, and far fewer opium dens. Until the 1860s, there were no more than around 100 Chinese in the country, climbing to only 1,100 in 1911.[53] In 1884 – almost twenty years after Dickens had made his investigative foray into Limehouse – there were an estimated six smoking establishments in East End London. 'It was not repulsive', concluded a calmer observer that year. 'It was peaceful. There was a placid disregard of trivialities . . . which only opium can give.'[54] Opium-smokers, reported another witness from 1908, were 'ordinary working people . . . they have their pleasure time . . . as long as their money lasts.'[55]

The deepest fear was that the Chinese would infect with their 'hideous vice' those on whom the protection and well-being of the empire and the white race as a whole depended: fertile white women and their vigorous sons. Opium-smoking, as one popular novel put it, is 'bad enough in the heathens, but for an Englishwoman to dope herself is downright unchristian and beastly'.[56] A stock character in opium-den reportage was the British wife of the Chinese proprietor, in whom (as described by appalled journalists) the dread processes of degeneration were visibly occurring. 'Her skin was dusky yellow,' sighed one pitying observer, 'evidently she had, since her marriage, taken such an Oriental view of life, that her organs of vision were fast losing their European shape . . . It was killing her, she said, this constant breathing of the fumes of the subtle drug her husband dealt in.'[57] The Chinese and their opium, as penny-dreadful and literary opinion saw it, were deliberately corrupting the vulnerable British race. Dickens' last, unfinished novel, *The Mystery of Edwin Drood*, began with a Kent choirmaster entering a London opium den, whose English proprietress 'has opium-smoked herself into a strange likeness of the Chinaman. His form of cheek, eye, and temple, and his colour are repeated in her.'

Back in 1883, commentators on the opium question could remember enough of Britain's recent activities in China to account for the intense unease that opium-smoking generated in British minds. 'We really have', warned a former missionary to Canton that year, 'a new habit, prolific of evil, springing up amongst us . . . It is coming close to us with a rapidity and spring undreamt of even by those who have dreaded its stealthy and unseen step.' This opium plague 'spreading and attacking our vitals', he explained, was the 'retributive consequence of our own doings.'[58] Within another twenty years, this historical consciousness had been obscured by the growing mass of journalism, fiction, plays and eventually films stereotyping the Chinese as an 'Oriental canker' plotting the destruction of the white world. 'Very many of these celestials and Indians are mentally and physically inferior,' an 1897 short story carelessly remarked, 'and they go on smoking year after year, and seem not very much the worse for it. It is your finer natures that suffer, deteriorate and collapse. For these great and terrible is the ruin.'[59] In the first two decades of the twentieth century, British tabloid readers were transfixed by a string of sensational stories in which beautiful young British women were seduced (sometimes with fatal consequences) by Asiatic drug-peddlers. In 1918, a wealthy Shanghai dilettante called Brilliant Chang was implicated in the death by overdose of the cocaine-snorting darling of the London stage, Billie Carleton. Four years later, three sisters, Florence, Gwendoline and Rosetta Paul, were found in an opium stupor next to a dead Chinese man in the bedroom over a Cardiff laundry. 'The features of the women were so yellow', their discoverer reported, that for a time he 'did not realise they were white girls.'[60]

Around 1910, a former clerk of Irish-Birmingham stock by the name of Arthur Henry Ward sat down with his wife Elizabeth to divine his future. Elizabeth was an aspiring West End artiste, balancing bird cages and spinning plates on the music-hall stage while she waited for her big break. Arthur's background was slightly more white-collar. His first career plan had been Egyptology. When this hope came to nothing, he wound up as a bank clerk, a venture that ended badly after he thought he might try to burgle the vaults by hypnotizing his colleagues. But like his wife, his sights were set on show-business: on trying to make a name for himself as a writer of short stories and comic songs for the musical theatre. Sick of rejection letters, he sat down with Elizabeth at the Ouija board, to work out his next step. Their hands, as Arthur later told it, spelt out 'C-H-I-N-A-M-A-N'. Three years later, after he had discarded Arthur Ward for the more Aryan 'Sax' (Anglo-Saxon for 'blade') and the more romantic 'Rohmer '('he who roams' – the born freelancer), the bestselling *Mystery of Dr Fu Manchu* resulted.

We would be wise to be sceptical of most of what Sax Rohmer has to say to us, either through his own books or his biographer, his acolyte Cay Van Ash, for he was a professional fantasist.[61] Alongside his fifteen bestselling volumes on Fu Manchu, Rohmer had an indulged passion for the inter-denominational occult, in works such as *A Guide to Magic, Witchcraft and the Paranormal: the Romance of Sorcery*. But this much is true: his novels about the insidious Dr Fu Manchu, plus their spin-off radio plays and films, made him a celebrity. Few authors are lucky enough to be posthumously remembered; and yet, thanks to Fu Manchu and his global Chinese conspiracies against the white race, Sax Rohmer is not yet forgotten, half a century after his death.

Some might argue that the view of the Chinese generated by his books does not merit earnest analysis. The formulaic cheapness of it all – the soothing repetitiveness with which Rohmer dwells on his villain's impulses to evil (this 'sinister genius', 'that awful being', 'the incarnate essence of Eastern subtlety'); the number of times the stories' white heroes are foiled, within feet of their Oriental prey, by the action of a button-operated trapdoor – seems to implore a twenty-first-century reader to see the funny side. Or perhaps we should just resign ourselves to Rohmer's prejudice: racism was depressingly normal in early twentieth-century European and American writing. John Buchan's anti-Semitism, for example, has not stopped his books slipping onto canonical lists of High Literature. Yet it is not easy to dismiss the popularity and durability of the Fu Manchu phenomenon, and the degree to which it exploited and reinforced anti-Chinese feeling at the time. At the height of Rohmer's fame, Fu Manchu novels occupied public libraries, cinemas and the book collections of liners carrying Westerners out to China, ensuring (in the words of one such young traveller of the 1920s) that they 'knew all about Chinamen; they were cruel, wicked people'.[62]

Sax Rohmer's Fu Manchu was only the most successful fictional incarnation of sinophobia. From around 1873, morbid fear of Chinese dastardliness (exploiting widespread concern about economic competition from Chinese immigrant workforces) had become a staple of schlock American fiction: in H. J. West's 1873 *The Chinese Invasion*, in Atwell Whitney's 1878 *Almond-Eyed*, in Robert Wolter's 1882 *A Short and Truthful History of the Taking of California and Oregon by the Chinese in the Year A.D. 1899*. (An 1887 example of the genre, *White or Yellow? A Story of the Race-war of A.D. 1908*, was penned by the founder of the Australian Labour Federation.)

1898 saw the publication of the work that helped popularize the term Yellow Peril, Matthew Shiel's *The Yellow Danger*, in which the brilliant Chinese prime minister Yen How (a half-Japanese, half-Chinese, wholly satanic embodiment of the East) conceives and executes a 'wilful and wicked conspiracy' to massacre Europe and repopulate it with yellow masses, for the blissfully simple reason that 'he cherished a secret and bitter aversion to the white race'.[63] Like the epitome of Chinese cruelty that he is, Yen derives an unholy pleasure from his vile plot, his eyes 'wrinkl[ing] up into delicious merriment' as he unveils his foolproof plan for destruction of the white man. In the dystopian invasion novels of the 1870s and 1880s, the fear had been a little uncoordinated and faceless. Shiel created, for the first time, a mastermind, premeditating the conspiracy in the highest echelons of the East Asian leadership. Shiel further fanned Anglo-Saxon anxieties by giving his villain a lust for white women: 'What was Dr Yen How's aim? Simply told, it was to possess one white woman, ultimately, and after all. He had also the subsidiary aim of doing an ill turn to all the other white women, and men, in the world. If the earth had opened and swallowed him, then he would have renounced his hope; but for no lesser reason.'[64]

At the time of its publication, there were plenty who found Shiel's visions amusingly melodramatic. '[Shiel] must certainly expect us to laugh,' *The Times* reviewer chortled insouciantly, 'but we laugh with him rather than at him.'[65] The climax of the Boxer Rebellion in 1900 made it hard to see the funny side any more. Yellow Peril fiction now began to merge with the vengeful soldiers', missionaries' and diplomats' accounts coming out of China, both sets of narratives authenticating and pushing one another to new professions of hatred.

'Well, what are we to say of such a race, men?' Yen How's heroic British nemesis, John Hardy, asks a crew of marines under his command. 'Do you not agree with me that the earth would be well rid of such a people?' 'Yes! Yes! Yes!' they chorus back. 'I, here and now, devote my entire life henceforth to their destruction.'[66] By 1904, the Chinese master criminal (with his 'crafty yellow face twisted by a thin lipped grin', dreaming of world domination by forcing 'innocent men to commit crimes by injecting them with germs obtained from criminals') had become a staple of children's publications like *Pluck* and *Magnet*, his Oriental villainy usually infused by opium: 'a measured dose', revealed one comic-book detective, 'lulls the moral sense . . . it makes the victim blind to common honesty and capable of any theft or unscrupulous piece of work.'[67]

Chinese invasion plots regularly cropped up across the pages of children's serials. In 'Terror from the East', the 'Yellow Peril that men had dreamt about broke loose at last', with cohorts of Scouts battling on Brighton's beaches a 'hissing crew of Orientals munching handfuls of rice'. In 1910, even *Girls' Own Annual* felt compelled to warn its innocent readers of the global conspiracy taking place around them (the 'readiness of the Chinese to settle in the midst of other nations, and the evils which may follow in its train . . . constitutes the "Yellow Peril"'[68]). That same year, Jack London's own fictional take on the Yellow Peril, 'The Unprecedented Invasion', imagined a China that in 1976 had at last 'awakened'. 'China rejuvenescent!' London breathed. 'It was but a step to China rampant.' At the end of the story, the West is driven to destroy the Chinese with biological warfare, dropping – in neat little glass tubes – 'every virulent form of infectious death' over the 'chattering yellow populace . . . The plague smote them all.' Those who try to escape China are slaughtered by waiting Western armies massed on the frontiers. 'Cannibalism, murder, and madness reigned. And so perished China,' the story concludes. 'And then began the great task, the sanitation of China . . . according to the democratic American programme.'[69]

Yet none of these scenarios captured the public imagination like Sax Rohmer's Devil Doctor. The Fu Manchu brand succeeded and lasted as it did for several reasons. First, it danced artfully between hysteria and plausibility, mixing vague, fantastical fears about the Chinese presence in Britain with topical headline stories and police reports – about alleged Chinese webs of organized crime, and the shadowy world of Chinese opium dens, Oriental curio shops and other small businesses. Secondly, Rohmer focused all this supposition on a single antihero, whose memorable attributes (his love of sinister scientific plots and of extraordinarily elaborate tortures) would be imitated by later writers such as Ian Fleming. (By the 1930s, legend goes, the Chinese Fu-Manchu-style super-villain had become so ubiquitous in British thrillers that new members of the British Guild of Crime Writers were forced to swear an oath that they would never try to create one themselves.[70]) Finally, Rohmer saw the long-term potential in his creation and made him indestructible (to fire, beheading and being shot through the skull at point-blank range), rather than impatiently killing him off after only one novel (as Shiel did with Yen How).

To understand how the Fu Manchu phenomenon expressed so many of the distorted ideas about China circulating since the Opium War requires a closer look at the view of the Chinese that it sold to its millions of readers. In form, the novels borrowed heavily from Conan Doyle's blueprint for Sherlock Holmes, telling of the struggles of the narrator, one Dr Petrie – a solid man of science – and his brilliant, mercurial friend, Nayland Smith, to detect Chinese conspiracies up and down the country. (The second Fu Manchu novel, *The Devil Doctor*, in which Smith and Petrie come within a whisker of being swallowed up by the bogs of the Somersetshire moors, offers a particularly impudent plagiarism of *The Hound of the Baskervilles*.) Near the start of each book, a pillar of the British empire is usually murdered by shadowy Asiatic forces. From here, Petrie and Smith quickly deduce who is behind the villainy: 'the sinister genius of the Yellow movement', Fu Manchu. 'Imagine a person,' runs Rohmer's first description,

> tall, lean and feline, high-shouldered, with a brow like Shakespeare and a face like Satan, a close-shaven skull, and long magnetic eyes of the true cat-green. Invest him with all the cruel cunning of an entire Eastern race, accumulated in one giant intellect, with all the resources of science past and present, with all the resources, if you will, of a wealthy government – which, however, already has denied all knowledge of his existence . . .

you have a mental picture of Dr. Fu Manchu, the yellow peril incarnate in one man.[71]

In case any reader missed them, Rohmer recapitulates the basic points of his characterization every few pages: 'the face of Dr Fu Manchu was more utterly repellent than any I have ever known'; 'that yellow Satan' was 'an emanation of Hell . . . an archangel of evil'; and so on. As with Shiel's Yen How, this is a man of mysterious, aimless malignance, possessed by an unexplained, vengeful hatred of Caucasians and desire for world domination: 'the great and evil man who dreamed of Europe and America under Chinese rule . . . this enemy of the white race, this inhuman being who himself knew no mercy, this man whose very genius was inspired by the cool, calculated cruelty of his race.' Despite the range and complexity of his impulses to evil, the doctor seems to suffer from a complete innocence of motive, vowing to wage war on the entire white race for the sheer hell of it.[72]

Fu Manchu is thus the perfect embodiment of the China fear: cruel, cunning, arrogant and foreigner-hating. On book covers and in films, he is imagined as a timeless imperial Chinese cliché: as the pantomime mandarin of Hollywood stereotype, with his long moustache and grotesquely extended nails, seated on thrones of decadent Asiatic splendour.[73] His plots scatter through London practitioners of the dark Oriental arts: barely human lascars, mulattos, hideous poison-beasts from Burmese jungles, Indian thuggees, the sacred Abyssinian baboon with its nine-foot-long arms and unbreakable death-grip. Quite often, his ploys are stupidly complicated: at one point, he tries to dispatch an enemy using a cat whose claws are loaded with poison. At another, he keeps unwanted visitors from his hideaway by placing mice with bells attached to their tails behind the skirting boards, to make the house seem haunted – a tactic discovered only when Nayland Smith lures them out of their holes with toasted cheese. At the same time, however, he is a man armed with the terrifyingly destructive weapons of the modern world: a Doctor of Science from the University of Oxford, always surrounded by 'scientific paraphernalia'. 'At a large and very finely carved table', Petrie observes while (once again) a prisoner in the villain's lair, 'sat Dr Fu Manchu, a yellow and faded volume open before him, and some dark red fluid, almost like blood, bubbling in a test-tube which he held over the flame of a Bunsen-burner.'[74]

Rohmer's heroes usually follow a trail of clues and corpses across London until their travails take them into the centre of the terrible doctor's operations. Not coincidentally, in the first novel this is a 'literally poisonous' opium den: 'a horrible place' littered with comatose smokers and idiot, simian Chinese chattering pidgin. 'Here an extended hand, brown or yellow, there a sketchy, corpse-like face,' Petrie relates, 'whilst from all about rose obscene sighings and murmurings in far-away voices – an uncanny, animal chorus. It was like a glimpse of the Inferno seen by some Chinese Dante . . . we were cut off, were in the hands of Far Easterns . . . in the power of members of that most inscrutably mysterious race, the Chinese.'[75] Rohmer's purpose here is clear: to fill his readers with panic at the thought of the strange and terrible foreignness ensconced in the very heart of Britain. 'Aliens of every shade of colour were heading into the glare of the lamps upon the main road about us now,' runs one description of a damp, dark, sinisterly multicultural London, 'emerging from burrow-like alleys. In the short space of the drive we had passed from the bright world of the West into the dubious underworld of the East.'[76] In Rohmer's England, the white sons and daughters of the British empire are nowhere safe: 'an elaborate murder machine was set up somewhere in London', gasps Nayland Smith, 'sleep is a danger – every shadow threatens death.'[77]

Naturally, Fu Manchu is himself an opium addict: when he smiles 'the awful mirthless smile which I knew', observes Petrie, he reveals 'the teeth of an opium smoker.'[78] The books' storylines are spiked with other stealthy poisons, too. 'In the distorting of nature, in the disturbing of balances and the diverting of beneficent forces into strange and dangerous channels, Dr Fu Manchu excelled . . . in the sphere of pure toxicology, he had, and has, no rival: the Borgias were children by comparison.'[79] Fu Manchu's murder scenes are steeped in toxins; his first victim, Sir Crichton Davy (head of the Colonial Office), is dispatched with the 'Zayat Kiss' – the bite of a particularly deadly scarlet centipede of the Burmese jungle; a mysterious green toxic mist from a mummy case sees off an Egyptologist's secretary. As with most features of the Fu Manchu stories, Rohmer lifted his villain's poison fixation from earlier models. Magazines such as *Chums*,

Pluck and *Marvel* had all thoroughly established the Chinese predilection for mass poisonings (by germ warfare especially) during the first decade of the twentieth century.[80]

In probably every decade since its invention, the Yellow Panic has featured in Western consciousness, regardless of the reality of China's own political, social or economic capacity to pose a threat. In 1898, as Matthew Shiel created Yen How, the Qing empire was still reeling from a shocking defeat in Korea at the hands of its former cultural tributary, Japan. As Sax Rohmer began generating his Fu Manchu canon in the 1910s and 1920s, ethnic Chinese populations in London arguably possessed the hardest-working and generally least threatening social and political profile of any non-white British group. The 1932 movie of *The Mask of Fu Manchu* (in which the eponymous doctor screams for the destruction of the white race while trying to resurrect Genghis Khan by sacrificing a blonde white woman lashed to a stone altar) was filmed as China's military energies were fully absorbed either in civil war, or in facing off the Japanese aggression that would culminate in the Second World War. In 1938, only months after many tens, and quite possibly hundreds of thousands, of Chinese civilians had been massacred by Japanese forces at Nanjing, Sax Rohmer was still suggesting the imminent rise of a 'Kubla Khan ... who by force of personality will weave together the million threads and from his loom produce a close-knit China', spreading dread through its white neighbours.[81] 'I love Fu Manchu novels', freely admitted a former US ambassador to China, Stapleton Roy. 'Nothing sends shivers up my spine like sinister Chinese men scheming to take over the world ... But when you look at what's happening in China in terms of history, and not fantasy fiction, you're forced to a very different conclusion.'[82]

To a far greater extent than discussions about the world's other potential new Great Powers (say, India or Russia), non-specialist press debates about China today often appear almost unthinkingly framed in terms of 'Is China a Threat?'[83] There is of course a need for careful work on, for example, the Chinese state's military build-up; or its 'soft power' aspirations through Asia; or its scramble to invest in

Africa while enriching dictators. Clearly, China's ambitions as a rising superstate can clash with those of the West. Competition for global resources, and the political and military tensions this could generate, are genuine causes for concern; such struggles, history tells us, have always accompanied the rise of new powers. But to dress up this matter-of-fact economic phenomenon as a mystically ordained clash of civilizations does not help. Non-specialist American commentators have long questioned the Chinese government's motives in buying up trillions of dollars' worth of US debt, as if this were a subtle, ingenious plot to bring America to its knees, rather than a simpler case of US over-spending and under-saving.

Fu Manchu has generated, it sometimes seems, a lingering Western fondness for ill-qualified scaremongering about China. 'The China threat is real and growing', announced Bill Gertz, one of America's leading China conspiracy theorists, in his 2000 book, *The China Threat: How the People's Republic Targets America*. 'The reality today is that China is a major threat to the United States, and a growing one', he repeated five pages later, before moving on to the revelation that 'China's rulers . . . remain communists'.[84] Back in 2005, he predicted a mainland invasion of Taiwan within another couple of years, likening the PRC to a Fascist state – even Nazi Germany. 'We once again will be fighting a war on multiple fronts,' responded one of his readers, 'against Islam, and against the fascist Chinese. I hope we are prepared.' 'I don't doubt for a minute', agreed another, 'the Chinese will launch a nuclear attack against us.'[85] Never mind that – despite the double-digit growth in Chinese military spending over the past decade or so – America's military budget remains around eight times that of China's.

In almost any trouble connected with China, the old fears resurface. A typical example is the hysteria in 2007 that spread the idea of China exporting 'poison' to the world through its faulty products: pet food, drugs, toothpaste, lead-painted toy trains. 'Is China trying to poison Americans and their pets?' asked one article.[86] 'The Chinese Poison Train is still out there,' warned one American consumer association, 'lurking on a container ship headed our way. Nobody knows when it will strike again.'[87] At the same moment, China's profit-hungry companies were busy poisoning far more Chinese consumers: around 300,000 babies were taken ill in 2008, the year that the scandal about milk-powder tainted with melamine belatedly broke. And after recalling around 21 million toys manufactured in China, Mattel publicly apologized to its manufacturing partners in China, admitting that the 'vast majority of those products that were recalled were the result of a design flaw in Mattel's design, not through a manufacturing flaw in China's manufacturers.'[88] China has also been fingered for polluting the world with its economic miracle (the so-called Green Peril) – when Western consumers have been the principal market for cheap Chinese manufactures while letting China's own natural environment absorb most of the damage. The survival of the Yellow Peril school of thought on Sino-Western relations indicates the resilience of the self-justifying ideas and arguments that drove Britain towards war with China in the 1840s and 1850s: a Western fixation on the idea of unthinking Chinese xenophobia, and on China's determination to wish the West ill.

The greatest credibility problem for the Yellow Peril is that, historically, it has developed in isolation from opinion and events in China itself. It has thrived on delusional stereotypes generated by Westerners uninterested in what the Chinese themselves have made of events such as the Opium War and their subsequent relations with European invaders – the subject of this book's remaining chapters. As Sax Rohmer himself proudly told his biographer, 'I made my name on Fu Manchu because I know nothing about the Chinese!'[89]

Chapter Seventeen

THE NATIONAL DISEASE

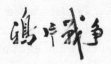

In the late 1870s, a bespectacled Chinese man in his mid-twenties passed a couple of years in London. Most weekdays he spent around the neoclassical heartland of British imperial technology: Greenwich Naval College. Most Sundays, he would drop in on the Chinese embassy, sometimes re-emerging onto the capital's gaslit streets only late at night. Who was he? What was he doing in England? Was he part of a sinister Qing plot to steal the military and scientific secrets of the West, decades before Sax Rohmer dreamed up the idea?

Yan Fu – the young man in question – was, like Fu Manchu, a son of imperial China: the twenty-seventh generation of a clan of eastern China that could trace its ancestors back to the tenth century and that, like most ambitious families in the empire, had for hundreds of years been fixated on pushing its scions through the civil-service examination system, and into a lucrative official posting. But three generations before Yan, the clan had begun to run short of money for the expensive business of examination preparation and started a successful doctor's practice in the deep, green, forested valleys of Fujian. As a boy, therefore, Yan had been schooled in both the Chinese classical and medical traditions.

In 1868, when Yan was aged fourteen, his conventional education changed course: he was sent off to the provincial capital to study at the Fuzhou Shipyard School, one of the new-style academies of Western science and technology that had sprung up after China's second war with Britain. In 1871, after five years studying English, arithmetic, geometry, algebra, physics, mechanics, chemistry, geology, astronomy and navigation, he graduated at the top of his class. After he had spent another five years putting his training to practical use on a Chinese military vessel patrolling between Singapore, Japan and Taiwan, the Qing government decided to dispatch him to England to study 'the newest and most ingenious arts of the West'. This enterprise was part of the 'Self-Strengthening Movement': a new Qing attempt – following a series of military defeats – to figure out how the West had achieved its scientific control of the world. China, pronounced Prince Gong (the brother of the emperor who agreed the Treaty of Beijing with Lord Elgin in 1860), must 'make a thorough study of the various kinds of [military] equipment to gain knowledge of all the secrets of the foreigners . . . Now that we know what they depend on for victory, we should try to master it.'[1] Europe's growing presence in China, declared one of the leading statesmen of the day, Li Hongzhang, 'was one of the great transformations of the past 3,000 years'.[2]

Up to this point, Yan Fu's education and career – with its loyalty to Chinese tradition and dedication to modern military science – bear passing resemblance to Rohmer's paranoid hypotheses about ambitious Orientals conspiring to beat the West at its own game. But here, Yan's life story departs from the Yellow Peril narrative. His decision to study Western science was not part of a grand, premeditated scheme – it sprang from economic necessity. After his father died when Yan was thirteen, the family finally abandoned all hope of supporting the boy through studying for the civil-service exams – in later life, Yan Fu recalled how his mother toiled at needlework to keep the family fed and clothed, and how he would be woken through the night by the sound of her weeping. The Fuzhou Shipyard, by contrast, could offer attractive incentives: free board and lodging, and a stipend of four silver dollars a month (with a bonus of ten silver dollars to students who came top in the quarterly exams).

The bribery was necessary, for in late-nineteenth-century China a Western education remained a disreputable life choice. 'Only the truly desperate stooped to studying Western sciences', remembered the writer Lu Xun, who took classes in medicine at one of the east-coast academies in the 1890s. 'By following the course I had fixed upon, I would be selling my soul to foreign devils'.[3] To praise the modernity of Western methods, to seek employment in the new Qing

Foreign Office or (even more unthinkably) in an embassy abroad, was to court career catastrophe. Guo Songtao, the Qing ambassador to London during Yan Fu's time in Britain, was a case in point. For his pro-Western views, he was physically assaulted, multiply impeached and eventually dismissed and sidelined from politics, while his house in China was vandalized. 'The empire cold-shoulders him', ran one contemporary scrap of doggerel. 'He cannot serve human beings / So how can he serve demons?'[4]

Secondly, Yan Fu had little interest in waging war on the white race. Quite the opposite: through his study of science and English, he fell in love with the West – and not just with the iron-plated steamers and guns that he was supposed to be studying, but also with its thinkers, writers and political and legal institutions. This, Yan concluded during his years abroad, was the foundation of Western strength. 'The reason why England and the other countries of Europe are wealthy and strong is that impartial justice is daily extended', he declared to Guo, during one of their Sunday conversations. 'Here is the ultimate source.'[5] Yan Fu remains a celebrity in China today for a remarkable series of translations that he completed after his return from England: Smith's *Wealth of Nations*, J. S. Mill's *On Liberty*, Montesquieu's *L'Esprit des Lois*. Yan Fu sought an idiom that would convince China's educated elites of the profundity of Western thought, rendering canonical texts of the modern West in the pure classical Chinese of the first millennium BC. 'The books with which I concern myself are profound and abstruse', Yan Fu reasoned. 'They are not designed to nourish schoolboys'.[6] But he is famed also as a leading representative of the first generation of Chinese men after the Opium Wars to launch upon a pointedly introspective quest – one of the country's key intellectual shifts of the nineteenth century – to understand China's weakness, and Western strength.

In their long discussions in London, Yan Fu and Ambassador Guo whiled away the hours assessing the virtues of the West and bemoaning the sins of China and the Chinese. For according to his diary, Guo shared with Yan Fu an extravagantly high opinion of China's imperialist adversaries (and of Great Britain in particular) – a fact that was all the more extraordinary given the discourteous reception that he received in Britain. On his arrival in London, *Punch* ran a

cartoon and seven poetic stanzas of impeccable offensiveness, in which
Guo was caricatured as a monkey ('With his eyes aslant, and his
pigtail's braid / Coiled neatly round his close-shaved head ... As
stubborn as pigs and as hard to steer / With a taste for cheap buying
and selling dear'), peering at the stately lion of the British empire.[7]
A week later, the magazine devoted a whole page of tasteless doggerel
to the bound feet of Guo's wife, whom it christened 'the tottering
Lily' and depicted as a décolleté Geisha.[8]

Yet Guo's enthusiasm was undented. Even on his voyage to
England, during which he suffered constant discomfort (in addition
to seasickness, he was afflicted by a sore throat, laboured breathing,
dizziness, swollen gums, toothache, a smarting nose and heart pain),
he sportingly retained an appreciation for everything Western that he
saw: the Europeans' 'ceremonial courtesies' he found 'refined and
civilised', their navigational techniques extraordinarily commend-
able. 'That country certainly produces admirably talented men', he
remarked, observing German officers seeking exercise in a game of
leapfrog. 'Admirable!'[9] Given Great Britain's not particularly creditable record in China, Guo also took a surprisingly positive view of
its long-term intentions towards his country. The British have, he
considered, 'surrounded China and press close upon her.

> With their hands reaching high and their feet travelling far,
> they rise up like eagles and glare like tigers ... Yet for all this,
> they have not the slightest intention of presuming on their
> military strength to act violently or rapaciously ... the nations
> of Europe do have insight into what is essential and what is
> not and possess a Way of their own which assists them in the
> acquisition of wealth and power ... Their governmental and
> educational systems are well-ordered, enlightened and method-
> ical.[10]

If Great Britain and the West were a repository of all that was
worth emulating, the (in Guo's view) stupid, smug Chinese were by
contrast a source of disgust. 'Surely this is not the time for China to
indulge in highflown talk and vain boasting in order to aggrandise
herself!' he sighed on the subject of anti-European prejudice. 'After
thirty years of foreign relations, our provincial authorities still know

nothing . . . The weakening of the Song and the downfall of the Ming, were both the outcome of the actions of such irresponsible and ignorant people.'[11]

Guo and Yan held in common another passionate belief: that opium lay at the root of China's problems. 'Personally,' analysed Guo, 'I think there is something in the Chinese mind which is absolutely unintelligible. I refer here to opium-smoking. Nothing the West has done has been more harmful to us than opium.' From here, it would seem an easy and logical step for Guo to lash out at the West for its behaviour towards China. But he took his argument in another direction. 'Even English gentlemen themselves are ashamed of the fact that they have used this harmful trade as an excuse for provoking hostilities with China, and are making a serious effort to eradicate the evil. Yet our Chinese scholar-officials complacently degrade themselves by smoking opium, and do so without remorse. This has been for several decades already our national disgrace, exhausting much money and man-power, and poisoning the lives of our people. And yet there is not one man who feels ashamed of it.'[12]

Opium, in Guo's opinion, was both cause and symptom of the rot in the Chinese national character. To him, the Chinese were doubly contemptible: for having allowed themselves to become addicted to opium, and for failing to feel ashamed of their weakness. Rather than dwelling on the fact that so much opium had reached China in British imperialist vessels, he saw the drug also as a self-inflicted poison. Yan was similarly concerned with Chinese culpability, proposing harsh punishments for officials who refused to give up the habit. Yan and Guo's identification of opium as the crucial national vice was another emblem of the pair's esteem for European opinion. For it was during these years that opium was reinvented in Great Britain as a social pathology: as China's own special disease of the will that it was threatening to export to the West.

Men like Yan Fu were responsible for propagating a new and influential set of nationalistic ideas for reforming China in the closing decades of the nineteenth century: ideas that were both intensely critical of their own country, and admiring of its redoubtable Western challengers. The years following the Treaty of Beijing had been difficult for the Qing empire. After the defeat of 1860, the Xianfeng emperor had been forced to accept the principle of a modern inter-

26. The British assault
on Chuanbi, some of
the forts near Canton,
in early 1841.

27. Liang Tingnan,
Cantonese scholar and
author of one of the key
first-hand Chinese accounts
of the Opium War, full
of acute and sometimes
acerbic insights into the
Qing war effort.

28. A late-nineteenth-century photograph of a Canton street;
its narrowness helps explain the claustrophobic panic of the battle for
Canton in May 1841.

29. Sir Henry Pottinger, a tough veteran of British operations in India who was appointed plenipotentiary in summer 1841 to replace Charles Elliot; in August 1842, he negotiated the Treaty of Nanjing that closed the Opium War.

30. A view of Ningbo, the trading city on the east coast that the British took without firing a shot in autumn 1841.

31. 'Repulse at Ningbo' in March 1842 – a single British howitzer creates a 'shrieking hecatomb' as the Qing counter-assault on the city begins to go wrong.

32. A peaceful view of Zhapu, the pretty east-coast town defended to the death by many of its Manchu garrison in spring 1842.

33. Qiying, chief Qing negotiator of the Treaty of Nanjing.

34. The signing of the Treaty of Nanjing in August 1842.

35. Harry Parkes: sinophone, sinophobe and architect of the second Anglo-Chinese War of 1856–60.

36. Lord Elgin, ambivalent plenipotentiary to the second Anglo-Chinese War.

37. Felix Beato's photograph of the walls of Beijing, taken on the final campaign of the second Opium War, 1860. Beato was an Italian war photographer of fortune, fresh from capturing on glass plates the killing fields of the Indian Mutiny.

38. Contemporary tourists at the ruins of the Yuanmingyuan, the imperial summer palace in the north-west of Beijing destroyed by Anglo-French forces in 1860; a key site of 'patriotic education' in contemporary China.

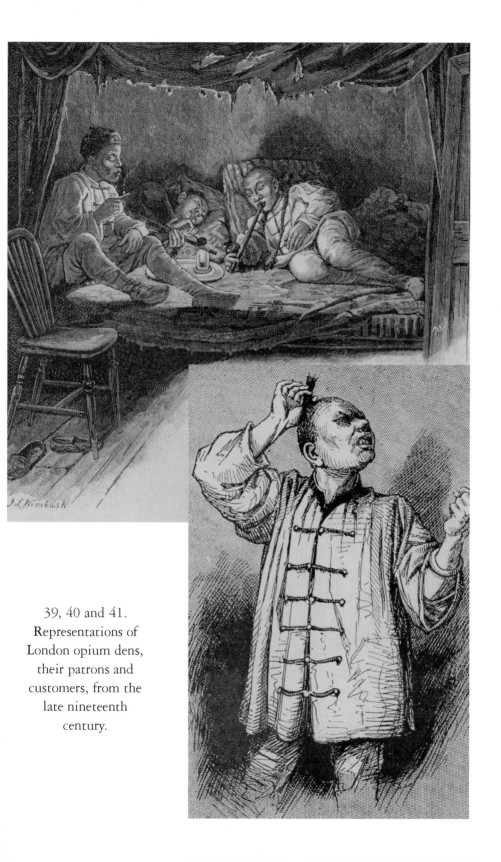

39, 40 and 41.
Representations of
London opium dens,
their patrons and
customers, from the
late nineteenth
century.

42. Public execution of Boxer rebels in Beijing 1900–1901 – a demonstration of Western 'pedagogical imperialism' (James Hevia's phrase) at work. The violence of the Boxer Rebellion and its aftermath fuelled Yellow Peril fears in the West about Chinese desire for vengeance for past humiliations and slights.

43. Boris Karloff as Sax Rohmer's 'insidious Dr Fu Manchu': 'Invest him with all the cruel cunning of an entire Eastern race, accumulated in one giant intellect, with all the resources of science past and present, with all the resources, if you will, of a wealthy government – which, however, already has denied all knowledge of his existence . . . you have a mental picture of Dr. Fu Manchu, the yellow peril incarnate in one man.'

44. Yan Fu – leading theorist of late-Qing nationalism, celebrated for his translations of Social Darwinist texts into Chinese – in Western dress.

45. Anti-opium remedies from the early twentieth century.

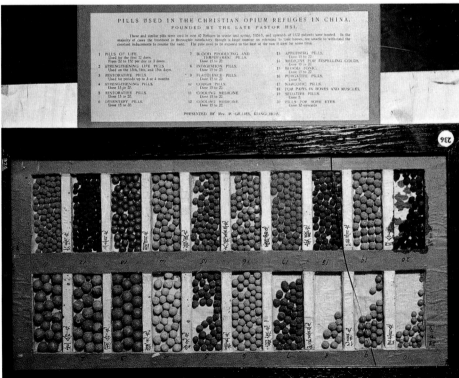

46. Poppy fields in early twentieth-century China.

47. Burning piles of confiscated opium pipes in China in the 1900s.

48. Sun Yat-sen, father of China's one-party state.

49. Two covers of the journal *Drugs Prohibition Monthly*. Left-hand image: the devils getting thumped are (left) opium and (right) morphine. Right-hand image: the figure pulling the child to the left is 'Evolution'; the child is 'China'; the hideous gargoyle is 'Opium'.

50. Akmal Shaikh, the British citizen executed in China in December 2009 for heroin-smuggling.

51. A Chinese demonstrator marching on the US embassy in May 1999, in protest against the NATO bombing of the Chinese embassy in Belgrade. His bandana is smeared with the characters reading 'blood debt'.

52. The Sea Battle Museum, on the south China coast, built in the 1990s to
commemorate the 1841 British destruction of the forts leading up
to Canton; another site of 'patriotic education' in the
People's Republic of China today.

national world system: 'England is an independent sovereign state', he pronounced. 'Let it have equal status with China.'[13] By 1884, the Qing had lost its old claims to authority over Indochina, following a disastrous naval engagement with France in which, within one hour, every Chinese ship had been destroyed, and at the end of which 521 Chinese (compared with only five French sailors) had lost their lives. Ten years later, China's defeat in the first Sino-Japanese War demolished the ritual facade of the old tribute system, as the Chinese empire found itself vanquished by a country that it had always viewed as a cultural tributary. In 1894, the Japanese government – hungry for its own colonies, with its own political and military modernization underway – seized upon the pretext of a domestic rebellion to dispatch troops into Korea. Within four months of a Qing force being sent to defend China's 'vassal', Japan's victory was so comprehensive that it could demand, as peace terms, 200 million ounces of silver in war indemnities, Taiwan and a substantial piece of the ancient Qing homeland, Manchuria.[14]

It is hard to overestimate the impact of this defeat on China's educated classes. It galvanized a nascent national press: news of the 1895 Treaty of Shimonoseki spread rapidly from the coastal cities (where most of China's newspapers and books were produced), and into the countryside, in second-, third- and fourth-hand copies of periodicals avidly read by anyone literate enough to understand their shocking message. Reports of the war moved the population at large in a way the Opium Wars never had. 'The Shanghai newspapers carried news about the war with Japan every day', remembered one provincial reader. 'Previously young Chinese people paid no attention to current events, but now we were shaken . . . [Now] most educated people, who had never before discussed national affairs, wanted to discuss them: why are others stronger than we are, and why are we weaker?'[15] Concerned Chinese drew one conclusion from the defeat: that the last thirty years of 'self-strengthening' had been full of futile half-measures, and that more urgent, more daring, more thoroughgoing reform had to take place.

The outcome of the war generated a new vision of a Western-dominated world in which China might quite simply be swallowed up by ambitious imperialists. 'They will enslave us and hinder the development of our spirit and body', Yan Fu worried. 'The brown and black races constantly waver between life and death, why not the 400 million yellows?'[16] It created new, anxious alliances of radical reformers who generated petitions and memorials protesting the humiliation and proclaiming the need to 'arouse the country's spirits' to protect it from imminent disaster.[17] Around this moment, Yan Fu and others like him responded with an ambitious blueprint for transforming China – this weak, loose empire – into a muscular, cohesive nation.

After a couple of decades spent languishing at the intellectual margins of Qing China in the unfashionable discipline of Western technical studies (sometimes less flatteringly translated from the Chinese as 'barbarian affairs'), Yan Fu now found his public voice and his audience, generating for the new press commentaries on and translations of key Social Darwinist tracts: Huxley's *Evolution and Ethics* and Spencer's *Study of Sociology*. In his exquisite classical Chinese, Yan described to a panicky readership the world of international warfare. 'In the so-called struggle for survival,' he explained, 'people and animals . . . compete for resources for their own survival . . . Races compete with races, and form groups and states, so that these groups and states can compete with each other. The weak will be eaten by the strong, the stupid will be enslaved by the clever . . . Unlike other animals, humans fight with armies, rather than with teeth and claws.'[18]

Like the Social Darwinist that he was, Yan was not particularly inclined to question the morality of the balance of power in this brave new world – to him, the foreign invasions that China had endured since 1840 were an inescapable phenomenon of nature. 'If a people is dispirited and stupid . . . then the society will disintegrate, and when a society in disintegration encounters an aggressive, intelligent, patriotic people, it will be dominated at best, and at worst extermi- nated'.[19] ('The tides of the world are unstoppable', agreed Guo Songtao.[20]) Instead, Yan believed that China must recognize its own flaws and remedy them with the ideas and culture of the West. 'What are China's principal troubles?' he asked. 'Are they not ignorance, poverty and weakness?'[21] Why, he wanted to know, had China failed to pick itself up since the defeat of 1842? 'The people's intelligence is not up to the task, and their physical strength and morality are not advanced enough to carry it through.' The West's 'expertise in machinery . . . their steam engines and weaponry' were only 'scratches on the surface . . . they are not the blood veins of strength.' No: the West owed its global supremacy to the two principles of 'truth in learning' and 'justice in politics'. In comparison, almost everything about Chinese tradition struck Yan as hopeless. 'There are almost innumerable practices in the customs of China, from law and institutions, scholarship and learning, to the ways we eat and live, owing to which the people's strength is enervated and the quality of the Chinese race debased.'[22]

If the struggle for survival depended on the cohesion of the group, the Chinese had to bond themselves into the same species of social and political unit that had worked so well for the West and for Japan: the nation. And to do this, the Chinese needed to discipline themselves. The Chinese body politic required a radical overhaul, to teach its constituents to 'live together, communicate with and rely on each other, and establish laws and institutions, rites and rituals for that purpose . . . we must find a way to make everyone take the nation as his own.' And the modern West was to be China's only teacher through all this; anyone who disagreed, Yan proclaimed, was 'a mindless lunatic.'[23]

The proposals of men like Yan were not only dependent on Western ideas; they relied on a new vocabulary translated into Chinese from European languages, via Japan. Even the early Chinese word for modern, *modeng*, was transliterated from the European term, entering China along with words such as bicycle, newspaper, democracy, party, election, telephone, international, photography and revolution. Through the 1890s and 1900s, a neologism, *Zhonghua minzu*, was adopted from the Japanese to refer to the concept of 'the Chinese nation' created by men like Yan Fu, and began to appear with increasing regularity in the writings of radicals and revolutionaries. Chinese nationalism was in important ways translated from the West.

Yan's sermons were imitated and amplified by his younger peers: by a rising generation of Chinese thinkers and activists who devoted themselves to educating the Chinese people into a modern nation. And of all these self-appointed engineers of Chinese nationalism, few were more influential than a young Cantonese scholar called Liang Qichao. Liang was a child prodigy who had rushed through to the penultimate stage of the civil-service exams by the age of seventeen.

That year (1890), however, he began to read histories of the world
and translations of Western works. 'As though with the thunderous
sound of the surf and the roar of a lion . . . as though cold water had
been poured over my back . . . and I had been hit over the head',
Liang later recalled, he turned against the 'useless old learning' in
which he had been schooled. 'Only then, for the first time in my life,
did I begin to understand scholarship.'[24] Through the 1890s, he
scolded those who 'thought that China was better in all respects than
the West, that she was only inferior in her military power . . .
Parliaments were the basis of a strong country'.[25]

In autumn 1898, Liang fled China for Japan with a price on his
head. That summer, he and his peers had briefly won the ear of the
young emperor Guangxu (1871–1908), who for three feverish months
had announced a range of Westernizing reforms overhauling education, commerce, the army, industry and government, before his
aunt, the Empress Dowager Cixi, had put him under house arrest and
executed those radical leaders who failed to flee her crackdown. But
Liang was not silenced. He spent the next decade generating polemics
on education, on historiography, on law, parliaments, taxation, freedom, oranges. By the early 1900s, Liang had established himself as
one of the most brilliant and influential writers of his generation –
perhaps, even, as the founder of modern Chinese journalism. Mao
Zedong admitted that he 'worshipped Liang Qichao' as a sixteen-
year-old, 'reading and rereading' Liang's essays until he 'knew them
by heart.'[26]

Like Yan Fu, one of the prolific Liang's favourite subjects was
China's deficiencies; both men were reluctant to view their country as
the blameless victim of Western imperialism. Although they could
be tainted by a crude ethnic pride that denigrated the 'black, red and
brown' peoples while proclaiming the Chinese race 'the most expansive and vigorous race on earth', Liang's sermons were rich also in
sinophobia.[27] The West might want to treat the Chinese 'as dogs and
horses', he analysed, but China was to blame for willingly becoming
their 'slaves, wives, and cows'. Why, he asked, 'are we so rotten and
dispirited?' It was, he concluded, China's corruption, selfishness, isolation, ignorance, cowardice and conservatism that had allowed the
West to take advantage of the country. The West can only 'humiliate
us, and annihilate other people and countries due to the superiority

of their own institutions (their parliament and newspapers) . . . and to their use of human and material resources.' 'The destruction of our country is not due to poverty, or to weakness, or to external troubles, or to internal divisions', he concluded in 1898. 'It's due to the mental weakness of our educated men.'[28]

Liang's critical approach was echoed by the late Qing newspapers that he had helped to popularize. 'Out of the 400 million people in our nation, half of them are weak women with bound feet', commented one disgusted journalist in 1904. 'Of the remaining 200 million, half again are emaciated and sickly opium addicts, and the rest are beggars, thieves, Buddhists, and Daoists, good-for-nothings from wealthy families, local bullies, the diseased, criminals, and actors and actresses.' 'The people of our nation do not know what rights are,' regretted another journalist in 1908. 'Alas! The dung beetle eats shit and rejoices. A fish swimming in a kettle forgets the water is boiling.'[29]

Men such as Yan Fu and Liang Qichao were not to be shaken from their negative view of their countrymen even after the imperialist rape of north China that followed the Boxer Rebellion. The revolt, Yan Fu decided, was an 'uprising of the superstitious mob and of ignorant and worthless armed bandits . . . It was certainly a disaster for our state.' Liang Qichao blamed the cataclysm not on Western brutality, but on the 'poisonous influence' of traditional Chinese fiction, which was responsible for leading the 'whole nation into great trouble.'[30] Editorials in the country's most popular newspaper, *Shenbao*, lambasted the dynasty's 'muddleheaded, common, false and reckless' ministers, who had encouraged the Boxers: 'if the Boxer rebels are not taken to task, all these [foreign] countries will bring out their military in great numbers and enter China'. China, in other words, had brought Western violence down on itself.[31]

Although this wave of Chinese self-recrimination crested in the decade after 1895, it had a much older pedigree. Between the Opium War itself and at least the 1910s, the Chinese (at the top and the bottom of the social scale) saved their most vitriolic attacks not for the foreigners who had brought destruction to the south and east coasts and to north China, but for their own poor leadership – some actually starved themselves to death in protest at the 'treachery' of Daoguang's 1842 negotiators. Even Lin Zexu – so often lionized by his fellow Chinese officials as a fearless patriot – suffered at the hands of public opinion. A victim of the Anglo-French looting of Beijing in 1860 offered the following analysis of the catastrophe. 'Some blamed Heaven for this unprecedented chaos but how, I say, can you deny it was brought upon us by human error?' His account of the painful events of 1860 – some 14,000 words long – principally directed its invective not at the British or French, but at derelict Qing ministers. 'Our nation's troubles began with Lin Zexu and Yuqian . . . Oh, I could eat their flesh! . . . Lin stole the foreigners' ships and destroyed their opium. As a result, they became angry and found a pretext for war.' In his estimation, the chief villain of the second war was the Qing commander, one Senggelinqin, who spent vast amounts of money on half-baked defence plans, then ran away the instant that they failed. 'He fled like a rabbit and hid like a tortoise . . . The great invasion [of 1860], the poison it caused the people and the disastrous burning of the Summer Palace were all his fault . . . If only we had had a decent commander . . . we would have seen the foreigners off with no trouble at all.' The people of Beijing, he remembered, all acclaimed him 'the King of Wobbles . . . how, I wonder, will he dare face the King of the Underworld after he has died?' Thanks to the incompetence of the leadership, this eyewitness concluded, 'anyone with a scrap of intelligence would have long known we were bound to lose . . . We invited disaster upon ourselves.'[32]

Xia Xie, a well-regarded 1860s chronicler of both China's wars with Britain, agreed that the Qing's troubles were self-inflicted: 'Worms only appear in a rotten carcass. It was not until exaction followed exaction, and justice was denied to creditors, that the foreigners turned upon us . . . opium only came because profits being impossible by fair means, the foreigners were driven to obtain them by foul means.'[33] Late-nineteenth-century accounts of the Opium Wars seemed less interested in the idea that dominates China's history industry today: that a global imperialist conspiracy was scheming to enslave the Chinese. Until the 1920s, the Chinese did not even get round to producing single, unified names for the war of 1839–42 and the treaty that concluded it. Often, discussions of these events refused to dignify them with the term 'war', preferring instead the old usage 'quarrel', 'provocation' or 'disturbance', while the British were identified dismissively as 'slaves', 'pirates', 'robbers', 'dogs', 'sheep'.[34]

The new opium-prohibition movement that developed within China around 1900 harmonized with the self-disgusted nationalism of the young century. With its fixation on 'renovating the people' into a modern nation, the patriotism of men like Yan Fu returned regularly to medical metaphors for the country's predicament. 'A nation is like a human', wrote Yan. 'If an individual is not active physically, the body will be weak . . . Does today's China look like a sick man?' 'Shame! Shame! Shame!' echoed other reformers. 'This great China, which for many centuries was hailed as the Celestial Empire by neighbours, is now reduced to a fourth-rate nation! The foreigners call us the sick man of East Asia: they call us a barbarian, inferior race.'[35] To strengthen the nation, Yan believed, the Chinese must first strengthen themselves by ridding themselves of their bad habits. And of all China's hideous vices, 'opium and foot-binding are the most destructive, and the most inveterate.'[36] Opium – this intellectual narcotic that was sapping the country's vigour, and putting its people to sleep when they needed to 'awaken' to a new national struggle for survival – became the perfect symbol of the Chinese sickness. 'Alas!' cried *Shenbao* in 1906. 'The poison of opium that has been flowing so long through China is the cause of our country's weakness, of our people's poverty. Every day our vitality ebbs and the day of our extinction grows closer.'[37] Even as opium remained a Chinese aspirin for the under-medicated masses, a fuel (as stimulant and appetite suppressant) for armies of cheap labour and a pleasure-giving narcotic for those with money and leisure, elite moral opinion was starting to move against the drug. The picture that the polemical press painted of opium addiction became desperate: perhaps '70 per cent', of Chinese, *Shenbao* announced, 'can no longer extricate themselves [from the habit] . . . Their lives fall drop by drop into the opium box, and their souls flicker away in the light of the opium lamp . . . When stung they feel no pain; when kicked, their wilted bones fail to rise. Since most of our countrymen wreck themselves by smoking opium, they represent our listless nation.'[38]

In the first decade of the twentieth century, in cities and towns across the country, opium-suppression societies denounced the drug in parades, meetings, journals and pamphlets. Hundreds of thousands of dens were shut down, while crowds gathered to attend burnings of confiscated opium and pipes. Investigators raided suspected illicit dens by night; vigilantes set upon inveterate smokers. Detoxification centres (often run by Western missionaries) did brisk business harassing smokers with a wide range of often untested, disgusting and potentially lethal cures. ('How strange it was', one observer of British missionaries' anti-opium activities mused, 'that the country which sends the poison should also send the antidote.'[39]) Some gave smokers miracle pills containing pomegranate skin, camphor, capsicum, quinine, belladonna, arsenic and cocaine; others subjected their patients to hypnotism, tai-chi, radio, religion and flannel underwear. Others again treated smokers with morphine pills, which the locals promptly christened 'Jesus opium'; red Heroin pills – rumoured to contain a virgin's first menstrual blood – were liked, too. One ex-smoker enthusiastically endorsed a Hong Kong clinician's cure consisting principally of morphine injections.[40]

The truly unfortunate were locked up, abruptly deprived of the drug and dosed with strong coffee. 'Opium took us to paradise', scrawled one unfortunate on the wall of a late-nineteenth-century clinic. 'Now we are tortured in hell.'[41] Those too poor or overworked to find an alternative, one missionary reported, simply died of the shock: 'When the opium dens were first closed the mortality among the poorer people was dreadful, for the opium smokers lived from hand to mouth, and, as they could not work without their usual opium, they died, partly of starvation, and partly from sudden deprivation of the drug.'[42] In 1906, the Qing government officially supported the campaign, announcing a new ban on opium and its intention to rid the empire of the drug within ten years. In 1907, Great Britain was somehow shamed into the Anglo-Chinese Ten-Year Opium Suppression Agreement, which pledged to cut opium imports into China by 10 per cent a year, if China cut back equally on domestic growth of the drug. (*The Times* responded to the news by sneering at the Chinese 'love of regulations' but 'abhorrence of regulation', and loftily calling on the British to take a lead, thereby displaying those 'qualities of humanity and altruism upon which we base our claims to a civilization superior to that of the East.'[43])

Like the Taiping Rebellion's ideologues and reformists such as Yan Fu and Guo Songtao, though, anti-opium campaigners seemed reluctant to blame China's opium habit exclusively on imperialism. 'The English use opium to speed China's demise', summarized a

Shanghai poet at the end of the nineteenth century. 'The Chinese do not understand and vie to smoke it; this can be called great stupidity.'[44] The origins of opium, then, had become clouded by the start of the twentieth century. Even if opium had originally been brought to China by foreigners, it was the weak Chinese who had seduced themselves into the habit; this weakness was in turn exacerbated by opium. 'To prevent worse to come,' ran one anti-opium manifesto, 'we have first to realize with sadness that in this world our race is the lowest.'[45] A throwaway remark about the Opium Wars in a history textbook of the 1900s catches the self-loathing: 'The empire grew addicted to smoking opium . . . The government tried all sorts of methods to curb the habit, due to the harm that it did to the population, but our people were too stubbornly stupid to give it up.'[46]

In a province like Sichuan, in any case, locals had some difficulty in viewing opium as a foreign commodity, because local production had long outstripped imports. Since 1860, opium duties had bought boats, guns and ammunition to help the Qing government suppress civil wars such as the Taiping Rebellion. After 1874, Li Hongzhang had argued that domestic cultivation should openly resume, while piously declaring that the 'single aim of my Government in taxing opium will be in the future, as it has always been in the past, to repress the traffic – never the desire to gain revenue from such a source.'[47] Nonetheless, during the 1870s south-west China alone began to produce more opium than the country was importing. Anti-imperialist passions in late-Qing China were often directed at issues other than opium. Through the 1900s, many regions of China were in the grip of a passionate Rights Recovery Movement, opposing European and American attempts to buy up the country's nascent railway system and Qing willingness to sell it: students threatened to starve themselves to death, soldiers wrote letters of protest in blood and one academic allegedly died of sadness on hearing the news that the government had accepted a massive foreign loan to build one stretch of track.[48] A cartoon from the 1908 Shanghai *Times* entitled 'Experts at Destroying China' pictured five pickaxes hacking at the characters for 'China'. Only one represented foreign interests (missionaries); the other four stood for soldiers, officials, political factions and bandits.[49]

From the 1920s onwards, China's young, authoritarian political parties would make much of the horrors of imperialism in China; the reality was more equivocal.[50] Certainly, there was much that was alarmingly foreign, or racist about the Western presence in China (concentrated in the concessions that developed in the treaty ports after 1842). Falling into the first category was the curious and disgusting food that the foreigners seemed to enjoy (the breaded cutlets, the curries, the rich soup, the butter, the pastries, jellies, custards, blancmanges); their habit of taking egg in their tea, if there was no milk to be had; their penchant for violent exercise ('shaking up the liver') in strange, uncomfortable clothes – one Chinese official is supposed to have once asked a British consul why he did not pay someone to play tennis on his behalf.[51] Falling into the second category was the effective apartheid of much treaty-port life: the spirit of exclusion expressed by the legend of the Shanghai park sign stipulating 'No Dogs or Chinese'; the condescending lectures delivered to 'hopeless' native servants. (The first chapter of the first Chinese-language textbook I ever picked up, printed in the 1950s, contained the all-important sentence construction: 'Tell the servant to . . . [open the window etc.]'.[52])

But the treaty ports were more than a symbol of imperialist oppression – they were also a symbol of progress. China's industrialization and modernization began in places like Shanghai, with banks, gaslights, electricity, telephones, running water and automobiles becoming part of the city between 1848 and 1901.[53] While some locals worried that in half a century Shanghai would be so overladen with skyscrapers that it would be swallowed up by the earth, elsewhere in the metropolis writers, artists, filmmakers and actors sipped chocolate and coffee in chichi jazz cafes, caught Tarzan movies or screwball comedies fresh out of Hollywood, shopped for high-heeled leather shoes and lipsticks in towering department stores, bought first editions of Joyce or Eliot in bookshops or enjoyed sauntering up and down the city's Parisian boulevards. Mesmerized by the cosmopolitanism of the place, Shanghai novelists of the 1920s and 1930s scattered their texts with chic foreign phrases: 'chicken a la king'; 'charming, Dear!', 'kiss-proof'.[54] The press explosion of the late Qing – the mass of newspapers that jibed at the establishment through the first decade of the twentieth century, creating a public opinion that made nationalism and revolution possible – could not have taken place outside the foreign concessions in cities such as Shanghai, where extraterritoriality permitted a degree of intellectual freedom not possible elsewhere in the empire. In 1904, the fugitive Liang Qichao risked his life to return to Shanghai – a price of 100,000 ounces of silver still on his head – to start a new paper. In 1911, the accidental bomb explosion that kicked off a nationalist revolution and brought to an end 2,000 years of imperial rule over China took place at a secret meeting in the Russian concession in the central Chinese city of Hankow.

And despite the anti-opium fury generated across the fin-de-siècle empire, plenty of people seemed unable to make up their minds about it or to treat it as a serious problem. The inconsistency of Sun Yat-sen, acclaimed on both sides of the Taiwanese straits as *guofu* (the father of the modern Chinese nation), was exemplary. 'Opium has caused more harm than war, plague and famine in China for more than ten years', he pronounced in the 1920s, perhaps forgetting that back in 1894 he had advised the Qing leadership to exhort the people to grow their own poppies to squeeze out the foreign competition, informing them that he had enjoyed much success persuading farmers in his home village in Guangdong to do just that. The bouquet of his local variety, he commented with authority, was 'even better than that of Indian opium, and far superior to that of Sichuan and Yunnan.'[55] Shanghai guidebooks vacillated over opium, exclaiming on one page about the wonders of the city's opium halls, while attacking the drug as a poison on another.[56]

In any case, there was too much money tied up in China's narcotic economy for it to surrender to prohibition without a fight. Although Alexander Hosie, the man whom Britain appointed to verify the Qing's claims of reducing opium production, reported that it had shrunk dramatically across China between 1907 and 1910, and in places been eradicated altogether, in 1908 a British missionary reported a case from north-west China in which 'the farmers, in spite of strongly worded proclamations and occasional demonstrations of soldiers, refuse to destroy it. Bands of their wives have gone to the magistrate's yamen, saying, "You may kill us, but we will grow opium." '[57] Anti-opium activists were periodically roughed up by angry, unemployed former den managers. Banquets and bribes, more-

over, usually offered a way out for those unwilling to give up opium
cultivation. If fed and remunerated well enough, poppy-extermination
squads would simply tap the flowers with their swords. The inconvenient fact was that by 1900, opium had become naturalized to
China: it was too useful, too prevalent to be easily uprooted. Even
after the Nationalist Party began executing smokers in the 1930s,
the Chinese attachment to opium remained hard to shake. As late
as 1944, a war fought by local farmers to protect poppy fields in
Guizhou left eighty killed or wounded. In 1939, an opium-prohibition inspector in Yunnan was reported to have died of a sudden,
mysterious illness; careful investigation (which his successor was
careful not to undertake) would have revealed that local bigwigs had
had him crushed to death under rice sacks.[58]

But our best example of early twentieth-century China's ambivalence towards opium is perhaps Yan Fu. Aged twenty-eight, he
acquired – to the tremendous disappointment of his later nationalist
biographers – the opium habit himself, thirteen years before he would
begin to characterize it as one of China's most pernicious customs. He
struggled guiltily with the habit for the rest of his life – even though
his breathing problems gave him a sound medical reason for taking
the drug as a cough suppressant. In 1921, a year after he had finally
succeeded in giving up his opium pipe, he died of asthma.[59]

Chapter Eighteen

COMMUNIST CONSPIRACIES

The 1850s were a trying decade for Karl Marx. Expelled from three countries (and barred even from Switzerland), in 1849 he had settled in London with his family. Not long after their arrival, however, the Marxes were evicted from their lodgings and their few possessions confiscated by bailiffs. In the next ten years, three of his children died, most probably from the strains of destitution, as Marx stumbled between financial crises, squandering his journalistic income and handouts from his friend Engels on maintaining a respectable middle-class facade (a useless personal secretary, seaside holidays, ball-gowns for his would-be debutante daughters), all the while agitating for the overthrow of capitalism by the global proletariat.

Despite the chaos of his own circumstances, Marx retained a robust belief in his ability to pronounce on the affairs of the world. And through the decade, his attention turned sporadically to China. The series of articles on the subject that he composed for the *New York Daily Tribune* had little good to say about Palmerston and his 'Christianity-canting and civilisation-mongering' government,[1] or about the merchant interests who were, by 1857, driving the two sides towards 'this most unrighteous war' that will lead the Chinese 'to regard all the nations of the Western World as united in a conspiracy against them.'[2] For China, Marx decided, the first Opium War had been an epochal catastrophe: 'The tribute to be paid to England after the unfortunate war of 1840, the great unproductive consumption of opium, the drain of the precious metals by this trade' had broken the country.[3] Worse than that, the

British had calculatingly poisoned an empire, for 'the opium seller slays the body after he has corrupted, degraded and annihilated the moral being of unhappy sinners, while every hour is bringing new victims to a Moloch which knows no satiety, and where the English murderer and Chinese suicide vie with each other in offerings at his shrine.'[4]

Yet at the same time, Marx was unable to muster much admiration for China, this 'giant empire,

> containing almost one-third of the human race, vegetating in the teeth of time . . . contriving to dupe itself with delusions of celestial perfection . . . Before the British arms the authority of the Manchu dynasty fell to pieces; the superstitious faith in the eternity of the Celestial Empire broke down; the barbarous and hermetic isolation from the civilised world was infringed . . . That isolation having come to a violent end by the medium of England, dissolution must follow as surely as that of any mummy carefully preserved in a hermetically sealed coffin, whenever it is brought into contact with the open air.'[5]

The inevitable result of this clash was 'one formidable revolution . . . afforded by the English cannon forcing upon China that soporific drug called opium . . . It would seem as though history had first to make this whole people drunk before it could rouse them out of their hereditary stupidity.'[6]

There was little that was original in Marx's conclusions about China and its Opium Wars. Key elements of his analysis – in particular, his scorn for the decadence of the Chinese empire – are to be found scattered across previous China-watchers' accounts. Heavily influenced by earlier European sinophobes of the nineteenth century, Marx propounded a vision of China that stripped it of both complexity and agency: that saw it as an inert empire capable only of being 'woken' by the West in the Opium War. The one novelty that Marx added to the standard racist repertoire of Victorian commentaries on China was a similarly intense disgust for Western imperialism.

By 1860, Marx had moved on from China, to concentrate instead on failing to complete Volume 1 of *Capital*; he seems never to have returned seriously to the subject. Less than a century later, however, his views would become enshrined in Chinese nationalist thought as the definitive account of 'the Celestial Empire' and the Opium Wars. This account would become the founding myth of Chinese nationalism: the beginning of the Western imperialist conspiracy against a rotting 'semi-feudal, semi-colonial' China, from which only communism could save the country. At the heart of anti-Western Maoism, therefore, lies a profound reverence for European opinion.

And to tell the strange story of how the opinions dashed off by a bourgeois from the Lower Rhine became holy writ in China, we must first return to the labours of another financially challenged chancer of the late-nineteenth century (and the architect of a one-party Chinese nation-state): Sun Yat-sen. It was Sun's late, ambivalent decision of the 1920s – taken in desperation to win Soviet funding for his faltering revolution – to name imperialism as the cause of all modern China's problems that transformed the Opium War into the inaugural trauma of Chinese history, and into a vital ingredient of twentieth-century patriotic propaganda.

Born in 1866 into a peasant family a little north of Macao, educated in Hong Kong and Hawai'i thanks to the generosity of a brother who had sailed off to make his fortune overseas, Sun was the archetypal product of China's forced opening to the West. By his late twenties, he had competent English, had graduated from a Hong Kong college with rudimentary knowledge of Western medicine and had converted to Christianity.

In 1894, he made a brief attempt at a more conventional career in the imperial bureaucracy, travelling north to deliver to the Qing head of state, Li Hongzhang, a long petition that offered his services to modernizing China. Preoccupied by war with Japan, Li did not make time to see him. This snub seems to have been enough to convince Sun that he must concentrate his energies on bringing down the entire edifice of Qing rule, and before the year was out he had founded a secret revolutionary cell in Hawai'i, the Revive China Society, dedicated to overthrowing the Manchus. After his first planned uprising in 1895 failed disastrously, he fled China with a price on his head and began a career as a professional itinerant revolutionary. Through this dispossessed period, Sun would develop his vision of a republican, nationalist state that would in later decades help win him a place in modern Chinese history as 'father of the nation'.

Over the course of the next sixteen years, Sun flitted between countries (Britain, France, Japan, the United States) and social groups (bandits, pirates, monarchists, anarchists, foreign ministers, missionaries, overseas Chinese businessmen, American mercenaries), begging for money and help for his anti-Manchu revolution, artfully telling each constituency what they wanted to hear. In London one season, he would extol the virtues of the British legal system; in Japan the next, he would excoriate the horrors of Western colonialism to Pan-Asianists. A year later, he would be wooing China's secret societies with toasts in pigeon's blood, while offering parts of south China to French imperialists if they first pledged to finance his 'federated republic'.

After a decade of failed rebellions, he read in October 1911 – in a newspaper, while breakfasting at the foot of the Rocky Mountains – that a string of revolutionary uprisings, beginning with a botched bomb explosion in central China, had brought down the Qing dynasty. (Sun was in the United States to work out the details of an anti-Qing conspiracy with a hunchbacked adventurer called Homer Lea, who was offering $3.5 million worth of soldiers and weapons in exchange for full economic control of the republic that would ensue.) Rather than rush straight back to China, however, Sun booked a ship ticket to London, where he promised the British government that in return for their support of the new regime he would appoint British officers to the command of the Chinese navy and enthrone a British official as his 'political adviser'.[7]

Finally returning to China on Christmas Day 1911, he accepted the presidency for thirty-four days, before handing over the infant republic to a former Qing general, Yuan Shikai, whose personal command over the Beiyang army in the north-east – the country's largest, most modernized military force – had enabled him to dominate negotiations between the Qing and the revolutionaries over the preceding weeks. In 1913, Sun found himself on the run again after Yuan had ordered the assassination of a newly elected prime minister, thereby destroying the new government's shaky democratic structures.[8] For the next decade, Sun returned to frequenting the drawing rooms of the international rich and powerful, offering slices of his future Chinese republic to the highest bidder.

But despite his promises to would-be foreign friends, he made little progress in finding funding for his republican dream. Following Yuan Shikai's death in 1916, his subordinates divided the country into personal enclaves and began battling each other for overall control. In 1917, after the warlord fashion of the day, Sun headed for his native Canton and, decked out in plumed helmet, fringed epaulettes and white gloves, proclaimed himself Grand Marshal of a cash-starved military government that existed principally on paper – he could muster, at the peak of his command, some twenty battalions and one gunboat. By 1922, even by the standards of his career to that point, Sun's position was looking precarious. On 16 June, his headquarters in Canton were bombarded by a former ally, Chen Jiongming, a Cantonese commander who objected to Sun's schemes to force Guangdong to pay for a northern expedition to reunite the country under his leadership. In the fire that resulted, Sun was forced to flee his house pursued by rifle shots and shouts of 'Kill Sun! Kill Sun!' He spent the next seven weeks sweltering on board a gunboat, waiting in vain for reinforcements to restore him to his seat of power, while his old friends the British did nothing except send a ship to taxi him to Hong Kong.[9]

Impelled at least partly by hopelessness, around this time Sun began to give thought to overtures from the Soviet Union. The Russians, it emerged, were willing to provide his fractious Nationalist Party (Guomindang or GMD – the organization that he had founded in 1912, to replace his similarly fractious Revolutionary Alliance of the 1900s) with funding, arms and political and military training. Sun, in return, would allow members of the young Chinese Communist Party (CCP), founded in 1921 with help from the Comintern, into the ranks of the Nationalists, to form a United Front. Sun hoped that the Soviets would make him a Chinese Lenin, injecting the cash, weapons and discipline necessary to turn the Guomindang into a force that could reunite the country by defeating the warlords who had carved up China. The Russians planned to further their long-term aim of world revolution by advancing in China the primary political stage – national bourgeois revolution assisted by Chinese Communists – from within which, they hoped, communist revolution would spring.

But to secure Soviet money, Sun had to make a stand on a handful of key Communist policies. Displaying solidarity with the proletariat was one: organizing strikes, reducing rents, redistributing land and so on. In theory, this step made good sense, promising to turn Sun's Nationalist Party into a genuinely mass organization. In practice, it would prove problematic, for Sun had little stomach for class struggle. Since 1905, Sun's political manifestoes had glibly called for the 'equalization of land rights', while failing to acknowledge the social and economic conflict this process would necessarily bring with it. As a man permanently short of funds, Sun was naturally drawn to the rich and powerful, within and without China: to politicians, merchants, industrialists and wealthy landlords.[10]

Resisting 'the world-suppressing yoke of imperialism' was a second important Soviet principle with which Sun needed to concur – for imperialism, Marx had upheld (and Lenin agreed), was the highest stage of capitalism.[11] Again, in theory, this stipulation should not have posed any great difficulty for a Chinese political movement aspiring to mass popularity. By the 1920s, China had been suffering from foreign aggression for some eighty years; the past decade alone had been studded with new outrages. Taking advantage of China's post-revolutionary chaos, the Japanese government had in 1915 served Yuan Shikai with their Twenty-One Demands, asserting economic and political sovereignty over slices of Manchuria and Mongolia. Four years later, the British, French and Americans at Versailles had rewarded Japanese naval assistance in the First World War with another large portion of north-east China. Indignant Chinese youth had responded by plunging into the protest of the May Fourth Movement – a surge of radical nationalism named after the violent anti-imperialist demonstrations of 4 May 1919.

Again, in reality, mobilizing and harnessing anti-imperialist zeal in Republican China was not so straightforward. Assuredly, certain groups in Chinese society were prone to fury about foreign aggression: in particular, the students, teachers and writers who, through articles, demonstrations and petitions, drew attention to the country's mistreatment at the hands of the Powers. They filled journals and newspapers with appalled editorials about China's international predicament; they voted to brand shop signs, textbooks, flags and packaging (for cigarettes, wine, straw hats, stockings) with the words

'National Humiliation'; they commemorated traumatic anniversaries as 'National Humiliation Days'. There was money to be made from the Humiliation industry, too. To celebrate the tenth anniversary of the Demands, one newspaper advertised a special souvenir product: 'National Humiliation' towels, to help remind the Chinese people (through daily ablutions) that the shame of foreign aggression had to be wiped away. Another company six years later tried a similar pitch for tooth powder: 'you will naturally associate this in your mind with the great "national humiliation" and ponder ways to brush it clean.'[12]

But this anger was mixed with fear that, without the vigilance of the nation's intellectual leaders, ordinary Chinese would easily forget the horrors of foreign oppression. The Chinese, editorialists complained through the 1910s and 1920s, had a serious national humiliation attention deficit disorder: 'an enthusiasm for things that only lasted five minutes'.[13] Fulminations against external aggression in early Republican newspapers frequently veered into denunciations of popular indifference. 'There are a great many Chinese citizens', one commentator of the early 1920s worried, 'who do not appreciate the seriousness of the current national crisis and their responsibility to do something about it. This is a new national humiliation and also a great crisis.' One newspaper cartoon from 1922 pictured a disapproving-looking individual standing by an enormous thermometer showing that the country's 'National Humiliation Commemoration Fever' had dwindled to almost nothing.[14]

Even China's most passionate anti-imperialists – those who threw themselves into the May Fourth Movement – were inconsistent in their attitudes to the West. On the one hand, the protests – which quickly developed into strikes and boycotts of foreign goods across China's cities – decried the Great Powers' partition of China. But on the other, May Fourth nationalists (just like their radical predecessors from the turn of the century) worshipped Western 'civilization': its science, its democracy, its literature and culture. The basic task, proclaimed Chen Duxiu, one of the movement's intellectual leaders, 'is to import the foundation of Western society, that is, the new belief in equality and human rights.' For people like Chen, the real enemy was not the West, but China's own Confucianism: 'We must be thoroughly aware', he reminded his readers in 1916, 'of the incompatibility between Confucianism and the new belief, the new society and

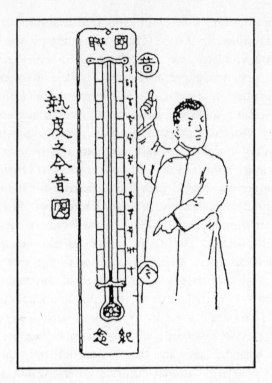

China's National Humiliation commemoration fever dwindles.

the new state.'[15] All that these nationalists could agree on was that something was intrinsically wrong with China and the Chinese – the country's sufferings at the hands of imperialism were consequences of this more fundamental malaise. 'The majority of our people are lethargic,' Chen worried in 1917, 'and do not know that not only our morality, politics and technology but even common commodities for daily use are all unfit for struggle and are going to be eliminated in the process of natural selection.'[16]

Sun Yat-sen had as much trouble turning on the imperialist powers as the next cosmopolitan patriot. This was partly for pragmatic, financial reasons: since he had fled China for his life in 1895, his revolutionary hopes had been kept alive by dollars, francs, pounds and yen. Sun owed the West not only an intellectual and emotional debt, but also his life. In London in 1896, he had been kidnapped by the Qing legation and threatened with deportation to China (and certain death), until a British media campaign on his behalf surrounded the embassy with crowds threatening to demolish the building unless the prisoner was released. (In Beijing in 1984 for fraught negotiations over Hong Kong, Mrs Thatcher took care to remind her Chinese counterparts of this merciful British intervention.) But his ambivalence also sprang from a realistic assessment of the relative importance of internal and international politics, and from a matter-of-fact refusal to blame foreigners for most of China's difficulties.

For most of his career, Sun was necessarily more preoccupied by his domestic political opponents than by foreign threats. Through the 1900s, he was careful to avoid open criticism of Western imperialism: his public statements always attributed the root of China's problems to the dictatorship of the Manchus (whom Sun excoriated for having failed to build a Western-style democracy).[17] In 1912, even as he declared opium prohibition to be one of the most urgent tasks of the new republic, he observed that 'Lin Zexu's burning of the opium generated unprecedented calamity for the country . . . it did not conform to treaties; it was uncivilized, illegal behaviour.'[18] To the end of his life, he considered his greatest mistake to have been to cede the presidency to Yuan Shikai in 1912 – rather than to have offered repeatedly to hand over large portions of the Chinese republic to would-be foreign backers. (In 1913 alone, he volunteered Manchuria to the Japanese government in exchange for 20 million yen and a couple of army divisions.) In 1923, Sun objected to a student slogan that exhorted the Chinese to 'Resist the Great Powers abroad and overthrow the warlords at home'. 'These two problems cannot be discussed in the same breath', he reprimanded the sloganeers. 'If the home government is good then foreign relations present no problem.'[19]

If, in the early 1920s, China's old Opium War adversary Great Britain had produced backing as substantial as that promised by the Soviet Union, Sun's budding agreement with Lenin might well have come to nothing. In February 1923, a mere month before the USSR pledged $2 million to his revolutionary government, Sun was taking tea in well-heeled Hong Kong drawing rooms and proclaiming that 'we must take England as our model and must extend England's example of good government to the whole of China.'[20]

But by 1924, his ongoing financial and political crises had persuaded Sun to complete the intellectual journey dictated by Soviet

backing, and in a series of lectures on his *Three Principles of the People*
– the text that would become a major part of his political legacy after
his death the following year – he began to identify imperialism as
Republican China's greatest enemy. By wresting control of Customs
from the Qing, the first Opium War had left China with a severe
'economic disability', resulting in the annual loss of $1.2 billion.
'China has suffered at the hands of the Great Powers for decades . . .
[It] has become a colony of the Great Powers.'[21] In fact, China was
far worse than a colony, he told his listeners – it was, he extemporized,
a 'hypocolony . . . not the slaves of one country but of all.'[22] The
'historic task', he decided, must now be to unite for 'the overthrow of
the intervention of foreign imperialism in China', for 'China's disintegration is not the fault of the Chinese, but, instead, is caused
exclusively by foreigners.'[23] Through his lectures, Sun painted a
simplistic picture of a peaceable, virtuous China surrounded by
rapacious foreign powers eager 'to destroy a nation in one morning.'
In order to rescue the country, he concluded, his Nationalist Party
was duty-bound to 'acquaint our 400 million people with our present
position. We are just now at the crisis between life and death.' If
the Chinese did not – under the leadership of the Nationalist Party
– recover their sense of nationalism and ready themselves to fight
imperialism, 'our nation [will] be destroyed [and our] race will be
exterminated.'[24] The Nationalists, in other words, were China's only
chance of salvation.

Once Sun's Nationalist Party had finally vowed to rally the
Chinese to the cause of anti-imperialism, however, it still had to find
the means to impress this new orthodoxy on the minds of its citizens.
By the early 1920s, it was clear to aspiring political elites that for
decades anti-Western feeling had ebbed and flowed in response to
particular crises, without coalescing into a unified political force.
A strong, cohesive nation required a one-party nation-state. The
problem with the Chinese, the supposed republican democrat Sun
Yat-sen concluded in 1924, was that they had too much freedom.
'We have had too much liberty without any unity . . . [B]ecause we
have become a sheet of loose sand . . . we must break down individual
liberty and become pressed together into an unyielding body like the
firm rock which is formed by the addition of cement to sand.'[25] The
Chinese people, in the estimation of the newly reformed Nationalist

Party, needed discipline. 'The masses', in an Orwellian phrase of the early 1920s, needed to be 'partified', Lenin-style; they needed a pervasive, unified national language of anti-imperialist slogans and symbols, clearly identifying the country's enemies (imperialism and its lackeys) and its saviours (the Nationalists and their sometime allies, the Communists).[26] At the First Congress of the reorganized Nationalist Party in 1924, anti-imperialism became one of the basic criteria by which Chinese citizens would be given membership of the national revolution to come: 'Those who betray the nation, those who give their loyalty to the imperialists or to the warlords, will be permitted neither freedom nor rights.'[27]

The task would prove beyond Sun Yat-sen. Soon after he had travelled north in 1925 to conduct talks with the warlord government in Beijing, he succumbed to liver cancer. Almost instantly, though, his successors embarked upon modern China's most humourlessly committed attempt at nation-building: 'with the president dead,' the Nationalists' Central Executive Committee quickly concluded, *party discipline* is the only thing that can protect . . . us.'[28] Sun's survivors began by reinvigorating its Propaganda Bureau, ensuring that a party line actually existed, that it was disseminated to all party branches, and that newspapers, magazines and public lectures toed it.[29] (This was a major achievement: as late as 1924, the newly appointed editor of the Nationalist Party newspaper had to work on ensuring that it stopped at least *openly* insulting Sun Yat-sen.) While Nationalist armies – trained and supplied by the Soviets – pushed up through the country between 1926 and 1928, fighting or bribing warlords into submission, Sun's successors (led by Chiang Kai-shek, the man who took over the helm of the party) deified their late, flawed leader as the political sage of a Nationalist Party that aspired to monopolize all claims to represent the 'Chinese nation'. As they surged north, fighting to reunify the country, Nationalist forces showered the country with tens of thousands of slogans, leaflets, images of the Great Leader and new blue-and-white Nationalist flags. Sun's anti-imperialist *Three Principles of the People* and last testament (drafted by subordinates desperate for a legacy and merely signed off by the semi-comatose dying man) became the soundtrack to public life in the Nationalist state founded in 1928. Every Monday, in offices, schools and garrisons, employees, students and soldiers would gather to bow

three times to his portrait, to listen to a reading of his Testament and
to contemplate silently for three minutes.[30]

But if the Nationalists were serious about engineering a nation
out of anti-imperialist feeling, tampering with history books was an
obvious step to take. 'Who controls the past, controls the future',
as Ingsoc put it in *Nineteen Eighty-Four*. 'Who controls the present
controls the past.' And it was thanks to the propaganda drive of the
1920s and 1930s that the events of 1839–42 stopped being a
quarrelsome side-story (a 'dispute' or 'expedition') of the nineteenth
century and became instead the aggrieved, unprecedented national
tragedy that the 'Opium War' remains in China today.

A touching illustration on page four of the sixth issue of *Children's
Magazine* (*Ertong Zazhi*) from 1936 shows two plump little brothers,
one a head taller than the other, standing with their arms around
each other, the older presumably imparting some fraternal wisdom to
the younger on the subject of the article's title: 'A Chat about the
Opium War'. The following dialogue between the two boys ensues.
'What was the Opium War about?' the little one wants to know.
Well, his big brother explains, it all started with Lin Zexu trying to
stop British opium imports.

> 'So they attacked Dinghai and Tianjin, and the Qing emperor
> was so useless he blamed Lin Zexu for causing the war, dismissed
> him and appointed Qishan instead to negotiate for peace.'
> 'What a silly emperor!'
> 'And because Qishan was so clueless, the English took
> Wusong and Nanjing. The Qing emperor was so surprised that
> he signed the Treaty of Nanjing that destroyed our sovereignty
> and humiliated the nation.'
> 'Those horrible fierce imperialists!'

The younger one – probably around seven years old – responds to a
description of the clauses of the Treaty of Nanjing with word-perfect
political correctness. 'Oh, I'm so angry I could die! The emperor
and his ministers were so stupid! I could kill them all! They deserve
to die!' 'Don't get angry,' counsels his sage brother. 'Just remember

everything that I told you – you'll take revenge when you get older.' 'Of course,' chirps the seven-year-old. 'This blood debt has to be repaid.'[31]

This exchange sums up what every schoolchild in Nationalist China was supposed to know about the Opium War: that it was a tale of evil imperialists and foreign poison humiliating China; and that all right-thinking Chinese people, of all ages, should be inspired to take revenge for it. Two or three decades earlier, what Chinese people today now know as the Opium War ('Yapian zhanzheng') remained an event in China's long, difficult nineteenth century, buried beneath the more general subheadings of 'Internal and External Troubles of the Nineteenth Century' or 'the Western Migration East', and sandwiched between difficulties in Xinjiang and the sprawling violence of the Taiping Rebellion. An average history textbook would run through a handful of factual details – the growing Chinese fondness for opium; the crackdown of 1839; the arrival of gunboats; the main battles; the treaty and the size of the indemnity – then move on to the next unpleasant nineteenth-century occurrence (usually domestic rebellions; occasionally sheep banditry in Mongolia).[32]

Through the 1920s, though, the historiography of the Opium War acquired a fresh sense of resentment. By the end of this decade, the conflict and the first 'Unequal Treaty' that Qiying and Yilibu had signed off with such careless haste had become the turning point in a modern history dominated by imperialist aggression. It was (ahistorically) named the 'beginning of China's diplomatic defeats' after '5,000 years of isolation' from the outside world; 'a humiliation to the country – the greatest ever in our history' that 'brought dishonour to countless descendants'.[33] 'The Opium War, for the first time, branded the iron hoofprint of imperialism on the bodies of our people', pronounced one history textbook.[34] 'From this time on,' observed another, 'the invasions and oppressions of the imperialists would daily encroach further on the Chinese people.'[35] 'The Opium War is intricately linked with the national fate of modern China', commented a 1931 tract on the conflict. 'At last, foreigners were able to realize their old dream of looting China; how furiously we sigh to remember it now. This book offers a warning to you all, to incite bitter hatred of the common enemy.'[36] 'Since the Opium War,' a magazine editorial analysed, 'international imperialism has forced opium on our country, miring our great rivers and mountains in black fog . . . we have been massacred, robbed of our sovereignty – we've become worse than a colony. We've become a poisoned people.'[37]

The aim was to persuade the populace to blame all China's problems on a single foreign enemy: to transform the Opium War and its Unequal Treaty into a long-term imperialist scheme from which only the Nationalists could preserve the country, thereby justifying any sacrifice that the party required of the Chinese. 'From the Opium War . . . the unanimous demand of the people has been to avenge the National Humiliation', Chiang Kai-shek informed his subjects. 'The success of the Nationalist Revolution [and] China's destiny depends upon the efforts of my countrymen.'[38] If something is not done, another essayist proclaimed, 'generation upon generation of our children will be enslaved for ever.'[39] Reassessment of the Opium War coincided with other anti-Western commemorations introduced after 1924: week-long anti-imperialism fiestas (orchestrated by the new Grand Anti-imperialist Alliance) protesting acts of foreign violence – such as the shooting of eleven Chinese protestors by British-led constables in Shanghai on 30 May 1925. Enlisted Nationalist soldiers were educated by four-hour lectures on the past and present oppression of imperialism: 'England imports opium into China', ran the official script for these talks. 'The British bombarded Canton, demanded indemnity and, moreover, occupied and still occupy Hong Kong.'[40] 'With their thirteen million square miles of colonies, the British imperialists are the leaders of world imperialism', exclaimed a party weekly in 1930. 'They've oppressed every small race to death . . . Because of British imperialism, our nation is neither free nor equal . . . if you want proof, just remember how the British have invaded us for the last eighty years . . . Let us lift the curtain on evil British imperialism, and reveal its viciousness.'[41]

Yet however hard Nationalist China's pedagogues tried to turn the Opium War into a monument to China's victimization by the West, the old self-disgust of earlier patriots crept back in. Reminders of British wickedness were accompanied by references to the war's 'failures' and 'defeats', caused by the 'arrogance', 'stupidity' and 'indecision' of the Qing government, by the 'slumbering, ancient, declining' and 'undisciplined' masses, and by the treachery of the 'bad merchants'. 'We weren't ready,' one 1936 analysis of the war concluded, 'we were divided . . . we were suspicious of each other . . . the responsibility lies, for the most part, on our shoulders . . . the Opium War is more useful than harmful to us – it can transform our thinking and correct our mistakes.'[42] 'It marked the beginning of our period of transformation and enlightenment', agreed *Drug Prohibition Monthly* in the same year. 'English imperialism was the induction injection for the reform of Chinese society.'[43] 'European and American imperialists invaded China,' an article commemorating the centenary of the war lamented, 'but the Chinese people were responsible for their own weakness – we can't blame other people.'[44]

In 1943, Chiang Kai-shek completed his own judgement of the Opium War, denouncing in his book-length manifesto *China's Destiny* the 'heartbreaking' and 'limitless evil effects' of the country's 'First National Humiliation', which 'cut off the lifeblood of the state' and 'threatened our people's chance of survival.'[45] Throwing off the enslavement of the Unequal Treaties was 'the most important objective of the Chinese Nationalist Revolution.'[46] In these same pages, though, he also made plain his contempt for the 'stupidity' of the Manchus and for the 'decadent habits and evil practices' of the ordinary people. 'The country was subjected only because it had subjected itself . . . Must we not tremble? Must we not be ashamed and disturbed?'[47] (His Western-educated wife, Song Meiling, took care to ensure that the government did not translate her husband's great work into English, for fear that its anti-Western message would alienate the Americans and British from whom the Nationalists desperately needed military aid to fight the Japanese.[48])

Coexisting with this still ambivalent vision of the Opium War was a set of similarly undecided attitudes to opium itself. In Nationalist declarations, opium was legally and morally beyond the pale: in 1928, Chiang's new government announced a 'total prohibition' (*juedui jinyan*). Unofficially, however, the Nationalists – like the warlord regimes they fought through the 1920s and 1930s – needed the opium trade for revenue. Between 1927 and 1937, the Nationalist government strove (often with surprising success, given appalling obstacles such as Japanese invasion and worldwide depression) to transform an impoverished, fragmented country into a modern unified state: creating national ministries, commissions, academies; building roads, railways, industries, dams.[49] In the absence of crucial resources such as income tax, opium duties would have to do instead. For the creative tax-collector – and Republican China was full of them – there was a wealth of surcharges to be extracted from opium: in duties on the drug itself (plus its transport and retail); and licences to sell and smoke it. The state even maintained a monopoly on opium-addiction cures.[50] The citizens of the republic dodged these taxes with comparable ingenuity: one filial individual smuggled opium between west and east China by concealing it not just inside his father's coffin, but inside his father's skull inside the coffin.[51]

In 1928, drug revenues helped keep the country's armies – at a total of 2.2 million, the largest in the world (costing $800 million a year) – standing. A 1931 cartoon entitled 'Shanghai business' pictured three figures: to left and right two dwarfs labelled 'industry' looked skyward at the towering colossus between them – Opium. In 1933, the size of the opium traffic in China was estimated at $2 billion annually (5.2 per cent of the country's gross domestic product). In many regions and contexts, opium was as good as, if not better than, money, and an essential commercial and social lubricant – 'light the lamps' was standard Chinese for 'let's talk business'; opium pipes were offered at weddings as conventionally as wine. The country literally reeked of the stuff, thanks to the vats of the drug publicly boiled in the streets of towns and cities: by the 1930s, China may have had as many as 50 million smokers (around 9 per cent of the population).[52]

Through the 1920s, concerned civilians organized themselves into a National Anti-Opium Association, launching special Anti-Opium Days, then Anti-Opium Weeks, and a monthly periodical *Drug Prohibition*, on whose covers righteous, muscular Chinese thwacked and thumped hideous tar-black monsters named Opium. (Four and a half million signatures were collected for anti-opium petitions in 1924 alone.) 'Why aren't our nation's merchants content with engaging in legitimate business activities?' the Association wanted to know in 1927. 'Why are they so willing to serve as the slaves of foreigners? As the running dogs of warlords? As those who injure both the people and the nation? . . . They curry favour with imperialists and warlords, and entice our male and female countrymen to smoke opium with devastating consequences.'[53] In the meantime, the Nationalist government identified offices for collecting opium tax as 'opium suppression bureaus', while opium merchant guilds could be euphemistically labelled 'medicinal merchants' friendship associations'.[54] 'Millions have been raised out of opium', remarked the International Anti-Opium Association in 1928. 'Nationalist Government monopolies exist in every large centre, and are so efficiently organised that enormous revenues result. And although the evil of the so-called "Opium Wars" has invariably been referred to on every Nationalist platform and in every proletarian demonstration, the Government is raising the very last cent out of the cultivation and use of opium.'[55] Not for nothing did the Cantonese have the saying, 'Opium addiction is easy to cure; opium tax addiction far harder.'[56]

Anti-opium activists reviled the government's pragmatic efforts to generate useful, state-building money out of the drug: 'As we look around at the conditions within China, opium is everywhere, how sickening! HOW SICKENING! We truly hope that the government authorities will . . . completely prohibit opium, and earnestly eradicate it in order to save the tarnished reputation of our country and forever consolidate the foundation of this nation.'[57] The government gave earnest public pledges that it 'will absolutely not derive one copper from opium revenue. If anything of this sort is suspected . . . we can regard this government as bankrupt and place no confidence in it.'[58] 'If we want to save China,' Chiang Kai-shek added, 'we must begin with prohibiting opium, and that prohibition must begin with the highest echelons of the leadership . . . Prohibit the poison if you want to save the country, the people, yourself, your sons and grandsons.'[59] 'The opium evil', he explained elsewhere, 'constitutes a greater menace to the nation than foreign aggression, because the former leads to self-degeneration and self-suicide, whereas the latter is invited by mutual dissension, weakness and degeneracy.'[60] In private, the regime did its best to silence inconvenient opponents by frightening off their sponsors, by smearing them with accusations of drug-smuggling, by sending them death threats; or simply by planting bombs in their houses. In 1931, the government was buffeted by one of its biggest drug scandals, when a group of Shanghai constables intercepted an opium shipment that a company of Nationalist soldiers were busy unloading. The men of the law were promptly taken prisoner until the precious drug had found its way to its gangland destination.[61]

In 1934, the government began to execute relapsed users of opiates, informing opium-smokers that they would 'be shot without further ceremony' if they returned to the habit after treatment. In 1936, nine such individuals were paraded through the streets of Xi'an then killed in front of thousands of spectators.[62] 'Opium is good for curing minor sickness, for dealing with boredom, and for helping you think', one of Chiang Kai-shek's 'opium-suppression' officials flagrantly contradicted government policy in 1940. 'Just light a pipe and you will be happy . . . your mind will open like a flower and you will be able to clearly distinguish things.'[63] 'In the country all that one can see is poppy growing everywhere,' observed a newspaper in 1932, 'in the cities there are opium dens along every street, government offices openly collect taxes on opium, and citizens openly smoke it . . . the whole of China depends upon opium . . . This condition is far more lamentable than the Opium Prohibition Memorial Day.'[64]

In the early 1940s, the north-eastern city of Mukden – the old Manchu capital – retained at least a touch of its old dynastic grandeur. In 1625, when the Qing were still only aspiring rulers of China, they had built themselves there a miniature replica of the Forbidden City (a diminutive seventeen acres, to the original's hundred and seventy) in which to perfect their practice of imperial rituals. Outside its palace complex, though, Mukden was heavily marked by the Japanese invasion of Manchuria. In 1942, the north-eastern edge of the city (just outside a thick, crenellated wall of Ming vintage) had acquired a prisoner-of-war camp, housing around 1,200 American, British, Dutch and Australian soldiers taken since the fall of Singapore; almost 40 per cent of them would be dead of malnutrition and ill-treatment by the time of the Japanese surrender. Along the grey streets of the city itself, a scattering of smarter establishments – newly, attractively spruced up in red and white paint – might have stood out. Their fronts proclaimed they were selling a mysterious substance called 'Official Paste' – opium. Elsewhere, a casual observer might have spotted a number of shacks – perhaps 200 – receiving dozens of visitors per day. These were, an eyewitness from 1931 had noted, 'dope huts . . . In a single shop, about forty to fifty persons come to receive [morphine] injections every day'.[65]

By 1942, the Second World War was going badly for Chiang Kai-shek and his government. In 1937, a Japanese move against Shanghai and Nanjing had driven the Nationalists from their seat of power on the east coast. As Chiang and his followers retreated into the hinterland, his armies destroyed Yellow River dykes to halt the Japanese advance – an act that caused at least half a million civilian deaths by drowning and disease. By the close of that year, Chiang had lost his industrial base and, four long years before the Americans joined the war effort, began struggling to reconstruct his regime in impoverished Sichuan. But as the Nationalists tried to build roads and rationalize taxes, they also found time to fight a new war of words on opium. In 1938, Madame Chiang Kai-shek accused the Japanese of a 'diabolically cunning' plot to 'drench' China with opium, with a view to 'demoralising the people until they were physically unfit to defend their country, and mentally and morally so depraved that they could easily be bought and bribed with drugs to act as spies when the time came in order that their craving might be satisfied.'[66] 'The Japanese are many times worse than the British ever were!' agreed a journalist two years later. 'Even at the time of the Opium War, some Britons criticized it, like true English gentlemen. The Japanese, by contrast, are trying to poison our people, to annihilate our race.'[67] Foreign correspondents in China through the 1930s denounced the 'ash heap of Mukden', littered with moribund drug fiends. The Japanese occupation government apparently encouraged opium use in Beijing by telling its police to turn a blind eye to proliferating dens in the former capital. Unpassported Korean and Japanese gangsters were, these same observers noted, busily peddling opium and heroin 'to the degradation of thousands of Chinese . . . sowing seeds of bitterness and hatred, which it will take years to eradicate.'[68]

The horror of the Japanese invasion and allegations of Japanese attempts to stupefy the country with opiates brought a new resonance to Chinese denunciations of the Opium War. (Whether or not Japanese-controlled regimes cynically pushed drugs to the Chinese to break their spirit of resistance, they certainly profited from them. The puppet state of Manchukuo in the north-east drew a sixth of its revenue from opium sales and exports.[69]) But the occupying Japanese and their Chinese collaborators also made use of the Opium War as a rhetorical tool to distract attention away from Japanese atrocities. In August 1939, by which point millions of Chinese had been killed or wounded in the war with Japan, Beijing's puppet government convened 'Down With Britain' rallies against the Opium War, arguing that they were merely giving an outlet to Chinese outrage that 'had been boiling since the Opium War'.[70] Stop fighting Japan, one Pan-Asianist editorial urged its Chinese readers the following year. 'Europe's disarray is Asia's opportunity . . . We've seized the opportunity for revenge. We should expunge the bloody humiliation [of the Opium War] with all determination! . . . We must recognize our true enemies and kill them with all our strength. Every Chinese person has the responsibility to commemorate the centenary of the Opium War and to remember that Asia is for the Asians!'[71] Meanwhile, occupied Shanghai – the headquarters of the Chinese film industry – planned an all-star-cast blockbuster about the war to 'encourage all Chinese people to oppose Britain and America.'[72]

Between 1925 and 1926, a tall, confident figure with a mop of black, swept-back hair sat in the director's chair of the newly reorganized Propaganda Bureau of the Nationalist Party, combing piles of newspapers for deviations from party orthodoxy. Mao Zedong did not have long in the job. Within another two years, there would be no place for a Communist like him anywhere in the Nationalist Party organization. On 12 April 1927, after months of secret negotiations with Shanghai's wealthiest financiers and their private underworld enforcers, the Green Gang, Chiang Kai-shek set an armed force of some 1,000 gangsters at the city's labour unions, the hubs of Communist activity; 100 unionists were gunned down at a single protest rally alone. Forces rallied by the Communists were similarly massacred in Changsha, Wuhan, Nanchang and, finally, Canton, where leftists were quickly identified by the dye marks left round their necks by their red kerchiefs and drowned in bundles of ten or twelve in the river by the city.

Over the next two decades, the civil conflict between the Nationalist and Communist Parties would dominate political and military life in China – sometimes to the extent even of sidelining the war with Japan. The Japanese invasion was, Chiang Kai-shek declared in the early 1930s, merely 'external . . . like a gradually festering ulcer on the skin. The [Communist] bandit disturbance is internal. It is . . . a disorder of the heart. Because this internal disease has not been eliminated, the external disorder cannot be cured.'[73] Violence would climax in the final stages of the civil war between 1945 and 1949, during which hundreds of thousands of civilians would perish; perhaps 650,000 died of starvation in the Communist siege of a single north-eastern city alone.

Despite their vicious political rivalries, China's new political parties concurred perfectly on how China was to be manipulated into an effective nation-state: through ideological discipline and unity. As Propaganda Chief Mao barked in 1925, 'either step right, into the counter-revolutionary faction, or step left, into the revolutionary faction . . . There is no third route . . . Anyone who offers support for counter-revolutionary actions . . . shall be counted as our enemy.'[74] And their populist rhetoric notwithstanding, at base both held similarly dismissive views of the Chinese people, and of their need for reprogramming with one-party nationalism. China, the Nationalist Party's first director of propaganda judged in 1925, was a 'blank sheet of paper. Colour it green, and it is green; colour it yellow and it is yellow.' Mao Zedong, his successor, agreed: the Chinese, he believed, were 'poor and blank. A clean sheet of paper has no blotches and so the newest and most beautiful words can be written on it.'[75]

Although, after 1949, the victorious CCP would expend much energy in excoriating the 'reactionary idealist, mechanical materialist, feudal, comprador, fascist ideology' of their old Nationalist enemies, both parties shared almost identical views of China's modern history.[76] The job of demonizing the Opium War was completed by the Communists, once most of the early work had been done for them by the Nationalists' official history industry. Many elements in the Communist version plagiarized earlier Nationalist models, portraying the war as the start of the plot by foreign imperialism ('the foremost and most ferocious enemy of the Chinese people') to 'impoverish . . . suppress . . . and poison the minds of the Chinese people', leaving them 'hungry and cold'.[77] But once Mao was done with it (going back to it in at least fifteen separate essays), the Opium War was no longer just a turning point in modern Chinese history; it was its inaugural event: 'the first lesson' of the Chinese revolution, and the start of a century of capitalist-imperialist oppression.[78] China's modern history now became, quite simply, 'a history of struggle by the indomitable Chinese people against imperialism and its running dogs'; the Opium War – this strange, ambivalent story of collaboration and civil war – became the 'people's unrelenting and heroic struggle', 'a national war' against imperialism.[79] 'For a whole hundred years,' a 1951 history recycled Mao's views, 'imperialism trampled our Chinese people underfoot. After 1842, China sank into a tragic state of slavery, and was transformed into a semi-colony by every imperialist country. The founding of the People's Republic in 1949, by contrast, is the most glorious achievement of this century; our will has been forged by the painful wound of suffering.'[80]

The point of remembering past bitterness was to remind the populace to savour the sweetness of the Communist present – even as the government itself caused tens of millions of deaths in man-made famines, in purges of counter-revolutionaries and in the civil war manufactured by Mao's Cultural Revolution. 'A young Chinese person in new China', explained a 1950 textbook in the preamble to its Opium War chapter, 'must have a basic understanding of modern history . . . and of the particular principles that governed the revolution . . . We must understand what our predecessors have suffered to establish the People's Republic so we love the motherland all the more, so we can contribute everything we have to the future of the motherland . . . We have to understand why Mao's thought is the only truth able to point out the way to revolutionary victory.'[81] By insisting on the malevolence of China's foreign antagonists, Mao's Communist Party legitimized its own use of violence, against both imperialists and their alleged Chinese allies (Nationalists, capitalists, landlords and anyone suspected of sympathizing with them): 'In the face of such enemies', Mao dictated, 'the Chinese revolution cannot be other than protracted and ruthless . . . In the face of such enemies, the principal means or form of the Chinese revolution must be armed struggle.'[82]

But Mao was as willing to profit from opium as the next warlord – even though he had officially banned opium production in Communist-controlled areas in 1939, asserting that it 'sickens the country and harms the people'.[83] Two years earlier, the Communists' finances – stretched by Mao's ambitions to expand militarily through the north-western province in which they had settled in 1935 – had briefly stabilized. That year, Chiang Kai-shek had called a second United Front – this time against the Japanese. Over the next four years, the Communist economy survived on annual handouts from the Nationalists and the Soviet Union.[84] After 1941, however, when relations between the two parties deteriorated back into effective civil war, the Nationalists severed their funding and blockaded the edges of the Communist zone, preventing essential imports from getting in. By the end of the year, the region's finances were millions of Nationalist dollars in the red.[85]

For decades, Communist propaganda held that the Maoists worked their way out of their predicament through frugality and popular democracy (by introducing rent reduction and cooperative farming practices), until a historian called Chen Yung-fa noticed at the end of the 1980s that account books for the period were scattered with references to a 'special product' that rescued the Communists from their trade deficit of the early 1940s and that, by 1945, was generating more than 40 per cent of the state's budget. A little more detective work revealed that this was opium, processed in 'Special Factories' and transported south and west to generate export revenue for Communist armies. ('Since opium entered China', a Communist editorial of 1941 explained, 'it has become the greatest source of harm to the Chinese people, inseparable from imperialist invasion . . . Imperialism has used opium to enslave and oppress the Chinese people. As the Chinese people have become ever weaker, ever poorer, opium has played a most detestable and poisonous destructive role.'[86]) But in 1945, as an American mission flew in to inspect Mao's kingdom, it found itself gazing over nothing more controversial than swaying fields of sorghum and wheat. The opium poppies had been uprooted just in time to maintain – for the next forty years at least – the propriety of the Chinese Communist wartime image.

After 1949, the new People's Republic declared a total rupture with the corruption and hypocrisy of Chiang Kai-shek's Nationalists and their opium policy. 'It has been more than a century since opium was forcibly imported into China by the imperialists', ran a General

Order for Opium Suppression. 'Due to the reactionary rule and the decadent lifestyle of the feudal bureaucrats, compradors, and warlords, not only was opium not suppressed, but we were forced to cultivate it ... Now that the people have been liberated, the suppression of opium and other narcotics is specifically stipulated to protect people's health, to cure addiction, and to accelerate production.'[87] In mass rallies and public trials, smokers were rehabilitated; thousands of pounds of opium were publicly burned; traffickers were imprisoned, dispatched to labour camps or executed. Only Western fellow travellers to Communism were welcome in China; foreign businessmen – seen as hangovers of the bad old Unequal Treaty days (the treaties themselves had been mostly revoked in the Second World War) – were harassed and even imprisoned, and their assets nationalized.

Popular enthusiasm could still have its old limits, though. Local government in the north-east remarked in the early 1950s that lecturing on 'the history of the Opium Wars or the opium policy of the imperialists was not an effective way to reach the masses.'[88]

Chapter Nineteen

CONCLUSION

The Opium War is a pretty shameful story. Perhaps it slipped
your memory? It certainly hasn't slipped [China's] and is still
unravelling.

Guardian, 2010[1]

On 28 December 2009, a prisoner of the Chinese state was driven
through the freezing streets of Urumqi to a Public Detention Centre.
The following morning, around 6.30, he was woken and offered a
breakfast of thin rice porridge, and the opportunity to brush his teeth.
By 10 a.m., he was delivered, under paramilitary guard, to a mobile
'death van', strapped to a trolley and given a lethal injection.

In some respects, the whole business was terribly mundane for the
People's Republic of China, which executes somewhere between 1,700
and 10,000 people every year. In its superficial particulars, the
sentencing would have looked uncontroversial. Smuggling any quantity above fifty grams of heroin automatically incurs the death penalty;
the condemned man had brought into the country a suitcase containing over four kilograms of the drug.

But in other ways, this was an unusual occurrence. The man,
Akmal Shaikh, was an ethnically Pakistani British citizen, and hence
the first European to be executed in China in almost sixty years. He
was, moreover, a Briton whose legal responsibility for the crime in
question was hotly contested by his family and friends. Shaikh, his
British defenders argued, was mentally ill, suffering from bipolar
disorder and manic depression. (He had originally travelled to China

in 2007 planning to become a pop star, bringing peace to the world with his atonal debut single, 'Come Little Rabbit'; his personal deposition in the Chinese court was so rambling and incoherent that his judges laughed at him.) He should, representatives of the British government had demanded, be given an independent psychiatric assessment by the Chinese authorities, a request that for months was stonewalled by the judges in the case.

Shaikh's death swiftly became a major international incident. 'I condemn the execution of Akmal Shaikh in the strongest terms,' said the British prime minister, Gordon Brown, 'and am appalled and disappointed that our persistent requests for clemency have not been granted.' Ivan Lewis, a Foreign Office minister, pronounced himself 'sick to the stomach . . . it's a deeply depressing day for anyone with a modicum of compassion or commitment to justice in Britain and throughout the world.'[2]

Chinese opinion responded with similar anger. The parallels were too obvious: a new British attempt to meddle with Chinese legal handling of an opiate-smuggling case. The media and Internet bubbled over with references to 1840 and all that. 'In China,' went the official government response, 'given the bitter memory of history . . . the public has a particular and strong resentment towards [drug smuggling]. In a recent web survey, 99% of the public support the decision of the Court.'[3] 'The execution of Shaikh is like the burning of opium stocks in Humen in 1840 during the Opium Wars', analysed one academic. 'This time, though, "gunboat diplomacy" could not work.'[4] 'England waged an Opium War against China', raged an anonymous Internet commentator. 'Does it feel "sick to its stomach" about having invaded us? . . . Lewis stands alongside Charles Elliot and Henry Pottinger: with the enemies of China.'[5] 'The words "England" and "opiate" equal "Opium War",' explained a blogger, 'the start of China's modern history of being bullied and humiliated. The English have forgotten that in 1840 their forebears began blasting open China's gates with opium. But the Chinese still feel the pain acutely.'[6] 'Kill kill kill kill', summarized another anonymous commentator.[7] The Chinese, it's worth pointing out, did not have a monopoly on memories of the Opium War. The same idea came to a handful of British commentators, one of whom denounced the fuss as 'hypocritical and insensitive'.[8]

This was the third piece of alarming news to come out of China in December 2009. The first concerned the failure of the Copenhagen Climate Change summit, following which European participants – bitterly disappointed that their hope for binding agreements on reductions of emissions had come to nothing – cast around for someone to blame, and found China. 'China wrecked the talks,' one impassioned environmentalist revealed, 'intentionally humiliated Barack Obama, and insisted on an awful "deal" so Western leaders would walk away carrying the blame.' China's only aim, he concluded, was to safeguard its own economic rise (reliant on free use of filthy, cheap coal), while encouraging the declining West to incinerate itself. The Chinese premier had not, moreover, even deigned to sit in the same room as leaders of the Western world – including Barack Obama – but had posted an underling to relay the negotiations back-and-forth by telephone.[9] To anyone with a touch of historical memory, this looked like an ominous return to the style of pompous, sino-centric diplomacy that had so enraged men like William Napier and Harry Parkes in the run-up to the first and second Opium Wars, as the emperor's officials refused to meet them in person, delegating instead the hapless Hong merchants.

Then, on Christmas Day, the Communist government (following months of illegal detention, and despite waves of international attention) sentenced to eleven years' imprisonment the celebrated veteran dissident Liu Xiaobo on charges of 'state subversion', as revenge for his authoring 'Charter 08' – an Internet petition calling for democracy and human rights for China. (Less than a year later, a group of Norwegians would enrage China by awarding Liu the 2010 Nobel Peace Prize in protest at his sentencing.) Eleven years earlier, Bill Clinton had lectured the Communist Party on its human-rights record, in person, in China. We're on the rise, the tune now seemed to run out of Beijing, and from now on you'd better get used to doing things our way.

The British press panicked. The foreign policy editor at the *Daily Telegraph* was swiftly grinding out invasion scenarios. 'The year is 2050, and a diplomatic dispute between China and Britain risks escalating into all-out war ... At the flick of a switch elite teams of Chinese hackers attached to the People's Liberation Army (PLA) launch a hi-tech assault on Britain's computer systems, with devastating consequences.' Recent clashes, he concluded, have laid bare 'the cold reality of China's attitude to the outside world.

> Rather than being a partner that can be trusted to work with the West ... the Chinese have demonstrated that their default position is that Beijing's only real priority is to look after its own interests ... Much of China's reluctance to engage constructively with the West on issues of mutual concern dates back to the psychological trauma the country suffered during the Opium Wars of the nineteenth century, when British gunboats routinely humiliated the Chinese government of the day ... To ensure that there is no repeat of a time when foreign powers could push the Chinese people around with impunity, Beijing is today investing enormous effort into developing technology that would render the West's superior military firepower useless.[10]

Drugs, revenge and Chinese plots for world domination: it was the Yellow Peril all over again.

Beneath the clash-of-civilizations rhetoric, things were more complicated. British commentators quickly assumed China's hard line was exclusively directed at them. But there was a domestic subtext to the government's lack of interest in compromising over Copenhagen, Liu Xiaobo or Akmal Shaikh. China's rulers are, for good reasons, intensely nervous of doing anything (such as restricting cheap coal emissions) that will jeopardize economic growth: their absolutist mandate to rule is predicated on their ability to deliver prosperity to their 1.3 billion subjects. The CCP's nervousness about domestic opposition showed in their grotesque treatment of Liu Xiaobo: China's Internet seethes with potential dissent and capacity to organize against the regime, with Liu only one representative of contemporary China's sizeable awkward squad.

Neither should it be forgotten that Akmal Shaikh's conviction and execution took place in Urumqi – the epicentre of violent clashes between Muslim populations and Han migrants in July 2009 that left 140 dead and many hundreds injured; it remained, as of January 2010, under tense paramilitary control. For years, China's preservers of law and order have connected drug-smuggling into Xinjiang via Central Asia with Islamic separatist terrorism. And in the couple of months preceding Akmal Shaikh's execution, Chinese newspapers were scattered with indications that Communist law and order was malfunctioning up and down the country: at least five deranged killing sprees, several of which involved multiple murders of family members – a sign that under the helm of the CCP, the moral fabric of society seemed to be in disintegration.[11] Look at us now, the Communist Party told their citizen subjects as they stood firm over Akmal Shaikh, we can keep domestic *and* international order. Where the West repeatedly saw deliberate, provocative defiance, the Chinese government also saw internal security issues. The whole sequence suggested another Opium War parallel: while seemingly at war with the West, China is also at war with itself.

It was worrying, though. It showed how edgy relations are, at base, between the West and a China that is clutching at superpower status; and how troubled these relations still are by a highly politicized historical memory.

One of the great clichés of non-specialist reporting on post-Mao China is that the place is changing, and fast. But through the transformations of the past thirty years, at least two things have remained reassuringly the same. One is the Communist Party's untiring claim to lead the country. Another is the airless account of modern Chinese history that the party constructed in the 1920s and 1930s, with significant help from the Nationalists, to shore up its own legitimacy and demand sacrifices from the Chinese people: namely, that the history of modern China is a history of imperialist victimization (from which only the party can save the country).

In the 1980s, though, this familiar narrative played to something of an empty house. For sure, the textbooks carried the old tune about 'the hideous sufferings' inflicted by the 'shameful opium trade', and 'the Chinese people's resolute will to resist foreign invasion.'[12] But this was a decade in which the government had trouble persuading anyone about anything. For many Chinese people, the volte-face from the Cultural Revolution was too dramatic for the regime to maintain its old credibility – former enemies of the people were suddenly rehabilitated; the vicious energies expended in persecuting and humiliating them were dismissed as an unfortunate mistake; the years that millions of urban intellectuals had spent 'learning from the peasants' were redefined as a waste of time. Even the once-deified Mao was pronounced in 1981 to have been only 70 per cent right.

A key element of the post-Mao change of heart was to admit that learning from the West – or parts of it, at least – was acceptable. But even as the government tried desperately hard to pick and choose what it imported – foreign investment, science and technology were fine; democracy less so – control proved elusive. 'Once you open the window,' as Mao's successor Deng Xiaoping famously commented, 'it's hard to stop the flies and mosquitoes coming in.' And when the party tried to block certain imports, ridicule resulted. In the early 1980s, it focused its energies on eradicating 'Spiritual Pollution': not only pornography and smuggling, but also less obviously criminal manifestations – long hair, flared trousers, slightly modernist poetry whose meaning was not as transparent as road-signs. By this point, although such campaigns could still chill the Chinese people with memories of the Cultural Revolution, they were far less successful at actually convincing anyone. Many urban Chinese recall the Anti-Spiritual Pollution Campaign as the single event that – through its sheer pettiness about things like hairstyles and clothing – destroyed their final shreds of intellectual respect for the CCP. 'Where shall we go and get polluted tonight?' mocked Yang Xianyi, one of the country's most famous literary intellectuals, down the phone to his friends as propaganda chiefs in the *People's Daily* railed against contamination by 'vulgar individualism'. Writers targeted by the campaign responded by cultivating Western support. 'Everyone I knew was disgusted with China, with the government', remembered Bonnie McDougall, a celebrated translator of post-Mao Chinese writing into English, and a resident in Beijing through the 1980s. 'I would be approached all the time by people asking me to get them invitations abroad ... they wanted to get out.'[13] The West was becoming no longer the root of all China's problems, but its saviour.

The authorities also seemed to lose some of their appetite for brainwashing the populace, through propaganda offensives, about their own infallibility. Many things were allowed to become publicly uncertain in the 1980s: how Marxist principles fitted with economic liberalization; how outrageous the government's vocal critics would be in their next essay or public lecture; how much cooking oil would cost next month. But as China stumbled towards a market economy and as inflation rocketed, one general conviction grew: the government's reforms weren't working and the leadership had not found a way to persuade the populace that they could lead. It was a decade in which almost everything and everyone Chinese seemed vulnerable to mockery and attack, and often from within the establishment. In 1988, as criticism fever ran high, Central China Television screened – not once, but twice – a six-part historical documentary entitled *Deathsong of a River* (*Heshang*), that scorned thousands of years of Chinese history and ridiculed the country's national symbols (such as the Great Wall and the Yellow River), while extolling Western-style trade, freedom, capitalism, science and democracy. The most avant-garde rebels – such as the 2010 Nobel Peace Laureate Liu Xiaobo – speculated that China could only experience 'great historical change' if it were colonized as Hong Kong had been.

The Opium War industry went into decline. The decade was littered with missed opportunities for commemorating Sino-British conflicts, with the neglected ruins of the old Summer Palace, to Beijing's north-west, a perfect example. During the Maoist period, the palace's pleasure gardens had become a treasure trove for pilfering farmers, questing for stone and bricks for pigsties and other useful buildings. Through the 1980s, administration of the place – crowded, as a couple of visitors noted, 'with heaps of rubbish, vegetable plots, pigsties and beancurd presses . . . fly- and mosquito-infested ditches' – was so slack that no one could be bothered to charge an entrance fee.[14] Fictionalized memoirs of the 1980s recalled a new, creative use for the dilapidated precincts: as a trysting location for the privacy- and sex-starved students of nearby Beijing and Qinghua Universities.

The neglect of political education had a direct effect on popular views of the CCP's legitimacy. From the mid-decade onwards, urban China was given pause, every year, by student protests: over the lack of government transparency; over the rising cost of food; over the rats in their dorms. Admittedly, some of these demonstrations seemed to be set off by anti-foreign feeling: most notoriously, the 1988 riots in Nanjing triggered by racist fury that African students were consorting with Chinese girls. But at bottom, these xenophobic eruptions were driven by acute domestic tensions. By the close of the decade, the leadership was unable to agree even in public on what it should be doing about the country's looming political and social crisis. Between 1986 and 1989, two of the men – Hu Yaobang and Zhao Ziyang – appointed by Deng Xiaoping to manage his socialist market economy were sacked for failing to come down hard enough on dissent (what the establishment had now started calling 'bourgeois liberalization'). The sudden death of Hu in April 1989 provided a focus for student dissatisfaction that led directly to the massive demonstrations of that spring and summer. After Zhao blanched at Deng's decision to send in the People's Liberation Army against the demonstrators, he would spend the next sixteen years (until his death in 2005) under house arrest, allowed out only for the occasional round of golf on one of Beijing's courses.

When a triumvirate of student leaders knelt on the steps to the Great Hall of the People in Tiananmen Square on 26 April 1989, to present the Communist leadership with a petition demanding democratic reforms, they had no idea that over the next two months their protests would fill the square with hunger-striking protestors, infect every major Chinese city, mesmerize the world's media and almost bring their Communist government down, before ending in bloodshed. (As the movement advanced, it became apparent that the students were clear about few of their aims, including democracy – many were distinctly lukewarm about the idea of giving the vote to the country's uneducated masses.) But whatever they did anticipate, no one could possibly have imagined – given how much emphasis the traditional Communist narrative of the Opium War had placed on taking the moral high ground over Western aggression – that it would be the government's most public act of violence against its own civilians (the suppression of the demonstrations on 4 June) that would restore the Opium War to its old, illustrious position as Pre-Eminent National Wound.

They were busy days in Beijing, just after 4 June 1989, just after the People's Liberation Army soldiers had lowered their rifle muzzles to chest height and begun firing at will on the people of Beijing. The military forces needed congratulating on national television on their triumph over the 'counter-revolution'; civilian bodies needed clearing from the streets; leading protestors who had not managed to smuggle themselves out of the country needed rounding up. But it was also a time for the leadership to reflect on what had gone wrong ideologically over the past ten years; on why the Chinese populace had seemed to stop believing in what the Communist Party told them; on why urban China had been on the brink of declaring war on the government; on why even the staff of the government's mouthpiece, the *People's Daily*, had joined the protestors, parading through the streets waving banners demanding 'No More Lies'.

Two answers were found – one public, one private. The public explanation was a reliable favourite: the turmoil was the result of foreign manipulation. 'Some political forces in the West', explained Chen Xitong, the Mayor of Beijing, 'always attempt to make socialist countries, including China, give up the socialist road, eventually bring these countries under the rule of international monopoly capital and put them on the course of capitalism. This is their long-term, fundamental strategy.'[15] A small group of counter-revolutionaries, he went on, had colluded with plotting foreigners, who had ploughed hundreds of millions of dollars into splitting the country.

In their more honest moments, though, China's hardliners might have concluded that they had brought it on themselves. Since Mao began his career in the Nationalists' Propaganda Office, the Communist Party had prided itself on its mastery of spin; on its understanding that in politics, surface is more important than substance. (In 1935, almost as soon as the ragged, starving remainder of Communist troops on the run from the Nationalist army limped into a new headquarters in the north-west, Mao had ordered underlings to get to work telling heroic tales about the trek, transforming it from a year-long rout into a triumph over adversity: the Long March.) But through the 1980s, that lesson had been sidelined in the interests of introducing fresh air into Chinese society: controlling public opinion had seemed less urgent than the drive towards a vigorous market economy. In spring 1989, as discontent climaxed, the party's propaganda chief extraordinarily lifted an initial media ban on reporting the protests, instructing newspaper editors to present 'the actual state of affairs' – to let the people make up their own minds; following which, journalists streamed into the square to join the demonstrations.[16]

The lessons were well marked by Deng Xiaoping. 'For many years,' he now sternly observed at a national meeting of propaganda department chiefs, 'some of our comrades, immersing themselves in specific affairs, have shown no concern for political developments and attached no importance to ideological work . . . Our gravest failure has been in [political] education. We did not provide enough education to young people, including students. For many of those who participated in the demonstrations and hunger strikes it will take years, not just a couple of months, of education to change their thinking.'[17] Deng's second-in-command, Jiang Zemin – who had scrambled up the party ranks on the strength of his muffling of 1989's Shanghai protests – was keen to show that the pendulum was swinging back. His predecessor, the disgraced Zhao Ziyang, had not even attended annual National Propaganda meetings; Jiang made a point not only of attending every one, but also of making the keynote speech.

Once the oversight had been acknowledged, though, the question was how to fill the propaganda vacuum. In declaring soon after Mao's death that 'practice was the sole criterion of truth', Deng had implicitly thrown ideology out of the window (perhaps the same one through which all the flies and mosquitoes were coming). The loss of Communist China's 'spiritual pillars' – the political, Marxist thought that glued the place together – had been the result. But now that the guns of the People's Liberation Army had been turned on the People, lecturing populations on proletarian principles was, realistically, going to be problematic – even though the conservative wing of the party remained in denial about this until around 1992, as they busily tried to orchestrate a return to old-style Maoism.

Some of the savvier elements in government had another idea: to combine recriminations of the West with a revamped patriotic propaganda drive – to reinvent the post-1989 party as defender of the national interest against Western attempts to contain a rising China. It was an almost improbably audacious plan: how on earth, a matter-of-fact observer might have reasonably asked at the time, was the party going to persuade its people – whom it had openly butchered through June 1989 – that it was, in fact, the country's saviour from evil Western schemes? The demonstrations' blood-soaked denouement was an international and domestic PR disaster of the first order: while

Western politicians and overseas Chinese called for economic and political sanctions and sinologists contemplated switching discipline in protest, hundreds of thousands of sobbing Chinese people came out in protest in Hong Kong, Macao, Taiwan and Western cities, comparing the PRC to Nazi Germany and spray-painting the national flag with swastikas. Surely, from here, there was no way back.

But one historical coincidence, at least, seemed to smile on the endeavour. The aftermath of the 1989 suppression fell upon an auspicious commemoration: the hundred and fiftieth anniversary of the Opium War. And through the months following June 1989, some of the country's modern historians got to work. While elsewhere in the world Communist states collapsed, academic hacks wrote and organized and wrote some more until, as the new year approached, they were at last ready. In 1990, China's establishment fought a vigorous campaign to remind the Chinese people of their history of oppression at the hands of West, through literally dozens of articles, conferences and spin-off books about the conflict.

'The Opium War', went *Humiliation and Resistance* – the book resulting from just one of the year's commemorative symposia – 'was the great event in China's modern history: not only the beginning of China's modern history of humiliation, but also the first glorious chapter of the Chinese people's struggle of resistance against foreign invasion. The War has not only branded an enormous, painful, unforgettable memory on the hearts of countless sons and daughters of China, but has also provided a hugely worthwhile lesson for later generations to reflect upon.' China's modern history was the story of the Chinese people suffering from, then resisting, (Western) imperialist aggression, beginning with the 'shameless' and 'filthy' Opium War, a concerted plot to 'enslave our people, steal our wealth and turn a great nation that had been independent for thousands of years into a semi-feudal semi-colony.' The Chinese people were also to remember that 'between the Opium War and the War of Resistance Against Japan, the Chinese people gradually awoke until, after many failed choices, they eventually chose socialism . . . and the leadership of the Communist Party . . . In recent years, some enemies of patriotism have been shouting about "total Westernization" . . . This is extraordinary . . . To forget history is treachery.'[18] 'Since the Opium War,' another conference paraphrased, 'history has shown that . . .

only the leadership of the Chinese Communist Party is the core power for the victory of the revolution ... only socialism can save and develop China.'[19]

The Opium War's birthday extravaganza of 1990 was the start of one of the Communist Party's most successful post-Mao ideological campaigns, Patriotic Education, a crusade designed – as the *People's Daily* explained in 1994 – to 'boost the nation's spirit, enhance its cohesion, foster its self-esteem and sense of pride, consolidate and develop a patriotic united front ... and rally the masses' patriotic passions to the great cause of building socialism with Chinese characteristics.'[20] The campaign encompassed three big ideas: first, to indoctrinate the Chinese in the idea that China possessed a unique, glorious, millennia-old 'national condition' (*guoqing*) unready for democracy; second, to remind them of their sufferings at the hands of the West; and third, to underline the genius of Communist leadership. In practice, this meant talking up the 'great achievements' of the Chinese People, Nation and Communist Party, in stirring films, in feel-good sing-songs, in top-hundred lists of heroes, great events and battles and in numbing references to China's 'century of humiliation' inflicted by foreign imperialism, always beginning with the Opium Wars, always passing slickly over the CCP's own acts of violence (the Maoist famine of the early 1960s; the Cultural Revolution; the 1989 crackdown). 'How can we give our youth patriotic education?' asked *Seeking Truth* (*Qiushi*), the party's leading policy journal. 'By teaching them to understand the historical inevitability and correctness of choosing the socialist road ... since the Opium War.'[21] Shortly after 1989, the Central Propaganda Department dubbed modern Chinese history 'a meaningful security issue.'[22] (In 2001, the official history of the CCP explicitly traced the party's period of pre-development back to 1840, 'in order to explain the historical inevitability of the CCP's establishment.'[23]) A rash of National Humiliation books erupted: *The Indignation of National Humiliation*, *A Dictionary of National Humiliation*, *A Simple Dictionary of National Humiliation*, *Never Forget National Humiliation*.[24] 'High schools didn't teach students anything about the Opium War until 1990,' a veteran author of history textbooks from the People's Educational Press recalled in 2007, 'when they brought it in to improve their patriotic education.'[25] As Francis Fukuyama pronounced the death of ideology, and both specialist and non-specialist China-watchers were predicting that China's famed propaganda system was in crisis, this machinery geared itself up for a new message.

Post-1989 China has bristled with new or improved tourist destinations commemorating the horrors of foreign aggression. The government finally mustered the will to capitalize on the propaganda value of the ruins of the Summer Palace, replacing the pigsties and piles of rubbish with new signs littered across the gardens reminding visitors of what would have been there, if the British and French had not burnt or stolen it first. The ruins of the Qing emperors' imitation Versailles, of course, were left in place – a handful of curlicued pillars looming up out of evocatively disarranged rubble – as if 1860 were only yesterday still. Before their groups scatter for photo-opportunities, Chinese tour-guides today make sure their charges have taken the point: 'This isn't history,' I overheard one party being told. 'This is a national tragedy.' After a solemn amble through the palace's remains, visitors eventually reach, along a fifty-yard walkway lined by notices detailing the location of items looted in 1860 in foreign museums ('the humiliated soul of the palace's remains is a constant imperative to reflect on history'), a courtyard museum in which a fifty-minute documentary film, *The Vicissitudes of the Summer Palace*, blares out on continuous loop: a masterpiece of shrill socialist realism graced by production values from the 1970s. 'Never forget history!' hectors its conclusion. 'Revive China!' (Naturally, there are no such publicly preserved ruins of the many historical sites destroyed by Chinese people, with full government encouragement, during the Cultural Revolution, or published listings of priceless artworks smashed or stolen by Red Guards.)

Inevitably, the first Opium War also did well out of the patriotic boom of the 1990s, with the redevelopment of a heritage trail around Canton and Nanjing. By the end of the decade, a new Sea Battle Museum rose, like a great barnacle, out of the Guangdong coastline, recounting British ships' 1841 destruction of the crucial forts that guarded the riverway up to Canton. The temple on the outskirts of Nanjing in which China's first 'Unequal Treaty' was agreed on 29 August 1842 had been destroyed during the Second World War; the site was reconstructed into the Museum of the Nanjing Treaty, in time for the all-important anniversary of 1990. In 1997, to mark the Handover of Hong Kong (the British occupation of which, pronounced Jiang Zemin, 'was the epitome of the humiliation China suffered in modern history'), six million *yuan* in public subscriptions were collected to pay for the forging of a massive 'Bell of Warning', which now stood at the entrance of the complex: 'to peal long and loud, lest we forget the national humiliation of the past.'[26] That same year, a blockbuster about the Opium War – full of tough, righteous Chinese officials and cruel, lecherous foreigners – hit Chinese cinemas.[27]

In 2007, a Central China Television documentary entitled *The Road to Revival* chronicled China's history since the Opium War, tracing out the horrors suffered before the joys of Communist victory in 1949. Near the entrance to the accompanying exhibition at Beijing's grimly Stalinist Military Affairs Museum, a vast flashing map ('The Historical Humiliations of the Chinese People') boggled visitors' minds with statistics about the millions of ounces of silver that the Unequal Treaties cost the country, while a video loop juxtaposed pitiful images of naked Chinese children with those of fully clothed Western soldiers. The briefest of nods to the glitches of communism were permitted. The exhibition offered one mention of the Great Leap Forward – Mao's fanatical 1957 farming revolution that led to some 30 million deaths in the man-made famine of the early 1960s – and glossed the decade of the Cultural Revolution with a three-dimensional display of China's first successful explosion of an atom bomb. The events of June 1989 were blotted out with images of happy Chinese people shopping for televisions through the 1980s, followed by even happier farmers, computers and skyscrapers through the 1990s. 'Remember our history of humiliation,' ran the closing display, 'build a beautiful future.'

Chen Xitong – Mayor of Beijing through the spring and summer of 1989 – termed Patriotic Education a 'systematically engineered project'; and it seems to have produced results. A survey of 10,000 young people in 1995 already found most of them expecting China's status to surge over the next thirty years; that year, patriotism rose to number two in the list of values important to China's youth, from number five only ten years previously.[28] In 2003, almost half of a 5,000-strong sample of students surveyed expressed confidence that in twenty years China should and would be able to become a leading military world power.[29] Popular, anti-Western nationalism has regularly erupted since the mid-1990s. In May 1999, as the tenth anniversary of the Tiananmen confrontation approached, tens of thousands of Chinese students spilled onto the streets of urban China roaring not for democracy but for revenge against America for the NATO bombing of the Chinese embassy in Belgrade. 'Oppose invasion!' ran one slogan. 'Blood for Blood!' ran another. Horrified apologies by the American government (whose Beijing embassy was besieged by protestors) that the bombing had been a mistake caused by CIA bungling and inefficiency meant nothing; the incident had instantly pressed the Opium War button in a Chinese public now seemingly conditioned to expect only the worst from the West. 'This is no longer an age', analysed the *People's Daily*, 'in which people can barge about the world with a few gunboats . . . no longer the era in which Western powers plundered the Imperial Palace at will . . . and seized Hong Kong . . . The hot blood of people of ideas and integrity who have opposed imperialism for more than a hundred and fifty years flows through the veins of the Chinese people. NATO had better remember this.'[30] There was, the instinctive reasoning went, nothing chance about it – it was the latest manifestation of the old foreign conspiracy against their country.

In April 2008, a similar outburst of Chinese nationalism was triggered by furious responses to Tibetan Independence demonstrations during the Olympic torch relay. While anti-Chinese protests spread through Tibet, *China Daily* blamed the unrest on British invasion following the Opium War.[31] On 7 April, when pro-Tibet protestors in Paris tried to grab the Olympic flame from a wheelchair-bound Chinese paralympian, the French leg of the relay broke down only half an hour after starting out from the Eiffel Tower. Around ten days later, civilian nationalists had mobilized protests around the French embassy in Beijing, and outside French supermarkets in at least five different Chinese cities. 'Protect Our Tibet! Bless Our Olympics! Boycott Carrefour!' ran banners displayed at demonstrations on the north-east coast. 'Say No to French Imperialists! Strongly Protest Britain and France Invading China in 1860!' As popular Chinese outrage grew about perceived anti-Chinese bias in Western reporting on the riots in Tibet, more than ten members of the Foreign Correspondents' Club of China received death threats.

'People who fart through the mouth will get shit stuffed down their faces by me! Foreign reporters out of China!' a posting on a popular news site owned by the People's Daily responded. 'These bastards make me want to throw up,' ran another. 'Throw them in the Taiwan Strait to fill it up. They're like flies – disgusting.'[32] Those without first-hand experience of or interest in China now encountered (either physically or on prime-time news slots) files of red-flag wavers in Australian, American and European cities occasionally prepared to kick and punch advocates of Tibetan independence. Things looked particularly ugly in clashes between Chinese and pro-Tibetan demonstrators at Duke University in the US, where one Chinese student who suggested dialogue between the two sides received death threats from compatriots. For a while – until the Sichuan earthquake revived global sympathy for China – dyspeptic chauvinism looked set to become the international face of this imminent superpower.

In the course of all this, a brash new persona in Chinese public life has emerged: the fenqing – angry, intensely nationalistic (predominantly male) youth.[33] Although they periodically spill out onto the streets, the favoured habitat of the fenqing is the Internet. One of the most impressive aspects of the CCP's post-1989 Patriotic Education campaign has been its ability to adapt new technology to its purposes. For sure, plenty of young Chinese nationalists' minds have been fed on old-fashioned, traditional media: on what one Chinese academic in 2006 controversially called the 'wolf's milk' of the PRC's nationalistically selective textbooks. The youngest self-proclaimed fenqing that I have encountered was a sixteen-year-old from Beijing, who told me that he had first learnt to become angry aged thirteen, in his modern Chinese history classes at junior high school. 'Our schooling taught us that China's misery was imposed by Western countries', observed one twenty-three-year-old in 2006. 'We were all strongly nationalist . . . We were bound to become fenqing.'[34] But the Internet in China has also become a crucial virtual meeting place for new extreme patriots: every nationalist flashpoint since the late 1990s has been stoked by, or organized over, the Internet.

For well over a decade, the Chinese government has been one of the world's most assiduous censors of the Internet, controlling the public's access to information through its 'Great Firewall': a handful of servers guarding the gateways at which the Chinese Internet meets that of the outside world, in order to block sensitive foreign sites.[35] Yet despite the regime's nerves about the Internet offering a free forum for exchange of political information and views, it has tolerated and even encouraged outbursts of angry nationalism, in the hope that anti-foreign sentiment will blur into state-defined patriotism. And on the face of it, the gamble has paid off. After the 1999 protests, the *People's Daily* set up the 'Strong Nation Forum': an official outlet for nationalistic postings. After the 2001 collision between a Chinese fighter plane and an American spy plane off the coast of southern China, the site raged with anti-US comments on the incident.[36] Aware that a great many Chinese Internet users are primarily interested in games, the propaganda department has ensured that rising generations can spend their leisure hours refining their patriotic instincts. In 2000, for example, an officially sanctioned news site featured games in which web-users could thump Lee Teng-hui (the President of Taiwan who oversaw the island's first democratic elections in 1995), stick silly noses on him or shoot at him as he jumped out of a plane. As the Hong Kong Handover approached in 1997, a software company launched an Opium War game whose players fought the British virtually: 'Let's use our wisdom and courage', ran the manual, 'to exterminate the damned invaders!'[37]

Unexpected breeds of angry young men have reinforced the CCP's messages. In the middle of the decade, popular nationalism hit China's bookshelves in the form of a series of bestselling volumes denouncing the West's dark conspiracy to 'contain' (*ezhi*) or even 'enslave' a rising China. Zhang Xiaobo, one of the co-authors of the earliest of these books, *China Can Say No*, was an improbable supporter of state orthodoxy: a veteran of the West-worshipping 1980s imprisoned briefly after 1989 for his involvement in the protests. *The Plot to Demonise China* (an account of the American media's conspiracy to blacken China) was put together by a group of young, Westernized intellectuals (one a professor at an American university). 'We were nothing to do with the party,' protested Zhang – now a highly successful independent publisher ambitious to produce China's first legal pornographic magazine – more than ten years later.[38]

In the late 1990s, as the Internet began to take off in China, George W. Bush predicted blithely that 'freedom's genie [is] out of

the bottle'. Within another ten years, such optimism was starting
to look misplaced, with a bullish Communist government defying
Western governments on key issues – the undervaluing of the *yuan*,
multilateral agreement at Copenhagen, freedom of speech – and
apparently cheered on by Internet-users who classified each collision
as an imperialist plot to keep China down. And the more that the
government and its netizens dwelt on Western schemes to intervene
in China, the more they fuelled old Yellow Peril fears in British and
American minds. In January 2010, after more than three decades of
market reforms and a decade of the Internet, Sino-Western relations
seemed as haunted by the Opium War syndrome as ever.

In winter 2007, finding myself in Beijing with some spare time on
my hands, I decided to take the temperature of Patriotic Education
for myself: to see whether it really was manufacturing furious chauvin-
ists. So I arranged to sit in on some high-school history classes. It was
surprisingly straightforward. If I'd been a Chinese researcher trying to
do the same thing in England, I would probably have had to wait
weeks or months for a Criminal Records Bureau check. A friend – a
clever and good-humoured thirty-something teacher with a degree
from an American university – contacted a couple of his friends, then
rang me back with a handful of phone numbers. 'Give them a call
and they'll tell you when to come.'

Arriving at the school early on a November morning, I was met
at the gates by another young, smiling history teacher, who took me
to the classroom. 'High-school education's politically very important,'
she told me as we walked over. 'That's where most people get their
ideas about modern history from.' And the class – on the Opium War
– did indeed kick off stolidly enough, with an introit about the evils
of British drug-smuggling and the damage done to the Chinese
people's dignity, and images of socialist realist sculptures depicting
muscular Chinese resistance. The lecture was accompanied – in an
emotive touch foreign to the history lessons I remember sitting
through as a teenager – by an atmospherically sinister soundtrack.
'To forget history is treachery', a PowerPoint slide reminded the
students – in case they hadn't heard it a hundred times before.

But there were surprises in the fifteen-minute discussion that followed, in which students were invited to debate why China was defeated, and the influence that the war had had on the country. One classroom wag hauled himself to his feet: 'As Chairman Mao said . . .' he began, in a deliberate parody of political correctness. Once his classmates' and teacher's gusts of laughter had died down, he made his point: 'We lost because we were too weak, too closed up.' His classmates agreed: 'The problem with us Chinese,' another went on, 'was that we had no backbone; we were all high on opium the whole time.' 'Our weapons were three hundred years behind the West,' observed a third, 'and we had no experience of naval war. We were too cowardly, too backward, too isolated.'

Despite the impressive efforts of the Propaganda Department to construct a China-as-victim account of modern history, commemoration of the Opium War is still saturated with self-loathing. 'We made *The Road to Revival*,' its director (a suave forty-something called Ren Xue'an) told me, 'because although we've solved the basic problem that led to the Opium War – that the isolated will be backward, and the backward will take a beating – there are lots of other things, such as national wealth and strength, democracy, harmony and civilization, that we haven't achieved yet. We're not obsessing about this period of history just for the sake of it, but in order to march forward, to tell the Chinese people to keep studying new things . . . the war opened up the rest of the world to us, and we began to learn from it.'[39]

Views are, in fact, very divided about the impact of Patriotic Education. History teachers on the front line of the crusade fret that, despite diligent reminders of the 'Century of Humiliation', 'the youth of today aren't very patriotic', as the teacher I saw in action complained. 'They're selfish. They have no sense of responsibility – they don't worry or think about things like Unequal Treaties. Some of them don't even know what the Boxer Indemnity is! Nothing matters to them, except passing the university entrance examination. If you tell them to be patriotic, they don't take any notice.' After one class, a group of Beijing sixteen-year-olds told me they hated modern history – it was so dark and oppressive. 'They all prefer ancient history,' their teacher told me. 'They like the sense of culture and the emperors.' I also observed some of the new compulsory modern history classes (that replaced older courses in Marxism-Leninism) at Beijing University. Soon, the only way I could keep myself awake was by sitting at the back and keeping a count on all the students who had obviously fallen asleep (some of them in the front rows).

A tour of some of China's sites of patriotic education intimated that the lack of enthusiasm was not restricted to students. A case in point was the Sea Battle Museum. The curators have made a stalwart attempt to fan visitors' sense of grievance through instructive captions ('the British colonialists attempted to open the door of China by the contemptible means of armed invasion and opium-smuggling . . . the sublime national integrity and great patriotic spirit of the Chinese people displayed during the anti-aggression struggle showed a national spirit that would never disappear'), and three-dimensional artists' impressions of the struggle: one's attention is grabbed particularly by a lurid waxworks of the fight for one of the forts, in which an unarmed Chinese man has wrestled to the ground an armed and apparently moribund British soldier, and is about to dash his brains out with a rock.

On the beach outside the museum, however, day-trippers seemed unperturbed by the events of 170 years past. As they laid out snacks and drinks, threw balls around and kicked shuttlecocks in the shadow of the forts that failed to protect China from British ships, tourists were far more interested in enjoying a few hours at the seaside than in contemplating the national tragedy. The largest and most accessible of the fortifications was Weiyuan Paotai (the Fort That Overawes to a Great Distance) just to the right of the beach: a long seawall regularly punctuated by large cannon, several of which were being straddled by young women in tight shorts who were having their photographs taken. I asked a young man watching his male friends scramble over the guns what he felt visiting the place: 'I . . . er . . . don't know. I haven't thought.' I tried goading him a little: 'I'm British, you know.' 'Really? I hear Britain's very advanced.' I gave him another opening: 'British as in "The Anti-British Invasion Museum" [another nearby site of Opium War-period patriotic education]. Wouldn't you like me to apologize?' 'Oh, that. That's just history.' Even the flagship monument to National Humiliation – the ruins of the Summer Palace – is patchy in its effects. 'Oh, yes, I'm very angry,' one male student visitor told me. A few minutes later, he tapped me on the shoulder to ask what country I was from and what opportunities there were for studying law in England.

For all the success of young Chinese nationalists in periodically grandstanding Western media coverage, almost every Chinese urbanite I have spoken to is embarrassed by them, refusing to admit they represent the mainstream. And in any case, most of China's patriots do not draw a clear line between themselves and the West. Significant numbers of China's angriest cyber-nationalists – denouncers of China's 'victimization' by the West and Japan – rank among the most enthusiastic exploiters of the wealth and opportunities generated by the opening up of post-Mao China to the outside world. A joke circulating in 1999 rumoured that demonstrators outside the US embassy in Beijing were lobbing into the compound stones wrapped in visa applications. Interviews I have attempted to conduct with *fenqing* have often been distracted by their earnest requests for advice about studying or getting published in the West. In one transcript, my interlocutor's speech on his readiness to send his army to the British Museum to recover the treasures looted from the Summer Palace is interrupted when he enthusiastically accepts a complimentary cup of Christmas coffee from a Starbucks waitress. Pragmatism, at least as much as patriotism, is the religion of the contemporary PRC.

Despite its fears that the population is oblivious to Patriotic Education, China's propaganda establishment is anxious also that the campaign might be too successful: that nationalist anger might prove uncontrollable.

Back in 2007, I encountered one of China's Angry Youth in person: a tall, rangy, mop-haired journalist, whom I will call Wang Ningwen.* I had first encountered him at a meeting at a small independent bookstore called Utopia (Wuyou zhixiang), just outside the western gate of Beijing University, that had established itself as a gathering place for left-wing nationalists. He was one of a group

* Not his real name.

assembled to discuss the patriotic problems in Li Ang's Oscar-winning sensation, *Lust, Caution* – a sex-stuffed tale of Japanese-occupied Second World War Shanghai, in which a female resistance worker ends up sacrificing herself for the political collaborator she is supposed to help assassinate. The discussion started off predictably enough: the film, the speakers agreed, was 'an insult to the Chinese people', a 'Chinese traitor movie', 'a sexually transmitted skin disease'. These denunciations out of the way though, things took a slightly surprising turn. What the speakers were really worried about was not the idea of a Hollywood cabal plotting to defame Chinese patriotism, but instead the utter spinelessness of the Chinese government's response to the film. Why hadn't they banned it? 'What did the censors think they were doing?' one speaker demanded, to enthusiastic applause.[40] China's problems, the group agreed, were the traitors within, not the enemy without: the 'comprador power-group' (*maiban shili*) at the heart of government, who identified with the West and Japan, who thought China would be better off today if it had been a colony for the last two centuries. These Chinese 'running dogs of capitalism' were turning China into the West's 'concubine'. I was struck by the fact that, although the speakers had no love of the West (Western culture, I learnt from one of them, 'is bestial – it turns everyone into animals. The West is infantile, savage and destructive; China is civilized'), their main quarrel was with the current Communist leadership. While the assembled had ostensibly gathered to condemn a non-mainland film, their anger quickly bounced back at the Chinese government.

I made an appointment to meet Wang Ningwen a few days later, to talk a little more about his Weltanshauung. (As a security check, I tested the depth of his anti-Western feeling over the phone by suggesting we met at Starbucks, to see whether his love of multinational lattes would triumph over patriotic principle.) Once we were sitting down over coffee, he poured out his grievances. They began with the West: 'All China's problems are connected to foreign invasion, starting with the Opium War . . . the British smuggled and stole – they behaved disgustingly . . . The accounts of history have to be settled . . . China's obsessed with getting an apology from Japan; they should get one from Britain, too.' But he was very clear about where the root of the problem lay: in the cowardice and treachery of China's own government. There was no such thing as patriotic education in China, he told me. 'It was all so boring we hated it – I called it anti-patriotic education . . . The average high-school student doesn't remember how badly the West behaved – all they know is that Japanese, American and European things are good . . . mainstream opinion in China today is trying to replace national identity with stuff about how we should be modern and civilized, like the West . . . The entire CCP today is basically a gang of traitors.'[41]

He was outraged by Yuan Weishi's criticisms of Chinese textbooks published in 2006 in *Freezing Point*: how could a Chinese scholar have allied himself with the Western imperialists? 'It was pure treachery – he was desecrating his own ancestors' graves . . . He should have been drowned in rotten eggs and spit . . . or maybe have had his house vandalized. It would have been completely right and proper.'[42] But even though *Freezing Point* was shut down by the government, Wang Ningwen was convinced the two sides were allies in the same conspiracy: 'Yuan's article is serving the current CCP, he's in cahoots with their treacherous bureaucrats.' At the end of our talk, Wang Ningwen had questions for me, too. The following day, he had been invited to an interview with the British Council for a scholarship to study in the UK, and he was wondering how best to present himself. 'Try not mentioning the [Opium] War,' I suggested. He must have controlled himself, for he won the award.[43]

Wang Ningwen's fierce anti-Western nationalism, then, was an odd hybrid. While it had swallowed whole the angry, victimized rhetoric of the Opium War narrative constructed by the CCP, it was far more concerned with opposing the current Communist government itself. Wang – as a graduate of Beijing University, a member of the country's intellectual elite – angrily attacked the regime's public monopoly on historical interpretations of the Cultural Revolution and of modern history in general. 'They don't want us to remember modern history,' he commented scornfully of *The Road to Revival*, 'they just want to make us realize how great the present is.'[44] Ren Xue'an – representative par excellence of the contemporary Communist media establishment so disliked by Wang Ningwen – was disapproving of *fenqing* nationalism: 'We should tolerate different voices, but their take on history is wrong. It doesn't resonate with many people in China today.'[45]

One of the reasons that the regime draws so much attention to the 'Century of Humiliation' is that it dreads the Chinese remembering man-made disasters of the Maoist period.[46] But the popular fury that is diverted into nationalism also reminds the establishment too much of the anarchic civil violence of the Cultural Revolution.[47] Ren Xue'an explained to me why commemorating recent domestic traumas was still out of the question. 'The Opium Wars were international issues, while the Cultural Revolution was an internal problem. China has to deal with internal turmoil in its own way . . . because the Chinese people aren't educated. If we said, let's sit down now and discuss the Cultural Revolution, all the settling of scores would mean we'd soon have a new civil war on our hands – it would be like the French Revolution. It would be awful.'[48]

For all its promotion of state-defined patriotism, the Chinese government has reason to be nervous of the feelings this can unleash. Attitudes towards Japan offer a good example. It's obvious that the post-1989 state has, with the help of the Patriotic Education campaign's emphasis on historical traumas, worked on generating anti-Japanese feeling. Under Mao, 'peaceful, friendly relations' with Japan had been state policy – no reparations or apologies required. Through the 1990s and 2000s, by contrast, hostility towards Japan grew in direct proportion to the CCP's expansion of public commemorations of the Second World War. A 2001 revision of high-school history textbooks toned down the old Marxist, anti-imperialist rhetoric on every one of China's former aggressors – except for Japan.[49] By 2007, textbook coverage of the Opium War had been slimmed down from eighteen pages stuffed with images of evil British plunderers to a sketchier four. Coverage of the Sino-Japanese War, by contrast, remained outraged: 'Burning, killing, raping, looting – there was no evil that Japan did not perpetrate', runs a caption directly opposite the photograph of a grinning Japanese soldier standing among massacred Chinese. 'What sufferings did Japan inflict upon the Chinese people between 1931 and 1945?' probes an essay question, instructing students to search out victims to interview.[50]

Apparently as a result of this patriotic education, in spring 2005 anti-Japanese demonstrations – fanned and organized by Internet activists – broke out across China's major cities, protesting (amongst other things) the publication in Japan of new school textbooks that hushed up wartime atrocities in China.[51] Yet although this movement began life converging with state-sponsored goals of anti-foreign nationalism, it was clear that the demonstrations quickly moved out of official control and into the hands of grass-roots organizations. As the protests spread to a third weekend, an uneasy note crept into the authorities' pre-emptive announcements: 'Express your passion in an orderly manner,' the police instructed would-be demonstrators on the Internet, warning that all street protests must be approved by the authorities and ordering well-known grass-roots campaigners to stay at home. Soon after, a major government newspaper denounced the anti-Japanese demonstrations as an 'evil plot' with 'ulterior motives' to bring down the Communist Party – an orthodox protest movement had clearly boiled over into civil activism and potential subversion.

Until 2009, one of China's most passionate anti-Japanese nationalists (founder of the Greater China Anti-Japanese Alliance) was a former criminal judge turned philosophy professor called Guo Quan, who won instant celebrity in 2005 for vandalizing the tomb of a Ming Dynasty merchant accused of collaborating with Japanese pirates. In 2006, his feelings started to take him in a new, anti-government direction. 'I am against Japan,' he wrote on the Internet, 'but also against the lack of democracy, freedom, and human rights in Chinese society.' By 2008, he had moved on to call openly for an overhaul of the political system, forming a China New Democracy Party. On 13 November 2008, he was arrested under charges of state subversion, and his computers, bank card and mobile phone confiscated; on 16 October 2009, he was sentenced to ten years' imprisonment.[52]

The curious thing about contemporary China's most intemperate nationalists, then, is how easily their anger turns against their own government and people. Public discontent about Japan's refusal to apologize for the Second World War, or claims to the Diaoyu Islands, often spirals into fury at the Chinese government for failing to defend the country's honour, or contempt for the indifferent general public. The government's tough stance on *Freezing Point* in 2006 was motivated at least in part by a desire to soothe cyber-nationalists outraged by the offending article's iconoclastic liberalism. Two days after the Carrefour protests erupted in 2008, the Chinese authorities moved to dampen their nationalistic ardour. 'Internet users are in an intense mood toward Western countries', noted government censors. 'Such information has shown a tendency to spread and, if not checked in time, could even lead to events getting out of control'.[53] 'It's good your hearts are patriotic,' one group of fledgling anti-Tibetan-independence demonstrators were told by Public Security, 'but you can't compromise social order and traffic flow.'[54] Chinese patriotism today must not imperil social stability, or frighten off foreign investment – the key to achieving post-1989 China's economic miracle and to persuading the population to keep trusting in the wisdom of the Communist Party. For China's current rulers, the Century of Humiliation is a tricky balancing act. Properly controlled, public memory of the Opium War and later acts of imperialism provides a politically correct pressure valve for venting strong feelings in the PRC's tightly controlled public sphere. Carelessly managed, these same feelings spill out into something dangerously subversive.

Contemporary China and its current surge of nationalism, then, are not as stable or monolithic as the CCP would ideally like. In the summer of 2009, Martin Jacques' carefully illustrated *When China Rules the World* suggested, over the coming decades, the decline of the West (with its model of liberal democracy) and the inexorable rise of a probably authoritarian, racist China that views itself as a 'civilization-state': homogeneous, unchanging over (at least) the past 2,000 years, and convinced of its own superiority over the rest of the world. But while political editorialists worried at the prospect of 'the rise of the middle kingdom and the end of the Western world' (the book's subtitle), other China-watchers saw things differently. Six weeks after the book was published, the political and environmental journalist Isabel Hilton pointed out, the Muslim-dominated north-western province of Xinjiang erupted into racial violence in which hundreds of Han Chinese settlers were killed or wounded; tense paramilitary control descended, and a communications cordon was drawn up around the region, cutting off Internet and mobile-phone connections. Hilton argued against 'a story that the Chinese government likes to tell: that China is the world's oldest continuous, unchanging civilization (the dates vary, according to the exuberance of the moment, from 2,000 to a mythical 5,000 years) . . . A more accurate description would be that it is a recently expanded land-based empire struggling to justify itself.'[55] For there is plenty of social and political volatility disturbing the twenty-first century's supposed new superpower (in the form of the tens of thousands of 'mass incidents' – strikes, street demonstrations and so on – that take place each year; an estimated 58,000 in the first quarter of 2009 alone); and around the patriotism that seems to be fuelling its confident rise.

China in the third millennium possesses (as it did in the nineteenth century) about as many reasons to fall apart as it does to stick together: banks riddled with bad loans, the challenges of finding employment and pensions for a massive, rapidly ageing workforce, severe social inequality (which, according to Chinese estimates, reached potentially destabilizing levels as early as 1994), government corruption (at the end of 2009, a Chinese newspaper directly blamed the country's rash of mass incidents on officials 'blindly pursuing profit' through 'expropriating land and demolishing houses'), environmental degradation.[56] There is general agreement that the country has grown extraordinarily, and with relative ease, over the past three decades. Consensus on what will come next is non-existent.

For 170 years, the Opium War and its afterlives have cast a shadow over Sino-Western relations, both sides tampering with the historical record for their own purposes. Influential nineteenth-century Britons worked hard to fabricate a virtuous casus belli out of an elementary problem of trade deficit: to reinvent the war as a clash of civilizations triggered by the 'unnaturally' isolationist Chinese. Joining this blame game, twentieth-century Chinese nation-builders in turn transformed it into the cause of all their country's troubles: into a black imperialist scheme to enslave a united, heroically resisting China. The reality of the war itself, by contrast, illuminated deep fault lines in the messily multi-ethnic Qing empire, as China's rulers struggled unsuccessfully to rally its officials, soldiers and subjects against a foreign enemy.

The West's public stance of self-justification over the war overlaid a moral guilt that has subsequently fanned further fears of, and tensions with, the Chinese state and people. Opium became a symbol both of Western malfeasance and of a sinister Chinese pollution, generating irrational clouds of Yellow Peril suspicion that arguably still haunt our media coverage. In China, meanwhile, opium, defeat and imperialism have manufactured an unstable combination of anger, self-loathing and pragmatic admiration for the West that continue to coexist uneasily in Chinese patriots.

Whether Western nations such as Britain have attacked the Chinese for their arrogance in refusing to pay them enough attention or respect, lambasted themselves for what they did or obsessed paranoically about Chinese retribution, one misconception has remained constant: that the West is central to China's calculations and actions. But both back in the nineteenth century and now, China's rulers have been primarily preoccupied with domestic affairs, rather than foreign relations. This refusal to look at matters from the perspective of the Chinese state's own prerogatives helped drive Britain towards war in the nineteenth century, and risks pushing relations towards confrontation in the early twenty-first.

In 1839, the Qing court was too distracted by fears of social unrest to come up voluntarily with a pragmatic response to Western trade demands; Britain interpreted this political paralysis as inveterate xenophobia. In 2010, the situation did not look so very different, with the government infuriating Western states over its rejection of climate-change legislation that might slow growth, its harsh stance on social control and its aversion to compromise on international-trade issues, such as strengthening the *yuan* relative to the dollar (thereby making exported Chinese manufactures more expensive, foreign imports less so). 'The current leadership', China-watcher Jonathan Fenby observed in January 2010, 'just want to get to retirement without the country collapsing. And their caution some-times leads them into conflict with the West. Take the question of revaluing the *yuan*. There'd be plenty of advantages: less danger of a trade war with the US, cheaper imports. But they're nervous of jeopardizing economic growth or looking like they were capitulating to the West – the public outcry in China might be too great.'[57] For the noisy anti-Western nationalism that the state has programmatic-ally engineered since the 1920s (and with renewed energies after 1989) regularly threatens to mutate into anti-government dissidence.

From the age of opium-traders to the Internet, China and the West have been infuriating and misunderstanding each other, despite ever-increasing opportunities for contact, study and mutual sympathy. Ten years into the twenty-first century, the nineteenth is still with us.

Principal Characters

LORD AUCKLAND (1784–1849): Governor-General of India between 1835 and 1841; cousin to Charles Elliot.

SIR JOHN BOWRING (1792–1872): fourth Governor of Hong Kong and Harry Parkes' co-conspirator agitating for a second war with China in 1856–57.

CHIANG KAI-SHEK (1887–1975): protégé of Sun Yat-sen, leader of the Nationalist Party, instigator of the anti-Communist purge of 1927 and President of the Nationalist regime in China and Taiwan from 1928.

DAOGUANG EMPEROR (1782–1850): the emperor who oversaw the first Opium War with Britain.

DENG TINGZHEN (1776–1846): Governor-General of Guangdong in the late 1830s; friend and ally of Lin Zexu.

DENG XIAOPING (1904–97): successor to Mao who oversaw China's transition to the market economy in the 1980s and 1990s, and who directed the crackdown of 1989.

LORD ELGIN (1811–63): British Plenipotentiary to China during the Second Opium War.

CHARLES ELLIOT (1801–75): Superintendent of Trade in China at the start of the Opium War, advocating armed conflict with China. After a year as plenipotentiary on the campaign, he was dismissed by Palmerston for disobeying official orders.

ADMIRAL GEORGE ELLIOT (1784–1863): until December 1840, joint plenipotentiary to China with his cousin Charles Elliot.

GUAN TIANPEI (1780/1–1841): admiral of the Qing fleet at Canton and architect of the city's river defences during the 1830s; killed in the battle for Canton's forts in February 1841.

GUO SONGTAO (1818–91): first Qing ambassador to London and passionate anti-opium campaigner.

KARL GÜTZLAFF (1803–51): missionary, exceptional linguist, assistant to opium smugglers, magistrate in British-occupied east China and spymaster.

HAI LING (d. 1842): unhinged defender of Zhenjiang against the British attack in spring 1842.

HOWQUA (1769–1843): the richest of the Hong merchants in antebellum Canton.

WILLIAM HUNTER (1812–91): New York merchant, Canton opium trader and author of a nostalgic memoir of antebellum Canton, *The 'Fan Kwae' at Canton before Treaty Days*.

WILLIAM JARDINE (1784–1843): with James Matheson, co-founder of Jardine–Matheson, the largest opium-trading house in antebellum Canton; lobbyist for war with China.

JIAQING EMPEROR (1760–1820): successor to Qianlong; author of several prohibitions against opium.

KANG YOUWEI (1858–1927): radical late-Qing reformer and mentor to Liang Qichao; driven into exile after the failure of the 'Hundred Days' Reforms' in 1897.

KANGXI EMPEROR (1654–1722): the second Qing emperor of China, first of the succession of three vigorous Qing rulers who oversaw a massive expansion of China's frontiers and population.

LIANG QICHAO (1873–1929): leading late-Qing radical journalist, celebrated for popularizing ideas about nationalism and political reform.

LIN ZEXU (1785–1850): Imperial Commissioner to Canton, dispatched in 1839 to crack down on opium smuggling.

GRANVILLE LOCH (1813–53): secretary to Sir Henry Pottinger in the closing stages of the first Opium War.

LORD MACARTNEY (1737–1806): leader of an abortive 1793 British trade mission dispatched to China by George III.

MAO ZEDONG (1893–1976): leader of the Communist Party from 1935 to 1976 and founder of the People's Republic of China.

JAMES MATHESON (1796–1878): with William Jardine, co-founder of Jardine–Matheson, the largest opium-trading house in antebellum Canton.

WILLIAM, LORD NAPIER (1786–1834): first British Superintendent of Trade to China, who died of fever in Macao following a clash with the Canton authorities.

NIU JIAN (d. 1858): Governor-General of Zhejiang in the closing stages of the first Opium War.

LORD PALMERSTON (1784–1865): British foreign secretary at the start of the first Opium War; prime minister during the second conflict with China.

SIR HARRY PARKES (1828–85): instigator of the Second Opium War and chief negotiator in the closing stages of the 1860 campaign in north China.

SIR HENRY POTTINGER (1789–1856): plenipotentiary who replaced Charles Elliot in August 1841 and who directed the closing negotiations at Nanjing; the first British Governor of Hong Kong.

QIANLONG EMPEROR (1711–99): after Kangxi and Yongzheng, the last of the vigorous Qing emperors who ruled over China's 'Prosperous Age'.

QISHAN (1790–1854): Manchu aristocrat appointed to replace Lin Zexu to oversee negotiations with the British in winter 1840. Arrested in March 1841 for ceding Hong Kong to Charles Elliot.

QIYING (1787–1858): imperial kinsman appointed as plenipotentiary to negotiate the Treaty of Nanjing in August 1842.

SAX ROHMER (1883–1959): born Arthur Ward, the creator of Fu Manchu.

SUN YAT-SEN (also Sun Zhongshan) (1866–1925): leading revolutionary, 'Father of the Chinese Nation', first President of the Republic of China and the engineer of the first United Front between the Communist and Nationalist parties.

YAN FU (1854–1921): leading theorist of late-Qing nationalism, celebrated for his translations of Social Darwinist texts into Chinese.

YANG FANG (1770–1846): veteran of the Qing dynasty's wars in Xinjiang, appointed commander of Canton's troops in February 1841.

YE MINGCHEN (1807–59): Governor-General of Canton during the second Opium War. Died in British captivity in India.

YIJING (1791–1853): nephew of the Daoguang emperor, appointed to manage the disastrous counter-offensive on the east coast of spring 1842.

YILIBU (1772–1843): imperial kinsman appointed as plenipotentiary to negotiate the Treaty of Nanjing in summer 1842.

YISHAN (1790?–1878): cousin of the Daoguang emperor, appointed 'Rebel-Suppressing General' in February 1841. Oversaw the ransoming of Canton to the British that May.

YONGZHENG EMPEROR (1678–1735): reigning after Kangxi and before Qianlong, the second of the three most successful Qing rulers and author of the first prohibition against opium.

YU BUYUN (d. 1843): commander of the Qing forces on the east coast 1841–42; executed by Daoguang for cowardice and incompetence in 1843.

YUQIAN (1793–1841): Mongolian imperial commissioner on the east coast who advocated war, not negotiations, with the British. Oversaw the Qing defeat in Zhoushan and Zhenhai in October 1841.

ZHANG XI (?): aide to Yilibu and key negotiator with the British in the run-up to the signing of the Treaty of Nanjing in 1842.

Timeline of Modern Chinese History
and of the Opium War

1644   the last Ming emperor hangs himself. The Manchus enter Beijing and found the Qing empire in China.

1661   the Kangxi emperor comes to the throne.

1683   the Qing occupy Taiwan.

1690s–1750s   Qing conquest of Central Asia.

Early 1700s   the Chinese begin to smoke tobacco soaked in opium syrup.

1720   founding of the Hong in Canton, a merchants' guild with a monopoly on trading with Europeans.

1722   the Yongzheng emperor comes to the throne.

1729   first Qing prohibition against opium.

1735   the Qianlong emperor comes to the throne.

1757   British conquest of Bengal.

1760   European trade with China limited to Canton.

1792–93   George III dispatches a trade mission, led by Lord Macartney, to China.

1793   British government establishes a monopoly over opium production in Bengal.

1799   death of the Qianlong emperor; the Jiaqing emperor takes power and purges Heshen.

1816–17   a second British embassy travels to China, led by Lord Amherst.

1820   the Daoguang emperor succeeds to the throne after the death of his father, Jiaqing.

1832   many of the Qing troops defeated by aboriginal rebels in Guangdong are discovered to be addicted to opium.

1833   abolition of the British East India Company's monopoly over the China trade.

1834   Lord Napier dies in south China while locked in conflict with Canton's authorities.

1836–38   intensification of Qing court debate about opium and escalation of legal measures against opium smugglers.

1838   Lin Zexu, one of the leaders of the opium prohibition party, is summoned to an audience with the emperor and dispatched to Canton to crack down on drug-smuggling.

1839

March Lin Zexu reaches Canton and threatens foreign smugglers with death if they do not hand over their opium stocks. The British superintendent of trade, Charles Elliot, and the foreign community are blockaded within the foreign factories. Three days after the start of the siege, Elliot agrees to surrender all foreign opium to Lin, who begins destroying it in May.

April to September diplomatic disputes continue over the British unwillingness to sign a bond pledging to give up the opium trade and over Elliot's refusal to hand over to the Qing judiciary sailors involved in the drunken manslaughter of a Chinese local,

Lin Weixi. British ships migrate to and effectively occupy Hong Kong.

August news of Lin's blockade of the foreign factories reaches England.

September to October a Cabinet meeting at Windsor agrees to send an expedition to China.

September to November the first shots are exchanged between British and Chinese warships, in the Battles of Kowloon and Chuanbi.

1840

April the Whig government's handling of affairs in China is debated in Parliament. The government narrowly wins a motion for war.

June a British force assembles off Macao; Charles Elliot serves as joint plenipotentiary with his cousin George Elliot.

July the British occupy the archipelago of Zhoushan and its principal town, Dinghai, on the east coast.

August the British force reaches the mouth of the Beihe, near Beijing, and hands over a letter from Lord Palmerston.

September to October Lin Zexu's replacement, Qishan, persuades the British to return to Canton for talks.

1841

January talks break down; the forts guarding the river approach to Canton collapse under British attack. Elliot and Qishan agree the Treaty of Chuanbi, which cedes Hong Kong and six million dollars to the British. The treaty is rejected by both Qing and British governments.

February British troops withdraw from Zhoushan, as part of the terms of the unratified Treaty of Chuanbi. Fighting resumes south of Canton.

March the British expedition reaches the foreign factories on the southern outskirts of Canton. Sino-Western trade resumes. Qishan is arrested and transported to Beijing in chains, to await trial for agreeing to cede Hong Kong to the British. His place in Canton is taken by the emperor's cousin, Yishan, and by a general, Yang Fang.

May Yishan launches a counter-assault against the British, which fails. The British retaliate and hold Canton to ransom. After skirmishes between the British and local villagers (the 'Sanyuanli incident'), Canton's authorities pay the ransom to rescue the city and order local militias to be disbanded. Palmerston dismisses Elliot as plenipotentiary and replaces him with Sir Henry Pottinger.

August Pottinger reaches Hong Kong. The expedition sails back up the east coast and takes Xiamen.

October Dinghai falls once more to the British, followed by Zhenhai and Ningbo, where the British force spends the winter.

1842

March the Qing counter-assault (directed by the emperor's nephew Yijing) against the British on the east coast fails.

May to August the British force embarks upon the final, Yangtze campaign. Manchu garrisons at Zhapu and Zhenjiang fall, with great loss of life.

July to August the Daoguang emperor authorizes two imperial kinsmen, Qiying and Yilibu, to act as plenipotentiaries, and to negotiate for peace at Nanjing. On 29 August, the Treaty of Nanjing is agreed on board HMS *Cornwallis*. Its principal terms include: the payment of twenty-one million dollars as indemnity; the opening of five ports (Canton, Xiamen, Fuzhou, Ningbo and Shanghai); equal diplomatic intercourse; the British right to install consuls at each of the five ports; Hong Kong to be ceded to the British.

1842–56   tension between the British and the Chinese escalates, over the Cantonese refusal to accept British entry into the city.

1850–64   the Taiping Rebellion leaves tens of millions of Chinese dead.

1856   Ye Mingchen, Governor of Canton, arrests the crew of the *Arrow* lorcha on suspicion of piracy. Acting-consul Harry Parkes seizes the pretext to call up a naval fleet from Hong Kong and bombard Canton.

1857   the government under Palmerston is dissolved after losing a parliamentary debate over going to war with China. After the 'Chinese Election', Palmerston is swept back into power and a joint Anglo-French force, under the plenipotentiary Lord Elgin, is sent out to make war with China. The campaign is delayed by the need to divert troops to India to suppress the Mutiny.

1858   the Anglo-French force captures Canton and Ye Mingchen. Lord Elgin signs the Treaty of Tianjin with Qing negotiators.

1859   hostilities resume, when Qing forces fire on the British fleet sailing to Beijing to ratify the new treaty.

1860   Lord Elgin leads a second expedition to north China. After a negotiating party is kidnapped and tortured, he orders the burning of the Yuanmingyuan (Summer Palace) north-west of Beijing. A new Treaty of Beijing is ratified, extracting from the Qing a large indemnity, opening the Chinese interior to Western trading and missionary activity and legalizing opium.

1882   the United States imposes the Chinese Exclusion Act, to bring a halt to Chinese immigration into the country.

1860s–90s   as part of the 'Self-Strengthening Movement', China attempts to modernize its armies and navies with Western science and technology.

1894–95   after the first Sino-Japanese War, China cedes Taiwan to Japan.

1898   the 'Hundred Days' Reforms' (advocated by pro-Western

intellectuals such as Kang Youwei and Liang Qichao) are
bloodily suppressed by Qing conservatives.

1900   Boxer rebels occupy Beijing and lay siege to the embassies. The
siege is broken by the arrival of an Eight-Nation Allied Force,
after which a vast indemnity is extracted by these nations from
the Qing government.

1901–11   the Qing embark upon a range of modernizing,
Westernizing reforms of government, army and education.

1906   the Qing government issues a new opium suppression edict.

1908   Great Britain agrees the Anglo-Chinese Ten-Year Opium
Suppression Agreement, pledging to cut opium imports into
China by 10 per cent per year, if China cuts back equally on
domestic growth of the drug.

1911   a republican revolution brings down the Qing dynasty.

1912   Sun Yat-sen briefly becomes first President of the new Republic,
before resigning his position to former Qing general Yuan
Shikai.

1914   Yuan Shikai dissolves parliament.

1915   the Japanese issue their 'Twenty-one Demands' to Yuan Shikai,
asserting sovereignty over parts of Manchuria and Mongolia.

1916   Yuan Shikai declares himself emperor. After China's provinces
declare independence from Beijing in protest, Yuan dies and the
country begins to fragment into enclaves of warlord power.

1919   the Treaty of Versailles grants Germany's former possessions in
China to Japan. The May Fourth protest movement erupts in
response.

1921   founding of the Chinese Communist Party in Shanghai. Sun
Yat-sen forms a Nationalist Party government in Canton.

1923   after winning the promise of support from the Soviet Union,
the Nationalist Party enters into a United Front with the
Chinese Communist Party.

1925   death of Sun Yat-sen.

1926   launch of the Northern Expedition against warlords, to reunify the country.

1927   Chiang Kai-shek begins a nationwide purge of the Communists ('the White Terror').

1928   official founding of the Nationalist government under Chiang Kai-shek in Nanjing. A National Opium Prohibition Committee is created, to implement the government's Opium Suppression Act.

1932   the Japanese establish an independent state (Manchukuo) in Manchuria.

1934   Communist troops break out of Chiang's encirclement of their Soviet base area in Jiangxi, and begin the Long March to Shaanxi. The Nationalist government starts to shoot relapsed users of opiates.

1935   Mao Zedong is established as leader of the Communist Party.

1937   war between China and Japan formally declared. Perhaps hundreds of thousands of Chinese civilians are massacred in the Rape of Nanjing. Chiang's Nationalist government is forced to retreat to an emergency capital at Chongqing, in west China. The Japanese control north and east China.

1945   Japanese defeat in the Second World War.

1949   Communist victory in the civil war. The Nationalist government flees to Taiwan. Mao Zedong proclaims the founding of the People's Republic of China.

1956–57   brief period of political openness during the Hundred Flowers Movement.

1957   the Anti-Rightist Campaign cracks down on criticism of the government.

1957–58   the Great Leap Forward – Mao's utopian plan for China to catch up with the industrial West within a few years and achieve Communism.

1959–61   famine, resulting in large part from the policies and
          brutality of the Great Leap Forward, causes the death of at least
          30 million Chinese.

1966   Mao launches the Cultural Revolution.

1975   death of Chiang Kai-shek in Taiwan.

1976   Mao's death brings Cultural Revolution policies to a formal
       end.

1978   Deng Xiaoping is established as Mao's successor.

1983   the Anti-Spiritual Pollution campaign targets corrupting
       influences from the West.

1989   pro-democracy demonstrations are violently suppressed by the
       People's Liberation Army. Jiang Zemin takes over presidency of
       the People's Republic of China but Deng Xiaoping continues to
       hold supreme power.

1992   while on his 'Southern Tour', Deng Xiaoping calls for faster
       market reforms in the Chinese economy.

1994   China's first Internet network is set up.

1997   Deng Xiaoping dies and Jiang Zemin succeeds to position of
       supreme power. Hong Kong returns to Mainland China.

1999   major anti-American protests follow the NATO bombing of the
       Chinese embassy in Belgrade. The Chinese government bans
       Falun Gong.

2001   the collision between an American spy plane and a Chinese jet
       fighter in China's airspace generates a serious diplomatic
       incident between China and the US, and national outrage in
       China.

2002–3   Jiang Zemin begins handing over power to his successor, Hu
         Jintao.

2005   Anti-Japanese demonstrations break out in cities across China.

2008   violent protests erupt in Tibet. The Olympic-torch relay is
       disrupted by pro-Tibetan independence demonstrators; urban

Chinese respond angrily to perceived Western bias in reports of the Tibetan unrest and the torch relay. Around 12,000 people die in the Sichuan earthquake. Beijing hosts the Olympic Games.

2009 violent protests break out in Xinjiang. Friction between Chinese and Western governments openly develops over the failure of the Copenhagen climate change summit. The Chinese government condemns the dissident Liu Xiaobo to eleven years in prison, for co-authoring the pro-democracy Charter 08. A convicted drug smuggler, Akmal Shaikh, is executed in Urumqi.

2010 Google withdraws its offices from mainland China. Liu Xiaobo is awarded the Nobel Peace Prize. China overtakes Japan to become the world's second largest economy, after the US.

Notes

INTRODUCTION

1 Glenn Melancon, *Britain's China Policy and the Opium Crisis: Balancing Drugs, Violence and National Honour, 1833–1840* (London: Ashgate, 2003), 34.

2 Frederic Wakeman Jr, 'The Canton Trade and the Opium War', in Fairbank, *Cambridge History of China: Volume 10, Late Ch'ing 1800–1911, Part I* (Cambridge: Cambridge University Press, 1978), 166–7.

3 See tables and figures in Man-houng Lin, *China Upside Down: Currency, Society and Ideologies 1808–1856* (Cambridge, Mass.: Harvard University Press, 2007), 89 and 95 and Hsin-pao Chang, *Commissioner Lin and the Opium War* (Cambridge, Mass.: Harvard University Press, 1964), 223. These two volumes offer very useful, detailed economic surveys of the opium–silver trade in late imperial China.

4 Hugh Hamilton Lindsay, *Report of Proceedings on a Voyage to the Northern Ports of China* (London: B. Fellowes, 1834), 86.

5 Quoted in P. P. Thoms, *The Emperor of China v. The Queen of England* (London: P. P. Thoms, 1853), 3.

6 Eliza Morrison, *Memoirs of the Life and Labours of Robert Morrison, D.D.* (London: Longman, 1839) Volume 1, 136.

7 'Introduction by the Reverend W. Ellis', in Karl Gützlaff, *A Journal of Three Voyages Along the Coast of China in 1831, 1832 and 1833* (facsimile reprint) (Westcliff on Sea: Desert Island Books, 2002), 54.

8 Ibid., 237.

9 See *Parliamentary Papers – Papers Relating to the Affairs of the East India Company 1831–32*, 4–14.

10 Melancon, *Britain's China Policy*, 35.

11 Ibid., 36.

12 Ibid., 37.

13 Priscilla Napier, *Barbarian Eye: Lord Napier in China* (London: Brassey's, 2003), 88.

14 Ibid., 101–2.

15 *Correspondence Relating to China* (1840), 13.

16 Napier, *Barbarian Eye*, 132.

17 Ibid., 159, 166.

18 Melancon, *Britain's China Policy*, 40.

19 *Correspondence Relating to China* (1840), 12.

20 It is with us still today, in recurrently edgy media discussions of how China's rise will threaten the West. Because of this old assumption of intrinsic Chinese hatred of the West, China's resurgence – the logic goes – will inevitably demand retribution for past humiliations.

21 *Chinese Repository* 5 (1836–1837), 177.

22 *Chinese Repository* 9 (1840), 106.

23 See a neat summary of this viewpoint in Frank Dikötter et al., *Narcotic Culture: A History of Drugs in China* (London: Hurst & Company, 2004), 1. For a thorough discussion of historical interpretations of the second Opium War, see J. Y. Wong, *Deadly Dreams: Opium, Imperialism and the* Arrow *War (1856–1860) in China* (Cambridge: Cambridge University Press, 1998).

24 The secondary literature – in English alone – on modern and contemporary Chinese nationalism is vast. Helpful primers on the historical and contemporary phenomenon include: Suisheng Zhao, *A Nation-State by Construction: Dynamics of Modern Chinese Nationalism* (Stanford: Stanford University Press, 2004); Jonathan Unger ed., *Chinese Nationalism* (Armonk: M. E. Sharpe, 1996) – see in particular essays by James Townsend, John Fitzgerald and Geremie Barmé; Henrietta Harrison, *China* (London: Arnold, 2001); Lowell Ditmer ed., *China's Quest for National Identity* (Ithaca: Cornell University Press, 2003); Christopher Hughes, *Chinese Nationalism in the Global Era* (London: Routledge, 2006); Yongnian Zheng, *Discovering Nationalism in China* (Cambridge: Cambridge University Press, 1999).

25 *Zhongguo jin, xiandaishi gangyao* (An Outline of Modern Chinese History) (Beijing: Gaodeng jiaoyu chubanshe, 2007), 1.

26 See Zhao, *A Nation-State by Construction* and 'Conclusion' above for further details on 'patriotic education'.

27 It should also be remembered that one of the aspects of the 1989 protests that deeply unnerved the Communist authorities was the student demonstrators' attempts to challenge the state's monopoly on defining nationalism by asserting their protests as independently patriotic – for example, by organizing a rally on 4 May, a key anniversary for modern Chinese nationalism.

28 *People's Daily*, 3 June 1990, 1.

29 'History Textbooks in China', at http://www.zonaeuropa.com/ 20060126_1.htm (accessed 3 March 2009).

30 See, for example, Liang Tingnan, *Yifen wenji* (Beijing: Zhonghua shuju, 1997), 82.

31 I owe this insight to Wakeman, 'The Canton Trade'.

32 Blackie Lau, 'Mistakes of the West', at http://www.chinadaily.com.cn/ english/doc/2004-04/27/content_326595.htm, 27 April 2004 (accessed 20 March 2009).

33 Paul Cohen, *Discovering History in China* (New York: Columbia University Press, 1986), 125.

34 See, for example, James Hevia's enlightening *English Lessons: The Pedagogy of Imperialism in Nineteenth-Century China* (Durham: Duke University Press, 2003).

35 On the subject of 'national humiliation' and China's modern uses of history, two of the key anglophone specialists are Paul Cohen in, for example, *History in Three Keys* (New York: Columbia University Press, 1997) and *Speaking to History: The Story of King Goujian in Twentieth-century China* (California: University of California Press, 2008); and William Callahan in, for example, *China: The Pessoptimist Nation* (Oxford: Oxford University Press, 2010).

One: OPIUM AND CHINA

1 See Keith McMahon's acute and detailed *The Fall of the God of Money: Opium Smoking in Nineteenth-Century China* (Lanham: Rowman and Littlefield, 2002), 193–201.

2 Ibid., 97.

3 Virginia Berridge, *Opium and the People: Opiate Use and Drug Control Policy in Nineteenth and Early Twentieth Century England* (London: Free

Association Books, 1999), 40. This is a highly informative cultural, social and political history of modern English opium use.

4 H. P. Rang et al., *Pharmacology* (Edinburgh: Churchill Livingstone, 2000), 595.

5 McMahon, *The Fall of the God of Money*, 79, 75.

6 Sascha Auerbach, *Race, Law, and "The Chinese Puzzle" in Imperial Britain* (Palgrave Macmillan: New York, 2009), 146.

7 Quoted in Edgar Holt, *The Opium Wars in China* (London: Putnam, 1964), 78.

8 Paul Howard, 'Opium Suppression in Qing China: Responses to a Social Problem, 1729–1906', unpublished Ph.D. dissertation (University of Pennsylvania, 1998), 30.

9 Zheng Yangwen, *The Social Life of Opium in China* (Cambridge: Cambridge University Press, 2005), 11.

10 For these and other extraordinary details of imperial China's opium use, see ibid., 10–24.

11 Howard, 'Opium Suppression', 70–71.

12 See Dikötter et al., *Narcotic Culture* for an eye-opening account of drug use in late imperial and republican China. This is a subject that has undergone a recent resurgence of interest; for a selection of notable contributions to the field, see works by Zhang Yangwen, David Bello, Alan Baumler, Joyce Madancy, Edward Slack, Jonathan Spence, Richard Newman, and Timothy Brook and Bob Wakabayashi, listed in notes below and in the bibliography.

13 W. Somerset Maugham, *On a Chinese Screen* (London: William Heinemann, 1922), 60–61.

14 Michael Greenberg, *British Trade and the Opening of China, 1800–42* (London: Routledge, 2000), 105.

15 Ibid., 106–7.

16 For biographical sketches of the two men, see (for example) Alain le Pichon ed., *China, Trade and Empire* (Oxford: Oxford University Press, 2006); A. R. Williamson, *Eastern Traders: Some Men and Ships of Jardine, Matheson & Company and Their Contemporaries in the East India Company's Maritime Service; a Collection of Articles* (Jardine, Matheson and Company, 1975); Robert Blake, *Jardine Matheson: Traders of the Far East* (London: Weidenfeld and Nicolson, 1999).

17 Greenberg, *British Trade*, 118.

18 Peter Ward Fay, *The Opium War, 1840–42* (North Carolina: University of North Carolina Press, 1975), 49. This is an excellent

account of the Opium War, told from the perspective of European and American participants and observers.

19 Quoted in Jack Beeching, *The Chinese Opium Wars* (New York: Harcourt, 1975), 56.

20 John K. Fairbank, 'The Creation of the Treaty System', in Fairbank ed., *The Cambridge History of China: Volume 10, Late Ch'ing 1800–1911, Part I*, 216.

21 Maurice Collis, *Foreign Mud* (London: Faber, 1997), 66.

22 Greenberg, *British Trade*, 139–40.

23 Collis, *Foreign Mud*, 68.

24 Ibid., 75.

25 See, for example, Gützlaff, *A Journal of Three Voyages*. Facetious cynicism aside, adherents to Qing China's various heterodox movements did eagerly consume Christian tracts.

26 Collis, *Foreign Mud*, 70.

27 Hunt Janin, *The India–China Opium Trade* (North Carolina: McFarland and Company, 1999), 82.

28 Ibid., 132–5.

29 Ibid., 28.

30 See Hugh Hamilton Lindsay, *Report of Proceedings*.

31 Charles Toogood Downing, *The Fan-qui in China, in 1836–7* (London: Henry Colburn, 1838) Volume I, 55.

32 Janin, *The India–China Opium Trade*, 71.

33 Dikötter et al., *Narcotic Culture*, 46.

34 Zheng, *The Social Life of Opium*, 83.

35 Ibid., 71–2.

36 See Chen Yung-fa, 'The Blooming Poppy Under the Red Sun: the Yan'an Way and the Opium Trade', in Hans van de Ven and Anthony Saich eds., *New Perspectives on the Chinese Communist Revolution* (M. E. Sharpe: New York, 1995), 263–98.

37 David Anthony Bello, *Opium and the Limits of Empire: Drug Prohibition in the Chinese Interior, 1729–1850* (Cambridge, Mass.: Harvard University Press, 2005), 168–9, 228 and *passim*. See also Joyce Madancy's highly informative *The Troublesome Legacy of Commissioner Lin: The Opium Trade and Opium Suppression in Fujian Province, 1820s to 1920s* (Cambridge, Mass.: Harvard University Press, 2003) for an account of opium suppression spanning the nineteenth and twentieth centuries.

38 Translation adapted from Zheng, *The Social Life of Opium*, 57.

39 Dikötter et al., *Narcotic Culture*, 34.

40 Howard, 'Opium Suppression', 86.
41 Ibid., 87.
42 Ibid., 92–3.
43 See table in Lin, *China Upside Down*, 89.
44 Chang, *Commissioner Lin*, 96 and McMahon, *The Fall of the God of Money*, 76.
45 Captain Arthur Cunynghame, *The Opium War: Being Recollections of Service in China* (Philadelphia: G. B. Zieber, 1845), 237.
46 Translation adapted from Dikötter et al., *Narcotic Culture*, 60–61.
47 McMahon, *The Fall of the God of Money*, 92.
48 Chang, *Commissioner Lin*, 96.
49 McMahon, *The Fall of the God of Money*, 78.
50 Ibid., 82.
51 Dikötter et al., *Narcotic Culture*, 74.
52 McMahon, *The Fall of the God of Money*, 83.
53 Dikötter et al., *Narcotic Culture*, 52–3.
54 'Admonitory Pictures', *Chinese Repository* 5 (1837), 571–3.
55 McMahon, *The Fall of the God of Money*, 78.
56 Dikötter et al., *Narcotic Culture*, 51–7.
57 Ibid., 34.
58 Howard, 'Opium Suppression', 88.
59 Ibid., 90.
60 Ibid., 60.
61 Lin, *China Upside Down*, 13.
62 Wakeman, 'The Canton Trade', 173.
63 See tables in Lin, *China Upside Down*, 89 and 95.
64 This section relies heavily on the analysis in ibid., 108 and *passim*, which offers a stimulating reappraisal of the global economic factors acting on late-Qing China.

Two DAOGUANG'S DECISION

1 Yan Chongnian, *Zheng shuo Qing chao shi er di* (Correct accounts of the twelve emperors of the Qing) (Beijing: Zhonghua shuju, 2006), 164.
2 James Polachek, 'Literati Groups and Literati Politics in Early Nineteenth-Century China', unpublished Ph.D. dissertation (University of California, 1976), 128.
3 Wan Yi et al., *Daily Life in the Forbidden City: The Qing Dynasty, 1644–1912* (New York: Viking, 1988), 312, 316.

4 Jonathan Spence, *The Search for Modern China* (New York: Norton, 1999), 114.

5 Joseph Fletcher, 'The Heyday of the Ch'ing Order in Mongolia, Sinkiang and Tibet', in Fairbank ed., *The Cambridge History of China: Volume 10, Late Ch'ing 1800–1911, Part I*, 364.

6 For these and other statistics, see Benjamin A. Elman's extraordinarily detailed account of the examination system in *A Cultural History of Civil Examinations in Late Imperial China* (Berkeley: University of California Press, 2000), 267, 134, 143.

7 Ibid., 291–2.

8 Pamela Kyle Crossley, *The Manchus* (Oxford: Wiley-Blackwell, 2002), 124.

9 This section is indebted to the marvellous reconstructions of Manchu life in Mark Elliot, *The Manchu Way: The Eight Banners and Ethnic Identity in Late Imperial China* (Stanford: Stanford University Press, 2001) and Pamela Kyle Crossley, *Orphan Warriors: Three Manchu Generations and the End of the Qing World* (Princeton: Princeton University Press, 1990).

10 Quoted in Elliot, *The Manchu Way*, 201.

11 Quoted in Wan Yi et al., *Qingdai gongtingshi* (A history of the Qing court) (Tianjin: Baihua wenyi chubanshe), 334.

12 Susan Mann Jones and Philip A. Kuhn, 'Dynastic Decline and the Roots of Rebellion', in Fairbank ed., *The Cambridge History of China: Volume 10, Late Ch'ing 1800–1911, Part I*, 127.

13 Betty Peh-T'i Wei, *Ruan Yuan, 1764–1849: The Life and Work of a Major Scholar-Official in Nineteenth-Century China before the Opium War* (Hong Kong: Hong Kong University Press, 2006), 284.

14 *The Analects of Confucius* trans. and notes by Simon Leys (New York: Norton, 1997).

15 See Polachek, 'Literati groups', 181, and also *The Inner Opium War* (Cambridge, Mass.: Harvard University Press, 1992), two pioneering examinations of internal policy debates in the Qing court before, during and after the Opium War.

16 Jonathan D. Spence, 'Opium Smoking in Ch'ing China', reprinted in Michael Greenberg, *British Trade*, 150.

17 Quoted in Collis, *Foreign Mud*, 82–3.

18 Quoted in Polachek, *The Inner Opium War*, 111.

19 For the full document, see Alan Baumler's invaluable *Modern China and Opium: A Reader* (Michigan: University of Michigan Press, 2001), 6–11.

20 Quoted in Chang, *Commissioner Lin*, 89.

21 See *Chinese Repository* 7 (1838), 271–80 for a translation of Huang's memorial.
22 Baumler ed., *Modern China and Opium*, 15–20.
23 Huang Jueci, 'Memorial Against Consumers of Opium', *Chinese Repository* 7 (1838), 271–80.
24 Mao, *Tianchao de bengkui* (The Collapse of a Dynasty) (Beijing: Shenghuo, 1995), 90–91.
25 Arthur Waley, *The Opium War Through Chinese Eyes* (London: George Allen and Unwin, 1958), 122.
26 P. C. Kuo, *A Critical Study of the First Anglo-Chinese War with Documents* (Shanghai: The Commercial Press, 1935), 220.
27 Mao, *Tianchao*, 92–3.

Three: CANTON SPRING

1 Yang Guozhen, *Lin Zexu zhuan* (Biography of Lin Zexu), (Beijing: Renmin chubanshe, 1981), 7.
2 For biographical information on Lin, see (in addition to ibid.) Qi Sihe et al. eds., *Yapian zhanzheng* (The Opium War) (Shanghai: Shanghai renmin chubanshe, 1954) Volume 6, 245–67 and Mao, *Tianchao*, 95–6.
3 Lin, *China Upside Down*, 287.
4 See Polachek, 'Literati groups', and also *The Inner Opium War*.
5 Chang, *Commissioner Lin*, 120.
6 Yang, *Lin*, 137.
7 Kuo, *A Critical Study*, 223.
8 Ibid., 226.
9 Yang, *Lin*, 134.
10 Kuo, *A Critical Study*, 215.
11 Qi, *Yapian zhanzheng* Volume 1, 314.
12 Waley, *The Opium War*, 24.
13 Liang, *Yifen wenji*, 23.
14 Figures from Chang, *Commissioner Lin*, 129.
15 *Correspondence Relating to China* (1840), 352–3.
16 Xiao Zhizhi, *Yapian zhanzheng shi* (History of the Opium War) (Fujian: Fujian renmin chubanshe, 1996) Volume 1, 194.
17 Waley, *The Opium War*, 30–31.
18 Chang, *Commissioner Lin*, 261.
19 Dai Xueji, *Yapian zhanzheng renwu zhuan* (Biographies of Figures from the Opium War) (Fujian: Fujian jiaoyu chubanshe, 1986), 1–3.

20 The literature on the British empire is predictably enormous. For a
    classic survey, see Ronald Hyam, *Britain's Imperial Century,*
    1815–1914: A Study of Empire and Expansion 3rd edition (New York:
    Palgrave Macmillan, 2002). For more recent accounts, see John
    Darwin, *The Empire Project: The Rise and Fall of the British World-*
    System 1830–1970 (Cambridge: Cambridge University Press, 2009)
    or Niall Ferguson, *Empire: How Britain Made the Modern World*
    (London: Allen Lane, 2003). For a good overview of twentieth-
    century scholarly theories of British empire-building, see David
    Cannadine, 'The Empire Strikes Back', *Past & Present* 147.1 (1995):
    180–94.

21 Clagette Blake, *Charles Elliot, R.N., 1801–1875: A Servant of Britain*
    Overseas (London: Cleaver-Hume, 1960), 2.

22 Ibid., 18–19.

23 Dai, *Yapian zhanzheng renwu zhuan*, 252–5.

24 Gerald Graham, *The China Station: War and Diplomacy, 1830–1860*
    (Oxford: Oxford University Press, 1978), 73.

25 *Correspondence Relating to China* (1840), 387.

26 Ibid., 190.

27 *Additional Papers Relating to China* (1840), 5.

28 See references in le Pichon, *China, Trade and Empire*, for example 479,
    497.

29 *Correspondence Relating to China* (1840), 188.

30 Ibid., 188.

31 Graham, *The China Station*, 81.

32 Melancon, *Britain's China Policy*, 76.

33 Chang, *Commissioner Lin*, 146.

34 Ibid., 147.

35 *Correspondence Relating to China* (1840), 356.

36 Ibid., 356.

37 Ibid., 357.

38 Chang, *Commissioner Lin*, 153.

39 For this description of the approach to Canton, see Downing, *The*
    Fan-qui in China Volume 1, 230–316.

40 Le Pichon, *China, Trade and Empire*, 499.

41 Chang, *Commissioner Lin*, 156.

42 *Correspondence Relating to China* (1840), 358.

43 Select Committee, *Report* (1840), 91.

44 Fay, *The Opium War*, 155.

45 Chang, *Commissioner Lin*, 163.

46 *Correspondence Relating to China* (1840), 372.
47 Ibid., 387.

Four: OPIUM AND LIME

1 Waley, *The Opium War*, 49.
2 See ibid. and Chang, *Commissioner Lin*, 172.
3 Tan Chung, *China and the Brave New World* (Durham: Carolina Academic Press, 1978), 203.
4 *Correspondence Relating to China* (1840), 375–6.
5 Qi, *Yapian zhanzheng* Volume 2, 16.
6 Chang, *Commissioner Lin*, 185, 269; *Correspondence Relating to China* (1840), 390.
7 For example, *Correspondence Relating to China* (1840), 387.
8 Chang, *Commissioner Lin*, 187.
9 *Correspondence Relating to China* (1840), 432.
10 Waley, *The Opium War*, 55–60.
11 Ibid., 62.
12 Ibid., 65.
13 See, for example, Chen Xiqi, *Lin Zexu yu yapian zhanzheng lungao* (Essays on Lin Zexu and the Opium War) (Guangdong: Zhongshan daxue chubanshe, 1990), 22–6.
14 *Chinese Repository* 8 (1840), 485.
15 Mao, *Tianchao*, 116.
16 *Lin Zexu ji (Zougao)* (Collected Works of Lin Zexu – Memorials) (Beijing: Zhonghua shuju, 1962–65) Volume 2, 676.
17 Mao, *Tianchao*, 118–23.
18 Waley, *The Opium War*, 67 and Qi, *Yapian zhanzheng* Volume 4, 167.
19 Waley, *The Opium War*, 67.
20 See, for example, *Correspondence Relating to China* (1840), 369–72, 396.
21 Mao, *Tianchao*, 123, from *Yapian zhanzheng dangan shiliao* (Archive Materials on the Opium War) (Tianjin: Tianjin guji chubanshe, 1992) Volume 1, 543.
22 Mao, *Tianchao*, 124, from *Yapian zhanzheng dangan shiliao* Volume 1, 723.
23 Mao, *Tianchao*, 124.

Five: THE FIRST SHOTS

1 *Chinese Repository* 3 (1834), 372.

2 Quoted in Thoms, *The Emperor of China*, 3.

3 Fay, *The Opium War*, 191.

4 Hugh Hamilton Lindsay, *Is the War with China a Just One?* (London: James Ridgway, 1840), 6–38.

5 Quoted in James L. Hevia, *Cherishing Men from Afar: Qing Guest Ritual and the Macartney Embassy of 1793* (Durham: Duke University Press, 1995), 67. This book offered a pioneering reappraisal of this key early encounter in Sino-British relations.

6 See citations in Raymond Dawson, *The Chinese Chameleon: An Analysis of European Conceptions of Chinese Civilisation* (London: Oxford University Press, 1967), 66.

7 A Resident in China, *The Rupture with China and Its Causes* (London: Gilbert and Piper, 1840), 59.

8 Quoted in Chung, *China and the Brave New World*, 1.

9 Without this rhetorical sleight of hand, we would be without a rich literature of racist generalizations about the 'Chinese national character'. We might never have had Arthur Smith's multiply reprinted 1894 classic *Chinese Characteristics*, which told you everything you needed to know about the Chinese in two dozen informative chapters (on 'Intellectual Turbidity', 'The Absence of Nerves' and of course, 'Contempt for Foreigners'); or Rodney Gilbert's irascible 1926 bestseller, *What's Wrong with China*. The country, Gilbert told his millions of readers, 'is already spoiled and capricious beyond words, simply because she has been consistently overpraised and overrated when she should have been spanked.' Cited in Robert Bickers, *Britain in China* (Manchester: Manchester University Press, 1999), 28. See also Bickers, *Empire Made Me: An Englishman Adrift in Shanghai* (London: Allen Lane, 2003) for an excellent portrait of one Briton in modern China.

10 Secondary research on the Qing dynasty has changed radically over the past two decades. Older views of the dynasty (both Chinese and Western, the latter represented by the work of John K. Fairbank, such as *Trade and Diplomacy on the China Coast* (Cambridge, Mass: Harvard Historical Studies, 1953–54)) tended to see the Qing as intensely sinicized and inward-looking. More recent scholarship has

emphasized instead the ways in which Manchu ethnic identity was preserved through the dynasty and the vigorous expansionism of the regime. For background and surveys of the period, Spence, *The Search for Modern China*, and relevant volumes of *The Cambridge History of China* offer very good starting points; the perspectives offered in Willard Price ed., *The Cambridge History of China: Volume 9, Early Qing* (Cambridge: Cambridge University Press, 2002) reflect the most recent trends in scholarship. William Rowe's *China's Last Empire: The Great Qing* (Cambridge, Mass.: Harvard University Press, 2009) is an excellent new one-volume book on the dynasty. See also the following for a further sampling of Qing scholarship: Crossley, *The Manchus* and *A Translucent Mirror: History and Identity in Qing Imperial Ideology* (Berkeley: University of California Press, 2006); Elliot, *The Manchu Way*; Hevia, *Cherishing Men from Afar*; Laura Hostetler, *Qing Colonial Enterprise: Ethnography and Cartography in Early Modern China* (Chicago: University of Chicago Press, 2005); James Millward, *Beyond the Pass: Economy, Ethnicity and Empire in Qing Central Asia 1759–1864* (Stanford: Stanford University Press, 1998); Peter Perdue, *China Marches West: The Qing Conquest of Central Eurasia* (Cambridge, Mass.: Harvard University Press, 2005); Evelyn Rawski, *The Last Emperors: A Social History of Qing Imperial Institutions* (Berkeley: University of California Press, 2001); Joanna Waley-Cohen, *The Sextants of Beijing: Global Currents in Chinese History* (New York: Norton, 1999) and *The Culture of War in China: Empire and the Military under the Qing* (London: Tauris, 2006).

11 Price ed., *The Cambridge History of China* Volume 9, 10.

12 Perdue, *China Marches West*, 205.

13 Translation slightly adapted from Jonathan Spence, 'The Kang-Hsi Reign', in Price ed., *The Cambridge History of China* Volume 9, 156.

14 Ibid., 291.

15 Quoted in Jonathan Spence, *The Chan's Great Continent* (London: Penguin, 2000), 60.

16 Hevia, *Cherishing Men*, 201.

17 Waley-Cohen, *The Sextants*, 97.

18 William Hunter, *The 'Fan-Kwae' at Canton before Treaty Days, 1825–1844* 2nd ed. (Shanghai: Kelly and Walsh, 1911), 26.

19 Ibid., 40.

20 Quoted in Chung, *China and the Brave New World*, 43.

21 Quoted in Lydia H. Liu's eye-opening book, *The Clash of Empires: The Invention of China in Modern World-Making* (Cambridge, Mass.: Harvard University Press, 2004), 58.

22 Quoted in Hostetler, *Qing Colonial Enterprise*, 40. I owe this insight to the enlightening accounts of Hevia in *Cherishing Men*, and Waley-Cohen in *The Sextants of Beijing*.

23 Quoted in Hevia, *Cherishing Men*, 179.

24 Quoted in Rawski, *The Last Emperors*, 6.

25 Hunter, *The 'Fan-Kwae'*, 61.

26 Chang, *Commissioner Lin*, 203.

27 Waley, *The Opium War*, 80.

28 *Additional Correspondence Relating to China* (1840), 10.

29 Kuo, *A Critical Study*, 252.

30 Lin Zexu, *Lin Zexu quanji* Volume 3 (Fuzhou: Haixia wenyu chubanshe, 2002), 216–18.

31 *Correspondence Relating to China* (1840), 474.

Six: 'An Explanatory Declaration'

1 Kenneth Bourne, *Palmerston, the Early Years: 1784–1841* (London: Allen Lane, 1982), 408. The following section on Palmerston's Foreign Office is much indebted to Bourne's lively and detailed account. See also http://www.fco.gov.uk/en/about-the-fco/publications/historians1/history-notes/the-fco-policy-people-places/the-buildings-fco (accessed 22 July 2009).

2 Bourne, *Palmerston*, 434.

3 Fay, *The Opium War*, 192–3.

4 Dai, *Yapian zhanzheng renwu zhuan*, 248–51.

5 Bourne, *Palmerston*, 459.

6 Ibid., 461.

7 Ibid., 470.

8 Ibid., 471.

9 Fay, *The Opium War*, 200.

10 Melancon, *Britain's China Policy*, 86; I am indebted to Glenn Melancon's careful unpicking of the background to the Whig Cabinet's decision for war with China.

11 For a tour-de-force account of the period, see Boyd Hilton, *A Mad, Bad, and Dangerous People? England 1783–1846* (Oxford: Clarendon Press, 2006).

12 Melancon, *Britain's China Policy*, 95.

13 Quoted in Bourne, *Palmerston*, 576.

14 Fay, *The Opium War*, 183.

15 Ibid., 183.

16 Melancon, *Britain's China Policy*, 99–101.

17 Le Pichon, *China, Trade and Empire*, 386–7.

18 Melancon, *Britain's China Policy*, 104.

19 Benedict Anderson, *Imagined Communities: Reflections on the Origin and Spread of Nationalism* (London: Verso, 1991), 91.

20 For accounts of this meeting, see Melancon, *Britain's China Policy*, 105–7; Lord Broughton, *Recollections of a Long Life* (New York: Charles Scribner's Sons, 1911) Volume 5; Bourne, *Palmerston*, 581–2.

21 http://hansard.millbanksystems.com/commons/1840/apr/07/war-with-china (accessed 15 July 2009).

22 Bourne, *Palmerston*, 582.

23 Ibid., 588.

24 Melancon, *Britain's China Policy*, 107.

25 Ibid., 107–8.

26 Fay, *The Opium War*, 195.

27 Le Pichon, *China, Trade and Empire*, 400.

28 'Opium Trade with China', *The Times*, 7 August 1839.

29 'Private Correspondence', *The Times*, 1 November 1839.

30 For Matheson's remark, see Janin, *The India–China Opium Trade*, 27; Algernon Thelwall, *The Iniquities of the Opium Trade with China* (London: W. H. Allen, 1839).

31 'China – Extinction of the Opium Trade', *The Times*, 30 August 1839.

32 'Proceeding with our View of the Opium Question', *The Times*, 23 October 1839.

33 'British Opium Trade with China', *Leeds Mercury*, 7 September 1839.

34 'Editorial', *The Times*, 25 December 1839.

35 'The Lord Mayor's Dinner and the Unpopular Ministers', *Northern Star*, 16 November 1839, 4.

36 'Parliamentary Intelligence', *The Times*, 6 February 1840.

37 'Editorial', *The Times*, 11 March 1840; 'Express from India', *The Times*, 12 March 1840.

38 'Editorial', *The Times*, 13 March 1840.

39 'The House of Lords Last Night', ibid.

40 'Editorial', *The Times*, 7 April 1840.

41 Shijie Guan, 'Chartism and the First Opium War', *History Workshop Journal* 24 (1987): 20.

42 http://hansard.millbanksystems.com/commons/1840/apr/09/war-with-china-adjourned-debate (accessed 15 July 2009).
43 Liang, *Yifen wenji*, 38–9.

Seven: SWEET-TALK AND SEA-SLUG

1 Waley, *The Opium War*, 108–9; Qi, *Yapian zhanzheng* Volume 4, 630.
2 Waley, *The Opium War*, 108.
3 Ian Nish ed., *British Documents on Foreign Affairs: Reports and Papers from the Foreign Office Confidential Print, Part 1, Series E, Asia, Volume 16, Chinese War and Its Aftermath, 1839–1849* (Frederick, Md.: University Publications of America, 1994), 12–20.
4 Polachek, *The Inner Opium War*, 153.
5 Lord Jocelyn, *Six Months with the Chinese Expedition* (London: John Murray, 1841), 52.
6 Ibid., 55–6.
7 Ibid., 56–7.
8 Crossley, *Orphan Warriors*, 103.
9 John Ouchterlony, *The Chinese War: An Account of All the Operations of the British Forces from the Commencement to the Treaty of Nanking* (London: Saunders and Otley, 1844), 54.
10 Fay, *The Opium War*, 215.
11 This section is indebted to the discussion in Mao, *Tianchao*, 33–73.
12 Ibid., 33.
13 *Chinese Repository* 5 (1836–37), 167.
14 Jocelyn, *Six Months*, 57.
15 *Chinese Repository* 5 (1836–37), 173–4.
16 Ibid., 169.
17 Crossley, *Orphan Warriors*, 86.
18 Mao, *Tianchao*, 63; and Crossley, *Orphan Warriors*, 85.
19 This was the case even though the British army entered a relative slump during these decades, following its triumph at Waterloo. For more details, see David Chandler and Ian Beckett eds., *The Oxford History of the British Army* (Oxford: Oxford Paperbacks, 2003); Allan Mallinson, *The Making of the British Army* (London: Bantam Press, 2010); Correlli Barnett, *Britain and Her Army* (London: Cassell, 2000).
20 Qi, *Yapian zhanzheng* Volume 4, 466–7.

21 Ibid., Volume 3, 469.

22 See account in the *Chinese Repository* 9 (1840), 222–8.

23 Respectively, Jocelyn, *Six Months*, 72; and Wei Yuan, *A Chinese Account of the Opium War: A Translation of the Last Two Chapters of the Shengwu ji* translated by Edward Parker (Shanghai: Kelly & Walsh, 1888), 17.

24 Waley, *The Opium War*, 73.

25 Mao, *Tianchao*, 160.

26 Ibid., 162; *Yapian zhanzheng dangan shiliao* Volume 2, 167.

27 Mao, *Tianchao*, 164.

28 Waley, *The Opium War*, 103.

29 Mao, *Tianchao*, 165.

30 Ibid., 166.

31 Ibid., 166.

32 Ibid., 166.

33 Waley, *The Opium War*, 111; Qi, *Yapian zhanzheng* Volume 2, 219–20.

34 Mao, *Tianchao*, 167.

35 John Elliot Bingham, *Narrative of the Expedition to China* 2nd ed. (London: Henry Colburn, 1843) Volume 1, 217.

36 Ouchterlony, *The Chinese War*, 58.

37 Nish, *British Documents*, 126.

38 See for example *Lishi* (History) Volume 1 (Beijing: Renmin jiaoyu chubanshe, 1960) or *Zhongguo lishi* (Chinese History) Volume 3 (Beijing: Renmin jiaoyu chubanshe, 1956).

39 See Mao, *Tianchao*, 1–23 for an expansion of this idea.

40 Mao, *Tianchao*, 168.

41 See ibid., 172.

42 Ibid., 172.

43 Ibid., 173.

44 Ibid., 174.

45 Ibid., 174.

46 Ibid., 155.

47 Ibid., 176.

48 Nish, *British Documents*, 130–1.

49 Ouchterlony, *The Chinese War*, 63.

50 Nish, *British Documents*, 136.

51 Mao, *Tianchao*, 180.

52 Jocelyn, *Six Months*, 114.

53 Nish, *British Documents*, 131.

54 Zheng, *The Social Life of Opium*, 107.
55 Mao, *Tianchao*, 179, 182.
56 Ibid., 242.
57 Jocelyn, *Six Months*, 138.

Eight: QISHAN'S DOWNFALL

1 Kuo, *A Critical Study*, 262.
2 Waley, *The Opium War*, 242.
3 Wei Yuan, *A Chinese Account*, 23; Liang, *Yifen wenji*, 50.
4 Bingham, *Narrative* Volume 1, 249; Volume 2, 41–2.
5 Wei Yuan, *A Chinese Account*, 23.
6 Bingham, *Narrative* Volume 1, 388; Mao, *Tianchao*, 134.
7 Liang, *Yifen wenji*, 51.
8 Bingham, *Narrative* Volume 1, 383.
9 Ibid., 408.
10 Ibid., 410, 413.
11 Waley, *The Opium War*, 124–6.
12 Nish, *British Documents*, 162–3.
13 Kuo, *A Critical Study*, 272.
14 Nish, *British Documents*, 167.
15 I am indebted to Peter Ward Fay's *The Opium War* for this insight.
16 Nish, *British Documents*, 176.
17 *Lin Zexu ji (Zougao)* Volume 2, 762.
18 Qi, *Yapian zhanzheng* Volume 2, 226; Waley, *The Opium War*, 114–15.
19 Mao, *Tianchao*, 223.
20 Liang, *Yifen wenji*, 52.
21 These two comments, respectively, are from Duncan McPherson, *Two Years in China: Narrative of the Chinese Expedition, from Its Formation in April, 1840, to the Treaty of Peace in August, 1842* 2nd ed. (London: Saunders and Otley, 1843), 74; and Ouchterlony, *The Chinese War*, 97.
22 McPherson, *Two Years*, 74.
23 W. H. Hall and W. D. Bernard, *Narrative of the Voyages and Services of the Nemesis* 2nd ed. (London: Henry Colburn, 1845), 5.
24 Ibid., 121.
25 Ibid., 126.

26 For reference to time, see Bingham, *Narrative* Volume 2, 29. See also Hall, *Narrative*, 128.

27 Waley, *The Opium War*, 123.

28 Qi, *Yapian zhanzheng* Volume 1, 409, Volume 4, 73.

29 Polachek, *The Inner Opium War*, 156.

30 Waley, *The Opium War*, 133.

31 Bingham, *Narrative* Volume 2, 406.

32 Mao, *Tianchao*, 225.

33 Wei Yuan, *A Chinese Account*, 24–5; Liang, *Yifen wenji*, 51–2.

34 Mao, *Tianchao*, 254.

35 Ibid., 212–13.

36 Hall, *Narrative*, 139.

37 Waley, *The Opium War*, 133, Mao, *Tianchao*, 214.

38 Hall, *Narrative*, 148.

39 Mao, *Tianchao*, 215.

40 Hall, *Narrative*, 158–9.

41 Hall, *Narrative*, 156 and Mao, *Tianchao*, 229–30; see also Liang, *Yifen wenji*, 54.

42 Liang, *Yifen wenji*, 58.

43 Ibid., 57.

44 Bingham, *Narrative* Volume 2, 88.

45 *Chinese Repository* 10 (1841), 182.

46 Hall, *Narrative*, 199.

47 Bingham, *Narrative* Volume 1, 411.

Nine: THE SIEGE OF CANTON

1 Liang, *Yifen wenji*, 58.

2 Mao, *Tianchao*, 260. My understanding of the sequence of communications between Canton and Beijing owes a great debt to the trenchant and entertaining analysis of Mao Haijian.

3 Liang, *Yifen wenji*, 58–9.

4 Mao, *Tianchao*, 261.

5 Liang, *Yifen wenji*, 59.

6 Bingham, *Narrative* Volume 2, 82.

7 *Chinese Repository* 10 (1841), 182.

8 Ibid., 234.

9 Liang, *Yifen wenji*, 58.

10 Waley, *The Opium War*, 137.

11 Mao, *Tianchao*, 268.

12 Ibid., 268.

13 Ibid., 269.

14 Ibid., 270.

15 Ibid., 271.

16 See Frederick Wakeman's inspiring volume on mid-nineteenth-century Canton and its clash with the British, *Strangers at the Gate: Social Disorder in South China, 1839–1861* (Berkeley: University of California Press, 1966), 46.

17 For more biographical information, see Arthur Hummel ed., *Eminent Chinese of the Ch'ing Period, 1644–1912* (Washington: Library of Congress, 1943), 391–3; and Mao, *Tianchao*, 272.

18 Mao, *Tianchao*, 273.

19 Ibid., 274.

20 Waley, *The Opium War*, 149; see also Liang, *Yifen wenji*, 64.

21 Mao, *Tianchao*, 328.

22 Waley, *The Opium War*, 142.

23 Mao, *Tianchao*, 275.

24 Earl Swisher, *China's Management of the American Barbarians: A Study of Sino-American Relations, 1841–1861, with Documents* (New Haven: Far Eastern Publications, 1953), 66–73.

25 Ibid., 70.

26 Ibid., 60.

27 Qi, *Yapian zhanzheng* Volume 3, 483–4; Swisher, *China's Management*, 71.

28 Swisher, *China's Management*, 74.

29 Liang, *Yifen wenji*, 73.

30 Bingham, *Narrative* Volume 2, 110.

31 *Yapian zhanzheng dangan shiliao* Volume 3, 363.

32 Swisher, *China's Management*, 75.

33 Qi, *Yapian zhanzheng* Volume 4, 617.

34 Liang, *Yifen wenji*, 73.

35 Swisher, *China's Management*, 68.

36 Ibid., 74.

37 *Yapian zhanzheng dangan shiliao* Volume 3, 363.

38 Swisher, *China's Management*, 71.

39 Ibid., 73.

40 Xiao, *Yapian zhanzheng* Volume 1, 410–22.

41 Bingham, *Narrative* Volume 2, 106.

42 *Chinese Repository* 10 (1841), 240.

43 Fay, *Opium War*, 288.

44 Wakeman, *Strangers*, 12.

45 Fay, *The Opium War*, 288.

46 Bingham, *Narrative* Volume 2, 113.

47 Wei Yuan, *A Chinese Account*, 31; Liang, *Yifen wenji*, 70.

48 Bingham, *Narrative* Volume 2, 132.

49 Liang, *Yifen wenji*, 71.

50 FO 17/52: 112–13 (dispatch of 29 May).

51 Liang, *Yifen wenji*, 71.

52 Wei Yuan, *A Chinese Account*, 32.

53 Liang, *Yifen wenji*, 72.

54 Wakeman, *Strangers*, 52.

55 Ibid., 53.

56 Liang, *Yifen wenji*, 71.

57 Ibid., 72–3.

58 Wakeman, *Strangers*, 56.

59 Bingham, *Narrative* Volume 2, 147.

60 Fay, *The Opium War*, 294.

61 Bingham, *Narrative* Volume 2, 147.

62 Wakeman, *Strangers*, 14.

63 Fay, *The Opium War*, 295.

64 Bingham, *Narrative* Volume 2, 150.

65 Ibid., 149–54.

66 Ibid., 155–6.

67 Quoted in Wakeman, *Strangers*, 19.

68 See account in Bingham, *Narrative* Volume 2, 162.

69 *Chinese Repository* 10 (1841), 530.

70 A Ying, *Yapian zhanzheng wenxueji* (Literary Anthology from the Opium War) (Beijing: Guji chubanshe, 1957), 1. See also translation in Wakeman, *Strangers*, 20.

71 Wei Yuan, *A Chinese Account*, 35; Liang, *Yifen wenji*, 75.

72 See discussion in Wakeman, *Strangers*.

73 Ibid., 61.

74 A Ying, *Yapian zhanzheng wenxueji*, 1.

75 Qi, *Yapian zhanzheng* Volume 3, 37.

76 Mao, *Tianchao*, 304.

77 Ibid., 305.

78 Liang, *Yifen wenji*, 76.

79 Polachek, *The Inner Opium War*, 175.

80 I owe this insight to Mao, *Tianchao*, 293.
81 See the account in McPherson, *Two Years*, 176–98. My attention was drawn to this issue by Mao Haijian's own acute analysis.
82 Qi, *Yapian zhanzheng* Volume 4, 240–41.
83 See, for example, Mao, *Tianchao*, 283, 288, 319.
84 Bingham, *Narrative*, 148.
85 Mao, *Tianchao*, 288–9.
86 *Yapian zhanzheng dangan shiliao* Volume 3, 462–3.
87 Ibid., 500.
88 Ibid., 547.
89 See, for example, ibid., 579.
90 Mao, *Tianchao*, 290.

Ten: THE UNENGLISHED ENGLISHMAN

1 For these comments, see Susanna Hoe and Derek Roebuck's fascinating biography of Elliot, *The Taking of Hong Kong: Charles and Clara Elliot in China Waters* (Richmond: Curzon, 1999), 188. My account of Elliot's China career in this chapter draws heavily on Hoe and Roebuck's use of Elliot's letters.
2 Nish, *British Documents*, 261.
3 Fay, *The Opium War*, 313.
4 Hoe and Roebuck, *The Taking of Hong Kong*, 136.
5 Ibid., 140.
6 Ibid., 141.
7 *The Times*, 8 April 1841, 5.
8 Hoe and Roebuck, *The Taking of Hong Kong*, 156.
9 Ibid., 157.
10 *The Times*, 15 April 1841.
11 Fay, *The Opium War*, 309.
12 Nish, *British Documents*, 186–7.
13 Hoe and Roebuck, *The Taking of Hong Kong*, 169.
14 Nish, *British Documents*, 283.
15 'Very Important from China, India and Egypt', *Freeman's Journal and Daily Commercial Advertiser*, 12 April 1841.
16 Fay, *The Opium War*, 276.
17 Hoe and Roebuck, *The Taking of Hong Kong*, 192.
18 Ibid., 192–3.
19 Ibid., 192.

20 Ibid., 224.

21 Ibid., 202.

22 Ibid., 210.

23 Ibid., 199–200.

24 Ibid., 206.

25 Nish, *British Affairs*, 261.

26 Cited in Wakeman, *Strangers at the Gate*, 46.

27 Nish, *British Affairs*, 178.

28 Hoe and Roebuck, *The Taking of Hong Kong*, 183.

29 Ibid., 180.

30 Edward Belcher, *Narrative of a Voyage Round the World Performed in Her Majesty's Ship* Sulphur *During the Years 1836–1842* (London: Henry Colburn, 1843) Volume 2, 214.

31 Hoe and Roebuck, *The Taking of Hong Kong*, 163.

32 Ibid., 209.

33 Ibid., 146.

34 Ibid., 150–1.

35 Ibid., 158.

36 'POISON UNPAID FOR', *Freeman's Journal and Daily Commercial Advertiser*, 12 April 1841.

37 Guan, 'Chartism and the First Opium War', 24.

38 Hoe and Roebuck, *The Taking of Hong Kong*, 163.

39 *The Times*, 8 February 1841.

40 *The Times*, 6 November 1840.

41 *The Times*, 14 June 1841.

42 'The Expedition to China', *The Times*, 17 April 1841.

43 *The Times*, 10 September 1841.

44 *The Times*, 9 November 1841.

45 For reports, see, for example, *The Times*, 20 May 1841.

46 Hoe and Roebuck, *The Taking of Hong Kong*, 150.

47 McPherson, *Two Years in China*, 74.

48 Fay, *The Opium War*, 312.

49 *The Times*, 9 July 1841.

50 *The Times*, 9 November 1841.

51 'A Field Officer', *The Last Year in China to the Peace of Nanking* (London: Longman, 1843), 137.

Eleven: XIAMEN AND ZHOUSHAN

1 *Yapian zhanzheng dangan shiliao* Volume 4, 17.
2 See Mao, *Tianchao*, 330–1, for a careful unpicking of these threads.
3 FO 17/54: 23.
4 Mao, *Tianchao*, 330.
5 Hall, *Narrative*, 270.
6 George Pottinger, *Sir Henry Pottinger, First Governor of Hong Kong* (Sutton: St Martin's Press, 1997), 15–23.
7 Ibid., 59.
8 Xiao, *Yapian zhanzheng shi* Volume 2, 448.
9 Mao, *Tianchao*, 341.
10 Bingham, *Narrative* Volume 2, 244.
11 Hall, *Narrative*, 281.
12 Qi, *Yapian zhanzheng* Volume 3, 514–17.
13 See Yuqian's memorials in Kuo, *A Critical Study*, 260–61, 275–7.
14 Mao, *Tianchao*, 349.
15 Ibid., 398.
16 Ibid., 352.
17 Ibid., 353.
18 Wei Yuan, *A Chinese Account*, 48.
19 Hall, *Narrative*, 308.
20 Mao, *Tianchao*, 356.
21 Hall, *Narrative*, 314.
22 Bingham, *Narrative* Volume 2, 263.
23 Mao, *Tianchao*, 363.
24 Qi, *Yapian zhanzheng* Volume 6, 302.
25 Mao, *Tianchao*, 368.
26 Bingham, *Narrative* Volume 2, 277–9.
27 Ibid., 280–1.
28 Mao, *Tianchao*, 373.
29 Ibid., 374.
30 Ibid., 367.
31 Liang, *Yifen wenji*, 99.
32 Wei Yuan, *A Chinese Account*, 51.

Twelve: A WINTER IN SUZHOU

1 FO 17/56: 38.
2 Qi, *Yapian zhanzheng* Volume 3, 181.
3 Ibid., 209.
4 Waley, *The Opium War*, 179.
5 Qi, *Yapian zhanzheng* Volume 3, 234.
6 Mao, *Tianchao*, 388–91.
7 FO 17/54: 237–8.
8 Mao, *Tianchao*, 382.
9 Qi, *Yapian zhanzheng* Volume 3, 229.
10 Hall, *Narrative*, 331–2.
11 Alexander Murray, *Doings in China: Being the Personal Narrative of an Officer Engaged in the Late China Expedition, from the Recapture of Chusan in 1841 to the Peace of Nankin in 1842* (London: Richard Bentley, 1843), 128.
12 FO 17/56, 144–6.
13 Waley, *The Opium War*, 164–5.
14 FO 17/56: 151.
15 FO 17/56: 145.
16 Qi, *Yapian zhanzheng* Volume 3, 186.
17 FO 17/56: 49; for an example of Yijing's rhetoric in Chinese, see *Yapian zhanzheng dangan shiliao* Volume 5, 55–61.
18 FO 17/56: 107.
19 *Yapian zhanzheng dangan shiliao* Volume 5, 61.
20 Bingham, *Narrative* Volume 2, 266.
21 Ibid., 285.
22 A Ying, *Yapian zhanzheng wenxue ji*, 24.
23 See, for example, FO 17/56: 33, 36.
24 Ibid., 41.
25 FO 17/54: 208–9.
26 FO 17/56: 52.
27 Waley, *The Opium War*, 235.
28 FO 17/56: 18.
29 Ibid., 47.
30 Ibid., 115.
31 Murray, *Doings in China*, 130.
32 Ouchterlony, *The Chinese War*, 225.
33 Murray, *Doings in China*, 73.

34 'A Field Officer', *The Last Year in China*, 102–3.

35 Ibid., 154–5.

36 Mao, *Tianchao*, 381, 405–6.

37 Ibid., 383.

38 Waley, *The Opium War*, 168–9.

39 Ouchterlony, *The Chinese War*, 239–40.

40 Ibid., 244.

41 Liang, *Yifen wenji*, 103.

42 Qi, *Yapian zhanzheng* Volume 3, 187.

43 Waley, *The Opium War*, for example 166, 174.

44 Ouchterlony, *The Chinese War*, 246.

45 Liang, *Yifen wenji*, 104; Wei Yuan, *A Chinese Account*, 55.

46 Mao, *Tianchao*, 387; *Yapian zhanzheng dangan shiliao* Volume 5, 85–6.

47 FO 17/56: 339.

48 Paraphrased from Waley, *The Opium War*, 173.

49 Ouchterlony, *The Chinese War*, 258–9.

50 Waley, *The Opium War*, 175.

51 Murray, *Doings in China*, 109.

52 'A Field Officer', *The Last Year in China*, 137.

53 Wei Yuan, *A Chinese Account*, 56–7.

54 Mao, *Tianchao*, 407; *Yapian zhanzheng dangan shiliao* Volume 5, 217–20.

55 Liang, *Yifen wenji*, 110.

56 *Yapian zhanzheng dangan shiliao* Volume 5, 248–50.

57 Wei Yuan, *A Chinese Account*, 60; Mao, *Tianchao*, 407.

58 FO 17/56: 337.

59 Summarized in Waley, *The Opium War*, 183–5.

60 Ibid., 170.

Thirteen: THE FIGHT FOR QING CHINA

1 Hall, *Narrative*, 385, 377.

2 See the wonderful account in Crossley, *Orphan Warriors*, 69.

3 See Peter Zarrow's eye-opening 'Historical Trauma: Anti-Manchuism and Memories of Atrocity in Late Qing China', *History and Memory* 16.2 (Autumn–Winter 2004): 77.

4 Crossley, *Orphan Warriors*, 25.

5 Ibid., 78.

6 Ibid., 105.

7 See figures from Fay, *The Opium War*, 341.

8 Murray, *Doings*, 138–9.

9 Quoted in Crossley, *Orphan Warriors*, 112.

10 Hall, *Narrative*, 383.

11 Granville Loch, *The Closing Events of the Campaign in China* (London: John Murray, 1843), 37.

12 See details in Crossley, *Orphan Warriors*, 112; Xia Xie, *Zhongxi jishi* (A Record of Sino-Western Relations) (Hunan: Xinhua, 1988), 106–7; 322–6; Qi, *Yapian zhanzheng* Volume 3, 267–9.

13 Hall, *Narrative*, 385–6.

14 *The Times*, 23 November 1842.

15 Loch, *The Closing Events*, 65.

16 Ibid., 4–35.

17 Ibid., 33.

18 Ibid., 44.

19 Ibid., 50.

20 Ibid., 75.

21 Ibid., 84.

22 Wei Yuan, *A Chinese Account*, 64.

23 Dai, *Yapian zhanzheng renwu zhuan*, 213.

24 Mao, *Tianchao*, 475.

25 Liang, *Yifen wenji*, 115.

26 Waley, *The Opium War*, 197.

27 FO 17/57: 118.

28 Waley, *The Opium War*, 200.

29 Ibid., 199.

30 Wei Yuan, *A Chinese Account*, 65.

31 Waley, *The Opium War*, 198.

32 Ibid., 198–203.

33 Liang, *Yifen wenji*, 117.

34 Waley, *The Opium War*, 203–5.

35 Ibid., 203.

36 Hall, *Narrative*, 429.

37 Waley, *The Opium War*, 205–6.

38 Waley, *The Opium War*, 207.

39 Hall, *Narrative*, 430.

40 Loch, *The Closing Events*, 107–13.

41 Ibid., 112.

42 Wakeman, 'The Canton Trade', 208.

43 Mao, *Tianchao*, 443–4.

44 FO 17/57: 23.

45 FO 17/57: 25.

46 See, for example, Susan Naquin, *Millenarian Rebellion in China: The Eight Trigrams Uprising of 1813* (Yale: Yale University Press, 1976); Lars Laaman, *Christian Heretics in Late Imperial China: Christian Inculturation and State Control 1720–1850* (London: Routledge, 2006).

47 Wei Yuan, *A Chinese Account*, 61.

48 Loch, *The Closing Events*, 104.

49 Hall, *Narrative*, 431.

50 Loch, *The Closing Events*, 117.

51 Waley, *The Opium War*, 213–14.

52 Ibid., 214–19.

53 Hall, *Narrative*, 432.

54 Bingham, *Narrative* Volume 2, 356.

Fourteen: THE TREATY OF NANJING

1 *Yapian zhanzheng dangan shiliao* Volume 5, 222.

2 See an interesting discussion of Liu's points in Mao, *Tianchao*, 414–20.

3 Ibid., 413.

4 Ibid., 413.

5 See, for example, ibid., 199.

6 *Yapian zhanzheng dangan shiliao* Volume 5, 86.

7 Mao, *Tianchao*, 428.

8 Ibid., 432.

9 *Yapian zhanzheng dangan shiliao* Volume 5, 306–7.

10 Ibid., 273.

11 FO 17/57: 9.

12 FO 17/57: 11.

13 Mao, *Tianchao*, 447.

14 Ibid., 446.

15 Ibid., 447.

16 Ibid., 447.

17 *Yapian zhanzheng dangan shiliao* Volume 5, 365.

18 Ibid., 364.

19 FO 17/56: 340; FO 17/57: 83.

20 FO 17/57: 79.

21 Ibid., 122.

22 *Yapian zhanzheng dangan shiliao* Volume 5, 428; Mao, *Tianchao*, 449–50.

23 Ssu-yu Teng, *Chang-hsi and the Treaty of Nanking* (Chicago: University of Chicago Press, 1944), 22.

24 Kuo, *A Critical Study*, 294.

25 *Yapian zhanzheng dangan shiliao* Volume 5, 701.

26 Ibid., 743.

27 Teng, *Chang-hsi*, 18.

28 Ibid., 19–20.

29 Ibid., 33.

30 Ibid., 35.

31 Ibid., 37.

32 Ibid., 38–40.

33 Ibid., 40–41.

34 Ibid., 43–5.

35 Ibid., 90.

36 Mao, *Tianchao*, 457.

37 Teng, *Chang-hsi*, 56–8.

38 Ibid., 56.

39 Ibid., 58.

40 Ibid., 59.

41 Ibid., 61–3.

42 Ibid., 65.

43 Loch, *The Closing Events*, 149.

44 Ibid., 151–2.

45 See Mao, *Tianchao*, 460, for a development of this idea.

46 Loch, *The Closing Events*, 152.

47 Ibid., 162–3.

48 Teng, *Chang-hsi*, 80.

49 Loch, *The Closing Events*, 170–1.

50 Teng, *Chang-hsi*, 94.

51 FO 17/57: 196.

52 Loch, *The Closing Events*, 172.

53 Ibid., 172–4, see also Teng, *Chang-hsi*, 69–70.

54 FO 17/57: 200.

55 Kuo, *A Critical Account*, 296.

56 Teng, *Chang-hsi*, 109.

57 *Yapian zhanzheng dangan shiliao* Volume 6, 136–8, 165.

58 Mao, *Tianchao*, 487–8.

59 Loch, *The Closing Events*, 187.

60 Teng, *Chang-hsi*, 88.
61 Loch, *The Closing Events*, 175 and Teng, *Chang-hsi*, 5.
62 Loch, *The Closing Events*, 187.
63 Ibid., 188.
64 Teng, *Chang-hsi*, 86.
65 Ibid., 93.
66 Mao, *Tianchao*, 504; Teng, *Chang-hsi*, 113, 108, 115.
67 Mao, *Tianchao*, 491.
68 Teng, *Chang-hsi*, 115.

Fifteen: PEACE AND WAR

1 'The China Ransom', 'The Chinese Treaty', *The Times*, 24 and 26 November 1842.
2 'Success in China and Affghanistan: Glorious News', 'The Treaty with China', *The Times*, 23 November 1842; 'The French Press and the Treaty of Peace with China', *The Times*, 25 November 1842.
3 'The Treaty with China', *The Times*, 23 November 1842.
4 Cited in Susan Thurin, *Victorian Travellers and the Opening of China* (Ohio: Ohio University Press, 1999), 5; I am also grateful to Thurin's book for bringing these images to my attention.
5 Patrick Wright, 'The Great Exhibition and London's Chinese Junk', at http://news.bbc.co.uk/nol/ukfs_news/hi/newsid_7450000/newsid_7457000/7457066.stm (accessed 17 July 2010).
6 'The Chinese and Persian Wars', *The Times*, 17 March 1857.
7 'The Birmingham Banquet to Mr Bright', *The Times*, 30 October 1858.
8 See reports in *The Times*, 9 and 12 August 1939.
9 'Official Secrets', *The Times*, 31 March 1934.
10 Stanley Lane-Poole, *Sir Harry Parkes in China* (London: Methuen, 1901), 3.
11 Ibid., 12, 29.
12 Ibid., 15–16; 29.
13 Ibid., 71, 48.
14 Ibid., 96.
15 Frank Welsh, *A History of Hong Kong* (London: HarperCollins, 1997), 140. See also Steve Tsang, *A Modern History of Hong Kong* (London: I. B. Tauris, 2004) for a very informative account of the island's recent history.

16 James Henderson, *Shanghai Hygiene, Or, Hints for the Preservation of Health in China* (Shanghai: Presbyterian Mission Press, 1863), 11.

17 John Nolde, 'The False Edict of 1849', *Journal of Asian Studies* 20.3 (1960): 299.

18 Wong, *Deadly Dreams*, 134. My understanding of the background to and discussion of the second Opium War in Britain owes much to Wong's painstaking research.

19 Howard, 'Opium Suppression', 180. On the subject of the Taiping Rebellion, see also Jonathan Spence's bold and evocative *God's Chinese Son: The Taiping Heavenly Kingdom of Hong Xiuquan* (New York: Norton, 1996); Franz Michael and Chung-li Chang, *The Taiping Rebellion: History and Documents* (Seattle: University of Washington Press, 1966–71).

20 Wong, *Deadly Dreams*, 139.

21 Lane-Poole, *Sir Harry Parkes*, 50.

22 Wong, *Deadly Dreams*, 135.

23 Wakeman, *Strangers*, 76.

24 Lane-Poole, *Sir Harry Parkes*, 107.

25 Ibid., 108 and 112.

26 Ibid., 145.

27 Wakeman, *Strangers*, 105; see also Wong, *Deadly Dreams*, 140 for a similar remark.

28 Lane-Poole, *Sir Harry Parkes*, 36.

29 Wong, *Deadly Dreams*, 434–8.

30 Ibid., 264 and 286.

31 Ibid., 211.

32 Reverend George Smith, *A Narrative of an Exploratory Visit to Each of the Consular Cities of China, and to the Islands of Hong Kong and Chusan* (London: Seeley and Burnside, 1847) Volume 1, 131.

33 Zheng, *The Social Life of Opium*, 107.

34 Wong, *Deadly Dreams*, 429.

35 Ibid., 409.

36 Ibid., 422.

37 Ibid., 54.

38 Ibid., 72–4.

39 Ibid., 71, 87.

40 Ibid., 76.

41 Ibid., 106.

42 Ibid., 88.

43 Ibid., 93.

44 Ibid., 101.

45 Ibid., 90–1.

46 Ibid., 288.

47 Ibid., 160.

48 Ibid., 157–8.

49 Ibid., 163.

50 Ibid., 81 and Hansard, 26 February 1857, Third Series, Volume 144, Column 1331.

51 Wong, *Deadly Dreams*, 186.

52 Ibid., 293.

53 Hansard, 26 February 1857, Third Series, Volume 144, Columns 1391–1446.

54 Ibid., 1461–1462.

55 Hansard, 3 March 1857, Third Series, Volume 144, Columns 1821–1830.

56 Wong, *Deadly Dreams*, 206.

57 Ibid., 208.

58 Ibid., 211.

59 Ibid., 216–17.

60 Ibid., 221.

61 Ibid., 320.

62 Ibid., 321.

63 Ibid., 230–1, 233.

64 Ibid., 236.

65 Hansard, 9 March 1857, Third Series, Volume 144, Column 2042.

66 Wong, *Deadly Dreams*, 261–82.

67 Ibid., 275.

68 Ibid., 79, 164–5.

69 See, for example, *The Times*, 4 February 1858.

70 See, for example, George Wingrove Cooke, *China and Lower Bengal: Being The Times Correspondence from China in the Years 1857–58*, 5th ed. (London: Routledge, 1861), 309.

71 Ibid., xi.

72 See *The Times*, 15 and 17 February 1858.

73 W. Travis Hanes III and Frank Sanello, *The Opium Wars* (Illinois: Sourcebooks, 2002), 205. See also Cooke, *China*, 349–51 and *The Times*, 26 February 1858.

74 J. Y. Wong, *Yeh Ming-ch'en: Viceroy of Liang Kuang 1852–8* (Cambridge: Cambridge University Press, 1976), 186.

75 Cooke, *China*, 349.

76 Lane-Poole, *Sir Harry Parkes*, 272.

77 *The Times*, 26 February 1858.

78 Cooke, *China*, 397–8, 402–3.

79 Lane-Poole, *Sir Harry Parkes*, 181.

80 'The Disaster in China', *The Times*, 16 September 1859.

81 'Allied Expedition to China', *The Times*, 16 September 1859; 12 September 1859.

82 Hevia, *English Lessons*, 35; Hanes and Sanello, *The Opium Wars*, 193; Wong, *Deadly Dreams*, 460. Hevia's book remains one of the most systematic explorations of the mindset behind Western campaigns against China in the nineteenth and twentieth centuries.

83 Douglas Hurd, *The Arrow War: An Anglo-Chinese Confusion, 1856–60* (London: Collins, 1967), 205.

84 Hanes and Sanello, *The Opium Wars*, 225.

85 Lane-Poole, *Sir Harry Parkes*, 178.

86 Hanes and Sanello, *The Opium Wars*, 234.

87 For Beato's photographs, see David Harris's fascinating *Of Battle and Beauty* (Berkeley: University of California Press, 1999).

88 Robert Swinhoe, *Narrative of the North China Campaign* (London: Smith, Elder and Co., 1861), 136–47.

89 Ibid., 145.

90 D. F. Rennie, *The British Arms in North China and Japan* (London: John Murray, 1864), 112.

91 Lane-Poole, *Sir Harry Parkes*, 227.

92 See, for example, Swinhoe, *Narrative*, 388; Garnet Joseph Wolseley, *Narrative of the War with China in 1860* (London: Longman, 1862), 209.

93 Wolseley, *Narrative*, 206.

94 Swinhoe, *Narrative*, 285.

95 Wolseley, *Narrative*, 220–4.

96 Ibid., 224.

97 Hevia, *English Lessons*, 79–81.

98 Wolseley, *Narrative*, 227.

99 Colonel J. FitzGerald, 'Incidents of the Last Chinese War', unpublished manuscript, reproduced by kind permission of his granddaughter, Jennifer Mackintosh.

100 Hevia, *English Lessons*, 98.

101 Wolseley, *Narrative*, 233.

102 Hevia, *English Lessons*, 100.

103 Wolseley, *Narrative*, 233.

104 Wolseley, *Narrative*, 259.
105 Hevia, *English Lessons*, 105.
106 Swinhoe, *Narrative*; 329; Hevia, *English Lessons*, 107.
107 Wolseley, *Narrative*, 280.
108 Swinhoe, *Narrative*, 330.
109 Cited in Hevia, *English Lessons*, 105.
110 Swinhoe, *Narrative*, 330–1.
111 Cited in Hevia, *English Lessons*, 111.
112 Ibid., 115.

Sixteen: THE YELLOW PERIL

1 *The Times*, 10 and 11 December 1860.
2 'Arrival of Mr Loch at Dover', *Morning Post*, 28 December 1860.
3 Henry Brougham Loch, A *Personal Narrative of Occurrences During Lord Elgin's Second Expedition to China* (London: John Murray, 1869), 289.
4 Hanes and Sanello, *The Opium Wars*, 94.
5 My particular thanks to Finlay McLeod for providing me with biographical information about Donald Matheson.
6 Quoted in Donald Matheson, *What is the Opium Trade?* (Edinburgh: Thomas Constable and Co., 1857), 5.
7 Quoted in Dikötter et al., *Narcotic Culture*, 54.
8 Karl Marx, 'Trade or Opium?' at http://www.marxists.org/archive/marx/works/1858/09/20.htm (accessed 17 July 2010).
9 Quoted in Dikötter et al., *Narcotic Culture*, 97.
10 Berridge, *Opium and the People*, 23.
11 Ibid., 45.
12 Ibid., 62–72.
13 David Wells, 'The Truth about the Opium War', *North American Review*, 162.475 (June 1896): 759–60.
14 Joseph G. Alexander, *North American Review*, 163.478 (September 1896): 381–3.
15 Zheng, *The Social Life of Opium*, 111.
16 Ibid., 154.
17 Ibid., 113.
18 Ibid., 155.
19 Ibid., 154–68, 175.
20 Kathleen Lodwick, *Crusaders Against Opium: Protestant Missionaries in*

China, 1874–1917 (Lexington: The University Press of Kentucky, 1996), 50.

21 Robert Montgomery Martin, *Opium in China* (Dowgate: Brewster & West, 1847), 5.

22 Lodwick, *Crusaders*, 40.

23 McMahon, *The Fall of the God of Money*, 56.

24 Lodwick, *Crusaders*, 94, 48.

25 Ibid., 99.

26 Ibid., 33.

27 Matheson, *What is the Opium Trade?*, 11.

28 Justin McCarthy, 'The Opium War', *Friend of China*, April 1880, 104–6.

29 *The Times*, 17 April 1840, 4.

30 Martin, *Opium in China*, 89–90.

31 McCarthy, 'The Opium War', 105.

32 C. F. Gordon Cumming, *Wanderings in China* (Edinburgh: Blackwood, 1886), 490.

33 For more on the Yellow Peril, see Auerbach, *Race*; Stanford M. Lyman, 'The "Yellow Peril" Mystique: Origins and Vicissitudes of a Racist Discourse', *International Journal of Politics, Culture, and Society*, 13.4 (Summer 2000): 683–747; Hevia, *English Lessons*, 315–45.

34 *Chums*, November 1892, 166.

35 Liu, *The Clash*, 189.

36 Hyam, *Britain's Imperial Century*, 139–40.

37 Ibid., 198.

38 Ibid., 191–2.

39 Ibid., 193. See Daniel Pick, *Faces of Degeneration: A European Disorder* (Cambridge: Cambridge University Press, 1993) for a brilliant survey of this question.

40 Liu, *The Clash*, 62.

41 Auerbach, *Race*, 39 and *passim*.

42 Ibid., 163–4.

43 Ibid., 66.

44 For more on the Boxer Rebellion, see (for example) Joseph Esherick, *The Origins of the Boxer Uprising* (Berkeley: University of California Press, 1987); Hevia, *English Lessons*; Cohen, *History in Three Keys*; and Robert Bickers and Gary Tiedemann eds., *The Boxers, China and the World* (Lanham: Rowman and Littlefield, 2007).

45 Hevia, *English Lessons*, 223.

46 Ibid., 221. Hevia's book offers an extraordinarily enlightening account of this 'punitive picnic'.

47 Cited in Esherick, *The Origins of the Boxer Uprising*, 310.

48 *The Times*, 17 January 1911.

49 Charles Dickens, 'Lazarus, Lotus-Eating', *All the Year Round*, 12 May 1866, 423.

50 'A Night in an Opium Den', *Strand Magazine* 1 (1891), 624–7.

51 Berridge, *Opium and the People*, 199.

52 Louise Foxcroft, *The Making of Addiction: The 'Use and Abuse' of Opium in Nineteenth-Century Britain* (Kent: Ashgate, 2007), 68.

53 Figures from Auerbach, *Race*, 52 and Foxcroft, *The Making of Addiction*, 65.

54 Berridge, *Opium*, 201.

55 Ibid., 202.

56 Auerbach, *Race*, 146.

57 Cited in Barry Milligan, *Pleasures and Pains* (Virginia: University of Virginia Press, 1995), 90.

58 Ibid., 83.

59 Berridge, *Opium*, 200.

60 Marek Kohn, *Dope Girls: The Birth of the British Drug Underground* (London: Granta Books, 1992), 144.

61 Cay Van Ash and Elizabeth Sax Rohmer, *Master of Villainy* (Ohio: Bowling Green University Popular Press, 1972).

62 Bickers, *Britain in China*, 23.

63 Matthew Shiel, *The Yellow Danger* (London: Routledge/Thoemmes, 1998), 37.

64 Ibid., 10.

65 *The Times*, 13 September 1898, 13.

66 Shiel, *The Yellow Danger*, 201.

67 Kathryn Castle, *Britannia's Children: Reading Colonialism through Children's Books and Magazines* (Manchester: Manchester University Press, 1996), 145–6.

68 Ibid., 136–48.

69 Jack London, 'The Unparalleled Invasion', at http://www.jacklondons.net/writings/StrengthStrong/invasion.html (accessed 17 July 2010).

70 Conversation with Sir Christopher Frayling, 2 December 2008.

71 Sax Rohmer, *The Mystery of Dr Fu Manchu* in *The Fu Manchu Omnibus* (London: Allison and Busby, 1995), 15.

72 Ibid., for example 32, 42, 412 and *passim*.

73 I owe this insight to Hevia, *English Lessons*, 319–20.

74 Sax Rohmer, *The Devil Doctor* in *The Fu Manchu Omnibus*, 345.

75 Ibid., 40.

76 Rohmer, *The Mystery of Dr Fu Manchu*, 161. Again, I owe this insight into Sax Rohmer's work to Hevia's *English Lessons*, 319. For further discussion, see also Urmila Seshagiri, 'Modernity's (Yellow) Perils: Dr Fu-Manchu and English Race Paranoia', *Cultural Critique* 62 (Winter 2006): 162–94.

77 Rohmer, *The Devil Doctor* in *The Fu Manchu Omnibus*, 320.

78 Ibid., 415.

79 Ibid., 318.

80 Castle, *Britannia's Children*.

81 David Scott, *China Stands Up: the PRC and the International System* (Abingdon: Routledge, 2007), 17.

82 'China Threat Debate', at http://www.youtube.com/watch?v=6hy_snHWdZE (accessed 17 July 2010).

83 Examples include a discussion on the BBC's *Newsnight* to cover Barack Obama's visit to China in winter 2009; or an article about trade relations with China in the British broadsheet the *Daily Telegraph*: 'Obama Faces Potential Chinese Death Trap', http://www.telegraph.co.uk/finance/globalbusiness/7536025/Barack-Obama-faces-potential-Chinese-death-trap.html30 March 2010 (accessed 31 March 2010).

84 Bill Gertz, *The China Threat: How the People's Republic Targets America* (Lanham: Regnery Publishing, 2000), xiv, 5.

85 http://littlegreenfootballs.com/article/16397_The_Chinese_Dragon_Awakens (accessed 30 November 2009).

86 http://digg.com/world_news/Is_China_trying_to_poison_Americans_and_their_pets (accessed 30 November 2009).

87 http://consumerist.com/2007/06/chinese-poison-train-defeats-fda-the-prequel.html (accessed 30 November 2009).

88 'Mattel Apologizes to China for Recall', at http://www.nytimes.com/2007/09/21/business/worldbusiness/21iht-mattel.3.7597386.html (accessed 30 November 2009).

89 D. J. Enright, 'Introduction', *The Mystery of Dr Fu Manchu* (London: Dent, 1985), viii.

Seventeen: THE NATIONAL DISEASE

1 Cited in Felipe Fernández-Armesto, *The World: A History* Volume 2
(Michigan: Prentice-Hall, 2009), 802. For more on late nineteenth-
century modernization, see relevant essays in *The Cambridge History of
China* Volumes 10 and 11 and primary sources collected in Theodore
de Bary and Richard Lufrano eds., *Sources of Chinese Tradition* (New
York: Columbia University Press, 2001) Volume 2.

2 Quoted in Wang Chengren, *Li Hongzhang sixiang tixi yanjiu*
(Systematic Research into the Thought of Li Hongzhang) (Wuhan:
Wuhan daxue chubanshe, 1998), 23–4.

3 Lu Xun, *The Real Story of Ah-Q and Other Tales of China*, trans. Julia
Lovell (London: Penguin Classics, 2009), 16.

4 J. D. Frodsham ed. and trans., *The First Chinese Embassy to the West:
the journals of Kuo Sung-t'ao, Liu Hsi-hung and Chang Te-yi* (Oxford:
Clarendon Press, 1974), xxxvii.

5 Benjamin Schwartz, *In Search of Wealth and Power: Yen Fu and the West*
(Cambridge, Mass.: Harvard University Press, 1990), 29.

6 Ibid., 94.

7 'John Chinaman', *Punch*, 10 February 1877.

8 'To the Tottering Lily', *Punch*, 17 February 1877.

9 Frodsham, *The First Chinese Embassy*, 75.

10 Ibid., 73, 43.

11 Ibid., 73, 100–101.

12 Ibid., 100.

13 Zhao, *A Nation-State*, 48.

14 For an overview, see Spence, *The Search for Modern China*, 220–2. See
also S. C. M. Paine, *The Sino-Japanese War of 1894–1895: Perceptions,
Power, and Primacy* (Cambridge: Cambridge University Press, 2003),
for a more detailed account.

15 Leo Oufan Lee and Andrew J. Nathan, 'The Beginnings of Mass
Culture: Journalism and Fiction in the Late Ch'ing and Beyond',
in *Popular Culture in Late Imperial China*, eds. David Johnson et al.,
364.

16 Frank Dikötter, *The Discourse of Race in Modern China* (London: Hurst,
1992), 75.

17 Jonathan Spence, *The Gate of Heavenly Peace* (New York: Penguin,
1982), 8. This is an excellent introduction to modern Chinese
cultural and intellectual history.

18 Yan Fu, 'Yuanqiang' (The Origins of Strength) in *Yan Fu ji* (Works of Yan Fu) (Beijing: Zhonghua shuju, 1986) Volume 1, 5–6.

19 De Bary and Lufrano, *Sources of Chinese Tradition* Volume 2, 258.

20 Quoted in Wah-kwan Cheng, 'Vox Populi: Language, Literature and Ideology in Modern China', unpublished Ph.D. dissertation (University of Chicago, 1989), 92.

21 Schwartz, *In Search of Wealth and Power*, 49.

22 Cheng, 'Vox Populi', 64–5, 69, 70, 77–8.

23 Ibid., 86, 84, 90.

24 See Li Yu-ning ed., *Two Self-Portraits: Liang Ch'i-ch'ao and Hu Shih* (Bronxville: Outer Sky Press, 1992), 5–6.

25 Philip Huang, *Liang Ch'i-ch'ao and Modern Chinese Liberalism* (Seattle: University of Washington Press, 1972), 31.

26 Joan Judge, *Print and Politics* (Stanford: Stanford University Press, 1996); Huang, *Liang Ch'i-ch'ao*, 7.

27 Dikötter, *The Discourse of Race*, 84.

28 See, for just one set of examples, *Liang Qichao quanji* (Collected Works of Liang Qichao) Volume 1 (Beijing: Beijing chubanshe, 1999) Volume 1, 101, 140, 99, 167.

29 Judge, *Print and Politics*, 96–7.

30 Schwartz, *In Search of Wealth and Power*, 142; Cohen, *History in Three Keys*, 224; Kirk Denton ed., *Modern Chinese Literary Thought: Writings on Literature 1893–1945* (Stanford: Stanford University Press, 1996), 74–81.

31 Barbara Mittler, *A Newspaper for China? Power, Identity and Change in Shanghai's News Media, 1872–1912* (Cambridge, Mass.: Harvard University Press, 2004), 365.

32 'Gengshen Yifen jilue' (A Record of the Foreign Affairs of 1860), in Qi Sihe et al. eds., *Di er ci yapian zhanzheng* (The Second Opium War) (Shanghai: Shanghai renmin chubanshe, 1978) Volume 2, 5–27.

33 Xia, *Zhongxi jishi*, 53–4; in English, see Edward Parker's abridged translation, *China's Intercourse with Europe* (Shanghai: Kelly and Walsh, 1890), 54.

34 See, for example, ibid. and also Qi, *Di er ci* Volume 1.

35 Xu Guoqi, *Olympic Dreams: China and Sports, 1895–2008* (Cambridge, Mass.: Harvard University Press, 2008), 18–19.

36 Ma Mozhen, *Zhongguo jindu shi ziliao* (Materials from the History of Drug Prohibition in China) (Tianjin: Tianjin renmin chubanshe, 1998), 351.

37 Ibid., 380.

38 Ibid., 395–6; Dikötter et al., *Narcotic Culture*, 109.

39 R. Bin Wong, 'Opium and Modern Chinese State-making', in Timothy Brook and Bob Wakabayashi eds., *Opium Regimes: China, Britain and Japan, 1839–1952* (Berkeley: University of California Press, 2000), 201.

40 See Lodwick, *Crusaders*, 35; Dikötter et al., *Narcotic Culture*, 156; Booth, *Opium: A History*, 91–2.

41 Dikötter et al., *Narcotic Culture*, 124.

42 Madancy, *The Troublesome Legacy of Commissioner Lin*, 124.

43 *The Times*, 4 April 1908.

44 Alexander Des Forges, 'Opium/Leisure/Shanghai', in Brook and Wakabayashi eds., *Opium Regimes*, 178.

45 Ma, *Zhongguo jindu shi ziliao*, 395–6; Dikötter et al., *Narcotic Culture*, 109.

46 *Gaodeng xiaoxue zhongguo lishi jiaokeshu* (High Level Primary School Textbook on Chinese History) (Shanghai: Shangwu yinshu guan, 1909), 82.

47 Zhou Yongming, *Anti-drug Crusades in Twentieth-Century China: Nationalism, History and State-Building* (Lanham: Rowman and Littlefield, 1999), 19.

48 See Mary Wright, 'Introduction' in *China in Revolution: The First Phase 1900–1913* (Yale: Yale University Press, 1971).

49 Joan Judge, *Print and Politics*, 86.

50 For key essays on this, see Paul Cohen, *Discovering History in China*.

51 Henrietta Harrison, *China*, 124. See also Frances Wood, *No Dogs and Not Many Chinese* (London: John Murray, 2000) for an entertaining and informative account of expatriate life in the treaty ports.

52 I use the term 'legend' advisedly, even while I would like to argue that the spirit of the sentiment existed; Robert Bickers and Jeffrey Wasserstrom have shown that no such exact usage featured on signs for Shanghai's municipal parks, in 'Shanghai's "Dogs and Chinese Not Admitted" Sign: Legend, History and Contemporary Symbol' in *China Quarterly* 142 (June 1995): 444–66.

53 See Frank Dikötter, *Things Modern* (London: Hurst, 2005) for a vivid account of the Chinese fascination with material modernity through this period.

54 See, for example, Mu Shiying, 'Five in a Nightclub', *Renditions* 37 (Spring 1992): 5–22. For an introduction to Shanghai's urban culture in the 1930s and 40s, see Leo Lee, *Shanghai Modern* (Cambridge, Mass.: Harvard University Press, 1999).

55 Dikötter et al., *Narcotic Culture*, 114; Alan Baumler, *Worse than Floods and Wild Beasts* (Albany: State University of New York Press, 2007), 54–5.

56 Des Forges, 'Opium/Leisure/Shanghai', 167–85.

57 Wong, 'Opium and Modern Chinese State-making', 192.

58 Lucien Bianco, 'The Responses of Opium Growers to Eradication Campaigns and the Poppy Tax, 1907–1949', in Brook and Wakabayashi, *Opium Regimes*, 307–9.

59 Dikötter et al., *Narcotic Culture*, 135.

Eighteen: COMMUNIST CONSPIRACIES

1 Karl Marx, 'Free Trade and Monopoly', at http://www.marxists.org/archive/marx/works/1858/09/25.htm (accessed 1 March 2010). See Francis Wheen, *Karl Marx* (London: Fourth Estate, 1999) for an enjoyable biography of Marx.

2 Karl Marx, 'Whose Atrocities?' at http://www.marxists.org/archive/marx/works/1857/04/10.htm (accessed 1 March 2010).

3 Karl Marx, 'Revolution in China and Europe', at http://www.marxists.org/archive/marx/works/1853/06/14.htm (accessed 1 March 2010).

4 Karl Marx, 'Trade or Opium?' at http://www.marxists.org/archive/marx/works/1858/09/20.htm (accessed 1 March 2010). These are the anti-opium campaigner R. Montgomery Martin's words, but Marx quotes them to stand for his own views of the drug trade.

5 Ibid., and 'Revolution in China and Europe'.

6 Marx, 'Revolution in China and in Europe'.

7 Marie-Claire Bergère, *Sun Yat-sen* (Stanford: Stanford University Press, 1998), 208. This is the most recent and complete biography of Sun, although biographies by C. Martin Wilbur and Harold Schiffrin are also informative and interesting.

8 C. Martin Wilbur, *Sun Yat-sen: Frustrated Patriot* (New York: Columbia University Press, 1976), 23.

9 Bergère, *Sun Yat-sen*, 303.

10 See 'The Manifesto of the T'ung-meng-hui, 1905', in Teng Ssu-yu and John Fairbank eds., *China's Response to the West: A Documentary Survey, 1839–1923* (Cambridge, Mass.: Harvard University Press, 1979), 227–9.

11 Wilbur, *Sun Yat-sen*, 118.

12 Paul Cohen, 'Remembering and forgetting', in *China Unbound: Evolving Perspectives on the Chinese Past* (London: Routledge, 2003), 158.

13 Ibid., 161–2.

14 Ibid., 163.

15 Lin Yu-sheng, *The Crisis of Chinese Consciousness* (Madison: University of Wisconsin Press, 1979), 76.

16 Spence, *The Search for Modern China*, 292.

17 Bergère, *Sun Yat-sen*, 158.

18 Ma, *Zhongguo jindu shi ziliao*, 594.

19 John Fitzgerald, *Awakening China: Politics, Culture and Class in the Nationalist Revolution* (Stanford: Stanford University Press, 1996), 170, 149. This is an excellent account of the modern Chinese nation-building project.

20 Wilbur, *Sun Yat-sen*, 135, 144.

21 Sun Yat-sen, *The Three Principles* (Shanghai: North China Daily News and Herald, 1927), 12, 16, 11.

22 Bergère, *Sun Yat-sen*, 361.

23 Dong Wang, *China's Unequal Treaties: Narrating National History* (Lanham: Lexington Books, 2005), 65.

24 Sun Yat-sen, *The Three Principles*, 33, 31, 39.

25 Bergère, *Sun Yat-sen*, 372.

26 Fitzgerald, *Awakening China*, 174.

27 Ibid., 173.

28 Ibid., 217.

29 Ibid., 214–60.

30 See a fine account of this in Henrietta Harrison, *The Making of the Republican Citizen: Political Ceremonies and Symbols in China, 1911–1929* (Oxford: Oxford University Press, 2000).

31 Lin Jiasheng, 'Tan tan yapian zhanzheng' (A Chat About the Opium War), *Ertong zazhi* 6 (1936): 4–7.

32 For a useful introduction to changing representations of the Opium War in Chinese history textbooks, see Liu Chao, 'Yapian zhanzheng yu Zhongguo jindaishi yanjiu' (The Opium War and Research into Modern Chinese History), *Xueshu yuekan* 6 (2007): 146–53. Late Qing and early Republican textbooks that I have sampled include: *Zuijin zhinashi* (A Recent History of China) (Shanghai: Zhendang shixueshe, 1905); *Zhina shi yao* (An Outline of Chinese History) (Shanghai: Guangzhi shuju, 1906); *Zhongguo lishi jiangyi* (Lectures on Chinese History) (Shanghai: Hongwenguan chuban, 1908); *Gaodeng*

xiaoxue zhongguo lishi jiaokeshu (High Level Primary School Textbook on Chinese History) (Shanghai: Shangwu yinshu guan, 1909); *Gongheguo jiaokeshu, benguoshi* (The Republican Textbook of Chinese History) (Shanghai: Shangwu, 1913); *Benguoshi jiaoben* (A Textbook for Chinese History) (Shanghai: Zhonghua shuju, 1917); *Zhongguo jin bainian shi gangyao* (An Outline of Chinese History over the Past Century) (Beijing: Zhonghua shuju, 1927); *Chu zhong ben guo shi* (Chinese History for Elementary High Schools) (Shanghai: Zhonghua shuju, 1934).

33 For these and similar quotations see Tian Longjun, 'Yapian zhanzheng ganyan' (Some emotional words about the Opium War), *Jiangsu sheng li di er nüzi shifan xuexiao xiaoyouhui huikan* 8 (1919), 4–5; Zhu Kuiyi, 'Kexue: Yapian zhi zhan' (Science: The War of Opium), *Jiangsu sheng li di yi nüzi shifan xuexiao xiaoyouhui zazhi* 3 (1920): 32–3; Zheng Hongfan, 'Yapian zhanzheng bainian jinian' (The Centenary of the Opium War), *Zhejiang chao* 108 (1940): 132–5; Pan Juemin, 'Cong Yapian zhanzheng dao wusa can'an diguo zhuyi de zui'e' (The Evil of Imperialism: From the Opium War to the Massacre of 30 May), *Jiangsu dangwu zhoukan* 17 (1930): 14–18; Fu Lin, 'Yapian zhanzheng shimo' (The Opium War from Beginning to End), *Wenxian* 4 (1925): 1–2; Bi Shuo, 'Yapian zhanzheng jiyu women de jiaoxun' (The Lesson that the Opium War Has For Us) *Mingde xunkan* 13.3 (1936): 7–8.

34 See Yang Ren, *Gaozhong benguo shi* (Chinese History for High Schools) (Shanghai: Beixin shuju, 1930) Volume 2, 55–61.

35 Zhou Yutong, *Kaiming benguoshi jiaoben* (Kaiming's Textbook of Chinese History) (Shanghai: Kaiming shudian, 1932) Volume 2, 75–6.

36 *Yapian zhanzheng* (The Opium War) (Shanghai: Shangwu, 1931), 1.

37 'Judu tekan fakan he' (An opening beration to this special issue of *Prohibition Monthly*), *Judu yuekan* 44 (1930): 28.

38 Chiang Kai-shek, *China's Destiny and Chinese Economic Theory* trans. Philip Jaffe (London: Dennis Dobson, 1947), 97, 105.

39 Dong Wang, *China's Unequal Treaties*, 67.

40 C. Martin Wilbur and Julie Lien-ying How, *Missionaries of Revolution: Soviet Advisers and Nationalist China, 1920–1927* (Cambridge, Mass.: Harvard University Press, 1989), 672–9.

41 Pan Juemin, 'Cong Yapian zhanzheng', 14.

42 Bi Shuo, 'Yapian zhanzheng'.

43 Wu Xuanyi, 'Judu pingtan: Yapian zhanzheng shibai de yuanyin ji

wo guo suo shoudao de yingxiang' (The Reasons for Our Defeat in the Opium War and Its Impact on China), *Judu yuekan* 98 (1936): 2–4.

44 Cao Han, 'Yapian zhanzheng bainian ji: bainian lai de xuezhai' (The Centenary of the Opium War: A Century-old Blood Debt), *Xingjian* 2.4 (1940): 29–32.

45 See, for example, Chiang, *China's Destiny*, 51, 55, 90, 84.

46 See also, for example, ibid., 83, 97, 155.

47 Ibid., 51, 89, 101, 90.

48 Jay Taylor, *The Generalissimo* (Cambridge, Mass.: Harvard University Press, 2009), 261.

49 Appraisals of the Nationalists' record in power have changed significantly over the past few decades. The highly critical view espoused by historians such as Lloyd Eastman (in, for example, 'Nationalist China during the Nanking Decade, 1927–37' in *The Cambridge History of China* Volume 13, 116–67) has recently been revised by more positive assessments that find the Nationalist regime relatively successful at state-building despite appalling difficulties, and that emphasize similarities rather than differences between the earlier Nationalist and later Communist states. Key points are made in works such as Hans van de Ven, *War and Nationalism in China, 1925–45* (London: Routledge, 2003); William C. Kirby, 'The Nationalist Regime and the Chinese Party-State, 1928–58', in M. Goldman and A. Gordon eds., *Historical Perspectives on Contemporary East Asia* (Cambridge, Mass.: Harvard University Press, 2000), and Rana Mitter, *Modern China: A Very Short Introduction* (Oxford: Oxford University Press, 2008).

50 Baumler, *Worse than Floods and Wild Beasts*, 90.

51 Edward Slack, *Opium, State and Society: China's Narco-Economy and the Guomindang, 1924–1937* (Honolulu: University of Hawai'i Press, 2001), 48.

52 These figures and details are drawn from ibid., probably the best, most detailed account of opium policy in Republican China.

53 Ibid., 45.

54 Ibid., 61.

55 Ibid., 83.

56 Ibid., 63.

57 Ibid., 91.

58 Ibid., 92.

59 'Judu tekan fakan he'.

60 'Opium Evil as China's Greatest Peril', *North China Herald*, 12 February 1936, 257.

61 Slack, *Opium*, 94.

62 Dikötter et al., *Narcotic Culture*, 143.

63 Baumler, *Worse than Floods*, 204.

64 Slack, *Opium*, 102.

65 See, for example, Mark S. Eykholt, 'Resistance to Opium as a Social Evil in Wartime China', in Brook and Wakabayashi eds., *Opium Regimes*, 362; and description in Dikötter et al., *Narcotic Culture*, 188. See Chiang, *China's Destiny*, 91, for a denunciation of Japan's 'poison policy'.

66 Timothy Brook, 'Opium and Collaboration in Central China, 1938–40', in Brook and Wakabayashi eds., *Opium Regimes*, 323.

67 Zheng Hongfan, 'Yapian zhanzheng bainian jinian', 134–5.

68 See John Jennings, *The Opium Empire: Japanese Imperialism and Drug Trafficking in Asia, 1895–1945* (Westport: Praeger, 1997), 85; 'Illicit Trade in North China', in *North China Herald*, 5 February 1936, 213; 'Korean Rascals in Tsangchow', in *North China Herald*, 13 November 1935, 273.

69 See, for example, Rana Mitter, *The Manchurian Myth: Nationalism, Resistance, and Collaboration in Modern China* (Berkeley: University of California Press, 2000), 118–19.

70 *The Times*, 9 August 1939, 12 August 1939.

71 Cao Han, 'Yapian zhanzheng bainian ji'.

72 '"Lin Zexu" gaiming "Yapian zhanzheng"' (*Lin Zexu* Changes Title to *The Opium War*), *Shanghai yingxun* 2.13 (1942): 307.

73 Parks M. Coble, *Facing Japan: Chinese Politics and Japanese Imperialism, 1931–37* (Cambridge, Mass.: Harvard University Press, 1991), 102.

74 Fitzgerald, *Awakening China*, 329, 257.

75 Ibid., 19.

76 Alisa Jones, 'Changing the Past to Serve the Present: History Education in Mainland China', in Edward Vickers and Alisa Jones eds., *History Education and National Identity in East Asia* (New York: Routledge, 2005), 72.

77 Mao Zedong, 'The Chinese Revolution and the Chinese Communist Party', at http://www.marxists.org/reference/archive/mao/selected-works/volume-2/mswv2_23.htm (accessed 10 February 2010).

78 Mao Zedong, 'Orientation of the Youth Movement', at http://www.marxists.org/reference/archive/mao/selected-works/volume-2/mswv2_14.htm (accessed 10 February 2010).

79 Mao Zedong, 'The Chinese Revolution and the Chinese Communist

Party'; Mao Zedong, 'On Contradiction', http://www.marxists.org/
reference/archive/mao/selected-works/volume-1/mswv1_17.htm
(accessed 10 February 2010).

80 *Bainian shihua* (A Narrative of the Past Century) (Shanghai:
Pingming chubanshe, 1951), 1.

81 *Zhongguo jindai jianshi* (A Concise Modern History of China) (Beijing:
Lianhe tushu chubanshe, 1950), 1–6.

82 Mao, 'The Chinese Revolution'.

83 Zhou Yongming, 'Nationalism, Identity, and State-Building', in
Brook and Wakabayashi eds., *Opium Regimes*, 381.

84 See Chen, 'The Blooming Poppy', 267; Jung Chang and Jon Halliday,
Mao: The Unknown Story (London: Jonathan Cape, 2005), 283.

85 Chen, 'The Blooming Poppy', 270.

86 Ma, *Zhongguo jindu shi ziliao*, 1611.

87 Zhou, 'Nationalism', 382.

88 Ibid., 393.

Nineteen: CONCLUSION

1 Michael White, 'Why Denouncing China is Hypocritical', at http://
www.guardian.co.uk/politics/blog/2009/dec/29/china-akmal-shaikh-
execution (accessed 12 January 2010).

2 http://www.fco.gov.uk/en/news/latest-news/
?view=News&id=21498748 (accessed 12 January 2010).

3 http://www.chinese-embassy.org.uk/eng/sghd/t648674.htm (accessed
12 January 2010).

4 http://china.globaltimes.cn/diplomacy/2009–12/495554.html
(accessed 12 January 2010).

5 http://news.xinmin.cn/rollnews/2010/01/02/3232072.html (accessed
12 January 2010).

6 'Zhongguo ren kan le gaoxing' (The Chinese People are Delighted),
at http://blog.huanqiu.com/?uid-89545-action-viewspace-itemid-
406290 (accessed 12 January 2010).

7 http://comment.news.163.com/news_guonei4_bbs/
5RMR30DG0001124J.html (accessed 12 January 2010).

8 White, 'Why Denouncing China'.

9 Mark Lynas, 'How Do I Know China Wrecked the Copenhagen Deal?
I Was in the Room', at http://www.guardian.co.uk/environment/

2009/dec/22/copenhagen-climate-change-mark-lynas (accessed 10 January 2010).

10 Con Coughlin, 'China Will Soon Have the Power to Switch off the Lights in the West', at http://www.telegraph.co.uk/comment/6924710/China-will-soon-have-the-power-to-switch-off-the-lights-in-the-West.html (accessed 12 January 2010).

11 'All Politics is Local', at http://www.newsweek.com/2010/01/03/all-politics-is-local.html (accessed 12 January 2010).

12 *Zhongguo lishi* (Chinese History) Volume 3 (Beijing: Renmin jiaoyu chubanshe, 1982), 3, 4, 7.

13 Bonnie McDougall, interview, 10 July 2002.

14 Haiyan Lee, 'The Ruins of Yuanmingyuan', *Modern China* (March 2009): 161. See also a special issue of *China Heritage Quarterly* on the ruined garden and palace (December 2006), at http://www.chinaheritagequarterly.org/editorial.php?issue=008 (accessed 21 August 2010).

15 *China Quarterly* 120 (December 1989): 919–46.

16 Anne-Marie Brady, *Marketing Dictatorship: Propaganda and Thought Work in Contemporary China* (Lanham: Rowman and Littlefield, 2008), 42. This is a fascinating account of how contemporary China's propaganda machine has adapted to new media since 1989.

17 Ibid., 45.

18 *Quru yu kangzheng* (Humiliation and Resistance) (Qinhuangdao: Zhongguo shehui yu zhongxue chubanshe, 1993), 1, 3, 45, 102, 4.

19 Zhang Haifeng et al., *Yapianzhanzheng yu zhongguo xiandai hua* (The Opium War and China's Modernization) (Beijing: Zhongguo shehui chubanshe, 1991), 3.

20 Zhao, *A Nation-State*, 219.

21 Zhang Jiangming, 'Aiguo zhuyi he jianshi you Zhongguo tese shehuizhuyi' (Patriotism and Building Socialism with Chinese Characteristics) *Qiushi*, November 1994: 22.

22 See Callahan, *China*, 34 and *passim* for a thorough and lively discussion of the discourse of national humiliation in modern and contemporary China.

23 Richard McGregor, *The Party: The Secret World of China's Communist Rulers* (London: Allen Lane, 2010), 236. This offers eye-opening insights into the workings of the Chinese Communist Party.

24 Callahan, *China*, 38–47.

25 Ma Zhibin, interview, 15 November 2007.

26 Callahan, *China*, 50.

27 See analysis in ibid., 4–52.

28 Zhao, *A Nation-State*, 338–41.

29 See tables in Martin Jacques, *When China Rules the World: The Rise of the Middle Kingdom and the End of the Western World* (London: Allen Lane, 2009), 392–4.

30 Han Zhongkun, 'Zhongguo, bushi yibaijiujiu' (This Is No Longer the China of 1899) *People's Daily*, 12 May 1999. The analogies during the 1999 protests to the Allied invasion of 1900 (during the Boxer Rebellion) were also marked. See discussion in Jeffrey Wasserstrom, 'Student Protests in Fin-de-siecle China', in the *New Left Review* (September/October 1999): 52–76; and *China's Brave New World and Other Tales for Global Times* (Indiana: Indiana University Press, 2007). Peter Hessler's *Oracle Bones* (London: John Murray, 2006) offers additional sharp analysis of these events.

31 'British Invasions Probed as Root Cause of Tibetan Separatism', 8 April 2008, at http://www.chinadaily.com.cn/china/2008-04/08/content_6598211.htm (accessed 2 March 2009).

32 'Patriotic Voices: Comments from the Global Times Online Forum', at http://chinadigitaltimes.net/2008/05/patriotic-voices-comments-from-the-global-times-online-forum/ (accessed 2 March 2009).

33 For a terrific introduction to the *fenqing* phenomenon, see Evan Osnos, 'Letter from China: Angry Youth', in the *New Yorker*, 28 July 2008, at http://www.newyorker.com/reporting/2008/07/28/080728fa_fact_osnos (accessed 17 November 2009).

34 Interview obtained by private communication with Evan Osnos, 14 November 2007.

35 For expertise on the Chinese Internet, visit essential digital resources such as China Digital Times, http://chinadigitaltimes.net/; Danwei, www.danwei.org; China Media Project, http://cmp.hku.hk/; Rebecca Mackinnon's blog, http://rconversation.blogs.com/. Among many fascinating works, see also Yang Guobin, *The Power of the Internet in China: Citizen Activism Online* (New York: Columbia University Press, 2009); Xu Wu, *Chinese Cyber Nationalism* (Lanham: Lexington Books, 2009); Shaun Breslin and Simon Shen, 'Online Chinese Nationalism', http://www.chathamhouse.org.uk/files/17307_0910breslin_shen.pdf.

36 Susan Shirk, *Fragile Superpower* (Oxford: Oxford University Press, 2008), 239.

37 Brady, *Marketing Dictatorship*, 55; Peter Hays Gries, *China's New Nationalism* (Berkeley: University of California Press, 2005), 51.

38 Zhang Xiaobo, interview, 30 September 2007.

39 Ren Xue'an, interview, 18 December 2007.

40 '*Lust, Caution* is rejected in Utopia', at http://zonaeuropa.com/ 200711b.brief.htm_008 (accessed 30 November 2007).

41 Wang Ningwen, interview.

42 Ibid.

43 Ibid.

44 Ibid.

45 Ren, interview.

46 Given the strictures currently governing public memory of Communist-manufactured traumas, it is not surprising, perhaps, that so much feeling is diverted into (authorized) recalling of the wounds, for example, of the Japanese invasion. See Vera Schwarcz, 'The Black Milk of Historical Consciousness', in Fei Fei Li, Robert Sabella and David Liu eds., *Nanking 1937: Memory and Healing* (New York: M. E. Sharpe, 2002), 183–204.

47 For insight into the anarchic world of China's young, Internet-savvy nationalists, see for example Mara Hvistendahl, 'China's Hacker Army', in *Foreign Policy*, 3 March 2010, at http://www.foreignpolicy.com/ articles/2010/03/03/china_s_hacker_army?page=full (accessed 21 August 2010).

48 Ren, interview.

49 Shirk, *Fragile Superpower*, 171.

50 *Lishi 1 – putong gaozhong kecheng biaozhun shiyan jiaokeshu* (History 1: Standard Textbooks For the Universal High School Curriculum) (Beijing: Renmin jiaoyu chubanshe, 2007), 76–7.

51 See, for example, James Farrer, 'Nationalism Pits Shanghai Against its Global Ambition', in YaleGlobal, 29 April 2005, at http:// yaleglobal.yale.edu/content/nationalism-pits-shanghai-against-its-global-ambition (accessed 21 August 2010).

52 For an introduction to Guo, see Mara Hvistendahl, 'Conscience of a Nationalist', at http://www.tnr.com/article/politics/conscience-nationalist (accessed 12 January 2010).

53 'Beijing Tries to Rein in Nationalist Beast', at http:// chinadigitaltimes.net/tag/carrefour/ (accessed 2 March 2009).

54 'Be Patriotic? First Be Cool!' at http://chinadigitaltimes.net/2008/04/ be-patriotic-first-be-cool/ (accessed 11 April 2009).

55 Isabel Hilton, 'Will China Implode?' at http://www.thedailybeast.com/ blogs-and-stories/2009-07-28/will-china-implode/ (accessed 1 July 2010).

Notes

56 'Blind Pursuit of Profit Causes Mass Incidents', *China Daily*, 25 December 2009 at http://www.chinadaily.com.cn/opinion/2009-12/25/content_9228967.htm (accessed 1 January 2010).
57 Private communication with Jonathan Fenby, 18 January 2010.

Selected Bibliography

The principal Chinese-language collections of primary materials on the Opium Wars are to be found in:

Qi Sihe et al. ed. *Yapian zhanzheng* (The Opium War) (Shanghai: Shanghai renmin chubanshe, 1954). A varied collection of official edicts and memorials, combined with personal diaries, narrative accounts, poems and letters, and translations of some British materials into Chinese.

Yapian zhanzheng dangan shiliao (Archive Materials on the Opium War) (Tianjin: Tianjin guji chubanshe, 1992). The most comprehensive collection of Qing official sources (memorials, edicts and so on) from the Opium War period.

Chouban yiwu shimo Daoguang chao (On the Handling of Foreign Affairs; Reign of Daoguang) (Beijing: Zhonghua shuju, 1964). A collection of memorials on the subject of foreign relations during Daoguang's reign.

Lin Zexu. *Lin Zexu ji* (The Works of Lin Zexu) (Beijing: Zhonghua shuju, 1962–65).

—. *Lin Zexu quanji* (Collected Works of Lin Zexu) (Fuzhou: Haixia wenyi chubanshe, 2002).

Qingshi lu (Annals of the Qing) (Beijing: Zhonghua shuju, 1986). The most complete, day-to-day record of Qing court business and notifications from the provinces sent to the court.

Qingshi gao (Draft History of the Qing) (Beijing: Zhonghua shuju, 1976). The draft 'official' history of the Qing based on the court annals and written up in the twentieth century.

A Ying ed. *Yapian zhanzheng wenxueji* (Literary Anthology from the Opium

War) (Beijing: Guji chubanshe, 1957). An invaluable collection of poems, essays and fiction about opium and the Opium War.

Liang Tingnan. *Yifen wenji* (Foreign Affairs) (Beijing: Zhonghua shuju, 1997). Liang's account, along with that of Wei Yuan below, offers one of the key narratives to the events of the Opium War.

Wei Yuan. 'Daoguang yangsou zhengfu ji' (Daoguang's Campaign Against and Soothing of the Foreign Boats) in *Wei Yuan quanji* (Complete Works of Wei Yuan) Volume 3 (Changsha: Yuelu shu she, 2005), 586–620. A slightly abridged translation of this text is published as *A Chinese Account of the Opium War: A Translation of the Last Two Chapters of the Shengwu ji* translated by Edward Parker (Shanghai: Kelly & Walsh, 1888).

Xia Xie. *Zhongxi jishi* (A Record of Sino-Western Relations) (Hunan: Xinhua, 1988). An abridged translation of this text (the original was completed after the second Opium War) is published as *China's Intercourse with Europe* translated by Edward Parker (Shanghai: Kelly and Walsh, 1890).

In addition, there are Chinese-language collections that focus on a particular geographical centre to the war, such as:

Sanyuanli renmin kangyi douzheng shiliao (Historical Materials on the Sanyuanli People's Struggle for Resistance) (Beijing: Zhonghua shuju, 1978).

Yapian zhanzheng zai zhoushan shiliao xuanbian (A Selection of Historical Materials from the Opium War on Zhoushan) (Hangzhou: Zhejiang renmin chubanshe, 1992).

English translations of some Chinese sources are available in the Parliamentary Papers and Foreign Office dispatches, and in some of the British army accounts listed below (such as Bingham's *Narrative*) and the *Chinese Repository*. But see also translations published in:

Kuo, P. C. *A Critical Study of the First Anglo-Chinese War with Documents* (Shanghai: The Commercial Press, 1935).

Swisher, Earl. *China's Management of the American Barbarians: A Study of Sino-American Relations, 1841–1861, with Documents* (New Haven: Far Eastern Publications, 1953).

Teng Ssu-yu. *Chang-hsi and the Treaty of Nanking* (Chicago: University of Chicago Press, 1944).

Waley, Arthur. *The Opium War Through Chinese Eyes* (London: George Allen and Unwin, 1958).

See also key Chinese secondary works for further guidance on the wealth of Chinese-language materials available on the conflict, for example:

Mao Haijian. *Tianchao de bengkui* (The Collapse of a Dynasty) (Beijing: Shenghuo, 1995).
Xiao Zhizhi. *Yapian zhanzheng shi* (History of the Opium War) (Fujian: Fujian renmin chubanshe, 1996).
Yao Weiyuan. *Yapian zhanzheng shi shikao* (An Investigation into the History of the Opium War) (Wuhan: Wuhan daxue chubanshe, 2007).

On the British side, many of the dispatches from China are collected together in relevant volumes of Parliamentary Papers through the 1830s and 1840s – see in particular *Correspondence Relating to China* (1840).

The Foreign Office microfilms of dispatches are available at the National Archives in Kew, London, in the FO 17 series. An edited set of these dispatches is published in Ian Nish ed., *British Documents on Foreign Affairs: Reports and Papers from the Foreign Office Confidential Print, Part 1, Series E, Asia, Volume 16, Chinese War and Its Aftermath, 1839–1849* (Frederick, Md.: University Publications of America, 1994).

Parliamentary debates are available online at:
http://hansard.millbanksystems.com/

In addition, there are many first-hand accounts written by those who participated in the campaigns, including:

'A Field Officer'. *The Last Year in China to the Peace of Nanking* (London: Longman, 1843).
Belcher, Edward. *Narrative of a Voyage Round the World Performed in Her Majesty's Ship* Sulphur *During the Years 1836–1842* (London: Henry Colburn, 1843).
Bingham, John Elliot. *Narrative of the Expedition to China* 2nd ed. (London: Henry Colburn, 1843).

Hall, W. H. and W. D. Bernard. *Narrative of the Voyages and Services of the Nemesis* 2nd ed. (London: Henry Colburn, 1845).

Lord Jocelyn. *Six Months with the Chinese Expedition* (London: John Murray, 1841).

Loch, Granville. *The Closing Events of the Campaign in China* (London: John Murray, 1843).

McPherson, Duncan. *Two Years in China: Narrative of the Chinese Expedition, from Its Formation in April, 1840, to the Treaty of Peace in August, 1842* 2nd ed. (London: Saunders and Otley, 1843).

Murray, Alexander. *Doings in China: Being the Personal Narrative of an Officer Engaged in the Late China Expedition, from the Recapture of Chusan in 1841 to the Peace of Nankin in 1842* (London: Richard Bentley, 1843).

Ouchterlony, John. *The Chinese War: An Account of All the Operations of the British Forces from the Commencement to the Treaty of Nanking* (London: Saunders and Otley, 1844).

For secondary English-language accounts of the Opium War, see the general bibliography below; books by Peter Ward Fay, Edgar Holt, Brian Inglis and James Polachek are, amongst others, particularly helpful.

In addition, the following works were consulted:

A Resident in China. *The Rupture with China and Its Causes* (London: Gilbert and Piper, 1840).

Appleton, William. *A Cycle of Cathay: The Chinese Vogue in England during the Seventeenth and Eighteenth Centuries* (New York: Columbia University Press, 1951).

Auerbach, Sascha. *Race, Law and "The Chinese Puzzle" in Imperial Britain* (Palgrave Macmillan: New York, 2009).

Bainian shihua (A Narrative of the Past Century) (Shanghai: Pingming chubanshe, 1951).

Barnett, Correlli. *Britain and Her Army* (London: Cassell, 2000).

Baum, Richard. *Burying Mao: Chinese Politics in the Age of Deng Xiaoping* (Princeton: Princeton University Press, 1994).

Baumler, Alan. *Modern China and Opium: A Reader* (Michigan: University of Michigan Press, 2001).

—. *Worse than Floods and Wild Beasts* (Albany: State University of New York Press, 2007).

Beeching, Jack. *The Chinese Opium Wars* (New York: Harcourt, 1975).

Bello, David Anthony. *Opium and the Limits of Empire: Drug Prohibition in the Chinese Interior, 1729–1850* (Cambridge, Mass.: Harvard University Press, 2005).

Bergère, Marie-Claire. *Sun Yat-sen* (Stanford: Stanford University Press, 1998).

—. *Shanghai: China's Gateway to Modernity* (Stanford: Stanford University Press, 2009).

Berridge, Virginia. *Opium and the People: Opiate Use and Drug Control Policy in Nineteenth and Early Twentieth Century England* (London: Free Association Books, 1999).

Bi Shuo. 'Yapian Zhanzheng jiyu women de jiaoxun' (The Lesson that the Opium War Has For Us) *Mingde xunkan* 13.3 (1936): 7–8.

Bickers, Robert. *Britain in China* (Manchester: Manchester University Press, 1999).

—. *Empire Made Me: An Englishman Adrift in Shanghai* (London: Allen Lane, 2003).

—. and Gary Tiedemann eds. *The Boxers, China and the World* (Lanham: Rowman and Littlefield, 2007).

—. and Jeffrey Wasserstrom. 'Shanghai's "Dogs and Chinese Not Admitted" Sign: Legend, History and Contemporary Symbol', *China Quarterly* 142 (June 1995): 444–66.

Blake, Clagette. *Charles Elliot, R.N., 1801–1875: A Servant of Britain Overseas* (London: Cleaver-Hume, 1960).

Blofeld, John. *City of Lingering Splendour: A Frank Account of Old Peking's Exotic Pleasures* (London: Hutchinson, 1961).

Boderhorn, Terry Wright ed. *Defining Modernity: Guomindang Rhetorics of a New China 1920–70* (Michigan: University of Michigan, 2002).

Booth, Martin. *Opium: A History* (London: Pocket Books, 1997).

Bourne, Kenneth. *The Foreign Policy of Victorian England* (Oxford: Clarendon, 1970).

—. *Palmerston, the Early Years: 1784–1841* (London: Allen Lane, 1982).

Brady, Anne-Marie. *Marketing Dictatorship: Propaganda and Thought Work in Contemporary China* (Lanham: Rowman and Littlefield, 2008).

Brook, Timothy, and Bob Wakabayashi eds. *Opium Regimes: China, Britain and Japan, 1839–1952* (Berkeley: University of California Press, 2000).

Lord Broughton. *Recollections of a Long Life* (New York: Charles Scribner's
    Sons, 1911).
Brown, David. *Palmerston: A Biography* (Yale: Yale University Press, 2010).

Callahan, William. *China: The Pessoptimist Nation* (Oxford: Oxford
    University Press, 2010).
Cambridge History of China (Cambridge: Cambridge University Press, 1978–)
    Volumes 9–.
Cannadine, David. 'The Empire Strikes Back', *Past and Present* 147.1
    (1995): 180–94.
Cao Han. 'Yapian zhanzheng bainian ji: bainian lai de xuezhai' (The
    Centenary of the Opium War: A Century-old Blood Debt)
    Xingjian 2.4 (1940): 29–35.
Castle, Kathryn. *Britannia's Children: Reading Colonialism through Children's
    Books and Magazines* (Manchester: Manchester University Press,
    1996).
Chandler, David and Ian Beckett eds. *The Oxford History of the British Army*
    (Oxford: Oxford Paperbacks, 2003).
Chang, Hao. *Liang Ch'i-ch'ao and Intellectual Transition in China,
    1890–1907* (Cambridge, Mass.: Harvard University Press, 1971).
Chang Hsin-pao. *Commissioner Lin and the Opium War* (Cambridge, Mass.:
    Harvard University Press, 1964).
Chang, Jung and Jon Halliday. *Mao: The Unknown Story* (London: Jonathan
    Cape, 2005).
Chen Xiqi. *Lin Zexu yu yapian zhanzheng lungao* (Essays on Lin Zexu and
    the Opium War) (Guangdong: Zhongshan daxue chubanshe,
    1990).
Chen Yung-fa. 'The Blooming Poppy Under the Red Sun: the Yan'an Way
    and the Opium Trade', in Hans van de Ven and Anthony Saich
    eds., *New Perspectives on the Chinese Communist Revolution* (New York:
    M. E. Sharpe, 1995), 263–98.
Cheng, Wah-kwan. 'Vox Populi: Language, Literature and Ideology in
    Modern China', unpublished Ph.D. dissertation (University of
    Chicago, 1989).
Chiang Kai-shek. *China's Destiny and Chinese Economic Theory* trans. Philip
    Jaffe (London: Dennis Dobson, 1947).
Chung, Tan. *China and the Brave New World* (Durham: Carolina Academic
    Press, 1978).
Coble, Parks M. *Facing Japan: Chinese Politics and Japanese Imperialism,
    1931–37* (Cambridge, Mass.: Harvard University Press, 1991).

Cohen, Paul. *Discovering History in China* (New York: Columbia University Press, 1986).

—. *History in Three Keys* (New York: Columbia University Press, 1997).

—. *China Unbound: Evolving Perspectives on the Chinese Past* (London: Routledge, 2003).

—. *Speaking to History: The Story of King Goujian in Twentieth-century China* (California: University of California Press, 2008).

Collis, Maurice. *Foreign Mud* (London: Faber, 1997).

Cooke, George Wingrove. *China and Lower Bengal: Being The Times Special Correspondence from China in the Years 1857–58* (London: Routledge, 1861).

Crossley, Pamela Kyle. *Orphan Warriors: Three Manchu Generations and the End of the Qing World* (Princeton: Princeton University Press, 1990).

—. *The Manchus* (Oxford: Wiley-Blackwell, 2002).

—. *A Translucent Mirror: History and Identity in Qing Imperial Ideology* (Berkeley: University of California Press, 2006).

Dai Xueji. *Yapian zhanzheng renwu zhuan* (Biographies of Figures from the Opium War) (Fujian: Fujian jiaoyu chubanshe, 1986).

Darwin, John. *The Empire Project: The Rise and Fall of the British World-System 1830–1970* (Cambridge: Cambridge University Press, 2009).

Dawson, Raymond. *The Chinese Chameleon: An Analysis of European Conceptions of Chinese Civilisation* (London: Oxford University Press, 1967).

De Bary, Theodore and Richard Lufrano eds. *Sources of Chinese Tradition* (New York: Columbia University Press, 2001).

De Quincey, Thomas. *The Confessions of an English Opium Eater* (Oxford: Oxford University Press, 1996).

Denton, Kirk ed. *Modern Chinese Literary Thought: Writings on Literature 1893–1945* (Stanford: Stanford University Press, 1996).

Dikötter, Frank. *The Discourse of Race in Modern China* (London: Hurst, 1992).

—. *Things Modern* (London: Hurst, 2005).

—. *The Age of Openness: China Before Mao* (Berkeley: University of California Press, 2008).

—, Lars Laaman and Zhou Xun. *Narcotic Culture: A History of Drugs in China* (London: Hurst & Company, 2004).

Ditmer, Lowell and Samuel S. Kim eds. *China's Quest for National Identity* (Ithaca: Cornell University Press, 2003).

Downing, Charles Toogood. *The Fan-qui in China, in 1836–7* (London: Henry Colburn, 1838).

Drumm, Anna. 'A study of contemporary Irish attitudes to the first Opium War, 1839–42', unpublished MA thesis (University of London, 2010).

Eastman, Lloyd. 'Nationalist China during the Nanking Decade, 1927–37' in *The Cambridge History of China* Volume 13 (Cambridge: Cambridge University Press, 1986), 116–67.

Elliot, Mark. *The Manchu Way: The Eight Banners and Ethnic Identity in Late Imperial China* (Stanford: Stanford University Press, 2001).

Elman, Benjamin A. *A Cultural History of Civil Examinations in Late Imperial China* (Berkeley: University of California Press, 2000).

Enright, D. J. 'Introduction', *The Mystery of Dr Fu Manchu* (London: Dent, 1985).

Esherick, Joseph. *The Origins of the Boxer Uprising* (Berkeley: University of California Press, 1987).

Fairbank, John K. *Trade and Diplomacy on the China Coast* (Cambridge, Mass: Harvard Historical Studies, 1953–54).

——. *The Chinese World Order: Traditional China's Foreign Relations* (Cambridge, Mass.: Harvard University Press, 1968).

——. 'The Creation of the Treaty System', in Fairbank ed., *The Cambridge History of China: Volume 10, Late Ch'ing 1800–1911, Part I*, 213–63.

Fay, Peter Ward. *The Opium War, 1840–42* (Chapel Hill: University of North Carolina Press, 1975).

Fenby, Jonathan. *The Penguin History of Modern China* (London: Allen Lane, 2008).

Feng Baoshan. *Yan Fu zhuan* (A Biography of Yan Fu) (Beijing: Tuanjie chubanshe, 1998).

Ferguson, Niall. *Empire: How Britain Made the Modern World* (London: Allen Lane, 2003).

FitzGerald, J. 'Incidents of the Last Chinese War', unpublished manuscript made available by kind permission of Jennifer Mackintosh.

Fitzgerald, John. *Awakening China: Politics, Culture and Class in the Nationalist Revolution* (Stanford: Stanford University Press, 1996).

Fletcher, Joseph. 'The Heyday of the Ch'ing Order in Mongolia, Sinkiang and Tibet', in Fairbank ed., *The Cambridge History of China: Volume 10, Late Ch'ing 1800–1911, Part I*, 351–408.

Foxcroft, Louise. *The Making of Addiction: The 'Use and Abuse' of Opium in Nineteenth-Century Britain* (Kent: Ashgate, 2007).

Frodsham, J. D. ed. and trans. *The First Chinese Embassy to the West: the journals of Kuo Sung-t'ao, Liu Hsi-hung and Chang Te-yi* (Oxford: Clarendon Press, 1974).

Fu Lin, 'Yapian zhanzheng shimo' (The Opium War from Beginning to End), *Wenxian* 4 (1925): 1–2.

Gaodeng xiaoxue zhongguo lishi jiaokeshu (High Level Primary School Textbook on Chinese History) (Shanghai: Shangwu yinshu guan, 1909).

Gertz, Bill. *The China Threat: How the People's Republic Targets America* (Lanham: Regnery Publishing, 2000).

Gongheguo jiaokeshu, benguoshi (The Republican Textbook of Chinese History) (Shanghai: Shangwu, 1913).

Gordon Cumming, C. F. *Wanderings in China* (Edinburgh: Blackwood, 1886).

Graham, Gerald. *The China Station: War and Diplomacy, 1830–1860* (Oxford: Oxford University Press, 1978).

Greenberg, Michael. *British Trade and the Opening of China, 1800–42* (London: Routledge, 2000).

Gries, Peter Hays. *China's New Nationalism* (Berkeley: University of California Press, 2005).

Guo Weidong. *Zhuanzhe: yi zaoqi Zhong-Ying guanxi he 'Nanjing tiaoxue' wei kaocha zhongxin* (Turning Point: Focusing on Sino-British Relations and the Nanjing Treaty) (Hebei: Hebei renmin chubanshe, 2003).

Gützlaff, Karl. *A Journal of Three Voyages Along the Coast of China in 1831, 1832 and 1833* (facsimile reprint) (Westcliffe on Sea: Desert Island Books, 2002).

Hanes III, Travis W. and Frank Sanello. *The Opium Wars* (Illinois: Sourcebooks, 2002).

Harris, David. *Of Battle and Beauty* (Berkeley: University of California Press, 1999).

Harrison, Henrietta. *The Making of the Republican Citizen: Political Ceremonies and Symbols in China, 1911–1929* (Oxford: Oxford University Press, 2000).

—. *China* (London: Arnold, 2001).

—. *Man Awakened from Dreams: One Man's Life in a North China Village, 1857–1942* (Stanford: Stanford University Press, 2005).

Henderson, James. *Shanghai Hygiene, Or, Hints for the Preservation of Health in China* (Shanghai: Presbyterian Mission Press, 1863).

Hessler, Peter. *Oracle Bones* (London: John Murray, 2006).

—. *Country Driving* (London: Harper, 2009).

Hevia, James. *Cherishing Men from Afar: Qing Guest Ritual and the Macartney Embassy of 1793* (Durham: Duke University Press, 1995).

—. *English Lessons: The Pedagogy of Imperialism in Nineteenth-Century China* (Durham: Duke University Press, 2003).

Hilton, Boyd. *A Mad, Bad, and Dangerous People? England 1783–1846* (Oxford: Clarendon Press, 2006).

Hoe, Susanna and Derek Roebuck. *The Taking of Hong Kong: Charles and Clara Elliot in China Waters* (Richmond: Curzon, 1999).

Holt, Edgar. *The Opium Wars in China* (London: Putnam, 1964).

Hostetler, Laura. *Qing Colonial Enterprise: Ethnography and Cartography in Early Modern China* (Chicago: University of Chicago Press, 2005).

Howard, Paul. 'Opium Suppression in Qing China: Responses to a social problem, 1729–1906', unpublished Ph.D. dissertation (University of Pennsylvania, 1998).

Huang, Philip. *Liang Ch'i-ch'ao and Modern Chinese Liberalism* (Seattle: University of Washington Press, 1972).

Hughes, Christopher. *Chinese Nationalism in the Global Era* (London: Routledge, 2006).

Hummel, Arthur ed. *Eminent Chinese of the Ch'ing Period, 1644–1912* (Washington: Library of Congress, 1943).

Hunter, William. *The 'Fan Kwae' at Canton before Treaty Days, 1825–1844* 2nd ed. (Shanghai: Kelly and Walsh, 1911).

Hurd, Douglas. *The Arrow War: An Anglo-Chinese Confusion, 1856–60* (London: Collins, 1967).

Hyam, Ronald. *Britain's Imperial Century, 1815–1914: A Study of Empire and Expansion* (New York: Palgrave Macmillan, 2002).

Inglis, Brian. *The Opium War* (London: Hodder and Stoughton, 1976).

Jacques, Martin. *When China Rules the World: The Rise of the Middle Kingdom and the End of the Western World* (London: Allen Lane, 2009).

Janin, Hunt. *The India–China Opium Trade* (North Carolina: McFarland and Company, 1999).

Jay, Mike. *Emperors of Dreams: Drugs in the Nineteenth Century* (Sawtry: Daedalus, 2002).

Jennings, John. *The Opium Empire: Japanese Imperialism and Drug Trafficking in Asia, 1895–1945* (Westport: Praeger, 1997).

Jones, Susan Mann and Philip A. Kuhn. 'Dynastic Decline and the Roots of Rebellion', Fairbank ed., *The Cambridge History of China: Volume 10, Late Ch'ing 1800–1911, Part I*, 107–62.

Judge, Joan. *Print and Politics* (Stanford: Stanford University Press, 1996).

'Judu tekan fakan he' (An opening beration to this special issue of *Prohibition Monthly*), *Judu yuekan* 1930 (44): 28.

Keswick, Maggie ed. *The Thistle and the Jade: A Celebration of 150 years of Jardine, Matheson & Co.* (London: Octopus, 1982).

Kirby, William C., 'The Nationalist Regime and the Chinese Party-State, 1928–58', in M. Goldman and A. Gordon eds., *Historical Perspectives on Contemporary East Asia* (Cambridge, Mass.: Harvard University Press, 2000).

Kohn, Marek. *Dope Girls: The Birth of the British Drug Underground* (London: Granta Books, 1992).

Kuhn, Philip. *Soul-Stealers: The Chinese Sorcery Scare of 1768* (Cambridge, Mass.: Harvard University Press, 2006).

Laaman, Lars. *Christian Heretics in Late Imperial China: Christian Inculturation and State Control 1720–1850* (London: Routledge, 2006).

Lane-Poole, Stanley. *Sir Harry Parkes in China* (London: Methuen, 1901).

Le Pichon, Alain ed. *China, Trade and Empire* (Oxford: Oxford University Press, 2006).

Lee, Haiyan. 'The Ruins of Yuanmingyuan', *Modern China* (March 2009): 155–90.

Lee, Leo Oufan. *Shanghai Modern* (Cambridge, Mass.: Harvard University Press, 1999).

—. and Andrew J. Nathan. 'The Beginnings of Mass Culture: Journalism and Fiction in the Late Ch'ing and Beyond', in *Popular Culture in Late Imperial China*, eds. David Johnson et al., 360–98.

Leonard, Jane Kate. *Wei Yuan and China's Rediscovery of the Maritime World* (Cambridge, Mass.: Harvard University Press, 1984).

Levenson, Joseph. *Liang Ch'i-ch'ao and the Mind of Modern China* (London: Thames and Hudson, 1959).

Li Yu-ning ed. *Two Self-Portraits: Liang Ch'i-ch'ao and Hu Shih* (Bronxville: Outer Sky Press, 1992).

Liang Qichao quanji (Collected Works of Liang Qichao) (Beijing: Beijing chubanshe, 1999).

Lin Jiasheng. 'Tan tan yapian zhanzheng' (A Chat about the Opium War), *Ertong zazhi* 6 (1936): 4–7.

Lin Man-houng. *China Upside Down: Currency, Society and Ideologies 1808–1856* (Cambridge, Mass.: Harvard University Press, 2007).

Lin Yu-sheng. *The Crisis of Chinese Consciousness* (Madison: University of Wisconsin Press, 1979).

'"Lin Zexu" gaiming "Yapian zhanzheng"' (*Lin Zexu* Changes Title to *The Opium War*), *Shanghai yingxun* 2.13 (1942): 307.

Lindsay, Hugh Hamilton. *Report of Proceedings on a Voyage to the Northern Ports of China* (London: B. Fellowes, 1834).

—. *Is the War with China a Just One?* (London: James Ridgway, 1840).

Lishi (History) Volume 1 (Beijing: Renmin jiaoyu chubanshe, 1960).

Lishi 1 – putong gaozhong kecheng biaozhun shiyan jiaokeshu (History 1 – Standard Textbooks for the Universal High School Curriculum) (Beijing: Renmin jiaoyu chubanshe, 2007).

Liu Chao. 'Yapian zhanzheng yu Zhongguo jindaishi yanjiu' (The Opium War and Research into Modern Chinese History), *Xueshu yuekan* 6 (2007): 146–53.

Liu, Lydia H. *The Clash of Empires: The Invention of China in Modern World-Making* (Cambridge, Mass.: Harvard University Press, 2004).

Loch, Henry Brougham. *Personal Narrative of Occurrences During Lord Elgin's Second Embassy to China, 1860* (London: John Murray, 1869).

Lodwick, Kathleen. *Crusaders Against Opium: Protestant Missionaries in China, 1874–1917* (Lexington: The University Press of Kentucky, 1996).

Lu Simian. *Zhongguo jindaishi* (Modern Chinese History) (Shanghai: Huadong shifan daxue chubanshe, 1997).

Lu Xun. *The Real Story of Ah-Q and Other Tales of China* Julia Lovell trans. (London: Penguin Classics, 2009).

Lyman, Stanford M. 'The "Yellow Peril" Mystique: Origins and Vicissitudes of a Racist Discourse', *International Journal of Politics, Culture, and Society*, 13.4 (Summer 2000): 683–747.

Ma Mozhen. *Zhongguo jindu shi ziliao* (Materials from the History of Drug Prohibition in China) (Tianjin: Tianjin renmin chubanshe, 1998).

MacFarquhar, Roderick. *The Politics of China: The Eras of Mao and Deng* (Cambridge: Cambridge University Press, 1998).

McGregor, Richard. *The Party: The Secret World of China's Communist Rulers* (London: Allen Lane, 2010).

McMahon, Keith. *The Fall of the God of Money: Opium Smoking in Nineteenth-century China* (Lanham: Rowman and Littlefield, 2002).

Madancy, Joyce. *The Troublesome Legacy of Commissioner Lin: The Opium Trade and Opium Suppression in Fujian Province, 1820s to 1920s* (Cambridge, Mass.: Harvard University Press, 2003).

Mallinson, Allan. *The Making of the British Army* (London: Bantam Press, 2010).

Mangan, James A. ed. *The Imperial Curriculum: Racial Images and Education in British Colonial Experience* (London: Routledge, 1993).

—. *'Benefits bestowed'?: Education and British Imperialism* (Manchester: Manchester University Press, 1998).

Martin, R. M. *Opium in China, Extracted from 'China: Political, Commercial, and Social'* (London: James Madden, 1847).

Marx, Karl. *Marx on China: 1853–1860: Articles from the New York Daily Tribune* (London: Lawrence and Wishart, 1951).

Matheson, Donald. *What is the Opium Trade?* (Edinburgh: Thomas Constable and Co., 1857).

Maugham, W. Somerset. *On a Chinese Screen* (London: William Heinemann, 1922).

Melancon, Glenn. *Britain's China Policy and the Opium Crisis: Balancing Drugs, Violence and National Honour, 1833–1840* (London: Ashgate, 2003).

Michael, Franz. 'Introduction', in Stanley Spector, *Li Hung-chang and the Huai Army: A Study in Nineteenth-Century Chinese Regionalism* (Seattle: University of Washington Press, 1964), xxi–xliii.

— and Chung-li Chang, *The Taiping Rebellion: History and Documents* (Seattle: University of Washington Press, 1966–71).

Millward, James. *Eurasian Crossroads: A History of Xinjiang* (New York: Columbia University Press, 2009).

—. *Beyond the Pass: Economy, Ethnicity and Empire in Qing Central Asia 1759–1864* (Stanford: Stanford University Press, 1998).

Mitter, Rana. *The Manchurian Myth: Nationalism, Resistance, and Collaboration in Modern China* (Berkeley: University of California Press, 2000).

—. *A Bitter Revolution: China's Struggle with the Modern World* (Oxford: Oxford University Press, 2004).

— and Sheila Miyoshi Jager eds. *Ruptured Histories: War, Memory, and the post-Cold War in Asia* (Cambridge, Mass.: Harvard University Press, 2007).

—. *Modern China: A Very Short Introduction* (Oxford: Oxford University Press, 2008).

Mittler, Barbara. *A Newspaper for China? Power, Identity and Change in Shanghai's News Media, 1872–1912* (Cambridge, Mass.: Harvard University Press, 2004).

Morrison, Eliza. *Memoirs of the Life and Labours of Robert Morrison, D.D.* (London: Longman, 1839).

Morse, Hosea Ballou. *The International Relations of the Chinese Empire* (London: Longmans, Green and Company, 1910).

—. *The Chronicles of the East India Company, Trading to China 1635–1834* (Oxford: Clarendon, 1926).

Napier, Priscilla. *Barbarian Eye: Lord Napier in China* (London: Brassey's, 2003).

Naquin, Susan. *Millenarian Rebellion in China: The Eight Trigrams Uprising of 1813* (Yale: Yale University Press, 1976).

Newman, Richard K. 'Opium Smoking in Late Imperial China: A Reconsideration'. *Modern Asian Studies* 29 (October 1995): 765–94.

Nolde, John. 'The False Edict of 1849'. *Journal of Asian Studies* 20.3 (1960): 299–315.

Owen, D. E. *British Opium Policy in China and India* (New Haven: Yale University Press, 1934).

Pan Juemin, 'Cong Yapian Zhanzheng dao wusa can'an diguo zhuyi de zui'e' (The Evil of Imperialism: From the Opium War to the Massacre of 30 May), *Jiangsu dangwu zhoukan* 17 (1930): 14–18.

Perdue, Peter. *China Marches West: The Qing Conquest of Central Eurasia* (Cambridge, Mass.: Harvard University Press).

Pick, Daniel. *Faces of Degeneration: A European Disorder* (Cambridge: Cambridge University Press, 1993).

Polachek, James. 'Literati Groups and Literati Politics in Early Nineteenth-Century China', unpublished Ph.D. thesis (University of California, 1976).

—. *The Inner Opium War* (Cambridge, Mass.: Harvard University Press, 1992).

Pomeranz, Kenneth. *The Great Divergence: China, Europe and the Making of the Modern World Economy* (Princeton: Princeton University Press, 2000).

Pottinger, George. *Sir Henry Pottinger, First Governor of Hong Kong* (Sutton: St Martin's Press, 1997).

Qi Sihe et al. eds. *Di er ci yapian zhanzheng* (The Second Opium War) (Shanghai: Shanghai renmin chubanshe, 1978).

Quru yu kangzheng (Humiliation and Resistance) (Qinhuangdao: Zhongguo shehui yu zhongxue chubanshe, 1993).

Rawski, Evelyn. *The Last Emperors: A Social History of Qing Imperial Institutions* (Berkeley: University of California Press, 2001).

Reins, Thomas D. 'Reform, Nationalism and Internationalism: The Opium Suppression Movement in China and the Anglo-American Influence, 1900–1908', *Modern Asian Studies* 44.3 (May 1985): 529–48.

Rennie, D. F. *The British Arms in North China and Japan* (London: John Murray, 1864).

Richards, John F. 'Opium and the British Indian Empire: The Royal Commission of 1895', *Modern Asian Studies* 36 (May 2002): 375–420.

Rohmer, Sax. *The Fu Manchu Omnibus* (London: Allison and Busby, 1995).

Rowe, William. *China's Last Empire: The Great Qing* (Cambridge, Mass.: Harvard University Press, 2009).

Schiffrin, Harold. *Sun Yat-sen and the Origins of the Chinese Revolution* (Berkeley: California University Press, 1968).

Schwarcz, Vera. 'The Black Milk of Historical Consciousness', in Fei Fei Li, Robert Sabella and David Liu eds., *Nanking 1937: Memory and Healing* (New York: M. E. Sharpe, 2002), 183–204.

Schwartz, Benjamin. *In Search of Wealth and Power: Yen Fu and the West* (Cambridge, Mass.: Harvard University Press, 1990).

Scott, David. *China Stands Up: the PRC and the International System* (Abingdon: Routledge, 2007).

Sergeant, Harriet. *Shanghai* (London: John Murray, 2002).

Seshagiri, Urmila. 'Modernity's (Yellow) Perils: Dr. Fu-Manchu and English Race Paranoia', *Cultural Critique* 62 (Winter 2006): 162–94.

Shiel, Matthew. *The Yellow Danger* (London: Routledge/Thoemmes, 1998).

Shirk, Susan. *Fragile Superpower* (Oxford: Oxford University Press, 2008).

Slack, Edward. *Opium, State and Society: China's Narco-Economy and the Guomindang, 1924–1937* (Honolulu: University of Hawai'i Press, 2001).

Smith, Arthur. *Chinese Characteristics* (New York: Fleming H. Revell Company, 1894).

Smith, Reverend George. *A Narrative of an Exploratory Visit to Each of the Consular Cities of China, and to the Islands of Hong Kong and Chusan* (London: Seeley and Burnside, 1847).

Smith, Steve A. *A Road Is Made: Communism in Shanghai, 1920–1927* (Honolulu: University of Hawai'i Press, 2000).

—. *Like Cattle and Horses: Nationalism and Labor in Shanghai, 1895–1927* (Durham: Duke University Press, 2002).

Spence, Jonathan. *The Gate of Heavenly Peace* (New York: Penguin, 1982).

—. *God's Chinese Son: The Taiping Heavenly Kingdom of Hong Xiuquan* (New York: Norton, 1996).

—. *The Search for Modern China* (New York: Norton, 1999).

—. 'Opium Smoking in Ch'ing China', reprinted in Michael Greenberg, *British Trade and the Opening of China, 1800–42* (London: Routledge, 2000).

—. *The Chan's Great Continent* (London: Penguin, 2000).

Sun Yat-sen. *The Three Principles* (Shanghai: North-China Daily News & Herald, 1927).

Swinhoe, Robert. *Narrative of the North China Campaign* (London: Smith, Elder and Co., 1861).

Tang Xiaobing. *Global Space and the Nationalist Discourse of Modernity: the Historical Thinking of Liang Qichao* (Stanford: Stanford University Press, 1996).

Taylor, Jay. *The Generalissimo* (Cambridge, Mass.: Harvard University Press, 2009).

Teng Ssu-yu and John Fairbank eds. *China's Response to the West: A Documentary Survey, 1839–1923* (Cambridge, Mass.: Harvard University Press, 1979).

Thelwall, Algernon. *The Iniquities of the Opium Trade with China* (London: W. H. Allen, 1839).

Thoms, P. P. *The Emperor of China v. The Queen of England* (London: P. P. Thoms, 1853).

Thurin, Susan. *Victorian Travellers and the Opening of China* (Ohio: Ohio University Press, 1999).

Trocki, Carl. *Opium, Empire and the Global Political Economy: A Study of the Asian Opium Trade 1750–1950* (London: Routledge, 1999).

Tsang, Steve. *A Modern History of Hong Kong* (London: I. B. Tauris, 2004).

Unger, Jonathan ed. *Chinese Nationalism* (Armonk: M. E. Sharpe, 1996).

Van Ash, Cay and Elizabeth Sax Rohmer. *Master of Villainy* (Ohio: Bowling Green University Popular Press, 1972).

Van de Ven, Hans. *From Friend to Comrade: The Founding of the Chinese Communist Party, 1920–27* (Berkeley: University of California Press, 1991).

—. *War and Nationalism in China, 1925–45* (London: Routledge, 2003).

Vickers, Edward and Alisa Jones eds. *History Education and National Identity in East Asia* (New York: Routledge, 2005).

Wakeman, Frederic, Jr. *Strangers at the Gate: Social Disorder in South China, 1839–1861* (Berkeley: University of California Press, 1966).

—. 'The Canton Trade and the Opium War', in John K. Fairbank ed., *The Cambridge History of China: Volume 10, Late Ch'ing, Part I* (Cambridge: Cambridge University Press, 1978), 163–212.

Waley-Cohen, Joanna. *The Sextants of Beijing: Global Currents in Chinese History* (New York: Norton, 1999).

—. *The Culture of War in China: Empire and the Military under the Qing* (London: I.B. Tauris, 2006).

Wan Yi et al., *Daily Life in the Forbidden City: The Qing Dynasty, 1644–1912* (New York: Viking, 1988).

Wang Chengren. *Li Hongzhang sixiang tixi yanjiu* (Systematic Research into the Thought of Li Hongzhang) (Wuhan: Wuhan daxue chubanshe, 1998).

Wang, Dong. *China's Unequal Treaties: Narrating National History* (Lanham: Lexington Books, 2005).

Warner, Jessica. *Craze: Gin and Debauchery in an Age of Reason* (London: Profile Books, 2003).

Wasserstrom, Jeffrey. *China's Brave New World and Other Tales for Global Times* (Indiana: Indiana University Press, 2007).

—. *Global Shanghai, 1850–2010* (London: Routledge, 2009).

—. *China in the 21st Century: What Everyone Needs to Know* (Oxford: Oxford University Press, 2010).

—. 'Student Protests in Fin-de-siecle China'. *The New Left Review* (September/October 1999): 52–76.

Wei, Betty Peh-T'i. *Ruan Yuan, 1764–1849: The Life and Work of a Major Scholar-Official in Nineteenth-Century China before the Opium War* (Hong Kong: Hong Kong University Press, 2006).

Welsh, Frank. *A History of Hong Kong* (London: HarperCollins, 1997).

Wheen, Francis. *Karl Marx* (London: Fourth Estate, 1999).

Wilbur, C. Martin. *Sun Yat-sen: Frustrated Patriot* (New York: Columbia University Press, 1976).

—. and Julie Lien-ying How, *Missionaries of Revolution: Soviet Advisers and Nationalist China, 1920–1927* (Cambridge, Mass.: Harvard University Press, 1989).

Wills, John E. *Embassies and Illusions: Dutch and Portuguese Envoys to K'ang-hsi, 1666–1687* (Cambridge, Mass.: Harvard University Press, 1984).

Wolseley, Garnet Joseph. *Narrative of the War with China in 1860* (London: Longman, 1862).

Wong, J. Y. *Yeh Ming-ch'en: Viceroy of Liang Kuang 1852–8* (Cambridge: Cambridge University Press, 1976).

—. *Deadly Dreams: Opium, Imperialism and the* Arrow *War (1856–1860) in China* (Cambridge: Cambridge University Press, 1998).

Wood, Frances. *No Dogs and Not Many Chinese* (London: John Murray, 2000).

Wright, Mary ed. *China in Revolution: The First Phase 1900–1913* (Yale: Yale University Press, 1971).

Wu Xuanyi, 'Judu pingtan: Yapian Zhanzheng shibai de yuanyin ji wo guo suo shoudao de yingxiang' (The Reasons for Our Defeat in the Opium War and Its Impact on China), *Judu yuekan* 98 (1936): 1–4.

Xu Guoqi. *Olympic Dreams: China and Sports, 1895–2008* (Cambridge, Mass.: Harvard University Press, 2008).

Xu Wu. *Chinese Cyber Nationalism* (Lanham: Lexington Books, 2009).

Yan Chongnian, *Zheng shuo Qing chao shi er di* (Correct Accounts of the Twelve Emperors of the Qing) (Beijing: Zhonghua shuju, 2006).

Yan Fu. *Yan Fu ji* (Works of Yan Fu) (Beijing: Zhonghua shuju, 1986).

Yang Guobin. *The Power of the Internet in China: Citizen Activism Online* (New York: Columbia University Press, 2009).

Yang Guozhen. *Lin Zexu zhuan* (Biography of Lin Zexu) (Beijing: Renmin chubanshe, 1981).

Yang Ren. *Gaozhong benguo shi* (Chinese History for High Schools) (Shanghai: Beixin shuju, 1930).

Yapian zhanzheng (The Opium War) (Shanghai: Shangwu, 1931).

Zarrow, Peter Gue. 'Historical Trauma: Anti-Manchuism and Memories of Atrocity in Late Qing China', *History and Memory* 16.2 (Autumn–Winter 2004): 67–107.

——. *China in War and Revolution 1895–1945* (London: Routledge, 2005).

Zhang Haifeng et al. *Yapianzhanzheng yu zhongguo xiandai hua* (The Opium War and China's Modernization) (Beijing: Zhongguo shehui chubanshe, 1991).

Zhang Jiangming. 'Aiguo zhuyi he jianshi you Zhongguo tese shehuizhuyi' (Patriotism and Building Socialism with Chinese Characteristics), *Qiushi*, November 1994: 18–22.

Zhao, Suisheng. *A Nation-State by Construction: Dynamics of Modern Chinese Nationalism* (Stanford: Stanford University Press, 2004).

Zheng Hongfan, 'Yapian zhanzheng bainian jinian' (The Centenary of the Opium War), *Zhejiang chao* 108 (1940): 132–5.

Zheng Yangwen. *The Social Life of Opium in China* (Cambridge: Cambridge University Press, 2005).

Zheng Yongnian. *Discovering Nationalism in China* (Cambridge: Cambridge University Press, 1999).

Zhina shi yao (A History of China) (Shanghai: Guangzhi shuju, 1906).

Zhongguo jin, xiandaishi gangyao (An Outline of Modern Chinese History) (Beijing: Gaodeng jiaoyu chubanshe, 2007).

Zhongguo jindai jianshi (A Concise Modern History of China) (Beijing: Lianhe tushu chubanshe, 1950).

Zhongguo lishi (Chinese History) Volume 3 (Beijing: Renmin jiaoyu chubanshe, 1956).

Zhongguo lishi jiangyi (Lectures on Chinese History) (Shanghai: Hongwenguan chuban, 1908).

Zhou Yongming. *Anti-drug Crusades in Twentieth-Century China: Nationalism, History and State-Building* (Lanham: Rowman and Littlefield, 1999).

Zhou Yutong. *Kaiming benguoshi jiaoben* (Kaiming's Textbook on Chinese History) (Shanghai: Kaiming shudian, 1932).

Zhu Kuiyi. 'Kexue: Yapian zhi zhan' (Science: The Opium War), *Jiangsu sheng li di yi nüzi shifan suexiao xiaoyouhui zazhi* 3 (1920): 32–3.

Zuijin zhinashi (A Recent History of China) (Shanghai: Zhendang shixueshe, 1905).

Acknowledgements

I would like to thank my agent, Toby Eady, for offering me the opportunity to turn his idea into a book, and for his support throughout the writing process. Many thanks also to Jamie Coleman and Samar Hammam, for their careful and astute readings of an early draft. Frank Dikötter, Lars Laaman, Joyce Madancy, Rana Mitter, and Jeffrey Wasserstrom all took the time to read the manuscript at very busy points in the year; the book has benefited greatly from their interventions. I am very grateful to Brian Callingham for pharmacological advice on opiates, and to Sean Brady for guidance on nineteenth-century British politics. Finlay McLeod and Evan Osnos offered much help on sources. Sam Humphreys and Nicholas Blake were meticulous editors, and Zhang Ruihua kindly provided calligraphy.

The primary research for the book was carried out in winter 2007 while I was a visiting fellow at Beijing University's Department of History. I owe enormous thanks to members of the department for the generous help and support that they offered: in particular Professors Guo Weidong and Mao Haijian. Their students Liang Minling and Li Kunrui gave invaluable assistance on classical Chinese sources. As will be apparent from my endnotes, my understanding and analysis of primary Chinese sources on the Opium War were greatly helped by reference to Mao Haijian's *Tianchao de bengkui* and its guidance concerning Chinese archival materials for the war. I have also learnt much from other historians of nineteenth- and twentieth-century China. As far as possible I have tried to acknowledge this in my endnotes; I offer grateful apologies to any names I have inadvertently omitted.

The book was started during a research fellowship at Queens' College, Cambridge, and completed after a move to the history department of Birkbeck College, London. I have benefited constantly from the supportive research atmospheres of both these academic communities.

My debt to my family is the greatest, and I would like to thank above all my husband, parents, brother and sister for their encouragement, advice and insightful readings of the manuscript.

PICTURE CREDITS

1 Courtesy of private collection.
2 By permission of the Syndics of Cambridge University Library.
3 By permission of the Syndics of Cambridge University Library.
4 By permission of the Syndics of the Cambridge University Library.
5 Courtesy of the Palace Museum, Beijing.
6 Courtesy of the Wellcome Library, London.
7 Courtesy of the Wellcome Library, London.
8 Courtesy of the Wellcome Library, London.
9 Courtesy of the Wellcome Library, London.
10 Copyright © National Maritime Museum, Greenwich, London.
11 Courtesy of the Wellcome Library, London.
12 Courtesy of the Wellcome Library, London.
13 By permission of the Syndics of the Cambridge University Library.
14 Courtesy of Martyn Gregory Gallery, London.
15 Courtesy of the descendants of Lin Zexu.
16 Courtesy of the National Portrait Gallery, London.
17 Photo supplied by, and by permission of, the Hong Kong Museum of Art.
18 WOA 5196, © Palace of Westminster Collection.
19 By permission of the Syndics of the Cambridge University Library.
20 By permission of the Syndics of the Cambridge University Library.
21 By permission of the Syndics of the Cambridge University Library.
22 By permission of the Syndics of the Cambridge University Library.
23 Courtesy of *Qingshi tudian*, Gugong Bowuguan.
24 By permission of the Syndics of the Cambridge University Library.
25 By permission of the Syndics of the Cambridge University Library.
26 By permission of the Syndics of the Cambridge University Library.
27 Courtesy of *Qingshi tudian*, Gugong Bowuguan.
28 By permission of the Syndics of the Cambridge University Library.

29 By permission of the Hong Kong Museum of Art Collection.
30 By permission of the Syndics of the Cambridge University Library.
31 By permission of the Syndics of the Cambridge University Library.
32 By permission of the Syndics of the Cambridge University Library.
33 Courtesy of *Qingshi tudian*, Gugong Bowuguan.
34 Courtesy of Private Collection.
35 By permission of the Syndics of the Cambridge University Library.
36 By permission of the Syndics of the Cambridge University Library.
37 Courtesy of the Wellcome Library, London.
38 Courtesy of William A. Callahan.
39 By permission of the Syndics of the Cambridge University Library.
40 By permission of the Syndics of the Cambridge University Library.
41 Courtesy of the Wellcome Library, London.
42 Courtesy of the Wellcome Library, London.
43 MGM/The Kobal Collection.
44 Reproduced with the permission of Zhonghua Shuju, Beijing.
45 Courtesy of the Wellcome Library, London.
46 By permission of the Syndics of the Cambridge University Library.
47 By permission of the Syndics of the Cambridge University Library.
48 By permission of the Syndics of the Cambridge University Library.
49 Courtesy of Beijing Library.
50 Courtesy of Paul Newbery.
51 Courtesy of AP/Press Association Images.
52 Courtesy of Brian Dell.

IN TEXT

Page 18, 'A late-nineteenth-century photograpch of Chinese opium smokers.' Courtesy of the Historical Photographs of China Project (http://chp.ish-lyon.cnrs.fr/)

Page 242, 'Chinese artillerymen'. By permission of the Syndics of the Cambridge University Library.

Page 261, 'Felix Beato's 1860 photographs of the Anglo-French fleet at Hong Kong and of dead Qing soldiers in the forts near Beijing.' Courtesy of the Wellcome Library, London.

Page 316, 'China's National Humiliation commemoration fever dwindles'. *Shenbao*, 9 May 1922.

Index

In Chinese names, the surname is given first, followed by the given name. Therefore, in the case of Liang Qichao, Liang is the surname and Qichao the given name.